A Letter From the Postman

A Memoir of the Original Lead Singer of the "Marvelettes"

Gladys Horton

Presented by Vaughn Thornton

Copyright © 2022 Vaughn Thornton
ISBN: 979-8-218-01979-2
Library of Congress Control Number: 2022910800
All rights reserved. No portion of this document may be reproduced in any form without expressed, written consent from the author. The authors have tried to recreate events, locales and conversations from their memories of them. In order to maintain their anonymity in some instances, the authors have changed the names of individuals and places. The authors may have changed some identifying characteristics and details such as physical properties, occupations and places of residence. This book was self-published by the authors.

"Free is what I've always been, that's why it's so easy to be me,"

—Gladys, Age 10

CONTENTS

GLADYS ACKNOWLEDGMENTS..................vii
A WORD ABOUT THE AUTHOR......................ix

PART 1: IN THE BEGINNING...GOD CREATED
"A MOTHERLESS CHILD"................................. 3
"THE MOTOWN ERA"..................................... 72
"POOR LITTLE RICH GIRL"........................... 105
"LOVE PUNCHES TOO HARD"..................... 182
"FREE TO BE ME AGAIN".............................. 236

PART 2: "WE GOT TO KEEP MOVING ON"
"PHILADELPHIA, PA – PHILLYTOWN"...................281
"INKSTER, MY HOME, SWEET HOME"...................343
"MOVING ON"... 426
"THE STREETS OF L.A."................................ 490

PART 3: "THE BEST TIME AROUND"
"SPOTLIGHT DATE: 1988"............................. 541
BACK ON TOP! AN AFTERWORD..................... 575
A TRIBUTE TO AL.. 583
LETTERS FROM GLADYS.............................. 605
VAUGHN ACKNOWLEDGMENTS..................... 615

GLADYS ACKNOWLEDGMENTS

My special thanks and acknowledgments go out to all the many people who came into my life enabling me to have a story to tell, especially to the ones who came to give my life some positive meaning. Most important to me are my three sons, who so many times were the reason I fought to survive.

Speaking of letters, to all the millions of people in the world who have come to realize through war, hospitalization, imprisonment, and far away relatives and friends, the magic of letters and just how much they mean, I also dedicate this book to you. Keep on writing them.

Other acknowledgments go out to the many Marvelettes fans who stood by us when there were no more hits; Sylvia Moy, who started me on my way to professional writing and producing while I was living in Detroit during the early '80s. Raynoma Gordy Singleton, who opened doors to my traveling and doing shows again in the late '80s; two journalists and friends Ron Brewington and his wife and publicity agent, Rich LaCaine, who first showcased me at the ever-popular Vine Street Bar and Grill in Hollywood, California, in 1988. To Manuel "Spooky" Esparza, who gave me lots of support through his Legendary Ladies Fan Club newsletter and Rudy Calville internationally known makeup artist. Also to one of my greatest fans David Horary, who gave me back Marvelette pictures, tapes, and items I had lost through constant moving around, especially to my friends and employees who work in the royalty department of Motown MCA Records in the California office. And to Mr. Ian Levine who brought the Motown artist back together through a reunion and recordings.

Special thanks to the original Marvelettes: Katherine Anderson Schaffner, Wanda Young Rogers, and Juanita Cowart Motley, whom all made my recent visit to years to Inkster, Michigan, a treat.

Thanks to David Tague, a former neighbor from Westland, Michigan, and Rosie Walsh-Tague for their support and Kevin Norwood for the preparation of my manuscript. Other further acknowledgments will go out to the people who wrote with me on this book: agents, publishers, and personal managers, whomever they shall be. And now for my story.

A WORD ABOUT THE AUTHOR

Gladys Horton *of the Original Marvelettes*

1945: Gladys Catherine Horton was born on May 30th, the original "Memorial Day", in Gainesville, Florida. At the tender age of 9 months, I was left to grow up in a number of foster homes, but never once being adopted by any one family. "I believe everything happens for a reason. Maybe my purpose for existence is to give hope, inspiration, and courage to all motherless or fatherless children. To let them know that life is the greatest gift anyone can give you. Eventually, you have to learn and live your own life without anyone else's decisions."

Gladys Horton achieved her first-world recognition, with a smash hit single shortly after her 15th birthday. She was the lead singer for The Marvelettes, the world-famous Motown Records supergirl group of the '60s and '70s. Her sassy lead vocals on "Please Mr. Postman" delivered that song up the charts, all the way to #1, and it's still classic today. It was her voice and sound that gave Berry Gordy Jr. and his company its first straight #1 in December of 1961.

Gladys Horton left the Marvelettes after an eight-year stint to become a full-time mother. It was at this time that her firstborn was handicapped with cerebral palsy. After having to give up her career on stage, she continued her hand at writing songs. Today, she is celebrated as an accomplished songwriter who kept those famous vocal cords in top form until her passing in 2011. Gladys Horton also wrote and sang the lead on "Playboy," another smash hit from The Marvelettes.

"I always knew I had some writing ability," she admitted. "When I was only in the fifth grade, I won first place in a Novel Writing Competition."

If you've never met Gladys or witnessed one of her performances, you're in for a treat. After just reading anything she has to say, you will feel like you've known her all of your life.

Ladies and gentlemen, teenagers, and children around the world...

Please, may I introduce you to the one and only... Gladys Horton.

A Letter From the Postman

PART 1:
IN THE BEGINNING...
GOD CREATED

CHAPTER 1:
"A MOTHERLESS CHILD"

The spell of daydreaming brought a wonderful world of make-believe to me. What a safe place to mentally play for a six-year-old who felt so alone and lost. Those days there seemed to be nowhere to go and nothing else to do.

I had been moved away from a beautiful town like Romeo and wound up in a place with old, rocky dirt roads and deep ditches. The houses were all built alike and too close together. Tall weeds were growing where there should have been flowers and grass. In fact, there were more flies and mosquitoes than there were butterflies. It was enough to make any kid want to escape from the reality that kept them bound.

So now, when I shut my eyes and start reminiscing back to my days in Romeo, I can still smell the apple orchards that grew for miles and miles across the vast countryside. I can still taste the warm, sweet raspberries we picked and ate in the midday afternoon sun. I can somehow feel the mild evening summer breeze that blew right through my bedroom window ever so often. I remember the big, white, plank farmhouse that sat way back off the street. It was surrounded by a tall, black gate, and the long walkway up to the front porch was lined with several tall trees across the large front lawn. The curved driveway went all the way around back to the farm sheds and chicken coops. There were swings in the back where the other children in the foster home and I played for hours. There was Irene, Patricia, and Janet, along with the twins, Marilyn and Marie, whose mother was one of the caretakers.

Those early years I sat perched on the pillows in the big oval window facing the street from our living room, watching who I called the happy little man. Every day, here he would come with this big bag on his shoulder. *I* thought he was walking much too fast. The little man steadily went from house to house. He never bothered to knock but always left something in the little boxes on the porches or the big metal boxes near the driveways. His head seemed to bob from side to side as though he was humming or whistling a tune.

He sure seemed happy all the time. Yeah, happy. Just like I was until the day I moved to Romulus. Yes, the names of the towns almost sound the same. Even the spelling with the first three letters being the same. Still, they were as different as night and day. And, as some folks like me would say, it was like going from heaven to hell.

"No, she is not my mother," I heard her loudly speak out, and I was suddenly jolted back to the reality of where I was. It was my new foster mother standing at the fence talking with her next-door neighbor. I looked up to see both women looking in my direction. I had been secretly hiding in the uncut grass on the front lawn.

Quickly, I thought about what she must have been telling her friend. We had all been returning on the bus a couple of days ago from a little weekend trip she had planned for the other two children in this foster home—a girl around my age named Sandra, a younger boy we called Junior, and me. For some unknown reason, a man coming down the aisle on the bus stopped and asked me a question.

"Is that your mother sitting behind you, little girl?"

Without hesitation, I loudly blurted out, "No, that is not my mother." These were words my foster mother did *not* respond to.

Afterward, I had wondered if she even heard me. Now she had confirmed my curiosity. Hearing my very own words coming back at me now should have made me feel ashamed and naughty. Instead, I felt I had more than enough reason to stand my own ground.

Oh, how I hated this place from the very first day I arrived. Somehow, I knew that I wouldn't be here very long. Everything spelled trouble right from the very beginning. I hadn't been here but a day or so when the foster mother asked me to collect the eggs from the chicken house out back. Even though we had chickens in Romeo, I had never been asked to gather the eggs before. Needless to say, I was all caught up in the excitement of it all.

I grabbed the basket and ran out to where the chickens had laid their eggs. After gathering all the eggs, I was on my way out to the picket fence that surrounded the chicken houses when up to me runs this fighting rooster with a big red crown flapping around on top of his head. He didn't waste any time in letting me know who was the ruler of those eggs, and *I* didn't waste any time in letting his eggs go. I dropped them to the ground without hesitation.

Still upset with me for just being on his property, the rooster showed signs of trying to fly up to my face—fussing, cackling, and making all kinds of loud chicken noises. I tried covering my face and turning in circles, but he still persisted in his fight to jump up at my face.

Suddenly, I just started screaming, "Help, help, help me, please!" That certainly brought everyone out of their houses to their backyard fences and more attention from the neighboring yards than I had bargained for.

"Why did you send her out there with that fighting rooster around?" I heard someone ask my foster mother.

She didn't say anything. We just looked at each other hard. So *now* I guess her little weekend activities had all been brought about to try and make up for that dirty little trick she played on me. So then afterward, I had to go and say something to mess it all up.

There were also other things quite different here than what I had been accustomed to. I don't know whether it was because *this* foster home was run by a husband-and-wife team, whereas up in Romeo, two women ran that home.

There was more than just the difference in the sizes of the two homes. There was too much of everything. There was too much furniture for such a small house and too much food all the time. Breakfast consisted of eggs, bacon, grits, toast, and sometimes scrambled pork brains, something I never knew of before now. Lunch brought on my favorite—split pea soup, sandwiches, hot dogs, hamburgers, French fries, and other side dishes, and *still* more to eat. For dinner, we had roast, chicken, fish, meatloaf, and potatoes, not to mention sweets and desserts of all kinds. This included delectables such as puddings, cakes, pies, jellies, cookies, and ice cream. It was just too much for my small frame.

Mrs. Clark and Mrs. Moore, the two foster parents who ran the home in Romeo, had a way of planning our activities where food was not the main pastime. We always ate light meals like buttered bread with applesauce. We played many games outside, picked fruit to eat, shucked corn, and kept so physically fit until I was never bothered with a weight problem. We just didn't learn to eat all day long.

Now, since moving here, I could feel the pounds mounting. My small, slim, girlish figure was turning into that of a round, fat, big, overfed female. I just *had* to get away. I know it wasn't the foster mother's fault. I guess her husband demanded to be fed, and unfortunately, I ended up getting too much of it all.

Like I said before, I knew I wouldn't be here in this place too long. But before I left, a couple of other changes took place in my personality. The early morning walks to school were usually filled with other children laughing, talking, or playing tag along the way as we all followed the same trail. Each day we trekked down the unpaved, bumpy roads and through the short cutoff path to the schoolhouse.

As it was, Sandra and I usually left the house together. Somewhere along the way, she disappeared among the different groupings of children, and I wouldn't bother to try to keep up or find her. Anyway, I wanted to stop by the small corner market store and see if I could get away with a "free" piece of bubble gum or candy.

Mmm… the smell of that chocolate and caramel went all through my nostrils as soon as I got within a few feet of the front door. The little old man who ran the store always seemed too busy sorting out his new stock of items or straightening up his store to strictly pay a great deal of attention to what I was doing. Sometimes, I don't even think he saw me come in. I knew exactly where the small candy treats were, and I was in and out of there before you could whistle Dixie.

Sometimes, other kids would have his attention at the cash register, which made my robberies even quicker. A little thief was what I was becoming. One day it was candy. The next day bubblegum, then potato chips or cupcakes. Anything pocket-sized, you name it, I stole it.

The awful thing about it was that I didn't have to steal. In my lunch every day, the foster mother had some kind of dessert. I guess it was just that I saw the other kids spending money for these things, and I never had any money to spend of my own. I never even thought to ask the foster mother for any. Maybe it was because I knew this was not my natural mother and that she didn't really owe me anything but shelter and food.

Besides not having the nerve to ask, I don't think it even entered my mind to ask her. Furthermore, she never offered me this commodity. My desire to carry on the trade and buy the respect that money creates among the consumer was what was missing those early years. So, I stole.

For some reason, there is a scary but good feeling about sneaking and doing things. I was so sneaky until I even kept my stealing a secret. I never told *anyone*. I didn't have very many friends at school either, because I had begun to feel ugly and fat. Once, I think I heard some boys laughing at me while I was eating lunch. I didn't exactly *hear* their words, but I imagined that they were laughing at my fat behind.

Girls *feel* when boys are talking about a part of their

body, and I sure knew mine wasn't one that they would be saying something sweet about. My hair had lost its length, it seemed, or maybe my head had just gotten fatter.

I remember how beautiful I used to feel after Mrs. Clark or Mrs. Moore used to keep my hair back in Romeo. Now, very seldom was my hair even being combed. *Especially* not every morning. How many times a week? I can't remember. For some reason, there is a blind spot in my mind as I try to recall how I got through a lot of episodes at this foster home.

I knew I didn't feel any love or compassion coming from anyone there. I do know I don't ever remember seeing Sandra's hair anything less than perfectly done or her clothes anything but pressed and ironed neatly. I have yet to remember a fuss being made over my looks or attire. Maybe that is why I used to find myself fighting back in a very awful way.

Sometimes, I would see Sandra's hair combed neatly. She'd have a beautiful dress on and would be playing with her doll outside. Out of spite, I would mess her all up. I'd tear the ribbons out of her hair and sometimes throw dirt on her nice clean dress. A few times, I even remember scratching her in her pretty face. Oh yes, I was fast becoming an unholy monster of a kid.

I can still remember how she wouldn't even fight back. She just would scream and cry and run to tell and show our foster mother what I had done. I would run off and hide in some of the tall bushes close by; I figured I would just wait a while before showing my face inside. Sometimes I would even cry myself because I would feel so miserable, ugly, ashamed, rotten, and fat.

These times only made me yearn for my Romeo days even stronger.

"Romeo, Romeo, where art thou, my sweet Romeo?"

***

I learned what unhappiness could do with children who had once felt like they were living in paradise. I was already feeling the hard bumps of life too early. I was even becoming worse than that little girl named Sue who once told a big, big lie on me not long after I started kindergarten there in Romeo.

I can remember it just as if it was only yesterday. The teacher had told us all to line up for lavatory time. Each week she picked a new monitor for the girls and one for the boys. This week she picked a girl named Sue. There were only four stalls in the bathrooms, so we went in fours. I was one of the last four girls. I used the bathroom and then came out to wash my hands.

Suddenly, I heard her voice behind me. "See, I told you Gladys peed on the floor. Look."

I spun around to see Sue with the teacher, pointing

to some water on the floor outside of the bathroom stall I had used. "I did not pee on the floor," I protested.
Still, the teacher chose to believe Sue. Quickly, she led me up the stairs to the principal's office.

It was against the rules to behave in any manner that was disrespectful to the cleanliness and morals of the school. The principal, who was a man, was very frightening to me. I had never been scolded or accused of any actions by a man before, and it scared me tremendously.

As I told you before, the foster home was run by two women who taught us girls very good manners and respectful ways. They never violently had to scold or chastise any of us in the process. Arguments and whippings were some of the things I hadn't had much experience with, being trained in such a proper and strict way. Believe it or not, and I laugh at this today, but even saying "shut up" was something our foster mothers would not allow or even hear of.

We even addressed a female as "Yes, ma'am" or "No, ma'am" and a male when answering or upon greeting as "Yes, sir" and "No, sir." I had not even heard any bold language. So, this day in the principal's office was certainly a dark, grim, gruesome experience for me. Until then, I don't even think I knew I was black. But, that day, the color barrier had finally been broken.

"You little black children have to abide by the same rules as our white children! Do you understand me?" he scolded me loudly.

"But I didn't do it!" I cried. "I didn't do it!"

I never understood until years later why Sue chose me to lie on. I was darker than the rest of the kids. There were very few black families living in Romeo, and I guess that is why I stuck out like a sore thumb. I had to remain in the principal's office that day until one of the foster mothers came to get me.

I still remember the grim look on Mrs. Clark's face as though she wanted to say more. After privately talking with the principal, I heard her softly say, "I am sure there won't be any more problems."

I thought that meant I would be punished greatly for something I didn't even do.

So, I just had to plead my innocence to her. As we walked home, I looked up at her and said, "Mom, I didn't pee on the floor."

She squeezed my hand just a little and smiled at me. "I know you didn't, Gladys," she said gently. "I know you didn't."

That is all that was said about it. I guess when she had mentioned that there would be no more problems, she was speaking about moving me to another foster home because I moved here to Romulus not long afterward.

Now, I understood that she didn't want to chance any more racial outbreaks on behalf of me attending An almost completely white school system. But the good it all did, because here I was now completely changed from my sweet, kind ways and manners from my earlier upbringing.

Sue had taught me white from black and right from wrong. Still, instead of me using what I learned to make myself a better person, here I was, changing for the worse. Oh, how I hated myself.

***

Going to church was something I was accustomed to but never one like this one. The music was loud, and there was a band. Some of the people got up and danced around. The preacher screamed and jumped up and down while the choir sang fast jerky songs. I couldn't take my eyes off all the excitement I saw and felt.

One Sunday, sitting behind me was a pew full of boys. The one who was directly behind my seat caught my attention. *Oh, he is cute,* I thought to myself. I wondered if he thought I was too. He seemed to have noticed me also. I kept turning around, giggling and acting silly, pretending to not be aware of the gleam I saw in his eyes.

I heard a couple of his friends teasing him, saying, "Go ahead, go ahead and ask her." *Ask me what?* I wondered. My panties began to feel wet with this unusual perspiration I was having. He seemed to be shy, so I took matters into my own hands and reassured him that I had noticed him and wanted to play too. I reached down between the church seats and started pulling on his pant legs.

Now the boys' laughter had gotten louder. But with all the racket they made in this church, I was sure nobody would say we were disturbing the peace. So, he leaned up behind me and whispered in my ear, "Please, little girl, stop."

Little girl! I thought. *I will show you about this little girl.* I felt like any woman who knew what she wanted. I continued to run my hands up his pants, pulling and stretching his socks, also feeling the masculinity of his legs. When I turned around to see what response he now had, I saw sheer desire in his eyes—a look that made me realize that he was ready for whatever came next.

And me? Well, I was now a little frightened by what I had stirred up. This time when he whispered in my ear again, I felt a chill run up and down my body that made me tremble a little. What he whispered to me next made me know he meant real business.

"Can you come outside?" he asked.

At that question, I froze. I didn't know what to do next because I was too young to be anything else but a virgin. I suddenly realized sex was something that you didn't have to be taught. You just followed Mother Nature's instincts. Oh, the things Mother Nature was telling me were about to happen were scaring the daylights out of me.

"Well, I hope to see you all back here next Sunday," I heard the preacher say loud and clear, now addressing the congregation. I was saved by the bell but not from the embarrassment I was soon to encounter from my foster mother. She had been watching me from one of the pews across the aisle. By the look on her face, I knew she had seen it all, along with a number of her church buddies. The way they looked at me made me feel nasty and unfit to be there in the presence of the Lord. Even the boys, who all had a ball at my kidding around that day, heard her scold me and call me a fast little hussy. I wanted to run away.

"You will hear more about this when you get home," she vowed. Even the spectators showed their dissatisfaction with my actions as they walked away. The one time I had ever felt wanted or needed by anyone in this town had been turned into a nightmare of embarrassment and laughter for me.

The foster mother gave me the first whipping I had ever had in my early years, and I knew she enjoyed every bit of it. I realized that I had it coming, though, for all the stealing, my fighting Sandra, and now from playing with sex in the church. What else could I do wrong? She knew it, and I knew it. I had to go.

I stayed there in Romulus until the school semester was out. And now I was moving to another foster home. A week before the day I was scheduled to be moved, my social worker came out and wanted to have a long talk with me.

"Gladys," she said, "I see in your records that you weren't with your natural parents for long and was too young to even remember or know who they are."

"That is right," I answered.

"Haven't any relatives or family friends ever tried to contact you?" she asked. This brought back memories of a weekend visit with some people I felt must have known me very well. It happened after I had been in Romeo about a year or so, making me around the age of four. So, I began to talk to my social worker, telling her about it.

I was being driven to the Children's Aid Society early one morning. The ride was long because Romeo was located near the Upper Peninsula of Michigan, and we had to travel almost all the way to downtown Detroit. While there, I was met and driven somewhere else by a large woman with a kind face, very cheerful ways, and a pretty smile. I can remember I was so little that I couldn't even see out of the car windows.

I just kept looking up at the lady who, every now and then, would give me a glance and a smile. The ride was somewhere far because I remember I fell asleep. When I woke up, we were driving around the back of a building that had a shed. There were stairs that led up to a door. I remember the first thing I saw when I got out of the car was the cow. It is funny how kids *never* forget the animals they see.

"Did you know that?" I asked the social worker as I paused my story.

"Yes, Gladys, now please go on," she encouraged.

I could see and feel that I had her full, undivided attention, so I continued on about that weekend. When we got upstairs, a lady greeted us at the door. She seemed very nice, although I remember her warning after showing my amazement at a beautiful candy dish sitting on a table. She opened it up to let me see all the pieces of candy in the dish. Then she said, "Gladys, do not steal any of this candy out of this dish. If you want a piece, come and ask me."

In some kind of way, I knew she really meant what she had just told me. And as much as I liked candy, I can't remember asking her for even one piece.

Later on, a lot of other people came over to welcome me. I had the feeling they knew who I was. I felt special and important to them because that is the way they made me feel.

My social worker seemed eager now to hear even more. So I went on.

They asked me questions that I can't remember. But whatever my answers were, it brought loud roars of laughter from them. So, I knew I must have been saying *something* right.

The next day, they really made a big fuss over me. They washed, straightened, curled, and cut my hair. Then they took me to this big mirror that sat on the floor and let me look at myself. I saw the straight, black, evenly cut bangs shining on my face and the pretty curled style they had given me.

"Oh, is that me?" I asked. They had made me feel so very beautiful inside and outside.

I don't know what the reason was for this short weekend visit, as I remembered it, but there were several other strange things about it. I can't remember how I returned from or ever leaving that place. I never saw that cow again after my initial arrival.

The social worker seemed to want to hear more, but I told her that everything was a complete blank after that. "You know, it is strange," I said to her, "how I can so clearly remember a lot of things that happened to me very early in my life."

She assured me that this sometimes happens when a child is taken away from their natural mother at such an early age. You have to grow up fast. You needed that extra sense in order to provide yourself with the protection that is usually given by the mother to the baby. Now, I was beginning to understand some things about myself. And as time would have it, I had much, much more to learn.

The next time I saw my social worker, I felt like I had found a friend. We had become better acquainted from the talking we had done. She even greeted me with enthusiasm.

"Gladys, I never knew you had such deep dimples,

and my, what a lovely smile you have," she beamed. It was true. I couldn't remember the last time I felt like smiling. But today, I was happy. I guess it showed all over my face. She had come to move me to my new foster home. During our drive there, we began to talk some more. I found it very easy talking to her.

"Gladys," she asked, "do you remember how many foster homes you have already lived in?"

"Well," I began thinking back. "Two or three."

"Well, this one will be your fourth foster home," she reminded me. "It will be the second time that you will have lived in this town."

"You mean I have been here before?" Excitement gripped my whole body. "Am I going back to Romeo?!" I shouted. The joy of it shot all through my mind so quickly until I was suddenly and uncontrollably filled with sheer ecstasy.

"Calm down, Gladys, calm down. I am sorry, but you are not going back to Romeo. You are going back to Inkster."

"Inkster," I repeated her pronunciation. *What kind of name was that for a town?* I thought to myself. As quick as I had felt that flash of joy, that is how quickly I now felt another dark cloud coming on. I guess it must have shown on my face, for the social worker tried cheering me up.

"It won't be that bad, believe me. You are bound to meet somebody who might remember you, although you were a baby when you lived here before. Only nine months old. It was the town of your very first foster home."

"Am I going back to that same foster home?" I asked quickly.

"No, I don't believe so," she answered me. "My records show that you never lived at this home before. I am not even sure if the first foster home you went to is still occupied by the same family or if they still live in that town. That was some years ago, you know. By the way, how old are you?"

"I am seven going on eight."

"That is a good age. I think that is around the same ages of the girls Mrs. Jones has at this home where you are going today."

I saw the sign as soon as we crossed the railroad tracks. It read, "Welcome to the Village of Inkster."

A village, I thought. *Sounds like someplace special.* As we drove up, I saw that there was a welcoming committee already there to greet me—a big group of kids that lived on the block along with the girls from the foster home. They were all waving, peeping through the windows, and running alongside the car as we drove into the driveway.

My social worker smiled at me and said, "Gladys, I think you are going to like it here."

All the kids were so friendly, making complimentary comments as they all seemed to be examining every inch of me. It took at least 10 minutes before the social worker and I could go inside to meet my new foster parents.

"What is your name?" they asked.

I told them, and they noisily began to comment on it.

"How do you spell that?"

"I have never known anyone named Gladys before, but I like it."

"Look how thick her hair is," I heard another voice speak out.

"I wonder does she go to the hairdresser," someone was whispering.

"Do you have lots of dresses?" one of the girls asked me. Before I could answer, they all started agreeing on how pretty the one was that I had on that day.

"Girls, introduce yourself, and then we must let Gladys meet her new foster parents," my social worker now interrupted.

"Okay," they all agreed at once, as though someone had mentioned a new game for everyone to play.

"I am Brenda, and I live here with you at this foster home."

"I do too, and my name is Christine," they went on.

"My name is Delores, and I lived here, but I am moving next week."

Then the others all began to give their names.

"I am Deborah. I live across the street. We are having dance lessons in my basement after you get your things put up, okay?"

"Okay!" I said cheerfully. It sounded like fun already.

"My name is Sylvia, and this is my brother Leon. We live next door."

I could see some of the parents from the houses on the block standing outside or at their front doors, all engaging in welcoming me to the neighborhood. Then I met Evelyn, Pinkie, and Geraldine, who all lived on the 36th block of Harriet Street, Inkster, Michigan.

I got a good look at the outline and architecture of the house as we drove up, even with all the racket the welcoming committee was making. I could see that it was a big two-story, red brick house with many rooms. Thank God for that. In no way did it remind me of the Romeo mansion, but I knew it wouldn't be as cramped as the one I just left.

We entered into a long screen porch that had a piano in the corner. Then there was another door that led into the house and the living room. I could see everything was neat and clean. Mrs. Jones came out of the kitchen to greet us. As she walked toward us, I could see that she had a limp to her walk. She was on the heavy side, but her complexion was nice, and so was her mannerism.

There was also something else about her that I picked up right away. She was the boss around here, whatever that meant. She told me right there in front of the social worker that all of her demands had to be met around her house and that she never had a child to leave who hadn't learned something to better their lives.

Quickly, she gave me a rundown of some of the things she expected of me. She went on to say, "You have some chores to do on a daily basis, like making your bed upon rising, keeping your clothes clean and ready for school, and keeping your bedrooms tidy. On weekends, the girls alternate with the chores here on the main floor, such as mopping, waxing, and vacuuming the floors, dusting and waxing, shining the furniture, and shopping for groceries." She laughed out loud as she saw my reaction as to how I was going to remember all of that and said, "Don't worry, there is still more to do. But I have saved the biggest job for myself."

"What else could that be?" I asked, puzzled beyond belief, and she pointed to the kitchen.

"That is my job. I do all the cooking around here. My husband works hard and insists on his meals on time."

I knew about that routine and how it worked. It seemed to be a happy home, even with all the talk about work and chores. I had a feeling that it would be easy for me to fit in here.

"You will be learning to do many things for yourself," my social worker mentioned to me before she left. "That is what growing up is all about."

Brenda was the oldest of us girls, although she couldn't have been more than 12 or 13 at the time. She was sweet and kind and had a very tender way of talking and discussing things with you. She came right up to me and volunteered her help in any way she could. "Come on, Gladys, I will show you to your room where you can unpack your things."

Upstairs there were four bedrooms. There was also a sitting room, or maybe you could call it a small den, and a bathroom. Downstairs, on the main floor, was a large living room, a formal dining room, a nice sized kitchen, another bedroom used by Mr. and Mrs. Jones, and another bathroom. The screened-in front porch was somewhat like a recreational room in the house with relaxing chairs and the old piano I first saw when I entered the house. There was also a full basement where all the washing was done. Clotheslines were all strung up for hanging the clothes to dry.

Brenda explained to me how sometimes, when all the washing was done, they used the basement for other activities like roller-skating, dancing, listening to records, or just plain entertaining friends.

You can see that this was in no way a little house. Everything and everyone seemed to have a lot of order about them. I could tell that these girls took pride in their homes and belongings.

"If you ever have a problem and Mrs. Jones is away

or busy, you can always come to me for help," Brenda assured me. I thought that was very grown-up for her to say. She certainly made me feel like I had found my big sister.

Later on, Christine offered to show me around the neighborhood, so off we went to meet the gang. After going from one house to another, meeting kids and their parents, we ended up at the dance party Deborah had told me about earlier.

"Let's see how she dances," I heard some kids whispering together in a group.

"Dance? Who me?" I questioned them. "But I don't know how to dance."

This brought on a chain reaction from them all.

"Where have *you* been?" The realization seemed to be something unbelievable to them all. "Everybody knows how to dance *here*," they all stated. Then someone put on the records, and they all began to show me the latest dances.

"Don't you ever go to dances?" I was asked by someone just popping and flopping around to the beat.

"No, I have never been to a dance in my life," I admitted.

"What?"

The mere mention of it brought other questions upon more questions about where I was before I came to Inkster. I talked about Romeo and Romulus and how we used to pick apples and berries and play in the back on the swings.

"Sounds like you have been nurtured in a real lily-white fashion all your life," someone blurted loudly.

They all laughed. I heard someone say, "No wonder she talks like a little white girl with her 'Yes, ma'ams' and 'No, sirs' and fancy talk about going uptown and coming downtown. Sister, don't you know? You are now in a *groovy* place," I was told. "You have got to learn to get down."

That first day they taught me how to shake my hips and do the bop. I had never popped my fingers to any dance music beat before. I tried a couple of times, but you could hardly hear my fingers popping. Come to think of it, I hadn't ever even played any records before. I really felt like an alien who had just come to earth.

I remember watching them and admiring how good they all knew how to dance. They even sang along with a lot of the songs. Songs I had not even heard of before that day, like *Dance with me, Annie; All Right, Baby; Don't Mean Maybe.* And then there was *Mamma, He Is Treating Your Daughter Mean.* Oh yes, this was a new time, age, and space for me, and I was soaking it all up. I wanted so desperately to be like them—to dance and to sing and know all the groovy words to say.

One thing I liked about these kids was that they were willing to teach me. Although I was different, they made me feel like I was still accepted into their club as long as I vowed to do better as time went on.

"I will, I will," I promised. And I really meant it. I had finally found a place where I *wanted* to be.

As the days went on, I found out more and more about the kids in Inkster. Number one, they were not lazy, sitting around idle, or waiting for excitement to come to them. Energy must have been discovered in this town because everybody had plenty of it. I noticed young and old alike were constantly creating new things to do. Many parents were just like the kids and kept events going on wherever they could get involved. There were church picnics, house parties, street baseball games, roller rink skating, theater matinees, group racing, and street corner singing sessions. Anything that meant getting together to have fun was there. You name it, and Inkster had it in those days. Unlike today's living conditions, I had never experienced any fist fighting or loud verbal abuse going on in any of the foster homes I had been in.

But it was at Mr. and Mrs. Jones's house that I began to watch and realize the roles males and females played in providing a well-rounded household. Mr. Jones was a tall, strong-looking, quiet man who was kind but hardly ever carried on any lengthy conversations with us girls. I can remember if he wanted you to do something, he would tell you once and never question you later about if you did it or not.

Under the strict behavior habits laid down by Mrs.

Jones, there was no doubt about it, I guess. He *knew* we had obeyed him. He went to work every day at the same time and came home exactly on time every evening. Dinner was always ready, and we all ate together at the big table in the dining room.

Mr. Jones put all his confidence in his wife that she would run the job of taking care of the bills and the other necessities. I know he always gave his paycheck to her to do as she wished, and she never let him down. Seeing the order and togetherness they had made me think that all marriages were that perfect.

Inkster was a family-oriented town anyway. In those early years, the men in this town knew their main role was to provide, while the women stayed home, keeping it very clean, neat, and tidy. As the housekeeper, their last words were final. Yes, in Inkster, the woman was the ruler. Everybody got used to it, especially the men. I think they even loved it that way. Or maybe they knew they just couldn't change the situation so easily.

Once I heard Mrs. Jones softly but firmly voicing her opinion about some matter, and *she* was all I heard. Like I said, the men here just didn't say much. I don't think I would call it being henpecked. I would rather say they intended on keeping the peace at whatever lengths they had to go to. Control was strictly something else widely practiced in this community. Along with Mr. and Mrs. Jones, many other parents belonged to the Masons and Eastern Star Auxiliaries.

I found out that Mr. and Mrs. Jones had been running the foster home for about nine years. Christine was the first to come to them when she was only a baby. Later, many girls followed. Some stayed a while and then left. Others came and stayed only months because of behavioral problems. Some were there only for a day or two because of some family member's hospitalization. I even saw several girls come in after I did. There was Shirley, Tyra, Pauline, Lily, Hilda, and Trula, just to name a few. Mrs. Jones never kept more than four girls at a time. So, for whatever reason, a lot of them moved in and then were out. Not long after came somebody new.

I had really learned the ropes and cornered all the loopholes of remaining there before I was 12 years old. The older we got, the more privileges we were able to handle. I was now getting my hair done by a hairdresser. On holidays, we were given money to buy special outfits for ourselves. New clothing was supplied to us yearly by the Children's Placement Agency.

***

Inkster had almost as many churches as it had schools. Although this town was called a village, its vicinity of a four-square-mile boundary covered a very large area of populated land.

Joining the choir at our church turned out to be exactly what I needed. I found out that I was musically inclined in using my voice. I had a natural instinct and an inborn sense of harmonizing.

We rehearsed every Saturday so that the songs would be fresh in your mind for the following day at the church services on Sunday. My strong vocal cords always stood out in the group. So, one day at rehearsal, the choir director asked me to lead a song. I had gained enough confidence from background singing, but I didn't know how I would do on my own as leading.

"I have been working for Jesus a long, Jong time. No, no, no, I am not tired, yet" were the words I led that Sunday. It was a real rocking, gospel type of tune. I think I made the congregation feel the spirit because they started clapping their hands and shouting afterward.

"Praise the Lord, praise the Lord," the preacher commented. He sure wanted the choir to sing more messages like that. So, every Sunday for almost a straight month, I had to lead that song. It was good for me because each time, I felt better about the sound of my voice, and I was learning to do more with my vocal cords and range. Thus, I began my early singing career, never knowing that I would gain world recognition from doing this in the future.

Besides Sunday school being a great learning experience there in Inkster, going to public school held a lot of joy, contentment, and positive makings for me. I never met a teacher who didn't like me. My aim was to impress, and that I did. In many ways, the teacher was like the mother I never had, telling me right from wrong and correcting me before I went on. I used to imagine that if I could see my own mother, I would want her to be just as pretty and neat and smart as they all were.

I was not a straight "A" student because I still daydreamed too much. But I did well in most of my subjects, never once being left a grade behind. I was great in spelling because of my extremely good memory track. I could look at a word once and remember its exact spelling. Reading was also a subject I excelled in. From the very beginning, I can never remember having a problem with learning to read or write.

Another big favorite of mine was telling stories. When I was only in the fifth grade, I won first place in a novel-writing contest. That was my first try at writing a book. I have always loved the task of tackling something I had never tried before just to see what I would come up with. Usually, it was the right stuff, and I would end up surprising myself as well as those around me.

For instance, at my grade school graduation, the teacher asked if anyone had something they wanted to do for the program. I raised my hand and offered to play a piano solo, never having a day of piano lessons in my life. I had to come up with a completely made-up song because I surely couldn't read a note of music. I had about two weeks to compose a tune.

It was frightening after I had lied because now, I realized how important this event would be with all the parents, teachers, school staff members, and kids attending. I had to look *and* sound like I knew how to play the piano. So, every day now after school, I was at the old piano on the porch.

First, I had to have a title for my song. So I called it *Evening Sunset*. I worked hard at it—messing around with the different keys and putting chords together to make up different sounds. It took a big effort, but I finally had it all together.

So now I had to practice it over and over, memorizing it from top to bottom. It wasn't hard, having the memory of an elephant like I did. The hardest thing I can remember was knowing that I had been faking it all. Each time a teacher, parent, or child came up and complimented me on my part in the program, I kept smiling nervously as they were saying, "Gladys, I never knew you played the piano, and you do it so well."

"Thank you," I replied, but I was a nervous wreck. That is what lying does to you, especially if you have to live up to your lies. You can bet that was the first and last time I volunteered to be a liar.

Even though that charade was over, I kept banging away at the piano, learning how to play different little songs by ear. Music was all so much fun, especially that old boogie-woogie. It was easy enough for anyone to learn.

Secretly, in the back of my mind, I think I have always

wished I could have had professional piano lessons. Even now, it is a real thrill for me to watch someone who can play. Truthfully speaking, the piano is my favorite musical instrument. This, along with the singing and the writing, all proved to be the many things I first came in contact with from living in Inkster with the Joneses.

But wait, there was more to be learned about myself in Inkster. I was nearly 12 years old when another secret was revealed. One day, soon after Brenda had taken a cleaning job outside the foster home, she came home full of excitement and very anxious to tell me something.

"Gladys, have I got news for you," she started telling me right as she saw me, not even waiting to catch her breath. "The lady I am cleaning house for knows you."

"Me? But how?" I asked.

"Mrs. McKay is her name. Today I found out that she was once a foster parent. She was talking about some of the children she once mothered, and your name came up. She couldn't believe it when I told her that you were now living in another foster home right here in Inkster with me."

Then it all came back to me. "My social worker told me that I once lived here in Inkster when I was a baby," I told Brenda. "But I never thought I would find out with who or where, so I never mentioned it."

"Well, I found her, and she wants to see you."

It didn't take long for us to arrive at Mrs. McKay's

house, as she lived on the very next street. It was a nice-looking white, two-story, medium-sized house, sitting on an evenly cut, beautifully manicured green lawn. The flower beds out front were enclosed by a small picket fence that went all along the front side of the porch. They were all in full bloom, and this gave it an appealing storybook type of setting.

It looked so clean outside, so it was not surprising to see how clean the interior was. *Brenda sure was doing her job well,* I thought, as I looked at the freshly polished look it had everywhere. The mirror over the pretty little shelf in the living room was almost blinding with its crystal clearness.

Even though there were no kids around now, the place had the love and feel as though it might have once been a nursery. You could tell Mrs. McKay was one who really loved babies. You know what I mean? The kind who still had a twinkle in their eyes and a shine all over their face, still laughing and smiling as though everything was still the same as it was then.

"Gladys, is that you? I never thought I would live to see you again. Come over here and let me look at you." In a childlike way, her smile made me feel like I was that young little baby again. "My, how you have grown. You were only nine months old when you came to live with me, you know."

At first, I felt speechless. But the more she talked, the more I began to want to know about her. She went on and on as though it had only been a day or so ago. "Then we used to call you 'Precious' because that is just what you were. Such a good little baby. You were hardly any trouble."

"Well, why did I have to leave?" The question just sort of popped out of my mouth.

"Well, my husband's health began to fail him, and I just couldn't give you all the need and attention with having to care for him all the time," she said solemnly.

"You mean there were other babies here with me?" I asked.

"No," she answered. "There were three little boys who were older than you, but they were also quite young, too." Laughing, she added, "I remember how bossy you were with them when you first started to talk."

"How long did I live here?" was my next question.

"I believe you must have been around three years old when they moved you up to Romeo."

"You remember Romeo too?" I really got excited now with the mention of that name.

"Yes, Gladys," she said softly. "That was such a lovely foster home. I came up to see you once after you left here. I guess you were too young to remember it. But I missed you so much, and I just wanted to know that you were in a nice home."

Then Brenda spoke up. "I sure would like to see this

place called Romeo. Gladys has talked so much about it since I met her."

Suddenly there was something else that gripped at my mind to ask her before I forgot. "Mrs. McKay, did my mother ever come to see me?"

"Yes," she answered right away.

"How did she look?" I asked anxiously.

"If I can remember correctly from the two visits, I distinctly recall that she was young, olive-brown complexioned, with a beautiful thick head of hair. She spoke very little to me. But from what she did say, I can see that she had a slight accent to her voice."

I wondered about that. But I couldn't stop to linger; I had to know more. "What did she do when she came to see me? Did she hold me or kiss me?"

"I recall that on both occasions when she came, she didn't stay long, nor was I expecting her," she reminisced. "It was kind of strange how each time when she visited, you were napping. She would pick you up, smiling, swaying you back and forth in her arms. As you would begin to awake, she would put you down quickly and head out the door, never saying another word about whether she'd return or anything else."

"That happened on both visits?" I looked puzzled now.

"I thought it was sort of weird too," Mrs. McKay

spoke up. "It was as though she didn't want you to get a look at her face."

"And maybe she didn't want me to look into her eyes," I proposed. "Maybe she thought she'd fall deeply in love with me and want to take me back?"

"Maybe so." Mrs. McKay had a look of concern on her face now. "But for whatever reasons, I am sure she'd be proud to see how you have grown up today."

We talked a bit more about some of the silly little things I guess all kids ask about when they are way beyond their baby years. Then she invited me back whenever I felt like coming. She insisted.

"Now, Gladys, you come and see me from time to time. I would like to know how and what you are doing."

"Okay," I promised, leaving there with a whole new perspective on who I was. Although it wasn't much, I was told about my parents. I felt like I was somebody who had a mother and, somewhere, a father. I was somebody who must have been loved very deeply and somebody who must have been missed and remembered to have been visited.

All these years had gone by, and for some unexplained reason, I never felt any real anger towards my parents for them giving me up. I was really too young to have been so understanding about it all. I had accepted being free and alone as though it was my very own will.

Sure, I felt different, but I enjoyed this feeling of complete freedom. No one to take me anywhere I personally didn't want to go, so to speak. I made up my own mind. I decided what I should do. Me, myself, and I, and I hope, God. More so than ever, as I look back now, I know for sure a Super Being was watching over me.

***

I made a lot of lasting friendships while growing up in Inkster, but for some reason, I was always a loner at school. By that, I mean I never hung around with just one group or set of individuals. I just kind of knew everybody and stayed on a pleasant, congenial, happy plateau with them all. Some of my friends dated back as far as the third grade. We went to the same elementary school right on to junior high and then on to high school together.

I always enjoyed my school days, mainly because the personalities of my friends were exciting. They always had fresh new ideas and things to talk about that really stirred my intellect. There was Margaret Williams, Sharon O'Neill, and Linda Allen, the three girls I used to walk to elementary school with every day. They lived right around the corner from me, and I spent a lot of time even after school hours with them.

Also in my same classroom were two other neighbors, Heather Burton and Annie Tripp, who lived on the street facing mine. I could see both of their houses from my front porch due to the big open field that separated the two streets. Heather also lived in a foster home, and Annie's mother was a seamstress who made me a dress for one of our school programs.

Some more of my friends from the earliest days were Teddy Reid, Ed and Mary McClendon, James Glaxe, Bob Patton, JoAnn Preston, Alice McClure, Odell Williams, Helen Pruitt, Delores Horne, Valerie and Marjorie White, Dorothy and Larry Murphy, Deborah and Frances Steel and their two brothers, Bernard and Howard, Juanita Gray, Georgeanna Ingrams, Mildred Rogers, Josephine Cargill, and still there are more I could name.

Inkster was the kind of town that didn't have many big crime stories to read about every day. So if something very drastic happened there, the news hit the town like a tornado. I remember the day when one of my classmates was hit and killed by a fast-moving freight train.

I was only in the seventh grade and had never before mourned the death of anyone who had been close around me. Even after hearing the news that she had been hit by the train, it never registered in my mind that she was dead. Hurt badly, I thought, but not gone forever.

It happened around 2:15 on a regular school day. Half of our school got out at 2:00 p.m., and the other half was released at 3:00. I was still in class when they brought us the news. It hadn't been the first time that the kids would all run and try to beat the train as soon as they heard the ringing bells at the crossing rails. But this day, as I understand it, Dorothy Murphy was teasing with her buddies who had already made it across. She bet that she could do it within minutes of the approaching train, waiting for it to get closer.

Well, she was a minute too late. The train knocked her up into the air, and she flew way across the tracks onto a nearby side street. Her body was covered by the time we were walking home after school that day. Shock, disbelief, fear, and grief filled the atmosphere there in Inkster. We just weren't used to having bad things like that happen in our village.

From that day on, the kids knew that playing on the railroad tracks was out for good. It is a shame that some lessons had to be learned with someone suffering destruction. It took some time for me to turn that dark, gray day back into the sunny days I was accustomed to. My life went on there in Inkster, and I grew up with a healthy outlook on it.

***

Oh, how I remember my first childhood sweetheart. I think every girl keeps this guy forever in the back of her mind, even after she has had her own children and they have grown up. It is something so sweet with that first love. Something so innocent about it until you find yourself following those memories almost forever, no matter how happy someone else might have made you.

I remember my guy was named Lonnie, Lonnie Sanders. I met him when I was in the eighth grade. It was during a basketball game one night at Inkster High School. I was still attending junior high school, which sat right across from the high school.

I had gone to the game with Christine, who was a freshman now and having her first year there. We were all sitting in the bleachers rooting for the home team when someone behind us caught Chris's attention. She later leaned over and whispered in my ear that a friend of hers behind us wanted to meet me.

I quickly turned around to see who, what, and why, when I was met by a set of beautiful hazel-colored eyes, reddish-brown hair, and a smile that would have melted a ton of ice.

"Hi," he spoke right up, showing no signs of even being the *least* bit shy like I was. I don't think I responded right away because I still had my mouth open with amazement at how attractive he was. *He sure was cute,*

I thought. *Why me?* No, no, it couldn't be true. Then he complimented me on my new haircut by running his hands over my neck and saying, "I like your hairstyle."

"Thanks," I managed to swallow hard to relieve the dryness that was all choked up in my throat now.

"What grade are you in?" he furthered the conversation. I can remember suddenly wishing that I was now in high school, although something in the back of my mind told me it didn't matter. He had his eye on *me*.

I could see by his legs that he was very tall and slim. His coloring was that of a high yellow complexion compared to my darker brown. He took my hand in his after the game was over and said, "I would like to walk you home if you don't mind?"

"No, I don't mind," I accepted, but I warned him that he would not be allowed to come inside. "My foster parents would never approve of it. You see, I am not dating anyone yet."

"Umm, too young, I guess," he laughed.

That night started it all. I didn't know what to say about myself. A *boy* walking *me* home! Christine, a few of her friends, and other kids who also lived in that direction were all walking out that way. I had a nervous feeling all over, not to mention that I was scared that Mrs. Jones would look out of the window and see us walking up to the house with the boys. *What would she do?* I thought. *Scold us right in the front of them?* The embarrassment was certainly something I didn't want to have to go through, so I stopped Lonnie at the corner, telling him he had walked me far enough.

Before I could turn and go, he quickly drew me close. In one swift motion, he firmly yet ever so gently kissed me. His lips were warm and soft, and I could hear his heart beating wildly against my chest. At first, I was lost in his kiss. It was as if nothing else existed except us. I was suspended in time until I heard Christine's voice say, "Hurry up, come on, Gladys. I think I see someone watching out the window." Forgetting to exchange numbers, I quickly darted to the house.

I didn't even know where he lived. I only know I spent that whole weekend with him on my mind. I couldn't wait until Monday morning for school. Chris and I had already planned it all. I was to meet her at lunchtime in the high school cafeteria.

"Just come. He will be there. I am sure."

"Okay," I agreed. "But don't forget to tell him when you see him at his locker that I am coming."

There's nothing quite like that puppy love. It's like a brand-new awakening you have for the love of school, your friends, and yourself when you find yourself in it. Everything takes on a whole new meaning, and your mere existence seems spiritually heightened.

As I reminisce through those memorable years, I realize that it is at this very moment when you discover your first feelings of love. It's now that you start to grow more mentally and physically stable. Suddenly, you care about what happens to someone else critical to your well-being. All those "grown-up" desires like getting married, having children, buying houses, and getting jobs become a major part of your future now. Your whole world is now full of pure magic and opportunity.

Yes, this is a happiness that you want to last forever,

and in some kind of way, you *know* it will. All you need is each other to live happily ever after. Your eyes shine with love, your life is so alive, and your world is full of all those wonderful, loving thoughts. Oh, the virtues of that first young love!

I met Lonnie that day at lunchtime as planned. After that, he met me almost every day after school unless he had something else very important to do. Some days we ate lunch together. Others, he would walk me home, or we would stop by the drugstore for sodas after school. We talked on the telephone daily, and we were nearly inseparable.

Even though I was still not allowed to date or have company, school was our outlet and one chance to see each other, and we did *plenty* of that. At first, kissing and holding hands was all we ever did. Then one day, he popped the big question.

"No," I said right away. "I might get pregnant."

"Please," he begged. "I can't stand it much longer. I have got to relieve myself of all this emotion I have got bottled up inside of me for you. All this longing and yearning you've caused me… I can't help it. Don't you love me too?"

"I do, I do. But I am scared."

"Scared of what?" he asked. "We love each other. If anything happens unexpectedly, we'll get married." Of course, that is what everyone in Inkster ever did in those days. Somehow meet, fall in love, get married, and have babies. *Lots* and lots of them. That was the biggest news event for the whole town.

Somehow, I escaped any real results from Lonnie's passionate "necking" and love-playing, and we had been together for almost a year. I was now in the ninth grade, and since we were both attending Inkster High, we decided we wanted to share lockers. This is what the kids did at our high school to show that they were going steady. It was like sharing a love nest together.

Everything with us was under control and going fine until a classmate of Lonnie's asked him if he could lock with us for a while. His name was Marvin Brooks, and all the kids around school called him "Meatballs." I knew there was going to be trouble when Meatballs found it necessary to gossip about Lonnie whenever he would catch me at the locker alone.

"What do you see in him?" he questioned me.

"None of your business," I snapped, turning him off right quick.

"I will show you what kind of man you got," Meatballs threatened one day.

I didn't pay him any attention until one afternoon when Lonnie didn't show up at the locker at our regular meeting time. I began to worry. It was getting late, so I just decided to walk home by myself.

When I got outside, I saw a large crowd of kids gathered at the corner store where everyone went for sodas after school. Usually, I would have kept on walking because I was never one to egg on the makings of a fight or dispute. But for some reason, this day, I felt an urge to see what the gathering was all about. Before I could reach the crowd, I saw Lonnie push his way out of the middle of them all and run down the street toward his house.

Meatballs and about two other guys were right behind him, shouting all kinds of insults. I was so outraged when I finally caught up with Meatballs and his group that I could have burst. At that point, they had stopped chasing Lonnie and were joking and laughing about it.

"Why are you picking on Lonnie?" I screamed. "You big bully!"

"Oh, are you going to do the fighting for that sissy?" he snorted nastily at me. "He sure can't fight himself."

I looked to see, but Lonnie was way out of sight.

"What do you need with a wimp?" he continued to put Lonnie down.

I knew Lonnie like the back of my hand, and I knew he didn't have a mean bone in his body. He was easy-going and just plain sweet. He was so easy to get along with—a peace-loving guy. I had been with him for over a year, and we hadn't even had one *real* quarrel. If we disagreed about something, he simply went along with me. From there, we would get on some other conversation. That is why I knew Meatballs must have provoked whatever fight had happened.

Later, I found out that this was Meatball's way of trying to belittle Lonnie in front of me so that I would see him as the better guy. In short, it didn't work. Lonnie was the *only* one for me. This feeling lasted with me until Lonnie changed it himself.

It happened one day at the movies. There was only one movie theater for us kids in Inkster to go to, the Melody Theater. Every weekend, it was the meeting place for us kids to hang out. Couples would meet and sit together and neck throughout the whole picture. I know neck is a little old school, but I think you know what I'm talking about. Truth be told, Lonnie and I never knew what picture was playing.

On this particular weekend, I had told Lonnie that I didn't think I was going to be able to come to the movies. Well...I changed my mind at the last minute. Usually, if I didn't go, Lonnie wouldn't go, so I didn't expect to see him there.

But oh, did I see him! I saw him sitting with another girl, kissing her, feeling on her breasts, and necking just like we had done so many times before. I was about two rows behind him, and he didn't see me when I came in. But I recognized *him* from the shape of his head as soon as I sat down. My foster sisters Christine, Trula, and Lilly all were with me.

"Be cool," Chris whispered to me. "Let's watch him awhile before you let him have it."

Chris was calm, but Trula was ready to get it on right away. She kept saying, "Don't let him get away with that!" she hissed. "He is supposed to be *your* man."

Me, I was "too hurt to cry and too much in love to say goodbye." Devastated was an understatement. The love of my life was lip-locked with another girl. What could I do? When I couldn't take any more of his deceit, I jumped up and ran towards the front entrance.

"Gladys, Gladys!" yelled Christine. "Don't leave, don't leave!"

On hearing my name, Lonnie ran back to where he saw me headed and stopped me before I could get outside. He knew I had seen him with the tears in my eyes as proof.

"I am sorry," he said. "But, Gladys, I am a growing man, and I needed to make love with someone. And she turned me on. That is the only reason I am with her. She gave me some, and I knew you wouldn't. Please understand," he begged.

"How long has this been going on?" I cried. I suddenly realized that it probably was not the first time. He confessed that she had given up her body to him numerous times for almost a month now.

I went love crazy. I started calling Lonnie names and saying things I really didn't mean.

He was still so sweet, even after getting a taste of my temper. He offered to stop seeing her and told me that she knew about me because he had told her. I couldn't see beyond my jealousy. I blurted out, "Go on back to her. I don't want you now, so just go on back in there to her."

Meekly and calmly, he said, "Are you sure, Gladys? Are you sure it's what you want me to do?"

"Yes, I'm sure!" I yelled out loudly. "I hate you!"

With these words, he slowly turned around and went back to his seat. I had too much pride to call him back, although I wanted to. He was too sweet for me to really hate. Still, just the thought of him going back in there to sit with her would not let me rest my case.

With a chip on my shoulder, I went back to sit two rows behind them where Chris and the rest of the girls still were.

"What happened?" they all loudly questioned me. Instead of talking about it later, we all started making loud insults about the girl and Lonnie, who were now just sitting there watching the movie. I knew they both heard every word because that is the way I wanted it. I wanted to hurt his feelings because I had been hurt.

Honestly, nothing compares to that *first* hurt. I think I even lost weight behind that heartache. It took me a while to forget and let my poor wounded heart heal. I discovered that heartache was part of growing up.

***

You've got to learn to be a good sport about losing, although living in Inkster made that quite difficult to do. One of the first negative things I learned about the kids in Inkster is that they hated to lose at *anything*. Additionally, they don't mind showing you their retaliation in person. Already, I had been at a few basketball and football games where Inkster High had lost and several big fights had erupted.

The girls in Inkster were as bad as the boys. They were all sore losers. Once, I remember when they caught a few of the visiting team's cheerleaders and cut their hair off. The kids were so bad that some schools even refused to play Inkster schools.

I had learned my lesson about trying to beat them not long after I first arrived at the foster home. We had a baseball game on our street one day, and my team was beating Christine's team.

When the game was over, she came up to me and said, "Why don't you go back to where you came from?"

Still smiling, I said, "I won, I won!" and she hit me hard in the head with the bat. I felt so dizzy that I thought I would blackout. Never once did I start to cry. The funny thing is that Christine started to.

"Are you all right?" some of the kids asked me as they helped me home. I guess with a blow like that to my head, they expected that I should have fallen. Christine apologized later on. After she hit me, she said that she was so scared that she might have hurt me badly. That's why she started to cry because she didn't know what was going to happen.

From then on, when Chris didn't get her way, she just slapped your face when you least expected it. I still hadn't joined in with the woes of the losing team as of yet, but I knew that there was no easy way to beat these kids. They were hard. If you happened to win and got away clean, you could *really* consider yourself the winner.

Yeah, winners. That is all I thought about when I heard the announcement on the school loudspeaker that day.

"The winners of the talent show will get a record audition with Detroit's Motown Records."

Another talent show! This time, I was going to have a group appearing on it. I had been to almost every talent show the schools there in Inkster had. It was something good about seeing what gifts the many students possessed.

I will get a group together today, I decided. I asked some girls from our school chorus because I knew they had some kind of singing ability. Mr. Phillips, our director, was always urging me to take part in their group ensembles and the school's musical competitions. Therefore, I figured I would start there. I saw Katherine and Juanita first.

"Girls," I asked, "Do you all want to be in my group for the talent show?"

"Sure," they said. "Who else do you have?"

"I need some more singers, so tell all your friends who might want to participate to meet over at my house this afternoon after school."

I called Rosemary, JoAnn, Georgia Dobbins—some other friends of mine who loved singing—until I was *sure* I had enough girls to pick from. It looked as though I was having a party going on at my house that evening. We were all in the basement singing and belting out some of the hit recordings of the day by The Chantels, The Shirelles, and The Bobbettes.

First, I was really concerned with who all could harmonize easily. One of the most important things about a singing group is knowing how to stay on your pitch. Georgia Dobbins was the first girl I picked. She was already out of school, but I had seen her several times in different talent shows. Therefore, I knew what she was capable of. Remember, I wanted *winners*. Then, I picked Katherine, Juanita, and Georgeanna. With myself, that made five. So now, we were ready to roll and start rehearsing for the 1961 Inkster High School Talent Show.

The girls who were not picked didn't make a fuss about it. Nobody expected anything big to evolve out of a mere high school talent show, not even me. We put in a full two and a half weeks of rehearsing and practicing some dance routines. Then we had to decide on costumes. I had pictured that Georgia Dobbins would lead the song we were going to sing, but she insisted that it might take away our chances of winning first place since she was out of school.

They were looking for student winners, so Katherine volunteered to lead the song. It was an original song that Georgia had come up with just for the show. The song had a lot of harmony and unison singing involved. Even then, she was already trying her hand at songwriting.

"Come to me, come to me. I want you, baby. I need you, baby, so come to me, come to me."

We practiced and practiced and practiced until it was perfect. The night of the talent show arrived. We were all gaily dressed in white skirts and pretty blue blouses. I am sure if there had been an award for best dressed, we would have surely placed first among the other acts.

The high school auditorium was packed with families, friends, and school faculty members. I thought I had conquered the battle of stage fright long ago from singing in church. Still, I had a bad case of the butterfly jitters.

Georgia Dobbins really had the confident look of a long-time star, and I think it was she who gave us the strength we needed to lean on. I know my knees were shaking like a leaf on a tree when they called our group on stage.

"And now, here they are, Inkster High's newest girl group, The Cassingyettes." The cheers from the crowd

Gladys Horton | 55

released my tension as we were walking on. Trying to remember my routines along with my own harmony voicing didn't seem as easy to put together as it had been at our rehearsals. Still, I got through it. Everyone seemed to be enjoying our act as I glanced every now and then into the faces of the smiling audience.

After we came off stage, I still couldn't seem to shake the nervousness brought on by seeing all my friends watching so intensely. There is no doubt about it; trying to impress your school buddies takes much more out of you than the Sunday church member crowd. Maybe it's because you fear your school friends' disapproval more than anything else during your teenage years.

Now, my greatest fear was going to be… maybe losing in front of *everybody*.

We just had to win. More than anything else, *I* knew I wanted to win it. I held my breath as the host announced the top three winners.

"Third place went to the female songstress, Miss Millicent Morris." The audience did a soft clap to congratulate the ladies.

"Second place was male soloist, Clarence Finch." Clarence was so good! I just *knew* we had him beat, though.

"And first place winners are…" It was so quiet you could even hear a straw drop. I held my breath to await the final result. "The Jazzmen Quartet."

If I had the power to just fade away, I think I would

have used it at that moment. To me, it was like a year's work all just vanished. I felt finished up, completely unnecessary, and a total failure.

We didn't say much on our way back to the dressing rooms where all the participants had dressed. I could tell by the looks on the rest of the girls' faces that we all felt some distress.

I guess some of that sore loser, no good sportsmanship manner I spoke about Inkster kids having had somehow rubbed off on me. As soon as I saw Millicent Morris, the girl who had won on female vocals, I walked right up to her and said loud and boldly, "You didn't sound like shit."

If Millicent had not been the sweet mannered girl she was, I am sure that night would have brought on the first fight I ever had at school. But she just humbly hung her head and walked away. I really felt rotten inside, but I needed to get mad in order to regain my strength of character. I guess that is an easy way of explaining the horrible feeling of defeat.

I was glad that the weekend seemed to drag by slowly because I really didn't want to face the following Monday morning at school. I knew that the talent show was going to be the main topic. Several of my friends made it easier for me by saying our group was the best dressed. Some even mentioned that they didn't agree with the contest voting. I just wanted all the talk of it to go away. It only made me wish more than ever that we could do it all over again.

I was headed to my first class when Mrs. Sharpley, my typing teacher, stopped me. "Gladys, I thought your group was marvelous Friday night on the show. I understand that you all placed fourth on the list."

"Oh, I didn't know that," I said, trying to look pleased with a half-smile.

"In that case, I am going to have a word with the principal about you all being able to make that audition," she smiled. I almost did a flip.

"Oh, thank you, thank you!" I wanted to jump up and down and hug her. She must have seen me come back to life because she added, "Let's wait and see what he says. Okay?"

"Okay," I agreed.

Again, I was living on high hopes and daydreams, just like a big secret. Something inside warned me not to tell a soul, so I kept it to myself all that day. Later on, around lunchtime, my wishes came true. When I saw Mrs. Sharpley's face smiling as I walked toward her, I knew that the principal had agreed to let us go to the audition.

"Gladys, the principal also thought that you sounded sensational, and he accepted the offer to let you all go along with the other winners." I gave her a big hug and ran off to tell the other girls.

"We have got to start rehearsing right away," I told

them. "We know what talent we are up against now, and we have got to be better than we were that night."

This time we picked a medley of songs to do. We started off with "I Met Him On Sunday" by The Shirelles, then onto "He's Gone "by The Chantels, "Come Go With Me" by The Del Vikings, and last but not least, Frankie Lyman's "Why Do Fools Fall In Love." We also picked the colors red and black for outfits that day—black skirts and red blouses. We were going to be hot stuff.

It was a warm, pleasant day in April of 1961, and it was the day of the grand audition at the only known recording company in the Detroit area, Berry Gordy's Motown Records on 2648 West Grand Boulevard. I remember driving up to the company that day. A group of three or four cars was our means of transportation.

"Look, there is Mary Wells," someone yelled. And sure enough, I saw Mary coming out of a building that read "Hitsville USA" on top. She went and got into a long black limousine that later drove off. Oh, how I wish that we could have been closer to her to get her autograph. That just started the excitement rolling.

Upon entering the studio, we saw the spitting image of a gorgeous recording artist with her long blonde hair and hazel eyes. She was built like a small, petite goddess with not an ounce of fat.

"Who is she?" someone asked.   We were later told that she was Mrs. Raynoma Gordy. *Rich and wealthy they must be,* I thought after looking at her.

Then someone took us on a short tour of the building. There were secretaries sitting behind typewriters who looked up long enough to smile as we were passing by. When we got to the recording room, they took us into the control room to see who was in session. No one was recording, but we saw Mabel John, "Popcorn" Wiley, and Andre Williams around the piano, creating some song or rehearsing a tune. I don't know which, but it was all so exciting.

Stars were all in my eyes. We all marveled at the pictures on the walls of all the artists now recording with the company. I saw professional black and white glossy photos of Marv Johnson, Barrett Strong, The Miracles, Jackie Wilson, Mary Wells, Mable John, and a gorgeous girl group called The Supremes.

Then came the audition. We met Brian Holland and Robert Bateman, two songwriters and producers who were conducting the audition for us. Need I say more than that? Even though everyone was terrific that day, Robert and Brian saw a place for our group in the company. They chose us, The Cassingyettes, to win the audition.

"But listen, girls," they warned us. "This is only the beginning, and it is up to you whether things go any further. We need hit song material around here. Being a success takes hard work. Do you girls have any original songs? You sing The Shirelles and Chantels really good, but they have already made those songs a hit. You need some songs of your own. Go home and put your heads together, and when you think you have something that might take you to the top, let us know."

I think that little pep talk—along with the producers telling us about the dynamic girl group they already had from the pictures—is what gave us the fuel we needed to really start our engines burning. Georgia Dobbins, who was the oldest and most experienced now in songwriting, automatically took over as our group leader and adviser.

"Oh, listen," she said before we went our separate ways later on that day. "I know a guy named William Garrett who has tons of songs he has written. I am going to call and make plans to meet him next week and see what we can come up with."

***

The next week found us all gathered around William Garrett and his briefcase of many songs. I watched Georgia as she seemed to be on a mission. Nothing could get in her way. She rambled through the songs, reading the titles quickly to herself. I saw her when she stopped at a page and slowly took it out from the others—"Please, Mr. Postman."

I looked at the title on the sheet music she was holding. "This is a catchy title," she told Mr. Garrett. "Will you sing a little of it for me?"

He began to sing the words. *"Please, please, please, Mr. Postman, my little girl done left me here all alone. So please bring me a letter to this unhappy home."*

It was real bluesy, something Cat Waller Brothers or Scatman Crothers would do in those days, but not five teenage girls. Georgia asked him if she could just use his title and compose a whole new story behind it.

William Garrett already heard the news of our new singing career with Motown. He assured us that he didn't care what we did with the song as long as he got credit for the title and his name on it as one of the writers. This we agreed on.

This is the true story of how the song "Please Mr. Postman" had its beginnings and was later taken down to Motown to be heard by our producers. I remember it sure didn't take Georgia long to come up with a new story for the song. A very cute and realistic one, everyone thought. She came over to my house about three days later, singing it to me. God knows how I admired her for her pure genius qualities and ability to quickly finish whatever she took upon her to do. She wasn't fooling around; she meant business. That is why I was so upset when she explained to me why she couldn't lead the song.

"But we need you, Georgia," I begged. "You are so good at all of this."

"You will be too if you just go ahead and give it your very best." She wanted me to lead the song. "I know you can do it," she told me.

Georgia went on to explain that there was no one to care for her mother at the time. She couldn't commit herself to the hard work of being a part of the group. We had to look for another member, it seemed. At first, I thought, *mission impossible.* I knew that there was only *one* Georgia Dobbins. When you have experienced working with the best, it is hard to accept anything less.

But as luck would have it, I heard it through the grapevine about another girl who was also out of school and had appeared in several talent shows in the area. Her name was Wanda Young, and I was told, "She can *really* sing."

"Well, I am going to find out," I said to myself aloud.

I knew it wouldn't be hard getting anybody to join our group, especially when the whole village knew that we had a record contract waiting to be signed as soon as we got our material together. So now I was going to be *very* choosy. They had to have something extra, something more than just the ability to sing. They had to look the part and be star material. They had to have personality, poise, and precision. I was looking for someone who had it all packaged perfectly and ready to go.

Wanda sure came close to fitting all those descriptions. You might say she was too good to be true. She fit right in with the rest of us girls.

"I am so glad you found me before I went away to

nursing school," she told me later on. "That is where I was headed if I didn't get a job soon. Now here I am doing exactly what I have always wanted to do, sing."

Yes, "Please Mr. Postman" seemingly started out with some sort of magical powers. Everyone who heard it fell in love with it right away. Brian and Robert instantly decided that we had a smash hit recording and that we shouldn't waste too much time before going into the studio to record it. They rehearsed us until we had it perfect, background and lead. Then the question came up about what we would put on the flip side of the record.

"Do you have another original song?" they asked.

No, we didn't, but we had a little more knowledge on how to remedy that situation this time.

Wanda brought it to our attention that her brother also was a lyricist. "He has got millions of words but no music," she explained.

"Fine," I said. "Bring them on over to my house. I am going to get on that old piano on our porch and make up some music to his words." I don't know what prompted me to do this. But I played, and Wanda sang the lyrics until we had another original tune. Wanda's strong falsetto voice proved to be another asset to our overnight success story.

The day of our grand first professional recording session had arrived. Everything so far had happened so quickly between the talent show and the winners' auditions. Both were held in April, and now around the last of May, we were about to create our first record. It's a wonder that we still had our heads on straight with all the hard work and preparation. Still, the time had finally come.

I remember it was on a warm Saturday afternoon shortly after 12. Katherine's parents came to boost our morale for the session. It was going to be a live recording with the musicians in the same studio as us. That is the way it was done in those early recording years.

That is also the first time we met Marvin Gaye, a musician and a singer who was the drummer on the session that day. Then there was Eddie Willis on guitar, James Jamerson on bass, and Dale Evans on piano. There were two soundproof booths set up for the vocals: the lead in one and the background singers in the other.

"Take one," the producer said in our earphones, and the magic began. After hearing that very first tape back, I knew it, and everyone else in the studio that day knew it too. Motown's first #1 was becoming a reality.

The more takes we did, the more confident I felt about the song. Just before we were finished, in walked two of The Supremes: Mary Wilson and Florence Ballard.

Their reaction while listening to what we were doing was one of disbelief and amazement.

"You all have a smash recording; do you know that?" they both spoke out loud in the control room for us to hear. It was music to our ears.

Then Florence, who seemed to be as excited as we were, asked if she could spend a little time with me to show me some ad-libs that would make the song more outstanding. This unpredicted, unpremeditated reaction might very well have been the beginning of that dedicated, undenying vocal spirit everyone seemed to later on possess, which helped all the Motown artists to achieve so much so fast. She came right in, wanting to do whatever she could to help, even if it spelled success for someone other than herself. I will never forget it.

Once I got the knack of what she was talking about, filling in the blank spaces with the "oh yeahs" and the "please, pleases," I started to loosen up and do a few things on my own, like adding that ever so popular phrase, "Deliver De Letter; De Sooner De Better."

Sure enough, our final taping proved to be the best one. Satisfaction showed on the faces of everyone there. Even the musicians had given far beyond what was required for a typical recording. So much love for what everyone was doing came out in the final product of that recording. It was as if a holy presence had been abiding there throughout the makings of it all.

Then suddenly, we heard a voice. It was the voice of Diana Ross coming through all the talk and excitement about our song.

"Who is that singing that song?" she demanded to

know. Such sass!

Thus began the meeting of Miss Ross, who even in those days carried a lot of authority with her in her attitude.

"It is only me," I wanted to say, but she recognized from seeing all of us together that we must be the new girls' group.

"Where are you all from?" she questioned us, eyeing us very closely now. "Inkster." We almost said it together in unison.

"Inkster!" She bugged her eyes wide now with a ridiculous stare. "Where is Inkster? I have never heard of it before."

Yes, even then, she held the power of reducing your ego to nothing. But for some reason, I liked her. She really made you feel like she knew what she wanted, and there was no one, not anyone, who could stop her.

Diane had to show us how good her group was as they sang a tune that had a perfect blend of harmony. They really looked professional with their make-up and clothes. These were no ordinary city chicks. They had been working at this a long time, and they sounded terrific—Mary, Flo, Diane and Barbara.

Diane and I became halfway friends that day. As I talked with her, I could see it in her eyes that what we had just walked right in and recorded was a smash #1 hit, which had been her long-lasting desire. She made it sound like a joke. Before we left that day, she laughed, "Who do you girls think you are coming in here and getting a hit record out before me?"

It was the beginning of many successful recording years for us and later, The Supremes and a host of other recording artists.

***

"Please, Mr. Postman" was released in August of 1961. It had found its way to the #1 spot in both Cashbox and Billboard Record review magazines by December of that year. It doesn't seem like so much could all have happened in just nine short months, the same amount of time it takes for a baby to be born.

Yet, here I was. I had a whole new life ahead of me, a brand-new career, and a great big world ready to be shown to me.

The radio stations everywhere were playing our song on the hour every hour. Sometimes we would turn to three different stations where they were all playing the song at the same time. I guess that was enough to blow anybody's mind, but I took it all in stride and remained under a controlled restraint.

The whole village of Inkster had lit up with our spotlight shining all over the place. The town was finally put on the map. No, we were no longer those small-town country girls anymore. Like they say, "When you're hot, you're hot, and you have got to move with the groove."

With each passing day, we were gaining more and more worldwide recognition, and the demands for our appearances on stage shows and at record hops were overwhelming. *Dick Clark* was one of the first big national television shows we appeared on. Everyone in Inkster knew we had gone straight to the top when we went to Philadelphia, Pennsylvania, to do his show live.

Our high school even canceled its all-time favorite homecoming game because the show was on the same date as the game. Everybody wanted to be home watching us on television.

Mr. and Mrs. Jones and all my foster home sisters were so proud of me. Even they couldn't believe all the success I was now having. Something like this had never happened in Inkster before. We were the "talk of the town" for years and years to come.

We were all still in school except for Wanda, and that alone was beginning to create many problems. It was hard for me to study and get my mind back into my schoolbooks after spending a weekend in New York City. Wow! Now *that* was a place that really blew my mind. It was like visiting another planet with tall buildings, skyscrapers, cars, and taxis everywhere. Oh, and millions and millions of people.

When I got back to Inkster, I felt like someone had

turned the lights out. The company was taking bookings for us only on weekends because of our school schedule. Once, our principal approved a two-week tour for us to go out on. The only catch was that we had to make both a written and oral report on all the things and places we had seen while traveling.

I can remember that tour took us to Washington D.C. first. We visited almost every tourist site there was to see: the Lincoln Memorial, the Washington Monument, the Pentagon, the United States Senate building, the tomb of the Unknown Soldier, the many different embassies, and last but not least, the White House.

We had to make the most of these tour spots early in the morning before our daily shows at the Howard Theater in D.C. This turned out to be very tiring for us nighttime show people.

Next, we went to the Royal Theater in Baltimore, Maryland, for another weekly stage show. Before we came back home, we did three nights as special guest artists at the world-famous Apollo Theater. This was an all-time treat and one of the greatest experiences and thrills of my first travels as a teenager and superstar recording artist.

I remember I had my whole class laughing at the embarrassing moment I had during our very first stage show appearance when we got to D.C. The announcer called The Marvelettes, and we had never been out on a stage that big before. So I stayed in one corner and led the song while the other girls stayed on their side of the curtains, all jammed up together, not knowing how to get to center stage on time for that first chord on "Postman."

We were just amateurs, and it really showed. After all, we were just kids trying to live the good life. Luckily, we cleaned up our act fast after seeing how polished and professional The Miracles, Marv Johnson, and some of the other artists on the show were. All the kids in my class at school really enjoyed my oral report. They could really relate to it and felt the stigma of our success. So, it was no surprise when I left school and moved to the big city.

Gladys Horton | 71

CHAPTER 2:

"THE MOTOWN ERA"

Moving to Motor City and into the hands of Motown Records was like a second phase in my life. It was one of the biggest and most important moves I could be making. There was no way for me to feel the great pressures upon me then because many things don't register so dynamically in your brain when you are young.

I was old enough to know that there were going to be many changes. And optimistically, I felt they all would be for the best. So, at least I was making a decision with a positive sense of view. It was hard to think any other way with all the great things that had already happened for me.

Record contracts had been signed by the other parents, but now there was a legal matter pending with the signing of my record contract. I needed an adult representative to legally sign as legal guardian over my business affairs. I was still very much a minor in the eyes of the law.

Because I was an orphan, a court-appointed guardian would have to be made. This was going to take some time to sort out. First, a court date had to be set for a hearing, and I had to send off a request for my birth certificate to use as proof of being born in the USA. Plus, I had to find a responsible adult that the court would approve of to manage my business estate.

Sending off for my birth certificate opened my eyes to some truths about myself that had been unknown until now. I was 16 years old. Imagine celebrating your birthday on the wrong date for all those many years. Yes, I found out that May 30th was my correct birth date. I hadn't been too far off, though. I had been celebrating on May 10th up until that time.

I hate to sound so completely ignorant, but I didn't even know that I *had* a middle name. My given birth name was Gladys Catherine Horton. My mother had been born in Montreal, Quebec, Canada. She had three names plus her surname—Dora Madalyn Catherine Lowman. And my father, who was born in Macon, Georgia, was good old John Thomas Horton. From the sound of his name, I thought he probably was a scientist or something. I smiled at the thought of having a genius for a father.

My birthplace was even a mystery to me. To my surprise, Florida was the state from whence I came, born in the beautiful city of Gainesville. Yes, that little document of my birth was somehow really a rebirth for me mentally.

Other information was now given to me by the supervisor and head authorities at the Children's Aid Society in Detroit. I got in touch with them to request a reading of my records. I was so curious now about whether they had a forwarding address on my legal parents. Unfortunately, nothing could be found. But there was some recorded information about my family history, which dated back to my grandparents from the West Indies Islands. Trinidad was the island mentioned. It seemed when they left the Islands, they went to Canada to live. There my mother was born, just as it was stated on my birth record. How she met my father and why I was born in Florida was not mentioned. Neither was any substantial reason given for my being placed in foster care.

"Maybe it was supposed to just be temporary," I was told. And in these cases, sometimes a full report on the family history is not requested. Nevertheless, I knew more now about myself than I had in 16 years. My true roots were from the West Indies Islands. The knowledge of this had added some background to my life. I felt I had found some depth to my character. I was somebody *real*, and I wanted to know more about my ancestors. So, I promised myself that as soon as I got a chance, I was going to the library to read up on the islands of the West Indies. I owed it to myself to try and find myself.

Berry Gordy's oldest sister, Mrs. Esther Edwards, played an important role in providing me with the proper court-appointed guardian. She was the wife of George Edwards, a Michigan State Representative. With a track record like that, no court would deny someone of that status the right to help serve and protect the interests of an orphan child who needed proper guidance.

So, after the legal proceedings that followed our request, she and her husband became my court-appointed guardians over my business affairs. They co-signed my record contracts, and now I was legally a member of the Motown family. My checkbook titles read "To the Estate of Gladys Horton, a Minor." Oh my, did I feel important and very, very rich.

One day Berry Gordy Jr. requested our group's presence at a meeting being held by himself up in his personal office. This really stirred our curiosity. The company president meeting with us? Until now, Berry had not made himself invisible to us, but he never had personally said more than "hello" or "I'm very proud of the work you are doing."

We all picked up from the very beginning that he demanded respect, and that is why he gave so much of it. So playing around with the artist needlessly and carrying on idle conversations was not a part of his character. Like I said, we didn't see him much. We just knew he was usually in his office attending to other business. Today he showed his friendlier side to us. He smiled a lot and asked us if we were happy being with the company.

"The main reason I asked you here today is because

the company is turning down lots and lots of jobs for your group because you are all still in school." He went on to say, "What we have decided to do, of course with your approval, is to send Gladys and Wanda out with three other girls until you finish school. A tutor will be paid from Gladys's estate to continue her education. But we need her more now because she is the main lead singer. After you all have graduated, your places will be welcomed back in the group."

"Oh my, oh no!" the girls protested.

"We don't want anybody else traveling in our places. Our parents wouldn't hear of it," they complained.

"How come we all can't have tutors?" someone asked.

I believe the question of the high cost and who would control the payments for this service came up. Finally, the girls were talking about quitting school.

"Well," Berry added, "just think about it this way. You aren't going to learn any more in a year than you already know now."

"But what if we don't have any more hit records 10 years from now? How are we going to survive?" we wanted to know.

Berry then told us that we would always have the company to fall back on for jobs. Later, I heard that the parents were so upset with that meeting that they allowed the girls to quit school to fulfill our show obligations.

We always carried a chaperon with us but never again were tutors mentioned. Besides not having the money to afford one, we didn't have the nerve it took to give up the limelight until we got our high school education.

For an orphan, opportunity sometimes only knocks once. I felt that if I could make enough money in this business, one day, I could further my education. But as for now, I had to take what was in front of me—a singing career.

Good luck seemed to follow us through the following years. We always worked, had constant hit releases, and were kept very busy recording, traveling, and learning the pros and cons of the business. It was the little things like our first record hops, our first outfits, and the first time we missed our plane to an engagement that stands out most in my memory. It was also all the in-between attention and love from some very influential role models that helped us grow into outstanding, respectable young ladies.

I remember the day Raynoma Gordy took our group downtown to buy us our first record hop uniforms. They were a two-piece skirt and jacket, emerald green with big gold buttons. She also made us realize that keeping your weight down was very necessary to be admired by your fans.

She was a perfect size 5 and always wore some fancy tailor-made suede or leather outfits that always fit her like a glove. Just looking at her made me want to be that slim, petite figure that always looked good in everything I wore. We were around this positive look, so it made us want to be that perfect size. By the time I reached the age of 18, I was finally a size 9/10. Wow! Did I feel good about myself.

Another influencing person in our lives during those years was Claudette Robinson. On and off stage, she was the shining sensation of The Miracles. Along with her smile being a key point, she was a perfectly well-groomed artist. Her size also was very neat, and her clean conservativeness was more than I could find the words to describe.

I just know I admired her for her sweet personality and the way she always watched us to make sure we were conducting ourselves in a ladylike manner. She believed in females acting like females, not men. That is one great lesson she taught us.

We were always asking her about the perfume she would wear. She would tell us the fragrance, and we would all run out and buy that same brand. As soon as we stocked up on one fragrance, I noticed that she would start wearing another scent.

One day I asked Claudette, "Why do you keep changing your cologne?"

She laughed at how I noticed everything. Then she politely said, "Because I want my husband to be able to smell me from all the rest of you." That made sense. I thought about it later on. We were just silly teenagers, and it is hard not to be big copycats. We admired her so much until we wanted to do *everything* she did, even wear the same cologne.

I know now it was all about growing up and seeing the right people to make you want to do the right things. All the things that being a part of Motown meant to me can be summed up in one word: living. Living a great life, living a prosperous life, living an adventuresome life, living at a joyful time, and a blessed one.

Motown may have been before its time. It was like an era from the future being swept down upon us so suddenly that its fire is still burning in the hearts of people everywhere. That is why even today, many still claim it to be #1 and the only one of its kind. Not only was it a sound, but Motown carried a certain feeling with its existence.

The life of a song is forever. That is why our songs will never die. The soul makes the heartbeat forever. That is why the love for it never goes away. Motown, Motown, always to be remembered.

Many times, I have been faced with the same question over and over again. "What made Motown so different from all the rest?" But, just like it is hard to define the mysteries of the universe or to question God's work, so it is answering that question.

But if I must speak out, I would say that no one man can take the credit for all the powerful and wonderful things Motown did to bring blacks out of the darkness when all most of us had were 9-5 factory jobs.

I believe that God uses people to bring about the goodness He wishes to bestow on this earth. He knew Berry Gordy, Jr. had a dream. He knew that dream, if it was fulfilled, would change the whole structure of the slavery environment most of us were still very much a part of. He also knew that Berry would need other people with dreams and desires to help build up this fantastic music empire for the earth.

So, he sent these talented but poor souls to seek the temple of the beginning of that dream, which was that first building on West Grand Boulevard in Detroit, Michigan. A temple that God used as a magnet drawing all the right pieces together to complete a puzzle. Every artist, every musician, every employee, every song and work of art; yes, every entity that walked through those doors was a part needed to complete that puzzle. That is why everything fit so perfectly together and worked out to be the greatest.

No earthly man had the power alone to do what Motown did for the whole world. Now the question may arise in your mind, what if Berry Gordy had not had the dream of a record company? Well, I say this supernatural power might very well have used Thelma Gordy's company, Wyngate or Fortune Records of Detroit as the temple provider. It was time for blacks to find a way of survival through the use of their own inborn talents. Luckily, Detroit was the center of this great beginning. If this city had not been ready, we would have lost our turn and someplace else would have been the starting point. I am sure.

I know we are all familiar with the words of a song that goes somewhat like this, *"You have got to be ready, or God will be moving on."* It is the same way when you are qualifying for a job. If you don't have the right qualifications, believe me, someone else does.

I know now what I hadn't even thought about at the time. The Marvelettes first recording of "Please Mr. Postman" opened the door to that temple so wide until I bet you nobody involved with Motown Records had to worry about ever looking back. It was the right song at the right time, plus it had an international, universal message that everyone could relate to—the postman and writing letters.

Some might say we may have only played a small part, but we also had a piece of the puzzle that needed to be fit into place. Take The Temptations hit recording, which said, *"Like a snowball rolling down the hill, it's growing. And where it's going to stop, nobody knows."* That is the story of Motown after their very first #1 tune by The Marvelettes.

Every group and every artist who followed continued on with nothing but top chart-busting hit releases. Billboard and Cashbox found Motown artists filling the top 10 spaces every month. Even the producers and writers seemed to be moved spiritually. There was magic and meaning to the words of their songs. And the different sounds that the producers came up with, like foot stomps and handclaps and finger-popping, sold millions of records. High energy was flowing all over this place, and you felt it as soon as you stepped inside the door.

The artists, we took it all over the country with us wherever we did shows. We made everybody feel that Motown spirit. It couldn't be hidden. Everybody just wanted to be a part of its happenings, spreading happiness and joy all over. If there was a depression going on, our music lifted everyone's spirit so high that it lightened the burdens of it all. People were *happy*. People wanted to sing and dance. People loved the life we were all living. Yes, Motown was my reason for living.

Sure enough, these were times when things were pure and simple. Man's desire for money had not been blown way out of proportion. Many of us were just happy doing what we loved best, even if we weren't becoming overnight millionaires.

Just think about it, when a record sold for only 45 cents and albums were $3 or $4, how long would it take for a group of four or five to get rich? Other charges, which included the price of recording, stage wear, road expenses like airfare, hotel, and food bills ate up your profits. Nobody was filthy rich in the beginning unless you had a job that didn't call for these types of expenses, such as people who worked behind the scenes and in the background. You wrote, produced, or arranged music. These people in the business usually stayed at home, making it possible for them to put their money into the nicer homes and the finer cars.

That is why we always saw Brian and Eddie Holland, Mickey Stevenson, Lamont Dozier, Norman Whitfield, Raynoma, and Berry Gordy, Jr. all driving big fine cars and living in the penthouses in those early days.

Nowadays, it is a whole new different story. Most artists now write, produce, arrange, and sometimes are even able to market their own material. It shows music has made a big step forward in advancing all its possibilities to its clients.

By 1964, I think Motown had signed over 33 acts and possibly more. These included five girl groups: The Marvelettes, The Supremes, Martha and the Vandellas, The Velvelettes, and The Andantes. The 10 male groups were The Temptations, The Four Tops, The Contours, The Spinners, The Valadiers, The Originals, The Satintones, Lee and the Leopards, The Love Tones, Sweet James and the Fantastic Four, and around the late '60s, The Isley Brothers.

There were four groups with male and one female member: The Miracles, The Monitors, The Elgins, and later, I believe it was, in 1967 that Gladys Knight and the Pips came to the company. Eight female artists included: Mabel John, Hattie Littles, Mary Wells, Chris Clark, Brenda Holloway, Kim Weston, Carolyn Crawford, and Tammi Terrell. Ten single male artists: Marv Johnson, Barrett Strong, Andrae Williams, "Popcorn" Wylie, Eddie Holland, Gino Parks, Shorty Long, Jimmy Ruffin, Marvin Gaye, and Stevie Wonder. Two recording bands: Junior Walker and the All-Stars and later, Rare Earth; and one ventriloquist, Willie Tyler and Lester. Several Motor Town Revues had toured the United States and Europe by then also. Our group had worked with almost every act I mentioned at some time or another during our career span.

While being interviewed, we were always asked how all those acts got along doing some of those month-long tours. "It was incredible," I would say. We had all loaded up on the bus out in front of the recording studio. Before we pulled off, the tour manager or either Mrs. Edwards would come on board and give us all a serious pep talk. Reminding us that we all had the obligation of representing the company and ourselves in the best of everyone's interest.

"People are going to talk, talk, talk," Mrs. Edwards would say. "It is up to you to make sure they remember the good things to talk about."

Those last-minute talks always left us looking forward to putting our best foot forward and giving our anxious fans everywhere we went a show that they could never forget. You can bet whenever a Motor Town Revue played a city or town, they always asked us back for more.

Besides putting on great shows, there was an amazing amount of respect given to all of us female singers on the tours. As you know, boys will be boys, but those guys from The Temptations, The Four Tops, and The Spinners, or whomever the male group was on those tours treated us like they were our big brothers. They made sure our luggage was carefully unloaded at the different hotels and never failed to ask throughout the tour if things were going well with us. They never allowed strangers to enter our tour bus, even if they were only in search of autographs.

I remember Melvin Franklin, with that deep bass Temptation voice, kindly telling a few excited male fans who had found their way to our hotel, "The ladies on this tour are chaperoned, and they don't sign autographs in the hotel lobbies." It truly was an unforgettable experience.

***

Traveling in the South in those days wasn't completely safe, no matter who you were. During this time, Martin Luther King was marching and fighting for the Civil Rights Act and demanding justice and equality for us all. I recall one incident where the bus got shot at during a stop to eat at a restaurant that refused to serve us upfront.

"Get down," Billy of The Spinners yelled to us ladies who were sitting by the windows. A couple of other guys in the group ensured that we were all safe from gunfire while driving off. Their concern and love were greatly appreciated.

The Four Tops were the oldest of the guys in the male groups on the tours, and they had a finesse and dimension about them that was hard to copy. The "Gentlemen Four" would have also described their group to a "T." They were professional, mature, and always showing that they considered us to be nothing more than perfect ladies.

We girls didn't do too bad either when it came to acting like sisters. Ordinarily, sisters do fight, you know, sometimes over little things like make-up and clothes. But it was never any of that gutbucket, downright jealousy being displayed among our girl groups. Instead, we all cheered each other on.

There were certain places like the civic auditoriums

and the convention centers where we all had one big, gigantic dressing room that we shared with ease. There were other moments when our disagreements hit the fan. These moments were usually experienced on the bus or some other time. *Never* during showtime. Nothing negative ever lasted too long with the Motown artists, simply because there was too much positive energy around us all.

The musicians on these tours were already acquainted with the music scores perfectly. Most of them had played on the original recording sessions, thus giving our shows the sounds of the actual recordings. Fans were always telling us that we sounded just like the records. I saw the band members signing almost as many autographs as the artists.

The Choker Campbell Orchestra, those musicians were fantastic on and off stage. They were always punctual and ready to hit it at showtime. They had a great bandleader, and it showed. There was never a problem with our music. Any entertainer can tell you that your performance is much smoother and more professional when you don't have to worry about your songs being played correctly. The critics all raved about the Motor Town Revues in the '60s.

"Outstanding!"

"Maybe the greatest show on Earth!"

It really was like living in a dream. There were other people involved in this Motown era. We had to reach a happy medium with the writers and producers at the company to keep the success story going.

"We want to come up with total smash hits," Berry kept stressing to everyone. To the writers, that meant getting the right artist(s) that could deliver their songs and their feelings the best. To the singer, that meant making sure the key was right for you and that you felt the song. It is hard to bring out or deliver the right message to a song that you're uncomfortable with or just don't like.

We were out to be #1, stay #1, and get the #1 hits. Working together with lots of understanding was essential, and getting the job done on time was demanded. We were able to achieve them both.

***

Raynoma Gordy kept us girls on our toes for being fashionable, but Mrs. Maxine Powell and Mr. Cholly Atkins taught female and male artists how to polish our stage routines. And as Mrs. Powell used to put it, "to bring some charm into our act."

So, to charm school and dance classes we all went. On the days that we weren't recording, we were exercising, learning new techniques for coming on and off stage, and how to handle the microphone correctly. Cholly also taught us how to gracefully get in and out of different routines, construct a unique, positive style for long medleys, and gracefully change from fast songs to slower tunes.

And, so you see, the Motown era was a busy era for me. It was Motown, Motown, all the time.

***

Our first year at Motown was a totally busy, successful one. We never dreamed that all of this would be happening to us as a result of a high school talent show.

Along with the success that came so fast that year was the news that Wanda was having a baby. It shook everybody up.

"So soon?"

"What!"

We had just gotten started and were really on the go when we had to stop. It turned out that she was already six months pregnant and would have to be away from the group for another six months. Florence Ballard of The Supremes traveled with us around this time until Wanda returned to the group around the middle of 1962.

This year had started out with no high expectations. Personally, I had started to count my many blessings for God had shown me many. For I was an orphan whom nobody knew existed until now.

The first Motor Town Revue went out in 1962. The joy of working with so much talent was indescribably fascinating. Somehow with this tour, I knew we were touching the face of history. Our group was really working hard in the studio, trying to come up with another chartbuster. Another big one like "Postman" was what we were looking for.

We weren't having much luck until I brought a song called "Playboy" to the producers' attention. They liked the title, the story, and even the way I sang it. It was immediately recorded and released.

Our new single went to #7 and was followed by Beechwood 4-5789, which was written by Marvin Gaye. This year we also recorded and released two more albums: *Playboy* and *The Marvelettes Sing*.

Our travels for this year included many of the Southern States: Alabama, Georgia, Texas, the Carolinas, and Virginia. Television shows included local shows like Robin Seymour, Detroit's own dance party, and we found ourselves for the second time on Dick Clark's *American Bandstand*.

That year also found us on our first Dick Clark tour. Some of the acts we performed with that year included the following: The Dovells, Gene Pitney, The Shirelles, Brian Hyland, The Four Seasons, Kitty Lester, The Falcons, The Ronettes, Little Eva, The Crystals Fabian, Bill Doggett, Solomon Burke, Dee Clark, Gorgeous George, The "Duke of Earl" Gene Chandler, Dee Dee Sharp, Patti LaBelle and the Bluebells, The Impressions, Little Anthony and the Imperials, Chubby Checker, The Orlons, Tommy Hunt, The Vibrations, The O'Jays, The Intruders,

Barbara Mason, Gladys Knight and The Pips. Also, artists: Aretha Franklin, Maxine Brown, Ben E. King, Jerry Butler, Betty Wright, Chuck Jackson, just to mention many of the groups around during the early '60s.

Our fame and popularity were growing fast, and we were well on our way to becoming superstars. Our act was more polished by 1963, but before the year was over, The Marvelettes had been reduced to three girls: Wanda Young, Katherine Anderson, and myself. The stress from the road and the wear and tear of show business had first interfered with the health of Juanita Cowart, who left the group first. Now it had taken its toll on another group member, Georgeanna Tillman, who suffered from sickle cell anemia.

Though being faced with these hardships, we had to go on. We had come far too far to turn around now. This year found us with our first two-sided hit, "Locking Up My Heart" and "Forever." Other releases for the year were "As Long As I Know He Is Mine" and "Strange I Know."

Berry Gordy tried something different and did something this year unexpected for our group. They released a song by us under another group name to see what the reaction would be with the fans. In November of 1963, we had a song released under the name of The Darnells entitled "Too Hurt to Cry, Too Much in Love to Say Goodbye."

92 | *A Letter From the Postman*

1961: The Marvelettes 1st Group Picture

Gladys Horton | 93

THE MARVELETTES Personal Management
BERRY GORDY, JR. ENTERPRISES, INC.
Detroit 8, Mich.

**1962: The group was now four members.
Wanda was out having her first child.**

Though the song, I thought, had a remarkable punchline and story, it didn't catch on fast enough for the company to really promote it. So I guess you could say it was one of those fly-by-night songs, here today and forgotten tomorrow.

Strange enough, though, many of our fans recognized that it was really our group by the sound of my voice. We got plenty of fan mail asking why a fictitious name had been put on our group to release this song. Yes, we found out early that you can't fool the public as easily as you wish you could in this business.

To stay on top, you have to keep coming up with smash tunes.

1964: The year we first went abroad. London, Holland, and Belgium were some of the places we played. Nothing it seemed could stop us now. We bought better dresses and used the proper stage make-up, giving us a much more professional look.

We tried every style of wig: long, short, medium. We changed our wardrobe and shows and were just more relaxed at entertaining our audience as a whole. We were truly living a more professional lifestyle with all the hotels, room service, and bellhops at our command.

1964 brought out songs like "He's a Good Guy, Yes He Is", "You're My Remedy", and the most popular that year, "Too Many Fish in the Sea."

To top it off, we had the first marriage out of the group.

Wanda Young married Bobby Rogers, a member of The Miracles. It was truly an experience being a bridesmaid for the first time in my life. Of course, you would think that her being a married woman would change things. Luckily, marriage in no way slowed down the lifestyle of the group. We were off and running at least two or more weeks out of every month.

By 1965, we had them all dancing to the beat of "I'll Keep On Holding On." We also were socializing or slow dancing as it was called to "No Time For Tears." Then we warned them all with "Danger, Heartbreak Dead Ahead" and later on too with "Don't Mess with Bill." Wanda's lead on this Top 10 tune gave our group a new contemporary, sexy sound style. On top of that, a good deal of attention was brought to Smokey Robinson as the writer of the tune. Therefore, Smokey Robinson asked for the exclusive writer's rights of our group. That meant that his songs would be prioritized over other songs for being first released.

We agreed. So, from now on, it was to be Smokey's songs that people heard us singing on the air. This proved to be the right choice because our record sales were back up again. Before this year came to an end, the group was blessed with another wedding. This time, Katherine Anderson married Joe Schaffner, a road manager for many of the Motown groups, including our very own at different times.

THE MARVELETTES

1963: The group had now been reduced to 3 members. Wanda was back. Georgeanna and Juanita were out for medical reasons.

THE ORIGINAL MARVELETTES
(Bottom Right) Lead Singer Gladys Horton
(Left) Wanda Young (Top) Katherine Anderson

1964: The year the Marvelettes first toured England.

Well, that was two down and one to go. Believe me, I was having too much fun to even *think* about being next. I hadn't met anyone who stayed on my mind long enough or kept my interest for over six months. There just wasn't enough time for me to get involved in much more than all Motown had to offer me. I had a great time this year, and the highlight was our trip to Bermuda and to the island of Bimini off the coast of Florida.

***

1966 started out with another release written by Smokey Robinson called "You're the One." This one was okay, but it just didn't do it for us the second time around. Later that year, Smokey's next written release put us back on the map at #13. That one was "The Hunter Gets Captured By the Game."

That year we went on the Otis Redding and Joe Tex tours. We celebrated my 21st birthday three times while we were on the one with Joe Tex. The tour included acts like Joe Tex headlining, Solomon Burke, Percy Sledge, and James and Bobby Purify, just to mention a few. The first surprise party they gave me was in Atlanta, Georgia. The second one, which I caught them putting up the decorations for, was in Pittsburgh, Pennsylvania. The third and final celebration was in Richmond, Virginia. I didn't know what to expect after that. I had never celebrated any one date so many times or even had anyone to do more than just wish me a happy day. It was one of the most exciting experiences of my life, to say the least.

I guess that contributed to my feeling that my meeting of Sammy Coleman, a trumpet player with Joe's band, was something far more important than it really was. Nevertheless, we started going steady, and I spent a great deal of my off days traveling around with Sammy on some of Joe's dates. We were seeing far too much of each other if you get my drift.

By 1967, I found myself repeating the marriage vows. Sammy and I had made our relationship official. Our group had always had Johnny Gilliam as the guitar player and band director. Now, even though we didn't need it, the group decided to hire Sammy as a trumpet player so that we could travel together. The good it did us. I ended up getting pregnant as soon as I started to share my bed on the road! I was scared, nervous, yet still excited. Being with child still didn't slow me down.

That year we had songs released like "When You're Young and In Love," "Keep Off, No Trespassing," and the last one for me was "My Baby Must Be a Magician." I continued to travel with the girls until my seventh month of pregnancy. We went out and bought some chiffon, which was a flowing type of stage wear that didn't show my pregnancy so much. We also calmed down a lot on our routines to make things easier for me.

Of all the times I could have gone to my mother's birthplace in Montreal, Quebec, it had to happen during my first pregnancy. I remember our dates there lasted for about a week, and I was so excited about seeing that city. It was fabulous. We joked about a street being named Catherine one day as we were riding around sightseeing. My middle name was Catherine, and then there was a Katherine in our group.

"The street was named after me," I insisted.

"No, it wasn't," Katherine Schaffner shouted. "It is *my* street."

I wound up winning the debate only because the spelling was closest to my own name.

That trip to Canada stayed on my mind long after we were back home. It had felt good to me to be in a place where my mother had once been. I even decided that maybe one day, I would like to live in Canada. It is such a lovely, peaceful place with many friendly people.

Gladys Horton | 101

1967
The Group Wore More
expensive Dresses Now
I Had got Married.???
And January 1968 I
Left to give birth to
my First Child

THE MARVELETTES
Tamla Recording Artists

Direction:
International Talent Management, Inc. (ITMI)
2648 West Grand Blvd.
Detroit, Mich. 48208

1967: The group wore more expensive dresses. Now I had to get married? In January 1968, I left to give birth to my 1st child.

***

January 1st, New Year's Day 1968, was the last show I did as a part of Motown. I remember it had been a 10-day engagement at the Fox Theater in Detroit, Michigan, starting just before Christmas until New Year's Day. On the show with The Marvelettes were The Miracles, The Temptations, Stevie Wonder, Willie Tyler and Lester, and Gladys Knight and the Pips. Wow! *What* a line up. I knew it was going to be my last show before the baby came. So, before the last night of the engagement, I told Gladys Knight, in front of my girls and her guys, that it was up to her to keep the name "Gladys" famous from now on. She just laughed it off as a joke, but never once have I failed to hear good remarks about anybody whose name was the same as mine. In fact, their group started a new day in their career there at Motown, which later took them to greater heights in their profession elsewhere.

Until that last year, Berry and I had never had an unkind word to say to one another. Unfortunately, that last show brought out an unforeseen argument between us. Whether he started it or I did is up to someone else to be the judge. The whole thing started over some light green dresses we had worn during one of the shows where he was in the audience watching us. Someone knocked on our dressing room door after the show and politely told me, "Berry says that he can see your stomach showing in those green dresses and not to wear them anymore."

"God forbid such a command coming from him," we all thought. But for the first time in our travels, all of our stage wear had been stolen while we were in New York performing. We were not able to replace all the dresses, with me being pregnant and all. So, our wardrobe was already reduced and limited to about only four changes. *Now* he was asking us to lower ourselves to only three changes for stage. Needless to say, we weren't hearing it.

"Well, you can just go back and tell Mr. Gordy," I angrily shouted, "that I am having a baby, and I am *supposed* to be showing by now! Nothing can hide that!"

Word came back to us that Mr. Gordy absolutely forbade us to ever wear those green dresses again. Defiantly, I sent the message back that we were going to wear the dresses at the very next show. You could *feel* the anxiety in the air backstage before the show. Everyone was patiently waiting to see if the sweet mannered, loving Marvelettes were going to go against Berry's last word. Well, we didn't wear the dresses. I was so angry with him that I wanted to cry. Wanda and Katherine both had talked me out of going ahead and wearing the dresses.

I never faced Berry or argued openly with him about the subject, but we both could feel the tension. We had had our first misunderstanding, and, of all times, it had to be at the time I was leaving.

Right now, to this very day, I will never understand why we were never awarded a gold record for "Please Mr. Postman." It sold well over a million copies; I know. But if for nothing else, but for all the energy, hard work, and time we put into those years at the company, it would have been something to show for it, because I sure didn't have any money.

I have no regrets though because these were wonderful years for me. Years with memories that will never die. All that I learned through the experiences I had can never be taken away from me. There's an old saying that someone said to me once that stuck with me forever. To own gold, something that can be stolen, can't be the *only* thing you will ever need. But to own your own *soul* is far better than carrying around that heavy load of gold.

CHAPTER 3:

"POOR LITTLE RICH GIRL"

"You don't have to leave the company and your career just because you're married and having a baby," said Wanda. She and I had had many discussions about it before now. I knew this was true because nobody ever came forth and said to me, "We expect you to leave if you are going to begin to raise a family, Gladys." It was totally up to me what I wanted to do. I just couldn't get past the thought of me finally bringing someone into this world that was of my own flesh and blood.

"Please try to understand," I begged Wanda. "I have been without any of my kinfolks these many years. I want to dedicate all my time now to that someone who will be *truly* related to me, my newborn baby." I knew Wanda was unhappy with my decision, but nothing could change my mind. I was determined to bring my child into this world the "right" way.

On second thought, maybe my husband could have changed my way of thinking. But he seemed perfectly satisfied with my decision to leave the group. I remember him saying, "I will be able to triple what you were making as soon as I get my business together."

His business, and only business, was playing that trumpet. I was soon going to find out how he was going to support me, a new baby, and make the payments on the new house we had just bought. Living in the limelight had distorted my vision of what the real world was all about. I had all the potential and opportunities for becoming a successful, rich person. Still, until now, I was still nothing but a "poor little rich girl." There was no doubt about it. I hadn't been singing long enough to be as rich as I felt inside.

Show business has a way of camouflaging all the flaws and scars of the true struggles most artists are up against. The fans see you being chauffeured and pampered and catered to as if you had the wealth and prestige of any queen or king. They only know that it takes a lot of money to live this way. They figure you *must* have it.

What most artists hate to admit is that they *don't*. So, they secretly live a lie, hoping and praying that one day their fans' beliefs of them will become a reality if they only hang on long enough. And that is exactly what you have to do—hang on long and tight.

That takes more than just strength. The frustrations of those days for me were going out on the road and spending most of the money made on hotels, food, clothes, transportation, and hired help. Then, after management fees and agent fees were taken out, we had to divide maybe $1,000 or less among a group of three or four. Then, when you received your share, you had bills at home to pay, which used up all or most of those earnings. Then you had to look the part of an entertainer, which took *more* money. Smiling all the time, all glittered up in silks and satins… but penniless.

I used to take the bus to and from the studio until it was brought to my attention that the public can't accept you being a star with you living such a common way of life. Yes, I had to pretend I had it made. In reality, all I had was a fascinating job for all to see. I was dressing up for my work but still paying taxes and more taxes at that. Despite what it may have looked like, I needed plenty of work like anyone else.

Now here I was after seven years of recording and still wondering how I was going to make it work. One of my biggest expenses for all of those years was all those session costs. We had recorded so many songs, and many of them would never be released. We were always in the studios recording, and that kept us always running up a big bill.

When our royalty checks came, you would have thought that it was Christmas around the company. *That* is the money you got the most of, enabling you to keep up the charade the public expected to see continuously. I was never one who liked putting on false airs or pretending that I had something that I didn't have. It was *that* part about show business that I hated the most. I wanted the things in life that didn't cost anything, like having someone to *really* care about you and love you enough to make you feel happy about just being alive. It was about being able to share your inner feelings with someone who felt the same way about you too. I wanted to live comfortably and not worry about a lot of bills.

Let's face it; I was used to a certain kind of lifestyle by now. Still, I was not spoiled by the superficialness of that style. I just wanted my husband to be able to feed and house me decently. Big diamonds, fur coats, and fast cars never excited me. I wasn't going to miss them. I just wanted a marriage that I could be proud of. I didn't want to think about it as being my #1 biggest mistake, but time certainly proved that to be true. You just don't give up a career like I had overnight and not expect to pay dearly afterward.

It is not like I hadn't been warned years before of what happens when you don't have a mate of your own caliber. I remember a lecture being given to our group once by Mrs. Edwards, who was trying to make us understand that we were young ladies who were in demand. "So, you just don't run off and marry a guy because you think you love him or he vows he will always love you," she warned. "You need someone who is going to be able to support you in ways that help you to keep your honor and pride always in life. Even if he is not a millionaire, the respect and love you are getting from everywhere you go and from all the people who know you won't last if they see you in any lesser light than they do now."

I knew she was right. But I felt like she was asking us to go look in the classified ad section of a directory for the right man. "But suppose you don't love him even if he can support you?" I asked her.

I remember how she laughed and said, "Gladys, you are going to see how fast love flies out of the window with someone who claims so much love but has no finances."

The whole idea was so depressing to me. It's hard to give up your dream of Prince Charming and living happily ever after with the man you truly love, regardless of the material things you may have or may never get from him. One thing now that was certainly true: I was married to a man I cared deeply for and respected, but I was *not* hopelessly in love with him... not even on our wedding day. That is when I should have had the courage to just say no. I always thought your wedding day is supposed to be the happiest day of your life. If that was the case, then why wasn't *I* really happy? I guess it was something telling me then I was making the wrong move. You can't buy happiness, just like you can't buy love. These are two things that no price can ever be put on. And for some reason, it is hard to have them both at the same time.

It wasn't that my husband and I didn't get along very well because we did. I remember how I used to love to listen to him talk on that tour when I met him. His ability to keep me wanting more mentally was one of the first things I noticed about him. He was like a preacher, and I was the full congregation. He would talk about the black brother and sister and how we had to come together because we held all the riches and all the knowledge of this wonderful land within our two unions. It was the white man who had separated us years ago and broke down our powerful family structure.

"Amen," I almost said plenty of times. *This sure was a good Christian man,* I thought. I even overlooked that big pot belly of his for his handsome smile and his seeming understanding of all things. What I forgot to look for were the things he *didn't* say. I had never even seen his mother or father until after we were married—another very ignorant gesture on my part. Nobody in their right mind should take such drastic actions without looking up the family tree and history. These people will be part of your children's personalities. It is very important to know whom you are really spending the rest of your life with.

The music part of our lives was the only thing that was compatible. Maybe if we had combined my singing with his playing trumpet, we could have found a reason to stay together. But his jealousy of me being out on center stage showed itself shortly after the honeymoon was over.

Come to think of it, there never really was a honeymoon. We were working in California at a club named

Guys and Dolls over on Crenshaw the week we got married. I will never forget how he started pushing me around as soon as we got back to the hotel from the preacher's house. It was our day off work and his aunt and uncle, who were then living in California at the time, offered to call a preacher they knew could perform the ceremony at his house.

For some strange reason, I just wanted to hurry up and get it over with. That wasn't a natural feeling to have on your wedding day. I didn't bother to even invite Katherine, Wanda, or Johnny to come and go with us so that they could be present during the marriage vows. I had built him up so big in the eyes of the group to the point that I knew I would feel like a fool if I didn't go through with it. Something in the back of my mind kept telling me to wait, just wait.

I know now that even if you have a church or a house full of people waiting to see you march down the aisle, if you are not feeling those glorious feelings of love, you'd better disappoint the world if you have to. It's your own life you are ruining, nobody else's. They will all go home and sleep well that night, and you, maybe you will get what I got.

I can remember him telling me to move out of the bathroom. When I took too long, he rudely pushed me out as if to say, "I don't have to pretend anymore. Here I really am." I didn't want to believe that his manners had changed so quickly. I didn't carry on any further discussions of his actions. I just quietly thought about his behavior for days afterward and wondered, *What have I gotten myself into this time?* I could feel that he was very proud of himself to have been the one to land the one and only Gladys Horton, and he was going to show me that the show was over. That is what *he* thought. But in many ways, it was really just beginning.

Dennis Edwards of The Temptations, who started out working as the house band for a nightclub called Mall's Lounge in Detroit gave my husband his first job with his band. What could have been more perfect for our situation! He didn't have to worry about traveling on the road making peanuts anymore and being away from the beautiful old English mansion we had just purchased through an FHA loan.

He was working six nights a week making a flat salary of $250 a week, which in those days was a lot of money for being a musician and working in a small intimate club. Along with his session work, I would say he was raking in almost $2,000 a month.

I had put about $5,000 in a joint bank account when we first settled in our home. It was just something to start us off with, hoping he'd keep saving his money and adding to it. I enjoyed keeping my house clean and immaculate, so I stayed home a lot. It was so big and roomy. I would sit for hours before the baby was born and draw up designs and plans on how I wanted to decorate every room.

We bought unfinished furniture for the baby's room

and waited to find out whether it was a boy or girl before we chose a color to paint it. We had moved into the house just before Christmas of 1967, and Sammie was born in March of the following year, which gave me time to have everything in place.

I was like a little girl with a real live baby doll. Sammie was all I thought about and all I even cared about. I just wanted to be left alone to be able to devote all my time to his survival. One friend of mine called to tell me one day that I had let my baby just take me away from *everything* else in the world. You know what? Her words had some truth to them because I had surely become overly neurotic with motherhood.

If Sammie opened his mouth to cry, I was instantly there to soothe him. His feedings had to be exactly on time. I never let him go with wet diapers no longer than minutes after I realized it. I rocked him to sleep. I kissed and hugged and spoiled him beyond comparison. For once, I felt that kind of happiness that makes you give and give of yourself without ever wanting to stop. My husband saw how wrapped up I was in the baby, but he didn't seem to mind.

When he'd come home after working the club around 3:00 a.m., he just naturally would go to one of the other four bedrooms. He would look in on me and see that Sammie, Jr. had so innocently taken up his spot. I tried to keep the baby in his own bed, but every night about an hour or so before my husband would come home, Sammie, Jr. would make such a fuss until I would have to put him in my bed if I was going to get any sleep.

My husband didn't seem to mind it at all, even though our sex life was now nonexistent. I later found out that he wasn't missing anything. He was having lots of fun out at the club every night. No wonder he never asked me to go. I wouldn't have anyway. Nothing was going to take me away from Sammie. He could do whatever he wanted to. Just leave me and my baby alone. Well, that was the story for about the first four months.

Then the next thing that happened drove me even farther away from ever getting close to him again. One night while we both were busy in the basement, a silly argument arose over something so small I can't even remember what it was. Sammy was ironing his band uniform while I was washing and folding up clothes. I must have been winning the debate over our dispute because it angered him to the point that he threatened to hurt me physically. He lashed out at me with a hardness in his eyes as he said, "If you don't shut up, I will stick this hot iron to your face." He moved fast towards me and was standing over me with the hot iron, ready to carry out his dreadful promise before I could even think about whether or not he was serious. As I looked back at him, I *knew* he was.

I couldn't believe my ears. Nothing had even been said that would have even brought on such a wish or desire for him to want to scar me for life. His words were that of a man full of hate who couldn't have felt anything good or decent about me to want to do that to me. I knew

I had to bite my tongue and show a humbleness like never before if I wanted to keep my body and facial features. But every inch of whatever type of feelings I had for him died that night with his threat. I hated him with a raging desire. If looks could kill, then he would have dropped dead that very next instant because my very soul was silently cursing him.

Here I was. I had given up a glamorous life and career to try and make some man on this earth happy and proud to be able to say I belonged to him. Now, he wants to make me ashamed to even be seen by other people. *Lord, help me to survive,* I prayed silently. It was tearing me up mentally that I couldn't say the words that were all bottled up inside of me. I knew that there were times when silence was golden, and *this* was one of those times.

I vowed to myself that very moment that I was getting away from this mad man one day. But for now, I had to play it safe and keep my mouth shut. I knew on my wedding day that I had settled for less than what my deepest desires had always been. That was to marry a tall, dark, handsome, intelligent, distinctive, and well-known, well-bred man. One who simply adored me and whose love and strength of character would carry me to the ends of the earth with him willingly. But somehow down the road, I began to think that this kind of man only existed in the fairy tales.

So, I had settled for someone who didn't have all those qualities. Instead, I thought we had a warm, sweet understanding of mutual trust and loyal friendship and togetherness, wanting the best for each other.

Now, I knew that even *this* was a mistake. So far in our relationship, I had always given him due respect and never nagged or bothered him about his nightlife

Up to now, we had never had any fistfights. We always talked calmly and maturely about any and everything. So, for him to lose control and show me that he was even capable of *thinking* such a horrid thing made me wish I never had to see him again. Something went out of our relationship that I can't define. From then on, I didn't trust him or bet on what he would do.

Maybe that is why I made a trip down to the bank one day where I was faced with another surprising fact about my husband. I hadn't checked on our savings account since I put the $5,000 in right after we moved into the house. I guess I secretly wanted to find out how much money my husband had been adding to it since his job at the club was going so well. He had been taking care of all the financial business since the baby was still so young. I just didn't get out to do as much lately as I had before.

It was no surprise to find the checking account was overdrawn. But when I was told that my savings had been almost completely washed out, I wanted to find a means of destroying him completely. I had foolishly opened a joint account with him, and he had been drawing money out of our savings without even bothering to ask or let me know.

Now I realized this man was really a stranger that I

didn't know at all. I had read somewhere about con artists like this that even go so far as marrying the woman just to make it easier for him to cheat her of everything she owns. I knew I had to put a stop to this whole situation. But how? He had already shown me a side of him that I didn't even know existed. Now, I was finding out something else. He couldn't be trusted, *and* he was a big liar.

When I calmly but firmly confronted him about my trip to the bank and my finding out about the monies that had been taken out of our savings, he just shrugged his shoulders and nonchalantly asked me, "What are you going to do about it?" The truth was written all over my face to see. There was nothing I *could* do.

"But what did you do with it?" I nearly broke down in tears with the thought of wanting to kill him.

He just walked away while saying something to the effect that he used it on a couple of car notes and some insurance that he had gotten behind in. "Don't worry about it. I will put it back in as soon as I can."

I knew how soon *that* would be. His drinking tab at the club nights had already begun to eat up half of his weekly salary. At least that's why he told me his checks had been reduced.

I was beginning to see the hidden light. So, I mentally started to plan my getaway when something else occurred, showing me that I better hurry up. This was no ordinary man I was married to. Besides being mean, jealous, a liar, and a cheat, I was also living with something evil and sinister.

I was in the basement again, which seemed to be where he stored all his deep dark secrets, looking for some gift boxes I had misplaced from that past Christmas. I had looked in every cabinet and storage space with no luck in finding them.

Maybe my husband had put them away somewhere in his little office down there. That was my last thought before giving up the search. I had never so much as *thought* about prying or going into his little private spot down there until this day. I had this strange feeling as I opened the door that *something* was in there that I should see.

Maybe some of my money was hidden in those desk drawers of his. I felt very inquisitive now. Suddenly, I didn't know what I had come in there for. The boxes and the money both seemed distant and irrelevant in my mind now. All I know is that I went through the drawers, the storage cabinets, and everything like a wife looking for some evidence of her husband's unloyalty or unfaithfulness.

I came to a drawer that had several drawing pads. As if something was moving my hands, I opened the pads to look at his drawings. I knew drawing was a pastime hobby of his. Many times, he had asked me to pose for a mood he was trying to capture of me on canvas.

"There is a certain air about your personality that no camera has yet brought across," he explained to me, "And I wish I knew how to express it through my drawings."

Of course, as I looked at his drawings now, I knew that his idea of capturing me on canvas was not meant to be such a pretty picture of me as he pretended. There I was, lines drawn through my face giving me the effect of an old woman. I quickly turned the page only to see other drawings where he repeated the same outline, causing me to look years beyond my age.

A cold terror gripped my heart, and my whole body seemed to quiver with fear. So *this* was his plan for me. To somehow draw me into a character of a woman who had lost her youth and composure. I saw how he had slumped my shoulders as if to show signs of surrendering to age. Was he really so jealous of me until he wished I would become like this? Maybe he felt that this way, he would never have to worry about me ever wanting to reach out again for the stage life.

I was for certain now that he was wicked and evil to the core. But again, I realized that being silent about the matter would be my best bet.

This poor little rich girl who tried to make him feel like a king,

filled his life with pride by standing by his side,

put him into a mansion,

and gave him a young son.

The same one who had shared her wealth and

> *herself with him… got this in return.*
>
> *This poor little rich girl could have kept it all.*
>
> *Her travels, her shows, when life was a ball.*
>
> *Instead, she let the curtains fall.*
>
> *And now, she's left with nothing at all.*
>
> *So poor little rich girl, go back to your world because his world is not your world,*
>
> *where you are just a poor, poor little rich girl.*

Seeing his drawings that day gave me a new determination that I never had before. I was determined to take care of my health and my body and fight the battle of aging every day of my life. There was a new awakening inside of me, a spirit that said to me, "Gladys, you don't ever have to look that way. God will show you the way. Just listen to your heart. His true plan was for man to improve with age, not to deteriorate. Treat yourself good, and you will look good. Treat yourself bad and you will look that way."

I never said anything to my husband about what I saw. I just watched his reactions more closely now. And to tell the truth, I was more suspicious of his voodoo and supernatural beliefs. Yes, we had often talked about my roots being from the West Indies, and he had made a statement to me that there was a lot of old voodoo tales and superstitions about the cultures of these people from the islands. My interest was suddenly piqued.

For some unexplainable reason, I now felt an urge to read up on some of the literary facts about this country. I had become aware that *somebody* had led me to the basement that day where I discovered those pictures. Somebody who *knew* me and my baby were not in the best of care. Maybe it was a relative of mine from the past or someone close to my family tree. Whoever it was had been putting all kinds of thoughts in my mind lately.

I had been watching my husband's potbelly, which seemed to be going away now. I questioned him about it saying, "Sammy, you used to look like you were pregnant when I first met you. Remember how I used to poke at your belly, teasing you and asking when were you going to have the baby? Well, since I have had a baby, I see that your stomach is a lot smaller now."

He didn't answer. He just rubbed his stomach while looking down at it.

"Maybe," I went on to say, "someone had a voodoo curse on you that made you carry the load of a baby until some maiden came along and gave you your own child."

He seemed quite interested now in my theory of his belly bulge. "What makes you think things like that?" he smiled as if the thought had perked up his imagination.

"I don't know," I said slowly. "It is as though something just told me that as I was looking at your reduced belly size. You had that belly for years. You know that, and you haven't stopped drinking beer. It disappeared after the baby was born."

He agreed, laughing heartily now. I knew he enjoyed anything that proved to be magical or mysteriously being done. Sammie, Jr. was getting bigger now, and I was taking him on daily strolls.

One day I decided to stop by the library. I had promised myself years ago that I was going to read up on my people and their land of the West Indies as soon as I had enough free time. Some strong force was moving me to do so now.

My God! I hadn't been in a library since I left school back in 1962. Just looking at all those books gave me the education blues. I knew my search was going to take more time than I had allowed myself that day. So, I applied for a library card and decided that I would take a few books home with me to read. The next couple of days kept me busy as I read up on the country of Trinidad, its agriculture and land, history, and some of the customs and beliefs of early primitive tribes.

I also read up on the city of Port-of-Spain, the islands of Tobago, the Virgin Islands, and Venezuela. From looking at the pictures, I could see that these islands were very resourceful and beautiful. I certainly would have loved a vacation touring this part of the world.

Then there was another book I took out on magic called *The Dark Secrets of the Early Tribes*. This book was too much for me to handle. First of all, there were so many beliefs and tribes and customs that I couldn't really attribute any one main fact or practiced belief to a particular tribe. They all had similar ceremonies and customs. Sometimes, it was called one thing in one area, and something else in another area. Regardless, the reasons and the results were all supposed to be the same, if you could understand that.

Witchcraft, voodoo, sacred ceremonies, tribal beliefs, and that old black magic had had its day with me. I was getting ready to clean up my house and filter out all the bad spirits if there were any. I only hoped that the one around me was a good one. It had helped me to receive a full summary on the roots of my beginnings. Now, I was hoping to gather up more information spiritually on what direction I needed to be headed in for my future.

***

I found myself more confused and puzzled as the days went by. What was going to happen to me and my child? Sammie was nearly nine months old, and he was making no real efforts to do anything. Not that I expected him to be a baby genius and do everything faster than other babies. But he'd sit in his playpen for hours and play all day alone if I let him.

"He doesn't even cry like babies usually do," I told his pediatrician during a visit.

His answer to me was, "He doesn't have to cry. I'm sure you are always there with his feedings and whatever else he may want. He doesn't have to have the need to cry out for you or anything."

I knew that I had done my share of spoiling Sammie, but there was a silence about Sammie that I recognized as being quite different in a young baby his age. He was now sitting alone and crawling. He could move around in his walker pretty fast, but he always seemed preoccupied in a little world of his very own.

One day I stood him up in his playpen, trying to get him to walk around the sides while holding on. He did this fairly well, so I decided to see if he would try to take a step while holding on to the big rubber ball in front of him. He screamed and cried so loudly until I knew that this was a game he did not want to play at all. I also recognized that it terrified him so much that he would start to tremble all over. I got this terrible feeling inside that Sammie felt like he was standing at the edge of a tall building. If he took one step out, he would fall off.

Something was wrong. I knew it. Never had I seen a child react so seriously to the game of trying to get them to take that first step. I think it was his shaking so much from fear that puzzled me.

"He shouldn't be that afraid to walk," I told his father.

"Just leave him alone," he told me.

Unconvinced, I brought it up again to the pediatrician. "He will walk when he is ready. Boys are usually lazy and walk later than girls do," he said nonchalantly.

Let me tell you something. With a mother's love and deep concern for her child comes a feeling when there is something not *quite* right. Even though it was my first child, and I didn't have much mother's wit, I *knew* Sammie had a problem. I didn't know if it was physical or mental, because he looked normal as a baby. He was always so sweet, charming, and adorable. Still, there was something very special about him. So special that it made him very different. Being a mother to a firstborn is a round-the-clock job with new things always happening that you hadn't anticipated, but I loved every moment of it. Staying home on a regular basis after all that traveling in my early teens didn't bother me one bit. I was obsessed with the love of my baby. If there was something wrong, I didn't want to know about it. I didn't want to hear anything but that everything was all right.

I needed to get my mind off what was troubling me and bring some friendly contacts back into my life. So, I had the thought one day to throw a party and invite The Marvelettes, the band members from the nightclub my husband was working at, and a host of other friends and acquaintances. Yes, that is what I needed—a big party to drown out all of my sorrows and suspicions.

My first step was to get on the telephone and start calling people. It had just dawned on me that I had hardly ever even used my own telephone anymore. I hadn't even given my number to more than 12 people. Every now and then, if I did get a call, it was always cut short with me always in the midst of doing something for the baby or having to complete some daily chore I hadn't done.

"Girl! Where have you been?" most of my friends asked. I had been in contact every now and then with the girls in the group. Wanda, Katherine, and my replacement Anne Bogan were all happy to hear that l was back in the swing of things.

"Sure, we're coming to your party, Gladys. We wouldn't miss it. When is it?" they asked. l figured around two weeks would give me the time I needed to perfectly plan everything.

"Be there, I can't wait," everyone told me.

I was going to have a party that would be the talk of the town with waitresses, cooks, and lots of food, drinks, and good music. I started on the guestlist immediately. I had to know just about how many people I could accommodate so that I could figure out a budget for the food and beverages. Then I had to plan my menu. This was not going to be just an hors d'oeuvre and liquor affair. I wanted a real soul food, music jamming, top choice, highly enjoyable grand bazaar. I had some friends I met years back who owned a soul food restaurant there in Detroit. Erlene and her husband, Fred, were famous for their home-style, southern barbecue pit. I hadn't seen or talked to them for some time, so I had to find out if they were still in existence. Hearing her voice over the phone brought back many happy, favorable memories.

"What storm blew you in?" Erlene laughed, as I filled her in on what was happening to date. "You? Married?!" she screamed. "Gladys, I have got to meet this man. He must have had a lot going for him in order to hook you."

I cleared up her curiosity immediately. "No, he didn't have that much going for him. I was just tired of all the traveling and foolishly wanted to try something else."

"You mean you feel you have made a big mistake now?" she asked seriously. I hadn't spilled the beans or let out my covered-up emotions and tensions for some time now. I just confided in her. I told her the whole story of how I was never deeply in love with him, and I only married him because I was so lonely and wanted a friendly, understanding companion. I also mentioned that I also wanted something of my own, a baby.

Hearing about Sammie, she insisted on coming over to meet my family. "That's sort of what I called you about," I informed her. "I am throwing a party, and I want you and your husband to cater it for me."

"Splendid," she said. "How long do we have to get ready for it?"

"About a good two weeks," I told her.

"Don't worry about a thing," she insisted. "We would be honored to do it for much less than you can imagine. All you have to do is buy the food, and we will throw in the help that night on the house for the fun of it all. I will get you three waitresses to serve your guests and my husband will handle the barbecuing. How is that?"

"Thank you, Erlene," I said. "That takes care of the most important part of the evening, the food." We both laughed.

I explained that I wanted the barbecuing to be done here at the house, out on the dining room patio. As the hostess, I wanted to prepare one main dish, which would be the potato salad, but I would leave the rest of the menu up to her. Barbecue beans, tossed and fruit salads, pastries and desserts, and meats of all kinds were discussed by us as part of her menu. "It is going to be jammin' and slammin'," we both agreed as we happily ended our conversation that day.

Planning this party was getting my very soul into the social life whirl of affairs. I began to feel the high spirit again of wanting to kick up my heels and celebrate. I was so thankful that I had lost all the fat I had gained during my pregnancy, and I was my own slim self again. I saw the looks my husband was giving me as he saw me dressing for the party that evening. I didn't know if he was proud of me or if he regretted seeing me using lipstick again and fancying up my hairstyle.

"What is the matter?" I asked, smiling as if I never saw his awful drawings of me. Then I sarcastically asked, "Don't I look like you want me to?"

"It is just that I haven't seen you dressed up for any social events in some time now," he faked a smile. "I forgot how perfectly you can fix yourself up."

"Oh, so that is it," I just dropped the subject not wanting to think about what I knew was the awful truth. He quickly finished dressing and went downstairs to meet some of the band members who had volunteered to work the bar that night. I could hear them arriving with all the cases of liquor and beer that my husband was in charge of getting ready.

The dress that evening was to be casual but neat. Nothing "after five" as I put it. I wanted the guests to feel comfortable but somewhat dressy too. So, the invitations read, "evening patio style attire." I had chosen a bright orange and white two-piece lounge outfit with earrings to match. I was all ready to be the prettiest hostess when I heard the footsteps coming up the stairs. It was Brenda, my foster big sister. She had volunteered to babysit Sammie in between enjoying the party herself.

"Is Christine coming too?" I asked her, as I was quickly showing her where all the baby's things were located.

"I think so," she told me. "I talked to her last week, and she was certainly planning on it then."

I wanted everyone I invited to come, and I made sure that I invited my friends from Inkster. The weather was good and everything was going along just fine. The rest would be up to me. I wanted to be the perfect hostess for the night. All of my hired help was right on time. The food was ready, and the coals on the barbecue pit were smoking. The music started playing and the mood was coming on. "It is party time!"

My guests started arriving around 8:30 p.m. By 10:00, we had a packed house. The party was not intended to show off my new home, but I found myself personally giving private tours of the place constantly throughout the night. Everyone loved my completely mirrored wall in the living room. It certainly made the room look twice as large as it already was. My husband also received praises for the walnut wooded items he had built himself for the den—the four-stool bar, the enclosed cabinets for the television, and the stereo console.

All the guests at the party were treated hospitably with the help of the waitresses from Erlene's place. They made sure to keep everyone's glass filled and the food served properly. Fred, I am sure, picked up dozens of more customers for their restaurant. The meats were so tender that they slid off the bone.

"Who made this sauce?" I heard the question asked over and over throughout the evening.

With the group being reunited for the first time since I had left, we sang songs all night. Everyone danced and had a good time throughout the evening. Before leaving, all my guests—some who had come as far as 30 miles—congratulated me on giving them the best time they'd had in quite some time.

"Gladys, you have *got* to throw another party soon," Christine, my foster cousin, pleaded. Others just stated that they hated to leave such a beautiful party but would be back as soon as I asked again. The following week I was flooded with calls telling me how much fun everyone had.

It really made me feel good inside to know that I had made others feel good too. The house seemed to have more spirit about it now. Like a colorful rainbow after the storm, I didn't seem to feel so alone now. Before, I thought the empty feelings I had came from so many empty rooms. After all, it was usually just the baby and me home most of the time.

***

It was the end of September, and I had just received a royalty check. Therefore, I decided to do some more house decorating. We had already painted Sammie's room in all the shades of blue there was. I wanted to finish it off with everything imaginable for a little boy. I added toys, some more furniture, and new sky-blue curtains. His room was so big even with a crib, swing, dressing table, full dresser, toy chest, and bookcase inside. With all that, there was still lots of room to roam around.

We had finally found a deep shag, two-tone carpet of light and dark blue for the room that made it feel like you were walking on a cloud. Sammie's room was simply marvelous.

"Too pretty for a little boy," one of my friends happened to say while having lunch with me one day. It was Delores Horn, one of my school friends from Inkster who now worked in Detroit at a nearby hair salon. Delores and I had always been close; closer than a lot of my other girlfriends because we met shortly after the first week I moved to Inkster. I could talk to her about almost anything.

"I still don't believe you gave up your career, Gladys," she started in on me. "You could have stopped just long enough to have your baby and then continued on. Don't you miss it at all?" she questioned.

The truth was, I hadn't been off the road long enough to miss it as greatly as most people thought I would. My love and dedication to my baby were so great and still brand new and exciting that I hadn't really even given it much thought about how rocky the road can become when you haven't got one thin dime.

So far, we have been able to pay our house note and buy food and clothing for the baby. I never was a big spender when it came to buying for myself. With that attitude, extra furs and jewelry and new dresses were not a problem for my husband to try and keep me up on.

"Maybe I will go back after the baby is older," I answered Delores's question, "but right now, I wouldn't give up raising my own child for all the tea in China."

"I hope you know what you are doing. It is still not too late to think about your career. Later on, it may be."

She was oh so right about that. "I don't think my husband wants to see me do it all over again. He hasn't said much about it, but he doesn't seem to mind me playing the role of the perfect mother and confined wife."

"Men, they are all the same," said Delores. "They cannot stand to see anyone else watching their woman."

"I wonder if it is out of downright cruelty or just plain jealousy that makes them feel this way?"

"I am inclined to believe that it is a bit of both," laughed Delores.

But it was no laughing matter to have to take the back seat and stay there. They say "I love you" so easily, I thought, when in the end, their actions say the reverse. "I don't think my marriage is going to last very long," I told Delores. "I should have read a book on understanding the male species of the human race *before* I chose any one of them to spend the rest of my life with. I am sure that he is not the one for me."

I told her about the savings account deal and how he wrote it off as being nothing at all. He didn't even appear to feel ashamed after I confronted him about it. He didn't *care*. I was the one who had worked hard for it. He probably felt quite clever about his deceit and glad to see me without my earnings. Now, I hear gossip about his affairs at the club.

"What have you said to him about them?" she asked.

"Nothing, nothing at all. That is how little I care. I just

let him think I don't even know about it. Besides, I have better things to think about."

She looked at me holding Sammie, and we both just smiled. She had to get back to work, and I had to get back to sorting out my plans for my baby and my future. I knew one day soon, it was all going to have to come to a turning point. I just wanted to be ready mentally and physically in dealing with the outcome.

I was trying to find a peaceful way of telling my husband that we needed to give each other some space to breathe, to find out what we really meant to one another. He goes his way and I go mine. If we wound up back together again, then maybe destiny had some plans unforeseen by us to try and stay together. But as for now, we were growing farther and farther apart. I was nothing more than a maid, cook, and mother of his child. There was no growing feelings of happiness or joy from just being together or true companionship. The only thing we shared was a roof over our heads to protect us from the rain.

We had grown so distant that I felt no concern for his safety or well-being. I didn't even care or hear him anymore, coming in at the wee hours of the mornings from the club. He had his room, and I had mine. No, he never even bothered to ask how I was feeling or what plans I had for the weekend when we did occasionally stop to talk. Our conversations were always quick, short, and to the point. "Yes," "no," "maybe," "so see you later."

Sometimes, he would mention how fast the baby was growing and scuffle around playfully with him a few seconds before he was off somewhere. Who cares, out the door. I stopped cooking every day too. Somehow, he didn't even notice. Eating meals outside somewhere else, I figured. Good for me. I would have more time to relax.

I wasn't really crying the blues over anything because I knew our failed sex life was as much a fault of mine as it was his, maybe more. *My* excuse was the baby. *He* never gave one. He just never asked anymore.

Lucky for him, I was not one of those wives easily aroused by the idea of making love whether she loved her husband or not. I am talking about those kinds of wives who demand that her husband satisfy her simply because she feels she deserves to get whatever she wants, whenever she wants it; sometimes even when she *knows* about an outside affair.

I, for one, have to feel those sexy feelings deep down inside me that make me actually yearn for a man. And I just wasn't getting any of those kinds of feelings for *this* man. I didn't feel any real hate for him either. I just felt like he had completed the job that he had come for and that was to conceive me with a child. Now, he could go. I just didn't care to be bothered with any further details.

It was understandable with this attitude that I was not acting like a real wife. But, on the other hand, I wasn't receiving the actions from a real husband. To be really frank about the matter, I really couldn't miss what I never had in the first place now, could I? I had already given my situation a complete rundown long ago. My husband had married me because he thought I had money. When he found out that my savings over the past seven years amounted to only a mere $5,000, it was too late for him to back out. So, intentionally, he helped to swindle me out of that, hoping that it would outrage me to the point where I would up and leave him. In doing so, I would be leaving him a mansion to live in and have all my personally designed, custom-made furniture to show off as his very own.

While secretly plotting my look of old age through his drawings, he wouldn't ever have to worry about me finding someone else to be happy with or admire me or want to marry me. Yes, he thought he had it all figured out—how to get rid of me and still be able to live the kind of life I had brought him into. Yes, the ruins and the end of his plans for such a "poor little rich girl."

I heard the voice of that spirit that had come to me before in my time of comforting needs saying, "That is what you get for not listening and obeying the warning you got while you still had your career going."

It made me think back to my legal guardian, Mrs. Edwards, when she was trying to save all of us girls from what she knew would happen if we didn't get our heads on straight and begin to first think things out before we actually did them. "You have got to be careful, girls," she warned. "You have got a lot of guys looking only at your pocketbooks."

But no, we thought we were *so* fine and beautiful and irresistible until men couldn't see straight or think about anything else but loving us. I knew now that "love" word carried a lot of weight with it. It means a lot of things we don't even think about, and it doesn't mean a lot of things we think we know about.

One thing I know for sure now was that if I ever got out of this mess I was in, I wasn't going to marry anyone else just because I had people waiting on me to do so. Even at the very last moment, when I am standing before the preacher with millions of people watching, if I don't feel the extreme happiness and joy that should be overflowing from my heart that day, I am going to call it quits and say "no way" and walk away this time. I surely hadn't been choosy enough. But even later on, I don't think I can ever marry a man just because he is rich.

I lived to be happy, and I am not ashamed to say I still believe that true love is out there somewhere. Somewhere waiting on those who are worthy of it. Yes, when I find my man, I am going to marry him because I love him and he truly loves me too. And if I am lucky in love, maybe he will always have what he needs to get me some of the things I feel I might want. But most of all, I will want *him*.

My prayers for ending this whole charade were soon to be answered in a way that I had not thought about. My husband had just hung up the telephone and seemed very eager to discuss something with me. Something that just couldn't wait, it seemed.

"Gladys," he said, "do you remember John and Odel, the couple who invited us to their home while we were working at that club out in Los Angeles, California?"

How could I forget, I thought to myself. They had shown us such a lovely home up in the Baldwin Hills area. "You mean that friend of yours who also plays trumpet?" I asked.

"Exactly," he stated.

Now, I saw a very anxious, excited look in his eyes as he asked me to sit down and talk. "Well," he went on to say, "that was John I was just talking to on the phone."

"Long-distance! All the way to California!" I shouted. Remembering the last telephone bill that almost didn't get paid made me wonder how and when this one was going to be taken care of. "You are going to have to give up something soon," I warned him. "Either the liquor bill on your tab at the club or talking all across the country any time you feel the need to. Have you ever thought about writing letters with your budget? It would be a lot easier on your wallet."

He realized I was angry and tried to calm me down by suggesting that I listen to a great idea that he had come up with.

"Listen, I think I have a plan where we wouldn't have to worry about paying any more bills around here. John just told me that he is starting his own group, and he wants me to play with him."

This was too good to be true, I thought. Talking *miracles*. It would be the perfect solution to our halfway separate live-in marriage problem. "So, you are going to move out to California, right?"

"Right," he answered. "But here's the terrific part. John and his fiancé own a liquor store. Right next door to it is a fish and chip take-out restaurant. To top that off, they are in the clothing business. They have their own factory. John has reassured me that I wouldn't have to worry about a job in between our club dates. And are you ready for this? They also have another house that we can lease from them until we decide on whether we want to make California our permanent home or not."

"We?" The words startled me. "What do you mean *we*? You expect me and the baby to move to California with you?"

"Of course, that is what I am saying. I am sure you will need time, and you will want to think about it first. But John told me that the house where we would be staying is in the same area where we visited them. Remember that gorgeous house?"

His smile was tempting now because he knew that there was no way I could have forgotten such a lovely home. Nevertheless, I still needed a clear head to think this thing out. He was asking me to pull up my roots from Detroit and plant them somewhere else. Somewhere strange to me, somewhere I didn't know a single soul. This was a big decision for me to make, and I had to be sure. Decisions, decisions… too quickly made decisions had been my biggest mistake up to now.

Amid all my jumbled-up thoughts, I could hear his voice pleading hard and trying to convince me that he was right. He was trying to say in so many words, "Let's take this opportunity now that is before us. It is a chance for us to find happiness and maybe a wealthy California lifestyle. Look at the weather. It is hot all year round, and it is a chance for me to be making three times the amount of money I am making now. Gladys, it is a chance of a lifetime. Let's take it. Let's move. Let's go out to California."

I still had my doubts, even with the overall beautiful picture he was painting about how wonderful it was all going to be. Not only were all my close friends there in Detroit and Inkster, but I had put time and money into my house. I couldn't just leave all of this behind me and move somewhere else at a moment's notice.

He could see that I was not totally convinced about the matter, so he added, "Gladys, you should have heard how John described the house where we are going to be staying."

"Now this better be good," I told myself. I was too curious with anticipation to hear all about the details. So I listened wholeheartedly to his exaggerations of the descriptions of it.

"It is sort of on the same style as John's house, but its

design is a tri-level complex. It doesn't have a swimming pool, but the ground layout is magnificent," he indicated. He described the front part of the house as being street level. Because it was built on a hill, the kitchen and rear side of the house slanted upwards and are built into the hill. The house is on a corner, making it a showcase of the neighborhood.

I think what made me believe that this house was just as he described it was that I remember the beautiful layout of the house that I had visited. If it was *anywhere* near the architecture of *that* house, I knew it had to be something great to look at. I began to imagine how it would be. I could see this fabulous, modern-day Hollywood Hills, bourgeoisie, dream house sitting in the warm California sunshine, with lots of greenery landscape of tall palm trees, orange bird-of-paradise flowers, and citrus fruit trees growing everywhere. Then, the thought of no snow, no heavy boots, no ice-cold water on my feet…oh, it had to be paradise.

I still wasn't altogether sold on the idea yet because the question came up of what would we do with our home we had now.

It was so easy for my husband to come up with the idea so quickly. "Just put the house up for sale."

"But what if I don't like California and want to come back to Detroit later? Where will I live?" I brought the question up immediately. He resorted to the idea that we could rent it out temporarily, but the wear and tear on it may not be worth it in the long run.

"If and when you decide you want to move back into it, you will probably have to do a complete remodeling job on it. That is going to cost you some big bucks." He had a point there. But something in the back of my mind kept me battling with the idea of not just giving it all up and having to start all over.

There had to be another solution. Getting FHA approved for buying a house is no easy thing. It only happened for me with this house because I had gotten several letters of recommendation from Motown's top executives, stating how much money from record sales and show engagements The Marvelettes had made over the past six or seven years.

Everyone knows that the credit ratings for entertainers have never been at an all-time high. Banks and other loan companies look at our jobs as not having a very promising outlook. You're hot today and not tomorrow. It isn't easy for them to take such risks when it comes to big investments like buying houses.

"Maybe I can rent it out to somebody we know, somebody who would take care of it," I argued.

But no, my husband wanted us to sell the house. "Anyway," he said, "we will need that money to get out to California and to buy other necessities after we have settled there." It was a pity and a shame. The house was the only collateral I had left. Both bank accounts were down to zero, and my husband was still struggling to bring home a full paycheck without a large liquor tab on it.

No wonder he wanted to move. I wish I could have seen the light of the whole story then like I do now. There was no more money left to splurge on. To get him away from the responsibilities of being a husband and father, he wanted me to sell my house to pay his way out of the mounting pressure of bills. He wanted to start fresh out in another state where he could assume his former irresponsible activities of doing and owning nothing.

I remember my foster mother, Mrs. Jones, always telling me while I was coming up, "Gladys, always remember, nothing from nothing leaves nothing. You can't get something from nothing." But I had *tried*. I tried to have something: a house, a home, a good way of life with someone who was used to nothing. And so, he had nothing to lose. As long as I was with him, I knew I would have nothing too.

But I made up my mind to leave because of a reason that had nothing to do with the house in California, his friends there, or the weather. It was simply because I knew soon that I would be faced with the awful truth—my baby was suffering from some kind of birth defect. I didn't know what was wrong yet, but I knew that I had to find out. I needed to be alone, away from my friends and the group members. It was going to be a shameful experience, I knew, with people expressing how sorry they felt for the baby and me. I didn't want to hear or see this type of reaction coming from the ones who knew me.

I didn't want to see the look on the faces of my friends as they voiced their pity for my child and me.

I knew I could find the strength to endure the heartache and depression I would be faced with among people who didn't know who I was or what I had done in my career as a singer. Leaving was a peaceful way for me to avoid all the controversy I knew would come up. All the gossip and misinterpretations of what happened would all be written out of my life's story.

Yes, I was running out on the truth. It was hard enough every day now, having to face the fact every time I looked at my baby that something was wrong. I was an important person. Important people are not supposed to make mistakes or have imperfect babies, whether it is your fault or not. People just don't accept the fact that entertainers or movie stars are fallible.

I *had* to get away. I guess to protect my baby and myself from all the propaganda I knew that staying in Detroit would deliver up to me. It had been a good home to me for too long. I wanted to remember it as a place where I was always able to hold my head up high and be proud to walk down the streets.

Call it selfish pride, but that is the *only* reason I gave in and put our house up for sale. In moving, I saw this was a way of keeping the truth hidden about what had *really* happened to my marriage and to my firstborn child. Maybe, later on, I would find the strength and courage to come back and pick up the pieces.

It didn't take as long as I thought it would to sell our house. In fact, the first people who saw it bought it. Our two-month wait was due to the paperwork on finalizing the sale with bank escrow and mortgage arrangements to be completed. I didn't make any special formal announcements about my move either. Only a few people were aware of it.

And even then, there were too many questions being asked. "Gladys, your house was so perfect, and you really had it together. I can't believe you're giving it up. Why do you have to move?"

And then there were those doubtful questions like, "Do you realize the difference in the cost of living out there in California?"

None of them seemed satisfied with the answer I gave about my husband finding a better job. All in all, they all said they wished the best for me but hoped I was making the right decision. I knew I was not making the right decision about giving up my house. But the decision I had made in the view of my baby's well-being was yet to be questioned. I could only hope and pray that it would be in our best interests.

***

It was March 1st, 1969, five days before Sammie would be a year old. It was our moving day, the day we were leaving Detroit and moving to California. The men from Bekins Moving Van were loading up our furniture and housewares onto the truck. We were driving out to California in the 1964 Ford Mustang my husband had purchased there in Detroit not too long after we had moved into the house.

I took one long look at the house before we drove off. I really hadn't been in the house long enough to have had the chance to enjoy its beauty and comfort. As we drove away, I wondered if I would ever have a big, big house again like this old English-style mansion was. Somehow, the spirit of that house was still with me. I could feel it everywhere.

I am inclined to believe that it followed me right on out to California. Whoever it was... constantly tried to tell me something all during our week-long drive out to the coast. Here's what happened.

I insisted that we stop every night at some traveler's hotel for safety precautions and to give my husband the rest he needed from driving all day. Our first stop was in Cincinnati, Ohio. The next morning we got up and started back on our journey, but my husband had lost his directions to Route 66. So, we drove around town a while searching for it and accidentally wound up at the gates of the town cemetery. "Now, *there* is someplace I am not dying to get to." I made a big joke of it. We both laughed and went on our way.

Our next stop was in the state of Missouri, somewhere around St. Louis. For some reason, we had a brief dispute about stopping to rest this night.

"I can make it a little further," my husband argued.

But I stuck to our former plans. "I need some rest myself from holding the baby almost all day. My arms are aching," I pleaded.

"Well, put the baby in the car seat in the back, and you get some sleep while I'm driving," he insisted.

"No," I strongly refused. Something kept telling me to try to stay awake while he was driving. I didn't want to chance falling asleep with him behind the wheel. Why suddenly I had no confidence in his ability to make those extra hours, I don't know. I only know we were soon checked into a hotel and spent the night there.

After feeding the baby and getting a bite to eat ourselves, we began looking for the proper highway to lead us to California. Would you believe that we went through the same thing as the previous morning? Clearly, following the right highway directions *wasn't* one of my husband's best qualities. Do you know what *was* easy as pie for him? Finding every city's burial ground. Yes, he seemed to naturally be drawn in *those* directions.

After the first few times, it became too much. We were lost again and again. I was tired of looking at stone heads on my right and him in the driver's seat on my left. This time, it was no laughing matter. I don't think we even spoke a word to one another about the repeated circumstances. As we were driving by this undesignated place, I gave him a look that said a thousand things. That spirit was speaking to me now, filling my mind with many suspicious thoughts. *There is something eerie and deadly about this man*, I thought. Something was trying to tell me where following him would get me, and I could hear it getting louder and louder.

Our next stop for the night was in Tulsa, Oklahoma. We had pulled in late that evening, but before we went to bed, I saw my husband checking out the map, trying to plan the correct route for the following day. I think those last two mornings with the same incident happening both times got to his brain. I am sure he wanted to avoid a three-time losing streak. I didn't know what to expect as we drove off the next morning. Surprises were something I was used to by now.

***

At last! We were headed in the right direction. No, we missed our turn, and now we were on a dead-end street. I could see the frustration in his face as he turned the car around and headed back in the other direction. I thought about the words we had just read a few blocks back: Dead-end. Yes, I was sure of it now. The spirit was trying to tell me that my life with him was headed for a similar outcome. What was I going to do? I was too far away from home now to turn back. I had to go on. I just kept my eyes and ears open, quietly observing his future plans for us.

Can you believe that we passed by *another* graveyard

before reaching the City of Los Angeles, California? I had just closed my eyes, saying a small prayer and thanking God that we had made it across the boundary line. We were just outside of Needles, California, where we had stopped the night before. As I opened my eyes, I looked up to see us passing that old familiar landmark—another cemetery. I tried to push the thought out of my mind that anything was out of the ordinary. I realized that millions of people must have traveled these roads and highways every day, and they all had to pass whatever scenery was along the way. This, of course, included graveyards. Still, I just couldn't shake the feeling that I was headed for trouble.

It didn't take long for my doubts to be verified. Before we reached Los Angeles, my husband stopped to call John and tell him that we were only hours away. That is when we got the news of the first big letdown.

"What's wrong?" I asked my husband from the look on his face when he came back to the car.

"John just told me that the house we are staying at is not ready yet. So, they had the Bekins movers take our furniture and belongings and store them in their garage."

"Their garage!" I shouted. "My brand-new furniture and my beautiful glass items in their garage?!" I wanted to cry.

Now we both began to worry. I wondered if the proper precautions had been made with the boxes marked "handle with care." Then the thought of where we *would* be staying suddenly crossed my mind. Before I could ask, my husband went on to say, "John said that we can stay with them until the people in our house have moved out."

"People! What people? You never mentioned anything to me about anyone already living in the home that we were supposed to occupy."

"I know," my husband softly spoke now. "John never told me about that on the telephone."

"I bet there are a lot of things John never told you," I warned him. We drove in silence the rest of the way. That sunny disposition we started out with had been launched somewhere into space. Now a cold, empty feeling filled the air around us. It was the feeling of not knowing what was coming next, and you can bet your bottom dollar that there was much more to come.

The next big letdown was the living conditions at the house that we had once thought was so immaculately clean. The maid actually quit the day after we arrived.

"Look at this kitchen," she told me with disgust. "It stays like this. No matter how much I clean it up, I only come back to find it in this same condition."

I looked around at all the junk on the cabinets and on the floor. Cans were everywhere, and watermelon rinds and other dirty dishes and glasses were in the sink.

"*Every* day?" I asked in shock.

"*Every* morning, it is the same thing. I wash up all the dishes and clean everything up neat and tidy the night before. And the next morning, it looks as though I did nothing at all. I am tired, and I am going to look for a new job."

Needless to say, I had to become the maid for about a whole month afterward. Of course, the owners never *asked* me to do it. Still, I quickly realized that if I wanted to be able to prepare my child's meals in a clean environment, I would have to clean up whatever was dirty around me. So, just like the maid warned me, I had a sink full of dishes to do daily. Other parts of the house weren't as bad as the kitchen, but I felt it my duty to try and keep things orderly as long as I was welcome in their home as a guest.

The third smack in the face came when John never asked my husband to work either at the liquor store or at the fish and chip fast food joint. The nightclub deal of playing his horn never took place either.

"What are you going to do now?" I asked him one day. Of course, he didn't seem to have an answer for me right away. I am sure he realized that the old jealousy game had been played on him. I imagined that my husband must have been bragging to John about the spacious, lovely home we had in Detroit. Through spite and jealousy, John had made him think that the grass was much greener on his side. In turn, it made my husband want to leave what we had behind and come out here after something that didn't even compare. I could see that my husband was feeling bad, but I just couldn't sit around and not say anything.

"I hope you can see the light now because John has really dogged you good. Has he even bothered to ask you *once* to start to work in one of their businesses?"

My husband just slowly shook his head, looking like a hurt puppy. I, for one, should have felt sorry for him because Sammie, Jr. and I would both be affected by this dirty trick. Deep down inside, I knew it was time for my husband to take a good look at himself. Maybe now he could see how evil the emotions of jealousy are. Jealousy doesn't even care about how much it hurts people. It breaks up happy homes. It has even ended people's lives. Oh, what a wonderful world this would be if jealousy had never existed.

I had to learn to live and survive under these un-Godly circumstances. It was my duty to keep smiling and entertaining as though the whole world was in love with me. Underneath it all, I saw how unreasonable and low-down that jealousy could make people.

That is precisely why right now I truly admire genuine humbleness coming from great people. I find it such a beautiful gesture to behold when they display this attitude. I have always refrained and tried my damnedest not to intentionally make others feel jealous of me. Jealousy makes you become an ugly person. People who go around purposely bragging and boasting with the thrill of trying to make people this way will someway, someday pay the price of the great wages of this sin.

I didn't have to ask that next question that I wanted to so badly because I already knew my husband had too much pride to beg John for a job. I was so glad now, though, that we hadn't come out to California with no money at all. Otherwise, we would have really been in trouble. Even though selling the house didn't give me a lot of money, I thought we would be able to have enough to hold us over until things picked up on the job front. Of course, now even *that* was uncertain.

We had already spent a good $1,000 just for the moving van. Our traveling expenses rounded out somewhere around $500. For the last four weeks, just from buying food, some light clothing, entertainment, and sightseeing, we had managed to flip through another $500 or more. On top of that, my husband's car note was overdue.

"I just don't see how we are going to have any money left to pay a couple of months rent whenever we do get to move in," I told my husband. "Has John said when we will be able to start moving into the house?"

"In about a week," my husband told me. He looked as though he had started to say something else but changed his mind. I caught on and quickly made him tell me what it was. That's when *another* shocking truth was about to unfold.

"I have been going over to the house where we are going to live every day now, trying to get it ready for you to see."

"Ready for me to see? What is so wrong with it that you have to get it ready?"

"Well," he hesitated. "The people who had to move out messed it up so bad that I knew you would have screamed 'mercy, mercy' if I had of let you seen how the place looked about a week ago. John and I have been painting and trying to make it look presentable."

"Presentable!" Those words made me know that this was *not* going to be the dream house described to me.

Besides it not being right around the corner from John's house, it had none of the Hollywood, Beverly Hills, or Bel-Air looks to it at all. In fact, it was not even a modern-day look. I think I had a minor nervous breakdown the day we drove over to move in. I couldn't believe my eyes.

"No!" I screamed. "You mean I left my big, gorgeous hunk of a house in Detroit for this?" I wanted to beat my husband up. "You fool!" I spat. "You big, stupid, foolish fool. How could you lead us into a trap like this?"

I thought the outside looked bad until I saw the inside. The people had poured acid on all the floors, and the kitchen and bathroom tiles were destroyed. Even the fresh paint job didn't do much to make it look better. The house was narrow and tight and without much room. I hated it, and my husband knew it.

"This whole house needs remodeling inside and out!"

I shouted.

He tried to keep me quiet and calm so he could explain. "We will fix it up. You will see," he promised. "But please don't show John your dislike. He volunteered to take off from his regular work to help me paint. If you had seen it the very first day I did, you would be back in Michigan by now. I *am* sorry I got you into this mess. I am sorry."

I just looked at him. I looked at him long and hard without saying a word. For the first time in his life, I think he really was.

You'd think that John would have had the decency to let us use the money we had to make it livable for humans before they stuck their hands out for first, last, and security. I felt like we had been baked, fried, roasted, and then burned all over.

We had been tricked out here to California, and now that same somebody was asking us to pay to live in this dump. We had to re-carpet the whole house, buy new drapes and curtains, and clean, clean, clean up *everything*. We spent an extra $3,000—putting a dent in our savings—for a place that wasn't even ours.

"There is no way I would even consider buying a house built like this one," I told my husband after we both stood admiring our newly decorated touches. It was April, and that meant royalty statement time. I hadn't given Motown Records my new address, so the trip to Hollywood this day would be worth the while.

Motown had just recently moved several of its offices to California, and how convenient this was for me now. I didn't have to wait on my checks to be mailed from Detroit.

"You'd better get on the move for finding a job," I told my husband. "We have got to get some steady income coming in soon, or we are going to be right back where we started."

It wasn't long before my husband started his own band of about five members. I can remember that he was able to find a steady weekend gig at some club for a while and was filling in with other musical jobs sometimes during the weekdays. This *barely* brought in enough to buy food and make utilities. We were really struggling with the rent payments, and he wasn't able to keep up his car notes. One morning, we woke up and found that the insurance company had confiscated his car from out of the garage. That was the first time I actually saw him break down and cry like a baby.

Sammie, Jr. and I hardly ever got a chance anymore to ride in it anyway because he stayed gone most of the time looking for work. So, we had gotten used to walking everywhere we went to the nearby stores, playgrounds, or whatever recreational plans I had made. *We* already learned to do without the car. Now it was his turn.

What else could happen? I wondered. He came back about a week later with an old used car. We laughed at it, but he just said, "I have to have some kind of way to get where I am going, or else we are going to be out on the streets."

Anyway, that was the next thing in store for us. We had only been renting the house for about nine months and were about two months behind in the payments when the owners paid us a visit one evening. They came in smiling, with John doing his buddy-buddy bit on my husband. I knew what was coming up next.

An argument arose when I frankly spoke out on how rotten I thought the whole deal had gone down from the very beginning. They threatened us with an eviction notice if we didn't have every last cent by a certain date. I don't know why I expected them to treat us any other way. I guess because they had been introduced to me as friends of my husband's, I assumed they'd be more understanding. Boy, was I wrong.

The next day, my husband went out in search of new living quarters for us. Sammie, Jr. was a lot bigger now, and in a matter of months, he would be two years old. He looked healthier and was much stronger, but he still wasn't walking or trying to talk. We had been so busy trying to pay the high costs of living in that area that I hadn't taken his slowness as seriously as I should have. He was such a happy, playful child and never seemingly sick. Therefore, it was much easier to just hope and wait for him to start to advance to these stages.

I told myself that as soon as we got settled again, I was going to get a specialist to look my child over. When my husband finally found an apartment, I had no idea where 39th and Normandie was until we got there. Liquor stores, pig feet meat shops, busy street corners, Salvation Army, and thrift shops were all close by to where I now lived. I had never seen this part of California before, but I knew I was in "Soulsville." Thank goodness I was black.

Once we arrived, I had only a couple of adjustments to make. My husband had brought me right on back home to my days before I ever recorded a song. I could tell by the smile on his face now that he was glad to be back. This was his kind of territory.

Talk about feeling like a has-been. I had to take a look in the mirror to see if I was the same girl who had traveled the world, stayed at the best hotels, ate with kings and queens, and had admiring fans and friends welcoming me back and asking for more. Was I the same girl whose voice had been heard singing great songs nationwide and internationally too? Oh! "If My Friends Could See Me Now" was the song playing in my mind now.

How could I have married such a loser? I must have been under some kind of spell to have not been able to see that he was no match for me. Now the spell had been lifted, and I could see. I could see *exactly* how blinded I must have been. The apartment was too small for all of my furniture. When we finished getting everything in place, it looked like a small furniture store with small narrow aisles leading in different directions—one to the kitchen and another to the bedrooms and bath.

Poor little rich girl; take a look at this world.

You don't wear pearls, and your hair's not in curls.

Poor little rich girl, I told you so.

He has got you so low; you're in the ghetto.

Yes, I was here, but that didn't mean I had to surrender to a life of having nothing else forever. As long as I could stay alive, I knew I would find the way back up on my feet. I just had to take one step at a time. And now, my first step was to find out what was wrong with my baby.

"How are you going to pay for the doctor bills?" The question was asked to me as I tried to get an appointment at the California Orthopedic Hospital. It was so stupid of me to not have thought about where the money would be coming from to pay for a specialist to examine my child. I knew my husband's salary wasn't going to do it. He hardly could pay the rent now, which had been reduced to almost three times less than what we were paying at his friend's house.

"It sounds like you are in a situation where you need assistance, Miss," the hospital operator spoke out.

"Assistance from where?" I wanted to know.

"Are you working now?" she asked me next.

"No, I have been in California for nearly a year now, and I haven't even looked for a job."

"Well, does your husband work?" she asked. "Usually, there is some sort of hospitalization plan set up through the employer, offered to the employees who hold jobs."

I explained to her what field of work we were in, and neither one of us had any hospitalization insurance.

"Well, that *is* really bad," she said. "I don't know what else to tell you to do. But from what I hear, you would probably be eligible to apply for welfare, and along with that, you will receive medical insurance for you, your husband, and your baby."

"What?!" I screamed. Along with feeling ashamed and a total outcast, I was speechless. The lady on the other end of the phone had spelled it right out for me to hear. I had just been in denial all this time. I was now eligible for welfare. And the worst thing about it was, it was true. How was I going to live in between my royalty check? Either I had to get a job or start receiving Aid to Dependent Families.

"Miss," she continued on speaking to me, "even *that* is going to take some time. So, when you are ready, call back, and I will be glad to give you an appointment."

I hung up the phone and just sat there and stared at the walls in front of me. I felt cheap and unimportant. How could I walk into a welfare office and apply for help after having all the fame I had experienced? Just the thought drove me into total depression for the moment.

"No," I told myself. "No, I *will* get a job." Then I started thinking about what kind of job. I hadn't even finished school. I couldn't even get a job mopping floors or waiting on tables without a high school diploma. A high-paying, more sophisticated job like a legal secretary, bank clerk, or business telemarketer all crossed my mind but were much too far out of my reach from a lack of educational skills.

"Maybe Motown will give me a job?" I was discussing the idea with my husband.

"They'll all laugh at you," he retorted. "How do you sound after all the money you have made for that company? What kind of job can they offer you?"

Yes, he was right. For me to come crawling back on my hands and knees would only prove that I hadn't earned the credits of becoming one of the top artists of the '60s. Then, a thought crossed my mind as though that spirit was still speaking to me again. If I was still in Detroit, the girls and I could easily reunite and start our careers again. It hadn't been that long since I left the group, and Motown wouldn't be against us. I'm sure we could have continued our success as an original group. Yet… here I was 2,000 miles away from getting myself or my career back together again. I needed some serious help and some answers to my problems quick. In order to help my child right now, I needed something to happen immediately.

Well, no sooner said than done. Help came through

the door almost the very next day. His name was Steve Thornton, and my husband had brought him to the apartment to talk about starting out a new job with Steve's band. I listened to Steve tell my husband about his concept of having musicians from different ethnic backgrounds playing together. He already had a Chinese, Spanish, German, and a couple of black guys rehearsing. He wanted nine members in total so he could call his group Concept 9.

"I am also looking for a girl to join the group, but I haven't had much luck. I need a girl with a certain sound, a sound that strikes out at the crowd."

My husband looked at me. I thought for a moment he was going to mention to Steve that I had originally been with a professional girls' group that had many hits and was an experienced entertainer. But he said nothing.

I knew then for sure that he really didn't want to ever see me performing again. *No wonder he had made it his business to make sure he got me away from Detroit,* I thought to myself. It would be so easy for me to step right back into the limelight after the baby was older and after the real truth had hit me about how I was going to be able to afford to continue to live as I had been used to. He knew he was not qualified to keep the fire burning long. This must have really made him overly jealous of my self-sufficient, independent career. I couldn't help but see the whole picture now. *You will never get away with it,* I silently vowed.

"I used to sing with The Marvelettes," I butted in now and told Steve.

"What!" He was shocked. He looked straight at my husband in such a confused, puzzled way. "Why? Why didn't you tell me? I could use that kind of professional profile in the group."

My husband tried to laugh it off by saying, "She has got the baby to look after, and she has never sung solo before."

"She can bring the baby to rehearsal. I'll pay a babysitter if you need one," he offered. "The Marvelettes," he repeated. "The Marvelettes. I remember The Marvelettes." Over and over, he began telling me how much he loved our songs. "I can't believe it."

He started to say something, then he started looking slowly around us. And I knew what was now on his mind. *What happened?* He might as well have asked it out loud. Instead, he was just polite and respected the fact that he could see that I was still able to maybe help myself back into a better lifestyle. "I would be glad to listen to you at our next rehearsal," he said to me before he left.

"Just let me know when and I will be there," I smiled, showing him that I was very much interested in his offer.

My husband went with Steve that night. When he came back, he said, "I went to one of their rehearsals to listen to them, and they can't play at all."

The little spark of joy that had arisen in me was suddenly put out with his words. I was feeling back down in the dumps again.

About two weeks later, while my husband was away one night, there was a knock at the door. It was Steve. "Why haven't you been coming to our rehearsals?" he asked me as soon as I opened the door. I didn't want to hurt his ego, but I had to tell the truth.

"My husband says that your band is no good."

"What!" He looked surprised, and then he just laughed. "Maybe that is why he has been playing with us for the last two weekends, saying nothing or complaining about the money he has been raking in."

"You mean he is now playing with your band?"

"Yes," Steve answered.

I invited Steve in, and we talked bluntly about what was happening here. Steve could see the picture clearer now also.

"I can't understand it," he shook his head. "Why wouldn't he wake up to the fact that you two working together would bring in even more money? What is wrong with him? He should be proud of your past, not trying to hide it. But listen, I will tell you the real reason why I came by tonight. I have got a promoter who has offered me some big money if our band can feature you as a guest artist. After this first show, it is no telling what all can happen for you. I could keep us working around the

L.A. area. I book my band almost every weekend somewhere."

"Oh, Steve!" I cried. "This is the answer to my prayers. Right now, my child needs medical help, and I can't even afford it without first getting on welfare."

"I am so sorry to hear that," he empathized. "And to see you down in this way... I would have thought that you would have made millions of dollars by now from your career of the '60s."

"I know," I sighed as I looked away, feeling the shame of how I must have appeared to be now. "I know. A lot of people figured that we artists had more profits coming from the business than we really did."

"I think I can learn a lot from you telling me what happened to you," Steve said. "So I can avoid the same pitfalls. But for right now, let me help you to get yourself out of here and into a home or something, somewhere better than this neighborhood has to offer. Will you come to our next rehearsal?" he added.

"Oh, yes," I answered quickly. "I will come if I can get there. I am not too sure my husband is going to volunteer to drive me there, let alone even advise me to where it is going to be."

"I will tell you what. If you need a ride, call me, and I will pick you up. When he sees how helpful and wonderful you'll both feel working together and being able to pay your bills easier, he will have a different attitude about the whole matter. You just wait and see."

His little pep talk brightened up the dull feelings I had been having lately about ever seeing my way clear again. Later on, when my husband came in, I cheerfully told him about Steve's visit and about the gig where he wanted me as a special guest attraction.

"He says I am to come to the next rehearsal so we can get ready for the show."

"My, you *are* in a good mood," my husband said. "Is all this about doing

the show?"

"I guess so," I smiled. Then I started reminding him of how it would be if we started working together, making more money so we could get the baby's proper checkups and have money to move into a nicer place. He didn't say very much, but I could tell that he was thinking hard and fast about something.

"So, when is the rehearsal?" I asked. "I need to know so I will be ready to go there with you."

"It is Wednesday night," and he left it at that. He didn't say he would be glad to take me or anything about whether he thought I should go or not. He just didn't say anything else pertaining to the conversation.

When Wednesday came, I was ready to go. Dinner was ready around 4:00. My husband was usually in the apartment from 3:00 in the afternoon until after he ate every day. Today, for some reason, he had left early that morning; I hadn't heard from him all day. Around 5:00 p.m., I called the number Steve had given me, telling him that I was pretty sure that I was going to need a ride.

"I will be there around 6:30," he promised. Steve lived with his mother and had rehearsals sometimes out in the back on their screened-in patio porch. Everyone showed up but my husband. He was not there that night. I knew he had purposely made himself unavailable, thinking that it would hinder me from going to the rehearsal. Steve felt the same way. All the group members welcomed me in and especially told me how honored they were to meet me.

"Your voice is too good to be true," Steve announced after I hit a few notes. He was pleased with my sound. I was happy about that, but I knew I couldn't take all the credit that night.

"You guys are terrific, and I couldn't help but feel like singing behind a group that plays so well." I could feel positive vibes coming from the group. In my heart, I knew that it was God working in His mysterious way of bringing me out of the dungeon where I had been carried.

"So you went to rehearsal anyway?" my husband questioned me when I got back to the apartment that evening.

"Yes, and they liked my voice," I said. "And may I ask what happened to you?" He came up with the old flat tire tale. I recognized that he was lying right away. I also recognized a small glint of hatred in his eyes. I knew he was not happy about it at all. For the very thing that he had taken me out of in Detroit had somehow found its way right back to me. I was now with another group getting ready to start back to work.

He didn't say anything else about it, but oh, did he have some plans for me. The show was two weeks away, so I was able to get in two more rehearsals. Then came the night of the show. It was at the Los Angeles, California Club. As we drove up, I saw my name on a big white club front poster in red letters. It said,

CONCEPT 9

FEATURING

GLADYS HORTON, LEAD SINGER OF THE FAMOUS MARVELETTES

The band had made my husband the regular emcee for the group, so he was the one introducing all the groups' numbers and telling jokes in between songs. I could hear the group getting impatient after the second set, asking my husband, "When are you going to bring Gladys on? Hurry up, man, and introduce Gladys." I was patiently waiting in the wings to come on stage.

I heard my husband laugh. He just kept laughing and

ignoring their pleas, calling out another band number to be played. This went on continuously all night until it was time for the club to close. The crowd had been quite noisy, and every now and then, I heard a voice louder than the rest saying, "On with the show. Let's see the show."

I was nearly in tears when the show promoter came backstage and told me to tell Steve that he was not paying what he had confirmed the date to pay because there was no extra added attraction. I told him who I was and how my husband refused to bring me on.

"You need to get yourself a new man, lady," he said. "He just fixed you all out of an extra $1,000."

Steve was so mad when he came off stage that I could see the fire in his eyes. "I never thought he was that ignorant and jealous. How did you get caught up with a man like that? I don't want him in my group with that attitude."

I told Steve about the reduced fee for the band that night. My husband heard me telling Steve that I wanted to remain with the group even if my husband wasn't going to be a part of it. That is when the flames started shooting. He called me all kinds of bitches and said my entertaining days were over. I cursed him back loudly and called him an all-time loser in everything he did.

Our argument was getting louder and louder. Some of the people who had been in the audience were getting to see the *real* show coming from us now. Some of the band members finally got us calmed down, but that wasn't all. On my way out of the club that night, he pushed me down on the ground and then kicked me as hard as he could in the ass.

I screamed so loudly until he threatened to do me more harm if I didn't shut up. I just kept screaming, "I hate you! I hate you! I hate you!"

The bass player with the band grabbed my husband and said some words that really made him feel like an ass. He said, "Man, if you feel this way about your famous wife, why don't you just let her go. You are making yourself appear like an insanely jealous husband with no respect, even for your manhood."

That speech took its effect in calming down my husband's verbal, brutal insult. Now, I had started crying and really boohooing out loud in spite of my efforts to remain in control and appear untouched by his beast-like behavior in front of all the club spectators.

Through all my tears, I was verbally trying to justify my reasons for being there. "I was only trying to help out so we could catch up on the rent and all the unpaid bills," I cried out. "I didn't mean to challenge your manhood and make you feel little if that is what you thought." I couldn't stop the tears streaming heavily down my face.

I heard voices in the crowd talking about what they had just witnessed. "That is Gladys Horton of The Marvelettes, and that man over there knocked her down and kicked her like a dog."

"What did she do?" I heard questions being asked. "Who is he?"

"I don't know, but it has something to do with why she wasn't on the show tonight."

He couldn't take the truth of my honest sincerity. After hearing somebody yell out from the crowd, "That dirty dog!" he jumped in the car and drove off, leaving Steve to take me home.

"You don't need that headache," Steve told me as he walked me to the door. "He is really afraid of you getting back out there again. It has nothing to do with you trying to help earn yourself a larger salary. You call me if you need me." Steve offered his support before he said good night.

I could see Mrs. Freedman, the lady upstairs who had babysat Sammie, Jr. for me, was still wide awake. She opened the door to see my face all covered and smeared with tears and make-up.

"What happened?" she asked. "Didn't the show turn out all right?" She was the only friend I had made in the whole building, and now I was so glad I had found the time to befriend someone close by. I really needed a shoulder to cry on and talk to now.

After listening to my embarrassing story, she said, "That often happens with black women who become well-known and loved by many people." She went on to explain to me that this had been happening to our race since the beginning of time. That is why many successful black women feel alone and unloved by her own black man. The black man refuses to worship this type of woman when it is his own wife. If you try to live with him, he will spend his whole life trying to make you feel belittled and no way up to his par. Now, if you are somebody he *can't* get close to, like some great lady he always sees on television or hears on the radio, he doesn't feel so threatened by your existence. He will proclaim you the greatest lady or entertainer he has ever known.

I knew it was true, but I went on to ask her, "Why did my husband feel this way when we both had been on stage together in the past? It wasn't like he was in the audience watching while I was up on stage performing. He was hired by The Marvelettes to play in our backup band."

"It only proves that this problem is far more serious than the human mind can conceive of it," she explained. "This man—our black man—is very complex. He hates competition from black women, and he only hates you more if it is the woman who has to bring him up to her level of living. So, the only thing that can save you from the results of this intimidation complex of his is to never marry a man. You have to only *help* do anything. He can only appreciate help coming from *any* other female rather than his wife. I think it's called the he-man ego."

No wonder, I thought, *that man has destroyed so much in his path just to be called the greatest ruler of all.* In the end, is it really worth all of that? So much of the good and pure all wasted or destroyed in the fight, and man ends up with nothing but his ego. Such a small reward.

I didn't see my husband again for almost two or three days, and even *that* was too soon for me. Oh, if you thought he had cooled off a bit by now, I am sorry to inform you that another fight evolved the moment he entered the apartment. This time, it was the last fight we were going to have. It would also be the last time I would ever see him again.

He came right in, warning me about trying to continue with Steve's band. I stood my ground and refused to buckle under his pressured threats. One thing led to another. Soon we were pulling and tugging at one another until we were out the door of the apartment, in the public's eye once again, broadcasting our business for the other tenants to see.

I was really no match for him, and I think getting out in the open was the only thing that saved me that day. A couple of the male tenants got him away from me and made him leave with threats of calling the police.

"Don't come back!" I screamed after him. He had torn my dress almost completely off of me, and I had hung onto his shirt during the scuffle until it was completely into shreds somewhere on the ground.

I called Steve, who volunteered to come and help me move my furniture into their back storage room. He said his mother had given her okay in letting me room with the family until I could get some help.

"Thank you, Mrs. Thornton, thank you," I said. "You just don't know how much this means to me and the baby. I don't have any relatives or any friends out here who could help me this way at a time like this. Plus, I don't have any money."

"Don't you worry about that," Steve vowed. "I will have you working so much that you will be straight again in no time."

I felt like a heavy cloud had been lifted from off my shoulders, allowing me to breathe again. Things started working out better than I ever had expected. The weekends found us playing clubs all over, clubs in Chinatown and downtown LA or Palm Springs or Bakersfield. Somewhere, somehow, we were on the go taking pictures, rehearsing, or just singing and writing new songs.

I remember what Mrs. Freedman had said to me about women helping men and how they rebel against it in many ways. So, I just let Steve lead the group completely. I didn't even mention to the audience that I was once with The Marvelettes. I didn't want anything to go wrong with my new job. So, I never insisted on being the star attraction of the group. I wanted things to be mellow and go smoothly like they were forever.

Annie, the neighbor across the street from Mrs. Thornton, had become my full-time babysitter, and she and Sammie, Jr. were really close now. I had made well over enough money, and I talked to her about Sammie's orthopedic appointment scheduled in about three days.

"I am so glad that you are going to have him looked at by a specialist," she was smiling and telling me. "They can do miraculous things nowadays in helping to cure whatever may be wrong."

Going to the orthopedic hospital that day had been a long-awaited goal of mine for some time, and I already saved almost $500 towards the hospital costs. I had been told that the treatments are so costly, but it is worth every cent to have my boy's needs taken care of.

Steve drove us to the appointment that day. I must have looked like a bundle of nerves because after we arrived, he looked at me and said, "Don't worry so much about it. I am sure Sammie, Jr. is going to be all right." The thought had never dawned on me before now. Still, suddenly I was hoping and praying that it was nothing so serious that would demand an operation for him.

The nurses and hospital staff there at Orthopedic were so concerned and polite to Sammie. He took his EEG test without a whimper, even when I saw them place all those needles in different spots on his head. I nearly fainted myself, but my baby was so cooperative. He didn't jump or move or show any signs of it being painful. The doctors explained that this test, which gives a brain wave reading, would tell them how much brain damage Sammie suffered during his birth. Also, it would let them know what activities, mentally and physically, he would be able to perform in his life. It was an all-day consultation with different physical and occupational therapists coming in to take a look at Sam and find out what his potential motor skills would be.

At the end of the day, the doctor who took blood tests and authorized the different examinations came to me and told me that Sammie's condition was termed cerebral palsy. It is where the brain is cut off from oxygen during the baby's birth. Sometimes not even for very long, but during whatever seconds or minutes this occurs, certain brain cells are destroyed, causing damage to some regions of the body. In Sammie's case, the muscles of his mouth and hips had been the ones affected.

"That is why he isn't walking yet or trying to talk," I was finally told.

"But will he ever walk and talk?" was the big question I asked.

"From the tests taken today," the doctor began to explain, "I can assure you that Sammie will walk. I can't say definitely when or how long from now that will be. But with a trained physical therapist working with him daily, it shouldn't be but a couple of years. Now, whether he will ever *talk* cannot be answered right now. There have been cases where these speechless kids grow up and become fully developed adults before they begin to talk. And then there have been cases where the individual never speaks. That is entirely up to time and the possibility that some of those brain cells may reproduce themselves.

"But mostly, it is up to God, who works many miracles as we all know. Now, your next step is to plan an individual physical therapy program for Sam here at the Orthopedic Hospital. We have counseling and support groups that you can contact to find out just what program will work best for his individual needs and circumstances. It is going to be a long and hard struggle, but you can make it. Just take one day at a time and keep the faith."

The doctor's words were very encouraging. Thus began Sammie's first day of treatment. I made an appointment to bring him back for therapy three days a week and for me to talk to a counselor. The counseling was excellent indeed. It prepared me for looking at the future with my boy, a future of bright new ideas and advanced planning for his academic programs and schooling.

Lately, I noticed Steve was looking at me longer. When I would cast my eyes in his direction, he would quickly look away or pretend that he hadn't been looking at all. It was quite obvious that he seemed to want to spend more "alone" time with me to go over the songs on the show.

Sometimes when rehearsals were over, he would want to continue on. He'd say, "Do you have a minute more? I would like to go over this new material." He would have his guitar in one hand and lean a little closer to me while playing and singing the songs he wanted me to learn. Finally, one day he couldn't hold back any longer, and he gave me a quick kiss on my cheek, saying, "That is for being indescribably good, as a singer, that is." Then he smiled that mischievous sexy smile that said he might also be talking about something else.

I tried to pass it on as just one of his fancy moods, but every day now, he would find more time to be alone with me. Finally, he asked if he could take Sammie and I out to the movies one night. I thought that was very sweet of him to include my child on our first date. I guess it was his way of showing me he accepted my child and was not ashamed to be seen with someone physically dysfunctional.

Sam was two years old now but taller than most his age. It was quite obvious that a kid this big should not be in a stroller. Whenever I had to carry him inside of places, he was at least two inches over my head. We surely got a lot of attention everywhere we went.

One night after we returned home after an engagement, Steve asked if he would come into my room and talk a while before I went to sleep. After I put Sammie to bed, we laughed and talked way into the wee hours of the morning. That is when he first asked me to have sex with him.

My answer, of course, was no. "Steve, we can't disrespect your mother's house like this after she was so kind as to let me stay here."

"I know," he agreed with me, "but you have become so much a part of my future plans now, and I just want you to know how I really feel about you."

He went on asking me if I had grown to feel differently about him since I had gotten to know him better by playing with his band and all. My answer was definitely yes. I explained that I couldn't help but love his genuine musical nature and his ability to financially keep me provided with the funds I needed to care for Sammie's treatments, babysitting fees, and proper living expenses.

I couldn't help but love him for the protection his family had rendered to me by giving us a roof over our heads. Still, I wasn't sure if it was the kind of love that called for the type of sexual behavior he wanted me to physically surrender to.

"But we work together so good as a team," he insisted. "Can't you see how much we can do together if we become even closer than close?"

My answer was still no for the next following weeks. I soon tired of his pleading and heckling and gave in. Maybe I wasn't head over heels in love with him, but he had made me feel wanted and needed like a female loves to sometimes feel she is. I had also thought about the possibility of truly finding out if I could have a normal baby.

This was something that bothered me terribly after Sammie started his physical therapy. I saw other children with birth defects. I wondered if something was wrong with my blood that really caused the big mix up or was it from Sam's father's side of the family?

In hindsight, it might not have been a good enough reason to have sex or to have a baby. But *if* it happened, I might very well get pregnant because I didn't use any birth control devices. I certainly would have the baby and finally, put my doubts to rest.

Mother Nature must have been right by my side because I am certain I must have gotten pregnant on the very first try. We were still doing shows on weekends, but Steve and I had moved out of his mother's house into a two-bedroom house around Figueroa Street and Gage Avenue. My first signs of being pregnant came one night while we were playing a club out in the Palm Springs desert area.

I had gotten so dizzy while we were up on stage performing that I felt like I was going to faint. Coming off stage, someone from the audience was asking me for my autograph. I couldn't stop to explain my ill feelings. I had to get to the dressing room and find a seat, so I just ignored their pleas.

"That was certainly rude of you," Steve came right in behind me, acknowledging that he had witnessed my actions.

"But I am sick. I am *sick*," I weakly tried to blurt out the words when all of my dinner came up all over the dressing room table. I guess that was enough proof that I hadn't become an egotistical superstar. A few days later, after seeing a doctor, we both heard the news at the same time.

"What are we going to do now?" Steve asked me.

"I am going to have this baby," I verified immediately.

He looked a little confused, so I added, "Everything will work out fine. I'll still be able to work with the group. You will see. It has been done before, you know."

With a new baby on the way and a new life, I was anxious yet excited to see what L.A. had for me.

CHAPTER 4:

"LOVE PUNCHES TOO HARD"

I don't know if it was because I already had a child with a birth defect or if I had gotten pregnant too soon after my first sexual encounter with Steve, but he showed me right from the very beginning that he had some doubts about whether the baby was really his or not.

"I just can't believe that I am going to be a father already," he said to me soon after it had been confirmed by the doctor.

I detected a note of sarcasm in his voice, and I picked up on his thoughts right away. "Well," I said, "you should have had those same doubts before you let your dick do your thinking for you."

He laughed at my bold, blunt statements and said, "It is just that it happened so soon. Are you sure you weren't pregnant when I met you?" He finally hit me with the big question that had been bothering him.

"No, I wasn't pregnant!" I screamed at him. "If I was, don't you think by now I would be showing?" Those final remarks seemed to end that conversation.

But before he entirely let the matter of his doubts cease, he apologized and explained to me why it had been a surprise for him. "You see, Gladys, the truth is, I was trying like hell to get my last girlfriend, Pat, pregnant, but it never happened. Finally, I gave up thinking that maybe I couldn't have any children. Then when it suddenly happened with you, almost on the first go-around, it has been hard for it to register in my mind that I am really going to be a father after all."

That was understandable, so I accepted his so sorry plea. One day I realized that I still had my secret spirit friend around; I guess watching over me. For some uncanny reason, I ran across an article that asked the question, "Can a baby have two fathers?" Right away, I could sense that someone else was in the room with me because I felt a quick flash of hot heat.

"What on earth could this all be about?" I thought out loud as I began to read. The article discussed a case where the seed was actually planted in the woman by one male whose sperm was not strong enough to fully fertilize it. Then, through sexual contact with another male, his sperm *finished* the fertilization process. This meant the baby would have two distinctly different fathers in scientific terms. It tells about how science is finding out new discoveries every day about human life and its extraordinary possibilities.

The article did exactly what it was supposed to do to me. It brought up those old doubts of Steve's again into my mind. I thought about it for a while, and then I remembered my husband and I hadn't had sex in three to four weeks before I left him. So, it couldn't be true. Then I heard that spirit speaking to me again saying, *"So what? Who cares whether it is true or not? You are having this baby to make sure you are able to produce normal children, aren't you?"* And it was true. I wanted this baby so much to be healthy and all right that I didn't care about anybody's doubts.

For some reason, I kept missing my doctor's appointments for monthly checkups. Once, I just plain forgot about it, and another time, I was too late getting there. The office had already closed. That is when I thought that I wasn't going to take any of the medicine that the doctors give you while you are pregnant.

That spirit had been talking to me saying, *"Remember all those pills that you were taking with Sam? Look how healthy he turned out to be?"*

Oh no, I thought. I have got to be sure this time, really sure that it is okay for me to be a mother. So, I explained to Steve that I wanted to start eating the right foods like fresh vegetables, fruits, and milk and not see a doctor until it was time for me to deliver. I thought that this idea of mine was going to be hard for him to accept. For some reason, he agreed with me and helped me out by sometimes cooking for me and making sure I ate right all the time.

I think it was in the back of both of our minds that this baby just had to be perfect. The group was still taking weekend bookings because I felt really good most of the time, and I was doing fine in keeping my weight down. Many times, I would get off my strict diet whenever I went over to Steve's mother's house. She was a Louisiana Creole girl. Her specialty was the spicy Cajun dishes and the Louisiana shrimp gumbo and fried oysters. I was getting to understand just why they say, "Those Louisiana folks sure can cook."

She and I had become very good companions because she was a humane person who understood people with difficulties. Being a schoolteacher in Watts, she heard family problems almost daily. Therefore, she had to deal with her share of lending an ear to the children's problems and trying to teach them the best she knew how.

She was always kind to Sammie and found ways to entertain him with her jokes. We used to always tease them about their names being the same. Hers was spelled with an "m-a-y-e" ending, while Sammie's had an "m-i-e" ending.

"What do you want this time?" she asked me about the baby.

"I don't care," I admitted. "As long as it is healthy, physically and mentally."

It was easy for her and I to communicate, especially with our birthdates being right together. Mine was May 30th, and hers was May 31st. We were both true Geminis.

Steve was her third son, and he had two older brothers, Butch and Michael. Things had gotten a lot easier for me on the pocketbook because I had gotten some hospitalization insurance for Sam and I. I didn't have to pay for those high therapy bills myself, and I knew having this next baby would also be covered fully by my insurance. So, now I was able to *see* my earnings being saved.

"After you have the baby, you are going to need some time to rest before you resume your place back in the group," Steve was telling me. "We are going to start rehearsing our act without you, so we will be ready to keep working." It was a good thing that Cornell and Perkins both had singing voices and could help Steve with the many songs I had led. I used to hear them backgrounding my songs, and I was really impressed with their unique harmony. It was always right and so close, one perfect pitch on top of the other. They had an ear for the right sound.

The months seemed to fly by, and when I knew it would soon be baby time, I went to Dr. Goodman's office for a checkup.

"Who has been taking care of you all these months?" he asked, noticing from my records that I had not kept one appointment.

"I have been taking care of myself," I answered, not knowing if he was still considering the job of delivering my baby or not. Steve had already warned me that some doctors will not.

"Well," he said, after listening to the heartbeat and measuring my abdomen size, "everything sounds good, and from the looks of you, your next visit will probably be to the hospital." He gave me the address of the hospital where he worked as a doctor on delivery days.

A good week went by when I awakened one morning with labor pains. I didn't even bother to tell Steve right away. I suddenly felt like an old pro at this game, and I knew it would be at least an hour or two before another one would come. So, I went back to sleep. I knew the important thing to do now was to keep calm and just relax.

By mid-morning, I had another one. This time, I told Steve that I was sure that I would have to go to the hospital before night fell. "The second child always comes a little quicker," I told him because the contractions experienced from the first child allow the body to respond to the procedures of childbirth faster.

I spent that day shopping for some toys for Sammie, Jr. I knew he was going to miss seeing me for a couple of days, and the brand-new toys would take his mind off my absence. Luckily, Steve had volunteered to watch Sammie, Jr. at the house for those days I would be away, so I didn't need a babysitter.

Around 4:00 that evening, December 15th, Steve took me to the hospital, where I was taken to the delivery room right away. The nurse there got me ready for bed. I had noticed that this hospital was much smaller than the one in Detroit, where Sammie was born. Maybe that was why

I thought there was hardly anybody in the labor rooms. I asked the one and only nurse in there, "Where are all the people?"

"What people?" she seemed puzzled at my question.

I knew that there was no way for her to understand what I was talking about unless I explained to her how busy my labor room had been while I was having my first child. "Well," I started on what now seemed to be a long-ago story. "When I was in labor once before, my room was like Grand Central Station, with nurses and interns constantly coming in and going out."

"Is that right?" she said. "Why was that?"

"I don't know," I answered, but I never gave it any thought before now. "I thought it was the normal procedure for all the labor rooms. Until I see now that yours is so different. It's so quiet without the hustle and bustle of a crowd."

She seemed interested in hearing more about it, and so talking to her took my mind off the contractions that were coming closer and closer together now. I explained how every time an intern came in to check me for dilation, it was a different intern and of a different nationality. That didn't even bother me so much as the interns in this hospital all being men.

"What!" she screamed. "That must have been very uncomfortable for you, especially with it being the first time you were going through the labor room procedures."

"Yes. And then the worst thing of all was that my husband was supposed to witness the birth but was talked out of it at the last minute."

"That usually means that they are having complications with the mother and child. Did you know that?" she asked me.

"I didn't until right now," I admitted. "But you are so right. My first child suffered brain damage during birth."

"Oh, that is too bad," she sympathized with me. "Don't worry too much about that happening here. We will be giving you and the baby the best of care. In fact, nobody else is going to even touch you besides the doctor and me."

Those words certainly put my mind at ease. "What kind of sedation are you going to give me for the pain?"

Before answering me, she asked, "Do you remember what they gave you before?"

"Oh, yes," I said. "I had a lot of things. A couple of doses of twilight sleep during the early stages of labor. Then in the delivery room, I had some gas and a saddle block, you know, that shot they give you in your spine."

"Oh, you poor dear!" she cried. "You must have been miserable! Not this time. I am going to give you one shot now in the hip. It is up to the doctor when he gets here whether he will give you anything else or not. You do want to be awake during the delivery this time, don't you?"

"Oh, yes. Yes, I do. I want to see that my baby is all right, right away."

It was now around 5:30 p.m., and my second son was born around 8:45 p.m. For many reasons, I will never forget the doctor's words as soon as the baby was out. "He is a perfect boy." As soon as the nurses washed him up, they laid him in my arms right there in the delivery room.

Later that evening, after Steve had seen the baby and was allowed to visit my bedside, he struck me with some words that were even more painful than the labor that I had just been through.

"He don't look nothing like me," was the first greeting I received from his mouth. I was too weak to say anything. I just closed my eyes very tightly, trying hard to fight back the agony of tears. I wasn't going to let anything or nobody scar the happiness I felt with my newborn baby.

He knew the damage his words had caused in just those first few minutes because he quickly left, saying he just wanted to make sure I was okay. "See you tomorrow," he said on leaving. I didn't even open my eyes to look at him or wave goodbye.

I could hear that voice of the spirit speaking to me again. It was comforting and telling me, *"That is all right. Whether it looks like him or not, you have your baby, and he is fine and healthy. There is nothing wrong with you. That is what really matters."*

When they brought my baby around to feed the next day, the nurses were all laughing and commenting on how strong his neck already was. "Look at him. He is already looking for you, Gladys," they said. And sure enough, Vaughn seemed to have more strength in his upper torso than most babies do. His head was peeking up over the blankets as though he was ready and willing to meet this new mom of his.

He was so cute and cuddly. What got me were his eyes. They were already opened wide, shining like two diamonds, which was very rare for newborn babies. Sometimes it took days before they opened their eyes to this degree. Everything went fine at the hospital, and so I was back home in three days.

Sammie was totally amazed and surprised when he saw this new baby. I told him, "Sammie, look here. You have got a brother now. This is your brother." A smile as wide as a mile came across Sammie's face. I think he realized instantly that he had a good friend now to play with. Someone that would be his partner for life.

"He is yours, Sammie. He is your very own brother."

Sammie knew that this meant Vaughn was going to be someone special for him. I let him watch me do everything for the baby. I knew right away that Sammie loved Vaughn from the very first time he looked at him.

Steve was showing no signs of regret, even if he felt like someone else was the father. He managed to prove to me that he planned on nothing else but being one of the best fathers a baby could have. Vaughn had been born 10 days before Christmas, and Steve's family had invited us over to welcome Vaughn into the family and also have the big holiday season Christmas dinner.

Mrs. Thornton had invited other neighbors and friends over. Steve's other two brothers also had their guests there. Everyone was already excited about the new baby's arrival. For the very first time, they were getting a chance to see Vaughn. I heard the knock on the door, but I didn't pay very much attention to the three extremely tall gentlemen who came in. I only glanced up once long enough to see that they all were well over six feet tall.

I knew I had never seen them before, and I didn't know whose company they were. They seemed to know the others there and was wishing everyone a happy holiday. Suddenly they came over to where I was holding Vaughn, who was still asleep, despite the noise of the music and laughter going on.

"My, what a fine baby you have," one spoke to me while the others all leaned down to take a closer look at him.

"May I?" I heard one ask to hold him. He gently picked Vaughn up, and now they were all standing tall, laughing and talking and making remarks you usually hear about newborns.

I heard one say, "He is going to be a big man." And at that remark, he put Vaughn in one hand and held him high up, almost to the ceiling. I jumped to my feet now with the fear of him maybe dropping my baby. I was only a midget compared to their height, but I didn't care. My maternal instincts had kicked in. I don't even think they noticed my quick gestures of protesting their action. He just handed my baby carefully back to me while they all joked about how Vaughn was not even disturbed one bit after taking that big height up in the air. He was still sleeping peacefully in my arms, unmoved by any type of interaction.

I saw the guys talking to Steve's mother and a few other guests, and then they bid everyone goodbye and left. We had a fine time that day, and the food was terrific. However, it wasn't until later that evening, when we were all about to leave, that I asked Steve's mother who they were. Come to find out, *nobody* knew who invited them.

"I thought they were friends of Michael's," Mrs. Thornton said. Michael thought they were friends of Steve's, and Steve said that he thought they were friends from the school where his mother teaches. We were all baffled and bewildered about the incident of the three seemingly wise men. Everyone was feeling so good because of the holiday spirit and because there didn't seem to be any harm done during their visit, nobody thought any more about it.

That is... nobody but me. I couldn't help but remember how easygoing and naturally they had come in, seeming to know everyone and mingling with the crowd. *Thank goodness they were good guys,* I thought, *because it would have been a perfect setup for a robbery.* And thank goodness they had been careful while holding my child. I guess I will just have to write it off as another strange supernatural episode in our lives.

***

Three months had passed, and I was now on the move again with the group. I knew my mistake from the past of stopping my career after Sammie's birth had not proved to be in the best of my interests. I wasn't going to make the same mistake again. So, I found a babysitter named Eileen, who lived right next door to help me out on the weekends. Again, I lost weight quickly after childbirth and was ready to take new pictures with the group.

Steve was really advancing more and more with his ability to write new material. He had a friend named Jack who had just started a new recording company. It was just a place where groups came in and booked his studio to lay down their master tracks. And so, I found myself there on plenty of evenings recording and singing leads to the new songs Steve was writing.

Something changed about Steve. I don't know whether it was because he was suddenly feeling the pressures of fatherhood or beginning to feel trapped with all the work he did in keeping the group together. I know he had dreams of becoming a big recording artist, and it seemed to be right within his reach. As a result, he was becoming pushier and less tolerant of the musicians' mistakes.

Studio recording was new to him and the group, but I had seen these days before. They now realized that making a record was much different than just playing on a live show. Steve had to understand that no group ever gets it right on the very first take. You have to do it over and over again. Sometimes, the pressure of this is more than you can stand. "But as the group leader, you have to excel in patience," I told him. Still, Steve had become just downright rude in his words of criticism of the whole group. He was getting on everyone's nerves.

The fellows had started to talk about it. "Just because he is a father now, he seems to think that we are all little children," I heard them griping one day.

They went on voicing their disapproval, saying, "We are all adults, and I demand to be spoken to like one."

I tried to add a little light to the subject by stating, "Steve just wants us to be the best. Sometimes, it takes someone being hard on us to make you tough and unbreakable. It is not easy making it to the top." Even when I stood up for him, he later said something to me that made me wish I hadn't said anything at all.

Once, when he thought I wasn't giving a particular song my all and all, he said, "Now I see why they gave Wanda of The Marvelettes all the better songs to lead." He knew he had hurt my feelings, and I could see it in his smile now.

"You're very good at hurting everybody's feelings," I told him. "Maybe you are in the wrong business. You should have a critic's column in the daily newspaper."

"Maybe we all just need a short vacation," one of the group members suggested after another disagreement during a recording session. We had all been working too hard and too long together, and we were beginning to get on each other's nerves. Steve let it be known right away that he was the boss, and he said when we would stop, nobody else.

Before now, Steve and I had gotten along just perfectly at home after our musical day was over. Recently, he had started to pick on how I did this and how I did that. At first, I ignored his grouchy nature because I knew he was more interested in the affairs of the family now and with bringing up the baby with Vaughn around. That is a phase I think *every* new father goes through.

But this particular evening, things just seemed to get out of control, and we both lost our tempers. For the first time since we had met, we had our first fight. I'm not just talking about a little fight. I am talking about my very first big black eye. Again, love had thrown a punch too hard in my direction. This time, it *really* hurt. I think more mentally than physically.

I had seen my husband's personality go totally on the blink. I assumed it was due to his negligent background of drinking and working for peanuts and not being used to the so-called good life. Now Steve, who had come from a long line of intelligent college graduates, had stooped to this low esteem activity of brutalizing and antagonizing this female species called me.

I couldn't take too much more of this side of love. These were love punches that were too hard for me to bear.

Love comes and throws a Knockout Punch.

A punch that just might be too much.

First, he sweeps you off your feet,

and later you find he has knocked you out of your seat.

Yes, the one you love has whipped you in defeat.

So, when love punches too hard,

You better start putting up your guard.

When love punches too hard,

You better start packing up your heart.

Be careful, girl, and please beware,

It has been known to get too rough.

Love can turn real mean and tough

If there is no one there to say what is fair.

When the only ring you see is in the fight

That has no referee.

You are up, and then he knocks you to the ground,

and you may not last to go nine rounds.

So when love punches too hard,

You better start putting up your guard.

When love punches too hard,

You better start packing up your heart.

I knew the tension had been building up for the last couple of weeks between Steve and me and the problems of recording with the group. But I never expected a performance such as this one coming from Mr. Steve Thornton. He hit me so hard I saw stars. It just wasn't like him. He also realized that it was way out of his nature to do such a thing, and the next day, he was all full of "sorry's" and apologies for his actions.

"I don't know what got into me," he explained. "I never felt so angry before. It is like I become someone else for a quick second. I just couldn't control myself."

Well, despite all his sorry pleas, it had happened at the wrong time. We had a wedding engagement party to play in one week, and my eye was so purple and blue that even a plastic surgeon couldn't have done much for me by then.

"If you could just get the swelling to go down, maybe you can camouflage the dark bruises with make-up," Steve suggested. I was in no condition to argue with anyone devising any means whatsoever to get me back to normal again. Witch hazel pads, ice packs, and lots of rest off of my feet are what Dr. Steve ordered for me.

He was the most attentive and overly concerned live-in nurse a patient could have asked for. He did all the cooking and took care of both of the boys. I think every time he looked at me, he apologized for the fight. I knew he was really sorry when he suggested that he move back over to his mother's house until he found a place of his own.

"You don't have to do all of that," I told him.

"I just want to be sure that something like this never happens again. I don't trust myself or my temper anymore, and above everything else, I am really ashamed of myself. I really am." He went on explaining, "We have got a good group now. And I'm not going to lose everything I have worked for on account of some negative vibes going around making us lose this chance for success."

He helped me to get my face back together well enough to do the wedding, and then days later, he moved back in with his mother. I had the house to myself with the boys, and to tell you the truth, I enjoyed having my privacy at last. Vaughn was about nine months old, and unlike Sammie, he did everything faster. I knew at the rate he was growing and learning that he would be walking soon.

Sam still wasn't walking yet, but they both were having races every day on the floors crawling. "It is great physical exercise," his therapist said. "I highly recommend it. It is exactly the type of motivation he needs right now. He is really learning from his brother's actions. When he sees his brother walking, he will feel the need and want to follow along and do the same." Yes, Sam was enjoying every minute of growing up with his brother.

***

I saw the ad in the paper one day. It read, "Want your divorce fast without the high cost of a lawyer? Call Legal-Aid today." I did just that.

"Here is what we do," I was told by a legal representative. "For a very low fee, we run an ad in the *Wall Street Journal* for three months so that your husband can legally protest the divorce if he wants to. After that time, if no one has answered the notice, you are given a court date wherein the judge grants you your final divorce."

"That sounds good enough to me," I said. Because I knew that my husband wasn't very likely going to buy the *Wall Street Journal* to read, my divorce was going to be a sure thing. All I had to do was be patient and wait. I was advised that sometimes these court dates take a while.

"But you're as good as a free woman after the three months publication has not been answered," the lawyer promised. I paid the legal fees, and the paperwork had begun.

Soon, no matter how long it took, I would be out of this mess called marriage. I felt like I was putting the pieces back together in my life again and getting my broken world repaired. Steve continued to pick me up for rehearsals and shows and saw to it that I got to the grocery store and out to pay my utilities at times. Other times, I just mailed in my payments because I was beginning to get some negative feedback on him having to drive me around to these different places.

One day, he just came out and said it straight. "I am tired of driving you around like I am your chauffeur." He accused me of making him feel this way. "Why don't you find yourself a handyman somewhere else."

I had really begun to feel like a bothersome household pest because it was true. I needed to have transportation. With two small children not walking, there was nothing else to do but keep requesting his services, despite his constant bickering of disliking it. What made me realize that he was serious about me cramping his style was when he came to pick me up one day in his new two-seater foreign sports car. "What happened to your old Chevrolet?" I asked.

"I traded it in for this," he said. "Don't you like it?"

Sure, it was more appealing for a single man and someone who didn't have people to drive around, but it was certainly too small for the two kids and me. "Just where are the kids supposed to ride?" I asked him.

I couldn't believe that he had grown to be so self-centered since we had separated. I knew that he had bought the car, hoping that I would now find it necessary to ask someone else for transportation to and from my different destinations.

This should have been my clue to get my license to drive and buy a small car for myself and the kids' recreation. But I just wasn't ready for the upkeep of a car yet, and I knew it. So, riding the bus was going to be my next best bet.

"You are going to have to let Sam spend some time away from you if he is ever going to learn to walk completely on his own," I was now being advised by his counselors. "There is a new childcare facility out in Hawthorne, California, that I think will be just great for him until he has learned to take those steps alone without your help. He will be getting physical therapy daily and learning independent living. I guarantee you if you let him stay there on a 24-hour basis, he will be walking alone very soon," they told me.

"What?!" I declared. "Let Sammie live somewhere away from me?" The thought of it was just unbearable and so depressing.

"I know it is going to be really hard on you both at first, but it is what he needs now to get going on his own. He will never step out alone as long as he knows you're right there to catch him if he falls. He needs to be away from you for a little while," I was finally told.

And just like a mother, far-seeing, and understanding, I knew that the best program was being provided for my son. All I had to do was be willing and strong enough to cooperate and help them provide these special training activities for Sammie.

So, the day after Sammie's fourth birthday, he went to live at the South Bay Center for Exceptional Children. The rules were that a child had to be there for two whole weeks before being allowed visitation rights. After that, he could even spend some weekends at home. Those two weeks without seeing Sammie at all were very lonely for Vaughn and me. Vaughn had grown so used to Sammie's companionship.

I tried to explain to Vaughn what was going on in a way that he could understand. "Sammie had become very confused when he saw that you were able to walk, and he still wasn't," I said confidently. "Seeing you made him realize that he had this problem. So now he is going to a place where they will make Sammie begin to walk on his own. Then, he will come back home and live with us." Even though he was young, Vaughn seemed to understand how much it meant to his brother to do the same things that he could. Within a short time, he quickly adapted to his brother's absence.

Besides, it wasn't very long before we had Sam back home on a weekend stay. Even after that, Vaughn went with me to see Sam on the weekends. They still kept in touch with one another. Sometimes, we would go out, get Sam, and go on a picnic for a day. Other times, we would just have an outing on the recreational court of the center. I made sure that Sammie knew that his family kept him in mind at all times.

Fortunately, I had met one of the mothers of a child who was also in placement at the center. We had become good conversational pals, talking about the different problems we both had with raising a handicapped child. Through those intimate moments, we sympathized with each other's difficulties. She also lived in Los Angeles and volunteered to give me a ride whenever she came out to the center.

"Just call me a day before you plan to visit, and if I am coming out this way, I will gladly pick you up," she offered. That helped me tremendously because it took me 45 minutes or more when riding the bus. Luckily, Vaughn never seemed to mind it. It must have been exciting for him to see all the different passengers coming aboard and then later leaving after reaching their destination points.

It is a good thing that I had never gotten my head so far up in the clouds from all of my success that I couldn't remember or face the everyday chores of the real world. I never told my friend about my career days as an entertainer because I had found out during these last four years away from Motown that it was easier for me this way. I didn't have to explain why this or that had not worked out for me. People didn't expect any more from me than from the next person. By being silent, I didn't have to be ashamed of not having this or wearing that. I could come and go as I pleased, just being an everyday person.

A month or so after Sammie went off to the center, we moved to a bigger place. It was a garage apartment around 61st and Vermont. Steve helped me move in, but he was still at his old job of making me feel like I was nothing but a big bother and total nuisance. "I will be so glad when you find somebody who will consider going steady with you," he would laugh and joke. Of course, he was referring to me still being single and without a steady fellow since we had separated.

The truth really was that I wasn't particularly *looking* for anyone else. I certainly was doing alright on my own. Our shows were enough to pay for my rent and food, which were the biggest bills in my living costs. And now, with Vaughn's birth, Steve was helping me with utility bills and whatever I may want to buy for the kids, like clothes, shoes, etc.

I think he thought that just because I was always alone—apart from when he stayed the night—that nobody else wanted me. I wanted to remind him so badly that it was because I *preferred* it that way, not because I was undesirable. I knew deep down inside that it would only spell trouble for me if he even *thought* that I was interested in anybody else. So, I never bothered to defend myself from his statements of pure speculation.

***

We had been in our new place for about three months when I met Al. He lived with his family right around the corner from me on Kansas Street. As I said, I sure wasn't looking for anybody else. But when I first saw Al, I had to take a double look. He was built like Adonis, the Greek god. And girls! Are you ready for this? He had green eyes and tall, dark olive-brown complexioned, and just righteously *fine*.

I had walked around the corner to the neighborhood supermarket. I noticed two guys were walking at a distance in front of me. One fellow was going into the store while the other remained outside by the entrance. I would never have even looked up at him, but his gentleman-like manner as he graciously stepped aside to let me enter caught my attention. I was startled to see such gorgeous green eyes smiling down into mine. It was very rare to see a guy that shade of brown with light eyes.

"Thank you," I blushed, wondering what planet this male species invaded us from. I am sure he knew what effect he was having on me. He certainly had that same effect on people everywhere he went. I never thought that I would ever see him again. He was like one of those fantastic figures you see only once. You never forget it, but you never even expect to see that grand attraction twice in your life.

That is why when I heard the knock at my door, I nearly fell to the floor when I opened it and saw his face.

"How did you find me?" were my first words. I was not only amazed, but I was shocked to discover that he had found out my exact address and where I lived. Being sought after really plays with the female mind. Never before had anything like this ever happened to me. I felt like the fairy princess who had finally been rescued by the handsome prince.

Romantic as it may seem, I soon found out I was getting involved in the opposite type of fairy tale. No way was this one going to be about Cinderella and her fairy godmother. Instead, it was closer to the tale about that tricky old wolf and Little Red Riding Hood.

"Well, aren't you going to invite me in?" He captured my heart with his smile as he spoke. But even with me being slightly hypnotized by his dramatically beautiful eyes, I was able to think clearly enough to heed the warning of my suspicious thoughts. I really didn't even know him. He may be a robber or something even worse: a rapist.

Instead of being in a daze, I ignored his question and started asking a few of my own. "How, what for, and why did you feel the need to try to find out where I lived?" I demanded.

He summed up all of my questions with a plain and simple answer. "I liked you the moment I saw you, but I really fell for the sweetness I saw in you. It is hard to forget someone who carries themselves like you, a perfect lady."

"Well, thank you," I said quietly, knowing very well that he must have had a lot of experience in saying the right things and displaying his very charming manners. "I bet you tell all the ladies the same thing?"

"No, I don't." He instantly took on a serious attitude now, and his smile was no longer apparent. "Believe it or not, I don't use my looks to entice anyone. The subject is very serious to me because I don't play. If I meet a female that I like, I go out of my way to tell her. Otherwise, it is hi and goodbye. I may look like a heartbreaker, but that is not my game. I don't have time for it. Up until now, even thinking about finding a mate has been secondary on my list."

"Oh, I see, Mr.—"

"Al, Alvin Morris is my name," he spoke up. "What is yours?" His smile returned again.

"Gladys."

I started to ask him another question, but he must have read my mind quickly as he added, "I live right around the corner with my parents. Do you trust me enough now to invite me in?"

I did, and so I said, "Come on in." He looked around at my belongings, and before he sat down, he said, "Somehow, I knew that you were a very neat girl. I like your apartment. Do you live here alone?"

"No, I have two children. One is away in a special care facility, and the other is playing with his friend in one of the front duplexes."

"How old are you?"

"I am 28 years old."

"Do you know how old I thought you were the other day when I first saw you?"

My interest was piqued. "How old?"

"I thought you were younger than me."

With that answer, I now had a few questions of my own to ask. "Well, how old are you?" I couldn't wait to hear this.

"I am 19 going on 20," he said truthfully.

"What!" My mouth flew open wide, and I knew my eyes were wild with disbelief. Not because I had been mistaken for a teenage girl but because I had figured him to be at least 30. Don't get me wrong; he didn't *look* old at all. It was his stature, so mature and well-rounded. The way he spoke was influential and intelligent, like he had years of knowing how to express himself.

He had thought that I was younger, and I had thought that he was older. *That* should have been my clue to say, "It was nice meeting you, Al, and goodbye," but I didn't. Instead, I enjoyed his company that day and his compliments on how nice I had kept my figure after having two children. Not to mention how he admired cleanliness in a woman. *That* was something new that had never been outwardly appreciated before.

He made no advances sexually towards me, nor even spoke of intimacy of any kind in our conversations that day or the next. In fact, on the several other times I invited him to come over, he never said a word. I admired that about him right away. He wasn't just after my body. I had found a new, exciting, and handsome suitor who loved my companionship.

At first, we just talked a lot, and he introduced me to some of his good close buddies. I found out one thing about Al early enough—he loved smoking marijuana. Eventually, so did I. At first, I was totally against it. I told him if he wanted to light it up, he would have to do it outside on the porch. There was no way he could do it in the house, especially with Vaughn there with me. He agreed to that policy and said he understood and respected my wishes.

One night after putting Vaughn to bed, I didn't make him go outside to smoke. Instead, I tried a little bit of it myself. After two or three puffs, I was *really* feeling good.

It wasn't like it was the first time I had tried marijuana. I had smoked some pot for the first time in my life when The Marvelettes had gone to Europe to perform way back in 1964. After we returned to the States, it did not become a habit or an everyday thing for me. Every now and then, I would take a puff while socializing or at a party with my friends. Our group never consistently used drugs while performing in the '60s. After I left show business, I had not even *seen* any until now.

I was learning to relax more with Al around me now. I remembered how much fun smoking was when you were in a happy and easy-going atmosphere, and we laughed at everything laughable. We had serious talks for hours about the world and its people. Sometimes, we would go out for a bite to eat, or I would fix us something right there at the apartment. He knew about Sammie and his difficulties in walking and talking. He knew about Steve and the group we both worked in. He knew everything about me before Steve found out about him. Until now, I had made sure that their paths didn't cross.

Al was nowhere around when Steve would pick me up for rehearsals or we had a show to play. But about three weeks after Al and I had become quite chummy, Steve showed up uninvited. It was early in the day and when I *least* expected him to. We were all in the kitchen—Al, Vaughn, and I—when I heard the loud knock on the door.

Who could that be? I thought. I put down the sandwiches that I was preparing for lunch and went to look out of the front room window before I answered the door. I saw Steve's dark green sports car parked down below. "It's Steve!" I ran back into the kitchen to warn Al.

"So what?" he remarked. "Go on ahead and let him in. It's time we met."

"But not right now," I begged of him. "I wanted to

discuss things with Steve quietly first before introducing you two."

"Well, what do you want me to do?" Al said. "Is there any place where I can hide?"

"No, no," I tried to calm myself because Steve was making more deliberate, impatient knocks. "Here! The back door!" I shouted. I had almost even forgotten I had one because we never used it. I opened it, and Al ran down the backstairs lined with uncut tree branches. I heard him complaining on his way down about the scratches he was enduring from the limbs.

By the time I got to the front door, Steve was aware that something was going on. His suspicious glare moved from my face to Vaughn's, who had been taking the whole incident in perspective.

"He went that way," Vaughn informed Steve. Vaughn was now pointing to the kitchen leading to the back door. Steve pushed past me and rushed into the kitchen. It was apparently obvious that the back door had been recently used.

"So *that* is how you have been spending your free time." He was now looking at the untouched sandwiches I had been making before he knocked.

"I-I-I-I-I—" I stuttered a bit as I began to tell him I had a friend over for lunch.

"If lunch is all you were having, why did he have to run off so fast?" He was beginning to start his probing and questioning. I knew from the look on his face that he was shocked. Vaughn was jumping up and down now, giving out more information willingly.

"His name is Al. Al is his name." Steve laughed, now reaching down to hug Vaughn. "That is my boy. My good boy. He tells Dad when Mommy has been bad."

That statement made me laugh. "What do you mean 'When Mommy has been bad?' Wasn't it you, as I plainly recall, who told me on numerous occasions that you wish I would find someone else and stop bothering you to take me here and there? Wasn't it you? Wasn't it *you*?"

Steve did not say a word at first. He just stared at me. Then he asked, "Does he know about the group?"

"Yes, he knows," I answered. "He has been watching Vaughn for me lately on our nights out to work."

"So he also knows about me?" Steve asked. "So, why didn't you tell me about him?"

My answer was quick and honest. "Because I didn't know how you would take it at first. Even with you always suggesting that I find someone else, I never really knew if you were serious or not. Men have been known to change when these things really happen. And I didn't want to upset you and the understanding that we have going."

"Upset me?" he echoed my words back to me. "It wouldn't have upset me. Sneaking behind my back is what has me upset. But now that I know, I wish you the best, and I hope he doesn't find it a problem with you and I still working together." He started to leave, but before he got to the front door, he turned around and asked me another question. "He does have a car, doesn't he? I was wondering if he could start bringing you to rehearsals? It would save me the trip of coming over here unless I am coming to see Vaughn."

I knew he was trying to find out more about Al. "No, he doesn't," I said. I felt ashamed, realizing that I had never even given it much thought until now. Steve sort of smiled as if to say I had certainly picked a lemon. "His car is in the shop right now," I quickly lied, hating to admit to what I knew he was trying to silently insinuate.

"Well, I will pick you up around seven tomorrow evening for rehearsal. Be ready," were his last demanding remarks to me.

***

"I hope you had that private talk with Steve?" Al later laughed about how he never wanted to have to make a dash for my backstairs again. He showed me all the scratches the tree branches had made on his arms.

"He knows all about us now," I told him. "And he wished me the best of luck."

"I hope I wasn't really breaking up anything serious?" Al looked at me with a big question mark in his eyes now.

"No, no," I said quickly. "Steve was quite tired of me, and he indicated it to me time and time again. I just think that deep down inside, he never expected me to actually look for somebody else."

Then Al quickly brought it back to my attention that *he* had found *me*. "Remember? You didn't have to leave your doorstep." We both laughed, thinking back to that first surprise he gave me when I saw him standing there in my doorway.

"How did you *really* find me?" I asked more seriously.

"It wasn't hard," Al joked. "I just asked a few people who lived in the neighborhood about the dark chocolate beauty who lived somewhere close around, and they all pointed back here to your apartment." Then he laughed and added, "You see, you were very well-known and didn't know it. You are not very hard to miss, you know. Or to forget."

And that is how our relationship finally got off the ground. Al was over every day. Soon after, we were having sex. I met his parents, his sister, and his two brothers. We all seemed to mix very well together, and soon they accepted me into the family as Al's girlfriend. His parents knew I was eight years older, but never once did they mention it being a problem. I think this is mostly because our age differences didn't show at all.

His sister once told me that we made a terrific-looking couple. She had started baby-sitting Vaughn for me, and the whole family fell in love with him. Vaughn loved all the extra attention he was getting now. He didn't seem to mind that Steve seemed only interested in keeping the group together and never came in to visit him anymore. Often, he would call on the telephone to speak to his son. Sometimes he would yell, "How is my boy doing?" from out of the car window up to Vaughn, who would be watching as we would be driving off to rehearsal.

Things went smoothly like this for about a month. Even during shows, I noticed that Steve and I avoided eyeing one another a lot like we used to. Then, it all came crashing down on me one day. Steve called to say that my telephone bill was higher than usual. I knew instantly what he was getting at, that somebody else must be making calls on my telephone.

Then he said, "Really, I don't feel like I should continue to pay any of your utilities anymore now that you have a guy of your own. And I especially refuse to pay for anyone else's calls." I could hear it in his voice that he was ready to get it on with the argument that we had deliberately been avoiding until now.

"Well, fine," I said shortly. "Don't pay any more bills for me."

"Your new guy," he continued. "He does have a job, doesn't he? Because if he is going to be the one fucking you, he should be paying for all of your added extras. I am through! And as for the group, I am taking a vacation. I am leaving and going back to Louisiana for a while. I need the rest."

So that is what he has been doing, I thought to myself now. He was planning a way to cut me off financially without a job. So now, he wouldn't be here to book the group. "What about Concept 9, your group?" I asked.

"All the fellows know what I am doing, and they understand. I hoped you would too. Goodbye," he said and hung up the telephone.

Later, after talking to the bass player, he told me that Steve had never gotten used to the idea of me dating someone else. "Gladys," he said, "Steve finally realized what he had in you after you found somebody else. Although it was too late then, I think he was secretly hoping that your affair wouldn't have lasted as long as it has and that you two would finally get back together. But it hasn't happened, and he is deeply hurt at losing you. That is why he is leaving."

I kind of felt sorry now that things hadn't worked out for us, but there was no turning back for me. I had to go on. The next thought that crossed my mind was how would I make a decent living for my kids and myself now? Although Al had recently found a job, he was not living with me. Therefore, whatever earnings he was making were going towards his family's household.

The way I got the job I did get about three weeks later was when a nicely dressed lady passed me her card in the supermarket one day. It read, "Celebrity Jewelry Shows at Homes, Businesses, and Special Events." Naturally, I wondered what it was all about, so I gave her a call.

"We go around to clubs and shops and businesses and put on jewelry and fashion shows," the woman informed me. "I have a girl who models my jewelry while also wearing clothes from a boutique shop owned by one of my customers. At these shows, I sell lots of jewelry and also give out cards in the boutique shop where the clothes can be bought. If you want to have a party in your home, we require that you must have at least ten guests on the night of your party. You also get a small commission on all the sales I make that night. Would you like to have a party?"

"Why not," I said enthusiastically. It might very well be a means for me to earn some money part-time. I was curious to find out just how much commission I could make at one of these parties. So, I got all the neighborhood ladies to come over, and they brought along some of their friends. I think I counted around 15 females in my apartment that night.

When the jewelry lady finally got there, I could plainly see she was upset. "Sorry I am late," she apologized, "but my model for the show was having problems, and she couldn't come."

"Don't worry," I reassured her. "I will model whatever jewelry you have." She looked me over quickly as if she wondered if I could successfully pull it off at a moment's notice. "Don't worry," I reiterated. "Everything will be fine." I just happened to have on one of my cute little dresses I had worn on stage with the guys. It went fine with being appropriate for the "after five" pieces that she had and the jewelry she was showing for the daytime wear.

Things worked out so naturally that night that you would have thought that I had been modeling jewelry and clothes all of my life. The ladies really put in enough jewelry orders until my commission for that one night was around $100. I was really pleased with the outcome of my party, and so was the jewelry lady.

"I am impressed," she said afterward, "but mostly with you. Are you working now?"

"No, I am not," I answered cheerfully with a smile, hoping that she would ask me to continue on with her doing this sort of work. I had really enjoyed showing off the fine, lovely jewelry that she had brought to my party. God knows I had been searching the papers day and night with hopes of finding some type of work that wouldn't make me feel like I had finally hit rock bottom.

In the papers, I had seen ads about becoming the Avon lady, selling clothes through a fashion catalog, and answering the phone for private party businesses. But now, right here in my own home, the perfect job had come to me. I had even had a formal and personal interview already with my employer. *How lucky could a person be?* I wondered.

"You certainly are exactly what I need," she went on, complimenting me on my posture and outgoing personality. "Do you have your own transportation?"

My heart just about fell to my knees as I answered no.

"Well, that wouldn't be a problem with me unless there is some reason why you couldn't be punctual for these shows. I can pick you up, but I can't afford to be late coming to these shows. My clients expect me to be on time, and I have been until recently when my last model kept holding me up with different excuses why she could or could not be ready. I fired her tonight. That is why I was late arriving for your party."

"I can be ready. I can be ready whenever you say," I eagerly spoke, almost begging her to hire me.

"Well, you have got the job if we can agree on a weekly salary for you." All of my guests had left now, and she and I had sat down to talk. She explained to me what was expected. "Fridays, Saturdays, and Sundays are the days we will be working. I usually book two shows a night. Very rarely, but sometimes there is only one. You will get paid $75 a show after taxes. That amounts to around $150 a night with two shows and $450 every weekend."

I couldn't believe my ears. I was thinking about what that would add up to monthly. Around $1,800. She went on to explain that the clothes that I would be wearing would be supplied by her and that I could purchase any of them that I wished to keep at half-price.

"Your total look is very important in selling jewelry. Everything has to look just perfect and good on you. I call it tempting the buyer. Some of the home shows I give are in the most exclusive areas and patronized by my very rich clients. You see, I do this for my living, so I have to keep it very professional and exciting so that my customers can continue to buy my jewelry and want to give more shows. At each show, I get bookings from new customers for more shows. That is how I keep it going. So can we call it partners?" She held out her hand as she stood up to leave.

"Yes, indeed," I said as I shook her hand. "And thank you very much."

"I hope you enjoy your work and enjoy working with me. We start next Friday."

***

"I got a job! I got a job!" I excitedly told Al on his next visit.

"Good, when do you start?" he asked.

"Next weekend," I happily danced around, feeling grand and proud of myself.

He wanted to hear all about it. Still, there was a lot about Al I hadn't found out about until we began to live together. My second common-law affair. You would have thought that I would have learned my lesson by now.

With Al, I found out that he wakes up in the morning in a bad mood. He is mean, grouchy, and extremely fussy. He would snap at me sometimes, ordering me to fix him some coffee. "Can't you ask me nicer than that?" I asked. Later on in the day, he would always apologize for his evil treatment toward me. Still, it would continue to happen over and over again.

"I can't help it," he tried to explain to me calmly after things really got out of hand one morning. We almost had our first big fistfight. "I just wake up on the wrong side of the bed in the mornings. I always get over it. So what is the problem?" He tried to play it off as something I shouldn't worry about.

"The problem is," I shouted, "that I am tired of hearing you say 'I'm sorry' over and over for the same thing! Only to repeat yourself the very next morning. You've got me walking around on pins and needles every morning, hoping we wouldn't have another dispute! I can't take it much longer," I went on. "You're killing all the good feelings I once had about our relationship. We just can't continue to live together much longer. It won't work. Either you go back home, or we are going to break up soon. I can feel it coming."

He promised that he'd monitor his actions and refrain from trying to converse with me right away in the mornings. That should help the situation and keep down the arguing. He begged me for another chance, and I gave in.

So now, for about one month, I noticed a new man in the mornings. As soon as I was satisfied with the new changes, he went right on back to his normal self. Only this time, *I* ended up on the floor. His punch had me unconscious for a few minutes. All I know is that everything went dark.

Blood was all along the wall above my head when I came to, and Al had run out of the apartment. He must have known that he had hurt me badly because he had run home to tell his mother. She was there by my side in a matter of minutes to help me.

> *Yes, when love punches too hard*
>
> *You better start packing up your heart.*
>
> *When love punches too hard,*
>
> *You better start putting up your guard.*
>
> *Here I was on my second go-round in the ring of love.*
>
> *Tell me, what was I thinking of?*
>
> *Love punches too hard.*

Al's mother got me an ice pack and helped me to get back up on my feet. Steve's punch had been nothing like this one was. A cut had been opened up over my left eye and was bleeding badly. I couldn't believe this was happening to me again.

"Do you want to go to the doctor?" she kept asking me.

"No, no," I kept repeating myself. I felt numb, dizzy, and I had a terrible headache. "He must have hit me too hard." I felt tired. It was like I only wanted to go to sleep, but she kept me awake by talking to me and making me tell her everything that had happened.

"That is too bad," she said as I was trying to fill her in on our recent difficulties.

Mrs. Morris was such a dedicated, loyal, and understanding mother with all of her children. I knew she was not one to speak out loud against them, regardless of the situation. And so, I didn't talk too much to her about her son. Instead, I just thanked her for coming to my rescue. Then, once the bleeding had subsided a bit, I told her that I could handle things from then on by myself.

Afterward, I took a look in the mirror, and I saw double. The left side of my face and forehead was double its size. My eye was closed completely. From what I could make out of my remaining facial features, I looked like a monster from outer space that had just landed on this planet.

"My job! Oh, God! My job!" I suddenly remembered. My brain had just focused on the next strike against me that I was about to receive: the most terrible blow of all. How was I going to be able to keep my job with me looking like I did now? I had to call my employer. She would be depending on me, and I couldn't let her down. It had only been two months working with her, and nothing could have been more perfect between us. I thought about all the pretty clothes I had been wearing—chiffon dresses, silk, lame', and many expensive jerseys along with the dazzling earrings, bracelets, necklaces, rings, and watches.

I remember how her personal hairdresser had given me such lovely hairstyles that enhanced my looks tremendously. She also gave me free make-up tips, cologne, and all sorts of beauty lotions and oils. Everything had been perfect. Now, *this* had to happen. How could all of this be happening to me? It just wasn't fair that I had to draw all the insecure men my way.

First, my husband couldn't take me being the star of the show. Then Steve, whose real problem I later figured out was because he hated the fact of being shorter than me. It made him feel less power over me. And now Al, who had everything going for him as far as looks, but he didn't know how to keep a happy medium going between us. Besides him being just plain moody and making me feel bad all the time, another thing that I recently found out about him was that before he met me, he had spent time in jail.

"Jail!" I shouted. "What on earth did you do to go there?" Al had been telling me one day about some of the changes he had been going through a year or so ago.

"I took a bum rap for one of my close buddies, and

since then, the cops seem to always be breathing down my neck. Like they were just watching and waiting to pin something else on me. Every time there was a robbery or someone got hung up, they came after me. Pretty soon, I got tired and started really doing some of the things they were trying to blame on me."

"Well, that is all over now," I remember telling him. "Now you have got a good job, and you got me. And we have better days to look forward to." As I looked at myself in the mirror *now*, it looked like I had spoken too soon.

I called the jewelry lady and told her about my misfortune. I knew it wouldn't be hard for her to find a replacement with such an exciting job like mine was. Still, I wanted her to know that I really wanted to keep my job. So, I asked her if I could return to work after healing my bruises.

"I am sorry, Gladys, I don't think so," she said sadly. "I would hate to chance it with you again. You don't know whether he will use his fists to disfigure you again. Even if he never does it again, it leaves such an uncertain cloud lingering over our heads. I would hate to have an unneeded worry always in the back of my mind about what is happening to my hired help. You understand, dear, don't you?"

I knew she was right. I never knew what to expect from the men who came into my life. It was as though they were all the same man, with the same reasons and with the same desires, only to keep me miserable and down on my luck.

I felt like if I could just scream to the top of my voice, it would release all the tension, grief, and sorrow I felt for myself. I had all these feelings that were now crowding my complete existence. Al stayed away for a couple of days. The next time he saw me, much of the swelling had left my face. Regardless, I was still a disaster zone. Despite the ugliness that lingered in my face from his punch, he pulled me close to him and whispered, "I love you no matter how you look. And I always will."

I wanted to just break down and cry because all I ever got from these men were they were sorry. "What about all the damage that has been done?" I wanted to scream. "What about me? Where can I go now? What can I do for myself? Sorry can't heal my wounds or heal my broken heart. If that is all you can say, you're killing me with all of your sorrow!"

I wanted to say a lot of things, but I was afraid. Afraid of those punches that came along with every "I love you." Things were calm for a while as my soul and body were healing. Al had found another part-time job since my job was no longer in existence. So I had *that* to be thankful for. At least he wasn't a lazy man. He was determined to keep some funds coming in to take care of us all.

It was late August, and I had begun to worry. I hadn't had my monthly yet. I told Al immediately, and his reaction was, "I sure hope it's a girl."

I was surprised to see him so happy. "I'm not sure yet," I admitted.

That doubt was all cleared up two weeks later after I got the final test results back from my doctor. Another baby. The strong realization was finally dawning on me. I was going to have my third child.

Sammie was still living in the Hawthorne Child Care Center. He was doing very well adapting to his new life by learning to feed himself, get dressed, and take those very important steps out on his own. I was still making as many visits to see him as I could, although my weekend job had been pretty much filled up doing the jewelry shows. Now, I was going to make up for many of those lost times.

Vaughn was reaching his third year and was experiencing all the joys and thrills of childhood. There were many kids around his age in the neighborhood, which helped me a lot. Of course, because most mothers held household child-rearing jobs, they looked out for all the kids in the neighborhood who came over to visit their own. They welcomed their children's friends and enjoyed the companionship the children found in one another.

As I sat thinking about how quickly the years had gone by since I had left Detroit, I realized that I had been living a fast life. Maybe *too* fast. Three babies were proof enough of that. What real progress was I *really* making? I had to stop and have a long talk with myself. It certainly was time for that. I had no husband, three children, and no financially built structure to lean on. Where was I going from here?

Such a big question for someone who had no answers. Times like these made me call on that inner voice or spirit friend I have spoken of many times before. I felt the energy of my meditations flowing all through my muscles and emotions now.

My inner voice said,

Relax and do what is right for you at the time being. Right now. Tomorrow will present itself with new things for you to wonder about. Let every 24 hours come naturally and without haste for looking into the future, which will present itself to you only in due time. Don't worry about what you don't know about. Take care of the things around you today and be good to yourself and your loved ones.

After these long talks with myself, I felt renewed and ready for the world again. With me going to have this third baby, the third time around made me realize that maybe these years were meant to be spent bringing my young ones into the world. I had to always be there for them while they were growing up. Nothing else was more important. How often had I vowed to myself to be the perfect mother to my child one day? Well, I should have recognized it before now, that maybe that one day is here.

***

Along with every perfect thought or situation, there seems to be a problem to be removed or resolved. In my case, I needed a man who was as much into being a perfect father for the kids as I wanted to be as a mother. That happy family does not grow without the help of all the family members. A house is not a home when there is nobody there.

I began to wonder if Al would be the last man ever to touch me sexually. I was beginning to feel like I had spread myself around too much already. With one husband and two common-law lovers in over six years, my life was beginning to sound like a real soap opera. To break that all down, it was like I had been sleeping with a different man every two years. Somehow, finding the right guy can sometimes make the woman feel cheap and disrespected.

Giving my body to this many guys and always ending up pregnant made me appear to be a sex-crazed female. Strangely enough, I really wasn't. I swear I wasn't. In fact, I always felt like there was something wrong with me because it took me so long to reach an orgasm. I can count the times my husband sexually satisfied me on one hand, and Steve didn't do much better either. Did I leave them because I wasn't being sexually satisfied? No. For some reason, I never felt like this was the biggest meaning or reason for a relationship to exist.

I always loved a man more for the everyday artistic things we could do together like decorating a house, growing a garden, creating a song together, playing checkers or chess, entertaining our friends together, or cooking up some recipe we both never heard of before. *That* is having fun for me. And naturally, the great joys of having children we can both watch grow up and teach the right way to do things.

Having a relationship like this takes two people really loving one another for who they are. Not for how much sexual satisfaction you receive from them in bed. Mental stimulation was number one in my book, but men just don't seem to believe this. Now I have Al, who was the only one who made it his business to make sure that I was satisfied sexually before he even turned over to go to sleep.

Still, even *he* had not changed my mind about what I really wanted from my man. I craved for us to spiritually and mentally do all things together—to have a oneness that nothing can come between. True love breeds a kind of protection that shields you from the idle thoughts of destroying one another. It prohibits any action that says fight. Your disagreements are aired out in a completely different manner. You never physically want to strike out and hurt one another.

Fighting is a selfish way of making the other person surrender and see things their way, which never really happens through abusive mannerisms. The person may give in but only because of fear. I noticed in my relationships every man who ever hit me had to be on his way out sooner or later. Even if I tried to continue on with the relationship after the beating had been done, something always happened that separated our paths.

And so it was with Al. We had moved into a home before my third son Alphonso was born and remained there for almost a year. That year was one of the worst times to be put down on record in my life's story. I experienced some days and nights that can never be erased from my memory. Through all of my suffering, I learned and understood why there is such a thin line between life and death and love and hate.

It was during this year that I had planned my own suicide. I just didn't want to live anymore under these tortured circumstances. I was being tortured by an evil spirit in the house that was trying through Al to make me take my own life. My weight was down to about 110 pounds, and I lived in fear of what the next day would bring.

The sad thing about it was that Wanda of The Marvelettes and I had started talking on the telephone a lot now. We realized that this same type of evil spirit was finding its way into both of our lives. She told me some things that her husband was doing, and I would have sworn that she must have been living with the same man that I was. "A spiritualist woman told me the other day that somebody has a death wish out on our group." I heard Wanda's words coming through loud and clear to me over the phone.

I had never been faced with any dilemma such as this. I was inclined to believe her with all my thoughts lately on trying to end my own life. *Who is it?* I wondered, and I wanted to know why. Wanda always asked me whether my children were alright when she called. I told her that I had to find a way to free them from the terrible situation I had gotten myself into. I didn't want them to grow up in this type of gangster atmosphere where there were always guns around and people with a chip on their shoulder.

I feared for my life and theirs, especially once I had to call the police during one of Al and I's really bad fights. They actually laughed at me when they arrived, even after seeing how badly I had been beaten up.

"Now calm down, calm down," was always their favorite punch line. "We can only ask him to leave, ma'am. If he comes back, call us."

What bothered me the most was how the police were smiling at a time like this. Why are all the neurotic looks of pleasure being passed amongst themselves? These were looks that they made sure were not hidden from their faces. It was at times like this when I would feel like all fairness in the world for women was lost. It was also at these times that I realized what the Bible meant when Jesus said, "Forgive them, for they know not what they do."

Al was too young to fight off this evil spirit, and so were all his friends that came around us. I saw our house being turned into a transit place for women and men to sleep over whenever they liked. It was a spot to just hang out—smoking marijuana, drinking, and having a so-called good time, all the time.

Al and I grew more distant as the days passed by because I wouldn't give up my duties of being an around-the-clock mother to my kids. This was no setting to raise children in, so I became a total bitch. I refused to surrender to the beer garden and smoking weed all day type of crowd. Although Al never gave up working and kept a job to pay the bills, he threw our relationship down the drain. He started hanging out with the wrong crowd, and that landed him back in jail. Al had always promised me that if I tried to ever leave him, he would find me no matter where I went. Despite his threats, I had finally found some free time to make my escape.

I didn't have any money, but now was the time that I received help from my friend Mary. She and I had met at the University of Southern California preschool program for kids where Vaughn had the privilege of attending. We were on campus every day with our children, so we used to talk a lot. I told her long ago about how I wished I could get away from the dungeon I had dug for myself and my kids. She assured me then that if I ever got the chance to escape, she would personally pay a moving van to get all of my furniture out of there. I could stay with her and her two kids until I got on my feet again.

I had no way of even knowing whether she really meant it or not, but I had to call and ask her for help.

She proved herself as being an angel in disguise for me because she did everything she promised she would and even more. Later she even loaned me enough money to move into another place out of the Los Angeles area for the safety of the kids and myself. She really proved to me what true friends and true people are really all about.

CHAPTER 5:

"FREE TO BE ME AGAIN"

F aith had played me a lucky hand too many times to count. Once again, I was now a free lady. I had been emancipated from the devastating boundaries of a common-law love affair. However, that was nothing compared to the fear that now took its place right next to me with every breath I took.

When Al was released from jail, I knew he would be out on a massive manhunt searching for his baby and me. So I had to take Vaughn out of the USC college preschool because I knew that would be the first place he'd stake his lookout. It is a shame how these ugly situations end up hurting many of life's opportunities for the children involved. I had felt so proud that Vaughn had been accepted to go to a preschool right on a college campus in his first year. It gave him such a wonderful head start in education.

My biggest struggle within was to keep a life going

for my children no matter what was happening on the home front. I enjoyed getting Vaughn ready in the mornings for school. At age 4, he was such a delightful and energetic little fellow. His hair was a natural dark chestnut brown and very curly.

I was always at the monthly sales to make sure he was able to wear the best-looking clothes I could afford. Vaughn used to look himself over before we took off for the bus every morning with that great big smile that he still has today. I could see that he was proud of himself and loved what school was all about. I think seeing his happiness at these times led me to hold on tight to my integrity and pride.

And now, I was having to explain to him why he couldn't go back to the pre school. Mary was still carrying her son Tony every day. Sure enough, she informed me one morning after she got back home that a big racket was going on inside the main supervisor's office. "I am sure it was Al," she told me. "I overheard him shouting about he wanted a forwarding address on where to reach you because he needed to see his son. His eyes were wild, and he looked like he hadn't shaved in days."

I felt myself start shaking. Just the *thought* of him brought fear to my body. "You must have been under some kind of strain," she noted sympathetically.

"Oh yes, he is crazy and unreasonable when he gets upset," I told her. "I can't imagine ever going back to live with him under his type of pressured lifestyle. You just don't know how happy I am and how good it feels just to be away from him. I am free to be myself again, and this time no man is ever going to live with me. I have learned my lesson well, and it will stick with me from now on."

Somehow my spirit had not been broken yet, even through all the arguing, bickering, and fights. My body was thin, and I felt sore from some of the bruises that I knew would take time to heal. My mental state had been one of great turmoil and confusion. Every time I heard his key opening the door, I felt like I lost 10 more pounds. All this, but I never broke down completely to where I was unable to deal with caring for my children.

I told Mary about the many moments when I just wasn't thinking straight or clear enough to imagine a new tomorrow for my kids and me. It was times like this that I would sit and mentally plan on taking Vaughn and Alphonso to a foster care program. Then I'd check into a hotel and take some form of poison that would just end it all. Constant threats of if I ever left him had made me feel like there was nowhere to run and nowhere to hide. Mary just stood there listening to the story of my horrid plans.

I saw that she was touched deeply by my testimony. I told her from the bottom of my heart how thankful I was for her befriending me at times like this.

"Mary," I said, "you may not realize it yet, but you have actually saved my life and whatever might have happened to my kids. How could I ever repay you? If I ever write a book, you can bet I would let the world know about your kindness. You are living proof that there is a lot of goodness and great deeds being done every day that never reach the newspapers or gain a reward. As long as there are people like you in the world, it gives the world a better meaning and reason for a lot of us to want to be here."

I know that we have all read many articles about whites killing blacks. Well, this one in my story is about a white girl saving a black girl's life and housing her family at a very stressful time. We both knew that there was no way I could remain living in the LA area. The fear of meeting up with Al was too great of a risk for me to take.

So after a month or so of looking on the outskirts of town, Mary helped me to move to the city of Lynwood, California. Thank God I was able to pay her back all the money I owed her. It was just a one-bedroom duplex, but there was enough room to suit all of my wants and needs. After all, there was really only one—having ourselves a place to call our own again.

Alphonso was just a little over a year old now, but he had been through enough with me already to be considered older. Babies who have to endure an environment where a battered lifestyle is going on learn quickly about the other side of this great big wonderful world. It is a shame and a pity that they come into the world seeing the bad before they even have a chance to see how good it can be to be alive.

Seeing their mother's face in tears most of the time gave them a clear understanding that life is not all about sweet little fairy tales and cake and ice cream. They have to grow up mentally quicker than Mother Nature required of them. Alphonso was a baby who showed he already had certain know-how and familiarity about his life and who he was. Just like his brother Vaughn, he was already walking and making his demands clearly understood with a few words now and then. I never got a chance to really spoil him either because of the constant battle I was always up against. I wanted to provide them with a home where they could be kids who knew about having a family with basic morals.

I was still bringing Sammie home on weekends when I could. I would sit and watch how perfectly matched they turned out to be as brothers who loved each other and got along well together. Soon, I was going to request Sammie to live back at home with us. He was already walking well enough to get around on his own. His counselor had mentioned the possibility of getting him right into an ongoing school program where he would be bused to school and back every day.

"That sounds great to me," I told Sam's counselor.

"It may take a month or so," he explained as he began to work on the release papers. "But Sam will soon be at home again."

It hadn't taken me very long to find a part-time job there in Lynwood after we got settled. Upon finding another pre-school for Vaughn, I ran across a job offer to help assist a Head Start program director in that area. The first day I went there to register Vaughn, the notice was on the bulletin board.

It read, "Do you love helping children and need a part-time job? We are looking for mothers to help assist in our program."

I immediately signed up for work after being told that I could bring Alphonso along every day. "Oh yes, we have an area for toddlers to play that is supervised. And you can look in on him during your break throughout the day."

I was glad to be working, but the pay was barely enough to get me by satisfactorily. Something else came through for me until I was able to have two jobs and start a savings account. I had called up my past employer just to say hello but also with the hopes that she might reconsider me for the same job I had before.

"Look, I have got an idea where you can start your own jewelry business through catalog sales," she explained. "You make a commission off all of your sales, plus the company pays you a complete salary every month for taking the job on a full-time basis."

We made plans for meeting together where I could submit a personal letter of application to the jewelry firm. The main office was in New York City.

"I will also give you a letter of recommendation coming from me stating that you were a great worker once hired by me and that I highly recommend your abilities as a sales person."

I was ecstatic about the new opportunity. A few weeks later, I received three big catalogs in the mail along with a complete jewelry kit, a suitcase full of samples, and cute little gift items for my regular customers. There were also instructions on how to become a successful jewelry retailer. It said to wear pieces of the jewelry samples around every day to show off your good taste and what you have to offer through your sales, and it worked.

Every day someone was asking me where I got this bracelet from or where those earrings I was wearing could be bought. I started carrying my catalog with me everywhere I went. Soon, I was having jewelry shows at the houses of many of the mothers who came to the Head Start program. Even my co-workers and supervisors put in orders from my catalogs.

Every time a man asked me for my phone number, I sold him a ring or a watch band instead. In many cases, they wanted to order gifts from me for special occasions like Mother's or Father's Day, or for some other female they just wanted to impress. I didn't care for what or who; I was looking to make a sale, not a date. In fact, I was having a wonderful time without any dates or any male in my life. It really helped my sales life and my world of working with the pre-schoolers to be able to keep up a cheerful, congenial, high-spirited attitude. People love you when they see that glow of happiness radiating from your smile. And they want to be part of whatever you are doing that makes you feel so good.

***

Before the summer was over that year of 1975, Sammie came home. I applied for him to start receiving a government fund given to handicapped children who are living at home. They called it SSI. Before now, I never even knew that this type of money was available for these afflicted children. Sammie started school soon after in Bellflower, California, a community to Lynwood. The bus picked him up every morning just before Vaughn. Alphonso and I went off to the school program, and everything was working out perfectly for us.

That same year, I accidentally ran into a member of one of Motown's recording groups of the '60's that hadn't really experienced a big hit as of yet. But as time would have it, he was still trying for that big one. Prentice Anderson of the group Lee and the Leopards was living right there in Lynwood with his wife, Dorothy.

Seeing him that day made me realize that I had not gotten in touch with Motown for receiving my yearly royalties for some time now. All the confusion and pressure made me totally forget about my royalty statements. I called the company right away and explained why and what had happened.

"We had no way of contacting you, Miss Horton, to even mail you your checks," I was told. "But if you will give me your current address, these money matters will be corrected, and your checks will be mailed out to you."

Soon and very soon it was like Christmas around our house. I made up for all the Christmases I just didn't have any extra money to splurge on toys for the kids. I also bought myself a few dresses and some needed items around the house. After our surprise meeting, Prentice and his wife had found their way into the lives of my family, and we suddenly had some good Detroit friends close by. Dorothy and Prentice didn't have any children together yet, but they still had Tina, Prentice's teenage daughter from another marriage. They all fell in love with my three boys. Before long, I felt like we were all one big happy family.

Dorothy had become just like a big sister to me, always giving me good advice on disciplining those now getting to be rather bad little boys. Boys get more adventurous as they grow up, so maybe mischievous might be a better word.

I could have bought a car with all the money I had saved in the bank. But I didn't have to because Dorothy and Prentice were always willing to involve the kids and myself in their weekend outings. Together, we went on picnics, to amusement parks, or maybe we just had a simple backyard barbecue. Dorothy and I even did our grocery shopping together. So, transportation for me just wasn't my biggest problem.

Prentice Anderson was always excited about some new song he had written. He was constantly moving to get my approval of the melody or the song lyrics. "It is going to be a smash tune," he proclaimed loudly about all of his writings. I tried to give him as much confidence as I could. I knew how much love he had for his music and the whole Motown story. He was like a live Motown robot.

Although his group never had a big nationwide smash, he was one person who was thrilled and excited about being there to see all the people involved in making the company run daily. He practically lived at the studios when everything was really going hot back in the '60s. He knew the years of the hits, the dates of the tours, the different groups, what ups and downs they were having behind the scenes, and all the successful moments the Motown Record Corporation shared.

Dorothy used to joke about Prentice never getting enough of Motown. She didn't seem to agree with how far he took it at times. She explained to me that at one time, all of their savings was being spent in recording Prentice's songs.

"Those recording session fees are so expensive," she argued. "I can't help it. It wouldn't be so bad if I could see some profit being made after spending so much money to get his songs recorded. But instead, there is just another song to be recorded that also winds up sitting up on the shelf. I try to stick behind him in this great dream he has to make it big in music one day. But on the other hand, I also want to see our earnings being used to make a home for ourselves. There is so much uncertainty in the music business…and I am a person who likes to have a firm foundation being laid under my feet. I want to know and to see clearly that my money is being spent wisely."

I understood her agony of not wanting to appear like a nagging wife, but she was right. Music had not yet paid off the kind of dividends most people deserved to acquire when dealing with it day and night. When Prentice came to me and asked me to record two songs he had written, I agreed, hoping that maybe I could change his luck. There was also a fat chance that *maybe* it was time for *his* big break to come. He certainly had labored long enough physically and mentally in this field to see the harvest of his works. I had nothing to lose either. Maybe, one of these songs would get my voice back on the air again. So I gave it a try.

For about a month every weekend, I would rehearse with Prentice on the tunes until we got them memorized just right. He hadn't bought much studio time, and having things perfectly rehearsed before our time started would make the session time run smoother and keep down costs.

Prentice showed himself as being a real businessman. He had rounded up a few musicians who were all there on time. They all seemed to have rehearsed the material and were ready to lay the music track down without any delays. Then came the recording of my lead on the tracks.

Give me a second chance

I will show you a new romance.

Give me another dance;

I need another chance.

It was a dance tempo, high-energy type of song. It had a cute little story to it about a girl who wanted another chance to prove to her guy that she would be a better lover the next time around. The other song was called, "I Won't Make No More Mistakes." It was slow and sexy, but it got straight to the point. This girl had had enough of love breaking her heart, so she was calling it quits. I *really* sang out the part that held a lot of meaning to me. It said:

I ain't looking for love no more;

Case closed, and I have shut the door.

I am through with the aches and the pains love makes;

And so I won't make no more mistakes.

All the musicians stuck around to hear what my leads were going to sound like on the music tracks. To my surprise, I came through with flying colors. "You still got it,

Gladys," one of the guys complimented me on my ability to still deliver "in that special way" as he called it.

"That is one thing I really liked about The Marvelettes," the sound engineer mentioned to me while we were listening to the playback of each song. "You girls always had a strong message in your music, and you stayed with a real commercial sound."

"That is what made the people listen to your music," I was told by another musician. "You had a certain rhythm and sound to your voice, Gladys."

I was grinning from ear to ear. "Thank you, thank you all," I smiled as I gladly accepted all their praises. At the same time, I quickly warned them that I refused to get a big head. They all laughed out loud and agreed that I still hadn't changed from being a sweet young lady.

Prentice was overjoyed with the outcome of the session. On our ride back to Lynwood, he rattled on and on about all his plans to get the songs distributed and into the hands of some very helpful people. "I wish you lots of luck," I told him after he dropped me off at my place. And I really did because I needed some luck myself.

***

The kids were growing like wild oats, and the daily thoughts of expanding crossed my mind. Soon we were going to need a much bigger house, but that would take more money. It was time to reorganize and start planning for something new in the future.

I still remember the day that certified letter came in the mail. I looked at the place of origin: Philadelphia, PA. *Who, what, and why?* I wondered. *It must be important*, I thought, *with all of these formalities*. I anxiously opened it and found out that it was a letter from a fan who had been trying to reach me or one of The Marvelettes since 1969.

It read:

> *Gladys,*
>
> *It nearly tore my world apart when I found out that you had left the group. Hopelessly, I have written Motown since then, trying to get some lead way on how to contact you. Just recently did I get a breakthrough in all of my correspondences, and an old fan club president from Motown wrote me and gave me your address. I knew if I sent the letter certified with a request of a return signature, I would know for sure you received this letter. I have every record, every album, every picture of your group that I found in magazines,*

> *books, on posters, and advertisements. Every time you came to Philadelphia, I made it my business to see your performance more than enough times.*
>
> *Why did you leave the group? What is the group doing now? Where is Wanda? Where is Katherine? Will you ever be getting back together again? I heard you were married. Is that still true? How many kids do you have, if any?*

Yes, this letter was full of questions and more questions. Then she asked before closing the letter out that I write her back.

> *Yours truly,*
>
> *Cynthia Trey.*

One thing was for sure, she was a very concerned and inquisitive fan.

Why I wrote her back right away, I can't really say. Maybe it was because it was the first fan letter I had received in all of those years that I had been away from

Motown. It was like I was suddenly reliving the past when we would get loads and loads of fan mail in the office. We would take turns reading the different messages the fans would write. You know, a certain feeling comes along with reading a letter from someone you have never seen. There is also a little magic that accompanies that feeling that is intoxicating and mystifying.

I figured it wouldn't hurt to take on a pen pal, especially someone who was so much into my career life as she talked about being. So, I wrote her back, and she responded immediately with a second letter. This time she had enclosed a photo of herself. She told me a little bit more about herself in this letter. She wrote she was a social worker there in Philadelphia. She was single, didn't have any children, and lived alone since her mother had died.

"I still listen to your records because I bought them all," she informed me. "But I have always wondered why, Gladys, you never looked the same in any two pictures. The other day, I was looking at some album photos of you and also some clippings I saved on The Marvelettes from way back. Your eyes remain the same, but there is something different about your poses in all of your photos. Did you realize this?"

No, I really hadn't. But after she mentioned it, I looked at several pictures I had and found her to be telling the truth. Before ending this letter, she gave me her telephone number and begged me to call her collect.

"Don't worry about the cost," she wrote. "I don't have any kids, and I can afford to spend a little extra here and there."

And so I followed up on her suggestion and called her long distance. She was very warm and caring and seemed very much concerned over the fact that I had been through so much since I stopped recording. I told her the names of the boys and their ages and birth dates. She said she wanted all of that information because she would love to send them little surprises on special dates. She did just that. For every birthday and every holiday, she sent them something. We became pen pals, telephone buddies, and she even named herself the kids' play aunt. Aunt Cynth we all called her. Months went on, and the day that Aunt Cynthia was coming for a visit finally came. During an Easter vacation, she had a week off work, and the kids were out of school.

"She's coming here to visit you!" Dorothy and Prentice both seemed shocked and alarmed by the news. "You shouldn't have invited her to your home this soon," Dorothy protested. "You don't know her well enough to have her around your children yet. People can turn out to be really weird at times."

Prentice added, "She must be some kind of neurotic fan to want to fly all the way from Philadelphia just to see you." I could read between the lines. Clearly, Prentice had doubts about her true feelings.

I tried to explain to them both that Aunt Cynthia and

I had talked many times over the telephone. She had sent the kids birthday cards and money on their special days. She just wanted to be a good friend and offer her companionship as a play aunt to the boys.

Dorothy, who also was leery of the situation, volunteered to be close by to make sure I hadn't involved myself in anything too crazy. In fact, she was there at the house with me when the cab brought Aunt Cynthia from the airport. She and Prentice had both got me all worked up, and now I was suspicious of what Cynthia's true motive of friendship might really mean.

All of that doubt disappeared as soon as she stepped from the cab that day. She was a conservative-looking woman with a sweet, honest-looking face and smile. You could see that she was intellectually inclined. She was much taller than I had imagined, and although she was younger than myself, she might have really been mistaken for *my* aunt instead of the boys. She leaned down to hug all the boys who were crowding around her, asking her little things like kids often do when they are meeting a relative of theirs for the very first time.

"How did you like riding in an airplane?"

"How far away do you live from here?"

Aunt Cynthia stopped all the questions when she handed them a big bag that had Easter baskets inside for them all. They thanked her and ran off to see what their different surprises were. That gave me the time to introduce Dorothy, who was already helping get her luggage inside. Dorothy seemed quite pleased to find out that Cynthia was a serious, mature-looking female who seemed to have the correct manners and style of a lady with some class.

"Gladys, you still look the same as you did all those years ago when you came to the Uptown Theater to perform. How do you do it even now with three kids?" Cynthia asked me.

"I really don't know," I humbly answered. "I am not using any special face creams or soaps if that is what you mean. I just keep my weight down and wear a little or no make-up and try to look presentable at all times. So there are no special tricks or antidotes to my method of survival."

"I am just thrilled to be in your presence again," she said, as she gave me a big hug. "I thought for years that I would never see you again."

The word Motown came up so much in Cynthia's conversation that day, that Dorothy told her that she needed to be talking to Prentice. "Now, I know he can out-talk *anybody* when it comes to answers and questions about Motown," Dorothy added.

Cynthia proved herself as being somewhat of an investigation squad on the many facets of that era of the music world. Stevie Wonder, Marvin Gaye, Mary Wells—she wanted to know about them all. The Temptations, The Supremes, The Four Tops—her interests grew with every passing minute.

Later, we made plans to show Cynthia the Hollywood shops, houses, film studios, and theaters. Dorothy said she would be back to take us sightseeing the next day. It had been quite some time since I had taken the kids to the Hollywood Hills area, so it was also a grand treat for them. I could see that Aunt Cynthia was very impressed with the Hollywood Walk of Fame. She took pictures of the names of the stars on the sidewalk in front of the Chinese Mann's Theater. She bought lots of souvenir gifts and postcards for her friends back in Philadelphia. We drove through the nicer neighborhood areas up around Sunset and Laurel Canyon and Mulholland Drive, not to mention Benedict Canyon and the Bel-Air Estates.

"This place is unbelievable," Cynthia marveled at the beautiful landscapes and mansion-type houses sitting on the hilltops. Yes, swimming pools and movie stars, *this* was California living for the rich.

After viewing the most glamorous sites of California, I am sure that Aunt Cynthia was more aware of just how much greener the grass was on the other side than where we were residing. I could tell by her conversation when we had returned to my place that she really felt sorry for the outcome of my successful singing career. She realized now more than ever how I had ended up on the short end of the rope.

"Isn't there anything that you can do to get the group back together?" she looked at me sadly as she spoke. I knew deep within her heart that she had really begun to feel sorry for me. I hated to think about how carelessly

I had just given it all up. "Your kids deserve more. They were meant to be living the type of life you have helped others to have." She looked as though she wanted to cry too. "I wish I could help to put you back up there some kind of way." Her words made me feel like I had truly found a real friend. Someone who would go all out just to give me back what we both knew I had lost: my honor, my dignity, my pride, and last but not least, my shining career.

That night, we made future plans of getting me back to Detroit. "It may take another year," she said, "but you are going back to Detroit to get Wanda and Katherine together. The Marvelettes will be performing on top once again."

Cynthia discussed her plans to move to Detroit as soon as she could sell her house in Philadelphia. "I have already put in for a job transfer. I am just waiting for the right buyer to come along and buy my property," she explained, informing me that it had been a long-time dream of hers to move to Detroit ever since the Motown days were going hot back in the '60s.

"I even have a few relatives already living there," she revealed. "So be patient and just wait. Because when it happens, you will have someplace to stay while you are getting back up on your feet. I can see it now," she started to smile. "The Marvelettes reunited, new album, new shows to do, and your own life brought back to you again." It all sounded so good and encouraging. I began to see that light in the forest shining brighter to show me the way out. I had someone working out plans *with* and *for* me. I was delighted that we had become friends. At last, I had found the help I needed to go in the right direction.

The kids were crazy about her, and I found out from her visit that we got along very well. Even Dorothy had mentioned to me later that she felt like she had misjudged Cynthia, who seemed to be a very caring and loving person. It was Prentice who still wouldn't buckle. He had greeted her with much speculation. Even though she appeared to be all right, he still had an uneasy feeling lurking within him about her.

"Just keep your eyes open, Gladys," he warned. "Everything will present itself in due time. Nothing ever remains hidden for long. And don't let nothing surprise you if you do find things are not what you expect."

"Don't worry, Prentice," I smiled confidently. "You'll see. Aunt Cynthia means none of us any harm."

Cynthia waved us goodbye and was gone after about five days of vacationing with us. It was now back to the same old routine of school for the boys, my little part-time jobs, and weekends with the Andersons. Dorothy worked daily as a receptionist and secretarial worker at a nearby hospital. Prentice held an office position at an insurance company in the greater Los Angeles downtown area.

So during the week, we didn't see very much of each other. Some weekends, Dorothy would just call in and ask how everything was going. I really appreciated having friends who always looked in on us and kept our safety and well-being in mind.

I was still writing and occasionally talking to Aunt Cynth on the telephone, but she never had any good news to tell me about the selling of the house. In many ways, getting back to Michigan was something I was really saving up for. I was really hoping it would soon come through like the answer to a daily prayer. I was growing more depressed and full of anxiety with every passing month; I just *had* to get away.

In the summer of 1977, I decided that the kids and I were going back to Michigan for a two-week visit. As soon as I started making plans, I could feel the excitement in the air. The joy of seeing all of my friends again was something I had looked forward to for eight years.

I suddenly realized that I hadn't written as many letters as I should have. I didn't even know if any of them were still living in the same town or not. After thinking about the many changes that occur as the years advance, I decided that I would make my visit a total surprise and be prepared to expect the unexpected.

While I was packing the kids' clothes, I came upon an old telephone book of mine. While looking through it, I saw my friend Delores Horn's number, who I thought would be able to keep my visit a secret. So I was tempted to call to see if she was still living in the Detroit area.

She was thrilled by the news. "You are what?!" she

shouted with excitement. "Coming back here for a visit? Gladys, I can't wait to see you! Have you decided who you are going to stay with?" she quickly asked me. Before I could answer, she said in a very inviting tone, "You and the boys can be with me for some of your stay."

"That will be great," I accepted her invitation right away. "The bus will be arriving there in Detroit on August the 16th, and we can get all rested up and ready before we head out to Inkster the next day."

"That is going to be a long trip for a bus ride, isn't it?" she asked. But I told her that we were going to enjoy every minute of it. The kids will love seeing the different highways and roadside scenery and making all the in-between stops in different towns and cities. They have never been on vacation before.

Delores and I got caught up on how many newcomers we both had added to our families since we last saw each other. Then before I hung up, I told her to keep my trip a secret because I wanted to surprise my old friends.

***

The day came, and we were all ready to start our bus trip all the way to Michigan. I locked up the place, and we took a cab downtown to the bus station. The kids were so happy to be going somewhere far, far away. I knew we were going to have a good time riding that bus even though it took three days. Eating snacks and meals at a different bus depot every day and night was certainly something the boys had never done before. Plus, seeing and meeting different strangers in every town along with boarding the many buses was very interesting to them.

"I love this," Vaughn told me very early in the trip. "I wish we could travel all the time." He laughed with excitement and curiosity as to where and what was coming next.

Alphonso was also getting his thrills and chills from the mystery that surrounded being in these new places. Sammie went right along with every new adjustment that riding these buses created. I was very much aware of how helpful people are everywhere when they see a mother with more than one child. Many of them, including the bus driver, seemed most concerned that the kids were really enjoying their long ride. I felt free again. Free to be me. No more arguing and fighting and depressing thoughts that come along with the battles of companions. Even though I had been living as a single person for the last two years now, I never felt truly free as I did right now. I didn't have anybody to answer to. Nobody but my children, and that was just fine with me. Traveling is so much fun, and that is what I felt like doing now.

***

When we arrived in Detroit that August morning, I felt blessed to feel my feet on Michigan soil again. Delores's husband, Will, was there at the bus station right on time to pick us up. It was great seeing Delores again and her family. She had a beautiful home there in Detroit. Parked in the backyard was a king-sized motor home, something I had always wanted to own. I used to always say if I had a motor home, I would live like a gypsy—here in one town today and somewhere else the next day.

"You will get a chance to ride it soon whenever you decide to go out to Inkster," Delores promised me. "Will will drive you there in the motor home."

"That is fine with me," I said proudly.

I couldn't wait, and neither could the kids. They kept saying, "We will be riding down the street in a house, won't we, Mommy?" That made me laugh.

Delores was still working in the hair salon business, and you certainly could tell it. Hers was magnificent from morning 'til night. I was now wearing my very first long-length weave, and she was telling me how natural it looked on me. I had really done it up for this vacation with new clothes, new shoes, and even new hair. I couldn't wait to show off my new California look. We had a nice quiet dinner that first night with Delores and her family.

The next day, I packed up some of our things to take out to Inkster. I knew that we would be staying overnight for a couple of days with some more of my friends, so I wanted to be prepared. You never know what might happen.

More and more surprises awaited us for the next few days. I was surprised to see how wonderful everything looked in Inkster. New townhouses had been built everywhere. Even some of the old houses had been remodeled and looked brand new. Little children I had known once were grown up, and some even had kids of their own. My old high school had become larger, with several new additions being added to its structure. The old neighborhood stores even had a new look. Everyone had built up their property and had made this once-called village a city. I was so proud to be able to show my kids this place as being the town where I had made a name for myself.

I saw my foster sister Christine first, although we went as cousins to everyone that we knew there in Inkster. Boy, had I surprised her. She had just fought with her boyfriend and was wearing a black eye. But it didn't matter; She looked beautiful to me. Everyone did.

Happiness filled my heart so much that nothing mattered but enjoying this reunion. I was surprised to see Sherry, Christine's daughter, and my goddaughter already carrying her first child. One thing was for sure. Inkster was still a family-oriented place, and people sure didn't wait forever on having babies. I visited one house after the other all day long.

I saw Katherine of the Marvelettes and her sisters and brothers and mother who all still lived in Inkster. Her father, I was told, had passed away.

"I am sorry, Katherine. I didn't know," I sympathized with her. I was also saddened by the news that my very own foster mother, Mrs. Jones, was gone.

Daddy was still there at the house, though, and invited me and the boys to stay over a couple of nights. He was so thrilled to see my three boys. He even gave me my old room back to sleep in. Mr. Jones had a big dog now for company, and he made sure that the boys got a chance to meet and play with him. "All growing boys need a dog to grow up with," he remarked.

Wanda of The Marvelettes was on my list, but I first visited all her family who was still there in Inkster. They were all overjoyed at seeing me again.

Juanita Cowart, another original Marvelette, said that she would have never known that it was me if I hadn't told her so. Apparently, I looked a lot different with longer hair and slimmer features. "How did you do it!" she exclaimed. "I can't believe it is you." Juanita had married a lawyer who was also a school friend of ours, Mr. Larry Motley. They had four very tall children who took their height from their parents who were both well over six feet tall.

Georgeanna of The Marvelettes was also a pleasure to see again. I visited her mother, sister Sharon, and all her nieces. Georgeanna had one son named Darrin who was practically grown now. It was a pleasure to see everyone doing so well.

Other school friends I saw again like Helen Jackson, Deborah Steel, Valerie White, and Margaret Williams were all delighted to see me again. Through all the cheery conversation, I was also met with sad stories of how so many of the youth in Inkster had died from drugs and drug-related crimes.

When you have been away as long as I had without keeping in constant contact with everyone, it comes as a shock to hear about people you just naturally felt were still living. Like Mrs. McKay, the very first foster home mother I had there in Inkster at the age of nine months, had passed away. So, along with the happy moments came some sadness. Still, our trip, on the whole, was very pleasing and satisfying.

After we went back to Detroit, I was able to visit Wanda. She seemed to be doing well, although she had been under extreme doctor's care. "It has been so stressful for me, Gladys, not being able to live the kind of life we had while the group was together," she explained.

I understood exactly what she meant and how she felt. Although I hadn't had the need to be hospitalized, I, too, had suffered such a depressing time until it was hard to even look forward to a new day coming. It was hard knowing that you wouldn't be doing the same great things we used to.

"If we could just bring it all back together somehow," I told her, "I know you will get well sooner."

"That is for sure," Wanda said. "I know I wouldn't

drink so much if I only had something to do."

She was surprised to see how big my three boys had grown. Although she had never met any of them except Sammie, we had talked enough on the telephone for her to be aware that I had two more sons.

I enjoyed reminiscing with Wanda about the good times, but I had to go back out to Inkster again before our vacation was over. This time we stayed at Christine's house a few days, then with Valerie, and later, a couple of more days with Daddy Jones. It was at this time that he begged me and the boys to stay there with him.

"I want you to be the one to bury me when the day comes for me to leave this earth," he honestly spoke out and told me his plans.

"But Daddy," I protested, "I don't want a job like that to look forward to. Please don't talk that way. Nothing is going to happen to you."

I knew he missed my mother very much. They spent so much time together when she was alive. I could almost still feel her presence all over that house. I guess it was true that real love is to the bone. It was obvious to me that Daddy just didn't want to be here alone without her. Still, talking about death was very upsetting to me. All of my life, I had never been bothered with this part of life. If anyone in my family ever died, I never knew about it, so I never had to feel the sadness and pain of it.

Coming back home was intended to be a glorious and

happy affair. However, I never thought about the changes that I would be faced with after learning about those loved ones who were now gone. Mr. Jones continued the conversation saying that he would leave the house for the boys and me to always have a roof over our heads.

"Don't go back to California," he begged. "Stay with me here and give the boys a place of their own."

"That is impossible, Daddy," I argued. "I have a bank account, two part-time jobs, and a lot of furniture, personal items, and business that needs to be taken care of before I can make a permanent move back here."

"How long would it take you to close out your business there?" he asked.

"I should be back within a year."

"Okay then," he agreed. "I think I can wait until then."

Mr. Jones had no idea of how sad he was making me feel. Just the thought of something happening to him filled me with deep sorrow. At that moment, I wished I had the power to bring my mother back so that he could be happy again and want to live again.

Georgeanna Tillman, the original Marvelette who had left the group because she had a trace of sickle cell anemia, had something to tell me before we left Inkster. We were just about to leave her house when she asked me to take a look at something.

"Georgeanna!" I screamed. "What happened?" She

pulled up one leg of her slacks to show me how one leg was the size of a small elephant.

"I had this jealous boyfriend," she began explaining. "Once we got into a big fight, and he knocked me down and made me cut the skin very deeply on my leg. I went to the doctor and had to have stitches. Soon after they healed, we got into another fight. This time he kicked me in the same leg and opened back up my stitches. I had to be hospitalized and given a blood transfusion." Georgeanna already had a blood cell problem, so I knew this must have been a setback in her ongoing treatment for sickle cell anemia.

"Then what happened?" I asked her to go on.

"A few weeks later, we made up, and I took him back on his apologies and insistence that he would never harm me again. Only to have him attack me later and do the same thing over again."

I couldn't stand to hear any more. The whole story was gross and so inhumane, with actions coming from someone who claimed that he loved her so much.

"Gladys," she started to almost cry, "I don't know what to do. My leg may never be the same again."

"I hope you are not going to see him anymore," I quickly added. Although the hurt had been done, I knew that the first solution to the problem would be to stay as far away from him as possible.

"No, it is all over," she insisted. "It took all of this to

happen, but now it is over for good."

I had to let Georgeanna know that she wasn't the only one who had sustained countless beatings from her mate. "Do you know that almost every female singer from Motown has had to undergo a series of unearthly treatments coming from whoever she was sexually involved with?" I asked. "That is why I am by myself now."

The strange thing about it is that none of them want to come forth and talk about it and bring the truth out in the open. Everyone wants to pretend that they have the perfect lover. Even if the man is not physically abusing her, he is mentally setting up barriers to break her down.

"I wonder why it is *us* who have to suffer like this?" Georgeanna asked seriously.

"Probably because we have shown ourselves to be stronger females than the rest. We were able to break away from the everyday cooking, kitchen, housewife stereotypes and provide an independent lifestyle for ourselves. Some men feel like that is too much power for a woman in this day and time to possess. It is like we are being punished for showing the modern female how to make it on her own."

Before I left Georgeanna that day, I made her promise me that she would be more careful about the company she decided to keep from now on. I knew it was none of my business to suggest that she try living her life without a man until she was certain she had found that special one. Georgeanna was always the type who felt like she was incomplete without some kind of male companion by her side. But my goodness, what good was it all doing her to have a man there if he was killing her?

I wish I could make all women everywhere understand that it is all right to be alone at some time or another in your lives. It is not a sickness if you don't care to be fucked all the time. All those old-time myths about going crazy without sex or a man are the biggest brainwashes that men ever thought up to dish out on the female. It is simply not true. I knew it now because I felt simply *marvelous* being free to be myself again.

Our vacation had finally come to its end, and it was time for us to take that long trip back to California. The boys had had the time of their lives, making new friends and seeing the old landmarks where I had grown up. They saw where I went to school, to church, and the homes where I had spent many happy hours playing with my friends.

They knew that Mr. Jones had asked us to come back to live, and already they were saying how they couldn't wait to return.

The long ride back home was welcomed by me, especially because I was going to use it to catch up on my rest. The constant moving around from house to house drained me of my energy. We were up late every night, and it was a non-stop roller coaster. I don't think I got a chance to close my mouth for not even an hour during the day with all the excitement and conversations our visit stirred amongst everyone who got a chance to see us.

***

The house was just as we left it, as I turned the key and opened the door. The kids all ran back to their bedroom to start unpacking their suitcases. More than ever before, I felt lonely. Already I missed Inkster. I felt the need to want to turn right around and go back.

After seeing people I hadn't seen in years, I realized how lonely my life was without the friends I had made while living in Inkster. No wonder the girls in my group never wanted to live anywhere else. Something about the people in Inkster made me feel extra good inside. This was a town where people didn't change so easily. Even with having all the fame and success with The Marvelettes, I never pictured myself as being any better than my buddies in Inkster. It was as though I couldn't lose that realness, honesty, or humbleness of just being Gladys. I partied with my friends during the years when the group was hot, and we still partied after we were not.

Yes, I always felt an understanding and some sort of connection there in Inkster. I knew I wasn't really going to unpack because, just like I promised my foster father, I was moving back there next year. I called Dorothy and Prentice to let them know that we had made it back safely. Then I called Aunt Cynthia. I knew she wanted to hear all about the trip.

It wasn't long before school had started back. Vaughn was now going to an elementary school close by in the first grade. He was growing fast and was a big boy, but just like all the other mothers in the neighborhood, I walked him to school every day. Sammie was still attending Pace school there in Bellflower with the regular bus service to and from school. Although he was only three years old, Alphonso had been in pre-school since he was a baby. I was still working there as an assistant mother. Since I was away nearly all of August, my jewelry orders had slackened up some. I had to call my customers to create another stir in their desire to see my new catalog.

The year seemed to pass by pretty fast without any new occurrences until I got the call from Christine that Mr. Jones had passed. "Oh no," I almost choked. I couldn't believe it.

"Guess what?" she went on to say, "I have got some more bad news for you." *What could be any worse*, I thought, *than this news about Daddy?* "Daddy's relatives are putting the house up for sale. So you can forget the promise he made to you before you left. I told you, you should have stayed when he asked you to. Maybe he would still be alive today."

Her words echoed over and over in my mind. Suddenly, I was overwhelmed with a dark, grim feeling like it was my fault. I wanted to cry out loud.

"But Christine, Daddy was as healthy and as strong as a bull. I didn't think that he would pass away so soon," my voice trailed off. I was hoping that my words would ease some of the blame off my leaving in her mind.

"I know that he was," Chris agreed, "but I think Daddy grieved himself to death over mother."

I remember how dedicated their marriage always was. He never even looked at another woman. And mother did everything for him. Cook, iron, sew, and clean. For many years while growing up, I always thought all marriages were this perfect. But I soon found that out to be a lie. Mr. Jones had morals and standards that he lived up to. You just don't find men like him around anymore.

With all the talk nowadays about men seducing their own daughters, you wouldn't have believed we would be lucky enough to have a foster father who never attempted to approach any of us girls living in the home. Respect was something he gave us all. You better believe we returned that respect to both Mr. and Mrs. Jones.

"Well," Chris started before she hung up, "they are together now, wherever they are. I know that for sure." The sun began to shine again. With those words, I felt nothing but happiness again.

Aunt Cynthia and I had been talking about the boys and me coming there to Philadelphia to live with her until she sold the house. At first, she was against it, saying things like, "You are not going to like living here in Philly, Gladys. Why do you think I am so anxious to move out of here?" But then, after she realized I just couldn't take the boredom of waiting as long as it might take her to sell the house, she agreed.

"I just want to be closer to Detroit," I insisted. "That way, I can at least visit more often, even if I can't move there immediately."

"All right, Gladys, have it your own way. But don't say I didn't warn you about this place."

My next task was planning how I would transport all of my furniture and personal belongings from California to Philadelphia. I called Bekins Moving Van since they had been the ones to move my things here back in 1969. I remembered they did an excellent job at not breaking or scratching anything. But after hearing just what the estimated price was, I decided that I would rather move it myself.

I had seen the big U-Haul truck advertising sign, "You move it, any time." But now, what would I do about a driver? I would have to get someone to drive the U-Haul truck back for me. Once again, having my own license to drive would have really come in handy in this situation. I began to read the many ads in the paper, and I immediately called two or three of the numbers. Suddenly the fear of traveling all those many miles with a total stranger crept into my visions. I started to imagine dreadful possibilities I would be putting my own self and children into. I had to stop and *really* think again about if this was the right way to do it.

When the telephone rang, I thought it was one of the truck companies I had just left a message with to contact me. Instead, it was Prentice Anderson, singing another song he had just written to me over the telephone.

Right away, I realized he was my answer for a driver. I wasted no time in directly asking him. "Prentice, would you drive a U-Haul truck to Philadelphia for me?"

"You have got to be joking," he laughed.

"Prentice, I am serious. The kids and I are moving to Philadelphia as soon as school is out."

"What! Does Dorothy know about this yet?" he asked.

"No, I haven't told anyone. But I am making plans now."

"Are you sure this is the way you want to go?" The sound and tone in his voice told me what he was thinking. He still didn't trust Aunt Cynthia's motives for befriending me. I don't blame him. It did seem a little odd to say the least.

"Prentice, I am only going to Philadelphia to live for a short while. My real destination is back to Michigan when the opportunity presents itself." I didn't want to leave any corners open for behind-the-scenes discussions later on. I explained to him how the death of my foster father had ruined my former plans.

"Because now we had no place to live if we went back there right away. So, I had decided to stop over in Philadelphia until Aunt Cynthia sells her property."

"So, despite the circumstances, you are leaving California anyway," Prentice finally realized that the real truth was that I refused to be stopped by my father's misfortune.

"That is right," I answered. "My vacation last summer helped me to make up my mind as to where I needed to be. All of my friends back home are living better than me. Do you know how it makes me feel to know that we inspired a lot of the families in our small town of Inkster to want to *be* somebody? Yet, now here I am, still with nothing to show for all of my work put forth in those early years. It was our songs and music that brought about many professional advancements for black people.

"Now I just have to take matters into my own hands and be the one to give myself another chance. And to start it all back over again, I can't very well do it way out here in California when the other girls are in Michigan. If I go back to Detroit, I might be able to pull our group back together again. But I need to know that I will have shelter and food for my kids back there. I don't want to go back there searching for a job to survive. That will only give people something to gossip about.

"Working in music is the only kind of work that I can do back there. It is the only thing they'll even accept coming from me. You understand, don't you, Prentice? I still have got my real pride inside. And I want to hold my head up in honor of my accomplishments. I need the support of anyone who offers to help me if I am going to get this thing together again. That is why Aunt Cynthia has offered us a place to stay with her when we finally move back to Detroit until I can get the show back on the road."

"I understand exactly what you feel," Prentice stated. "Let me talk to Dorothy about me driving you back there. It will mean me having to miss some days off from work. It will also mean that you will have to provide me with an airline ticket so that I can fly right back here to resume my job responsibilities."

"That can all be arranged," I agreed.

"What day had you planned to start moving?"

"On July 1st, we are leaving."

"Great, that is close to the 4th of July weekend. I will probably already have a couple of days free. Call you back later," he promised, and I knew he would.

Dorothy agreed that it would be wiser and safer to have someone I knew to drive the kids and me for that length of time and so great of a distance. "I am going to miss you and boys, but I understand. You got to do what you got to do. I have had many dreams of returning back to Cleveland, Ohio, myself. California takes its toll on you and your pocketbook after a certain amount of years of coping with the pressures." We both agreed that the weather and the winters without snow were the most convenient to us northern residents.

I had to rent the largest-sized moving van that U-Haul makes to accommodate all my belongings. After the truck had been securely packed, there was enough room left to lay out a couple of mattresses on the floor. We could park out at the roadside campsites to get our needed rest and not have to pay the extra expense of hotel accommodations.

The boys were all excited and happy about riding in such a big truck. They had had enough experience with the adventures and fun of traveling from our last vacation, and nothing could stop them now. They were all re-energized and ready to go. All of my personal and private businesses had been closed out, and I had given notice to my jobs. We had said our last goodbyes to neighbors and friends, and we were ready to hit the road again.

It is interesting how you feel the heaviness of your burdens and problems lifting whenever you are moving from one place to another. It certainly is a feeling of freedom, the beginning of a new day. And wow, after all that has been said and done, I am still free. Free to be me.

PART 2:

"WE GOT TO KEEP MOVING ON"

CHAPTER 6:

"PHILADELPHIA, PA – PHILLYTOWN"

Moving everything out to Philadelphia took us about four days, so you know we were really hitting the road, Jack! The kids were really riding the saddle again and were full of excitement and laughter with joy-filled eyes to be on the move again. Me, myself, I wasn't able to relax and enjoy this long journey on wheels like I had during the bus ride on our vacation a year ago to Michigan. Right from the very start, Prentice Anderson had this rush, rush, rush attitude. When I knew it was time for us to pull over and rest, he argued the point that he wasn't tired yet and wanted to go on.

"I've got to get back as fast as I can."" He kept mentioning something to the effect of him getting fired if he wasn't back at work on time after the 4th of July holiday. I was so grateful that he had taken on the responsibility of doing this job for me. At first, I did everything I could to keep down an argument over how much our safety depended on him getting the proper sleep. *I'll just stay awake and keep him alert*, I thought secretly to myself. So I talked to him all the while about his favorite subject: Motown. That should do the trick in keeping him wide awake and alert.

Well, it did for a couple of times when I knew he really needed to pull over and sleep. But unfortunately, one night, I dozed off myself. When I finally came to and realized that I had taken a quick doze, I jumped. Immediately I turned my gaze to Prentice, who had his eyes closed and was still driving. I screamed his name out so loud that I'm sure it would have awakened the dead.

"What, what, what's wrong?" he tried to pull himself together to appear to be under full capacity of his waking senses.

"Prentice, I woke up and looked at you, and you had your eyes closed. Thank God something woke me up."

"Nonsense," he replied. "I've been awake all the time."

"Man, you know you're lying!" I shouted. "Pull over right now!" Prentice simply ignored my demands and kept on driving. I was furious with him. "Stop this truck right now, and I mean it!"

The kids were fully awake now, trying to silently figure out what all the racket was about. Prentice and I argued back and forth for about another hour while he continued to drive on.

"I'm not going to lose my job doing you a favor!" he yelled out.

"And I'm not going to let you kill us trying too fast to get to Philadelphia."

We yelled and screamed more unmentionable insults to each other. And when he finally did pull over, we both were boiling hot under the collar and needed an extra long rest to iron out our grievances.

Prentice got out fast and went to make a call to Dorothy, I presumed.

Whatever she told him must have calmed him down a lot because he came back and apologized for our heated conversation.

After getting ourselves a bite to eat, we parked the truck in the back of a fully lighted restaurant hotel combination. The kids and I had gotten in the back of the truck to go to sleep, but I found I had far too much on my mind to sleep that night. Prentice had stretched out over the front seat of the truck and was snoring much too loudly from the lack of sleep. The kids were now all snuggled up close to one another and in dreamland.

I just lay there, looking up at the sky. A feeling of great loneliness accompanied by fear of the unknown days ahead for me and my kids seemed to be growing slowly inside me. Did I really know what I was doing, moving around so freely in this great big world as if I didn't have a care or a worry to be bothered with?

In many ways, I was still shaken by what could have happened to us all that night. I wondered how long Prentice had been driving with his eyes closed, and what great force had jolted me awake so suddenly. I remember feeling like someone had hit me hard on the shoulder. At times like these, one has to stop and realize that there is someone greater than yourself who is always watching and protecting you. Silently, I said my "thank you" prayers as I looked at the peaceful faces of my three boys.

"Thank you, God. Thank you for loving us so much that you took over the steering wheel for I don't know how long. Thank you for keeping us alive."

For the rest of the trip, I felt uneasy and pressured. Prentice and I were only speaking now when it was utterly necessary. But you can believe that there was no more nighttime driving when I was asleep.

The morning that we reached the Philadelphia state line drew a lot of questions from the boys. I told them that it wouldn't be long before we'd be at Aunt Cynthia's house.

"Does she live in a big house?"

"Will we have a big backyard like we saw at Christine's house?"

"Does she like animals?"

"Hold it, fellas. Hold it now. You've got to remember that this is *my* first time visiting Aunt Cynthia, too. Let's just wait and see what it's like when we get there."

"But she must have told you something about the house," Vaughn pressed on, still wanting some firsthand information.

Remembering a conversation once over the telephone, I recalled she had mentioned that hardly anyone in Philadelphia had a big backyard. But in her neighborhood, the backyards were relatively larger than the average family yards. She had also described her mother's house as being fairly larger than most of the homes with four bedrooms upstairs, her own living and dining room downstairs, and also a basement. Taking all of this into account, I told Vaughn, Alphonso, and Sammie that their Aunt Cynthia lived alone in a fairly big house, and they certainly would have a big backyard to play in.

"Now, the rest remains a secret. We'll all find out as soon as we arrive." From where we entered the city of Philadelphia, the scenery could not have been better.

"Ooh! Look at those big beautiful houses." I heard the questions being asked by the boys again.

"Which one is Aunt Cynthia's?"

"Are we going to live in a house that looks like that?"

I gazed out of my window to stare at a string of rich-looking villa-type mansions that all seemed to be right out of a Hans Christian Anderson's European fairy tale.

They all had lawns that were flowing and long and ever so green. All the shrubbery couldn't have been cut more evenly and perfectly if mere time depended on it. In all the years when The Marvelettes had come here to perform, I never saw *this* side of Philadelphia. Oh, how I wished that we could have been so lucky and that my traveling could have brought the boys and me to a neighborhood such as this.

The longer we drove through Philadelphia, I could see that the neighborhood's scenery was changing. We were now amongst the taller red-brick row houses on both sides of the streets, getting deeper and deeper into the city's residential areas. When we finally reached the address of Aunt Cynthia's house, I think I experienced a temporarily mental breakdown. It was *nothing* like I had imagined it to be. I looked at Prentice and then the kids, who all seemed to have the same thoughts I that did.

"Is *this* what we left sunny California for?"

I knew it was up to me to keep the morale of the boys up. I quickly pulled my mental facilities back together again enough to say to the boys, "Cheer up. We're only going to be here for a short while, and then it will be back to Detroit for us." With this happy thought in mind, the boys seemed to come alive again with their cheery depositions.

Aunt Cynthia had seen us drive up, and before we could all climb out of the truck, she was on the front porch to greet us. But I noticed right away that there was something missing—that great big happy smile of hers. Instead, she had this stern, grim look as though she had just received a bad telegram or something. Even the kids noticed the change in her attitude. There were no welcoming arms or kisses for them like she had demonstrated at the times when she had visited us. Before they started asking her millions of questions, I quickly asked her was everything all right.

"It's just my sinuses," she answered. "I've been up for two nights now, and then today I had to miss work because I didn't want to be gone when you all arrived. I'm glad you had a safe trip. Bring your things on in."

Prentice spoke up right away. "I'm not going to have time to help you unload all the furniture, Gladys, but I'll help you bring in some beds and some of your clothing for overnight. I've got to be on my way to the airport this very evening." Then he added, "I'm sure Cynthia has some friends in the neighborhood who can help you all finish moving your things in tomorrow."

Aunt Cynthia nodded. But then I remembered that we had to have the truck turned in on time or else I'd have to pay more money for it. "Prentice," I started to remind him about it, but he had already read my mind.

"Gladys, here are the papers you need when returning the truck. I'm sorry, but I can't stay. I must leave immediately."

Right away, Prentice started unloading the things he said he would while the kids and I went inside Aunt Cynthia's house. For some reason, I walked straight through the house to the back door to take a look at the backyard.

I knew it would be where the kids would spend much of their playtime, so I wanted to see her bigger backyard than the average Philadelphian had.

My heart fell through to the floor. The backyard was so small that there was only enough room for the dog that she had back there. The kids who were right behind me also stared in amazement at their playground—or lack thereof.

She had lied to me. *Why did she lie to me?* The thought brought on a dreadful fear that clenched at my heart. For some reason, I felt like a mouse who had just been caught in a trap. The kids had become so busy playing back and forth with the dog through the screen that it made it easy for me to hide my grief-stricken feelings. This also gave me a chance to turn my gaze to the other portions of the house.

Everything was neatly in place, but I noticed that the house was naturally dark. Even now, in the daytime, because of the lack of windows, which made it impossible for much sunlight to come in. I saw boxes in the dining area Aunt Cynthia had packed in preparation of her move to Detroit. Just seeing those boxes gave me an urge of inspiration just to know that this would not be a permanent place for us to live. It was so dark and haunted-looking.

Aunt Cynthia seemed to read my thoughts now as we avoided each other's eyes as she spoke to me. "You can go upstairs and pick the bedrooms you want to use," she told me since Prentice was already bringing items inside.

Quickly I made my way upstairs to find one great big unfurnished room and three other bedrooms completely decorated. I told Prentice to put everything in the big room. Aunt Cynthia had come up to tell me that I could take one of the furnished bedrooms for myself after fixing the big one up for the kids. I assured her that the one big room would be enough for all of us. She seemed disappointed that she could not convince me that I needed a room for myself.

"Thanks for being so kind, but I really need to be with the kids," I explained. "It's a new place and town for them. Until they get used to it, I'd rather sleep in the same room with them."

Without another word, she went back downstairs to let us finish organizing our bedroom.

On finishing, Prentice convinced Aunt Cynthia to drive him to the airport. Before he left, he said his goodbyes to all the boys and then turned to me to say, "I wish you lots of luck, Gladys. Remember, if you need Dorothy and I for anything or for any reason, please don't hesitate to call."

The look in his eye told me that he didn't expect this venture to be an altogether happy one. There was something in the air here that gave me the same feeling.

When Aunt Cynthia returned from the airport, she found us all asleep. It had been days since we had slept in a bed. As soon as I washed the kids and myself up, we fell right asleep.

When I awoke, it was night and so quiet until I wasn't even aware if anyone else was even in the house or not. I tiptoed downstairs to find Aunt Cynthia sitting in her chair in front of the television set. I'm sure she heard me coming down the stairs, but she never turned her gaze from the TV set until I spoke.

At first, I didn't even know what to say. I could feel a cold, distant air coming from her. I was in her house. *She should have made the proper advances of coming forth and speaking to me first*, I thought. But this great silence I was experiencing from her was not like her at all. No, I was sure of it. Something *was* wrong. Usually, the house hostess is busy welcoming her in-home guests with the details of where this and that can be found, especially knowing someone is new to the environment. But I couldn't just stand there waiting for her to break the ice, and so I said, "Well, we made it!"

At first, I didn't even think she was going to respond to that. She took her time joining in on a conversation. She turned and looked at me without getting up and without even giving me a smile to make me feel like at least she welcomed me in her home. Instead, she said, "Gladys, when I got home, I noticed your kids had their handprints all over my front door glass. Please remember that I am used to living by myself, and I don't have a lot of extra cleaning to do. If we're going to make it work under these circumstances, you're going to have to keep your kids intact and watch their activities."

"Oh, don't worry," I reassured her. "I always clean up after my kids. It's just that we all fell asleep, and I didn't get a chance to come back down here and check for anything being out of place or dirty."

And she went on in the same unconcerned, blunt, flat attitude. "If you're going to let the kids go in and out of the refrigerator, be sure you also wipe their fingerprints off the front of the door."

"Ok," I answered. "Is there anything else I should be aware of?"

"Only that I buy a small amount of food. Usually, it's my lunch meat and whatever I'm going to fix for dinner in the evenings after work. So, I'd appreciate it if you made sure you purchase whatever food you may want to feed your kids yourself. I'm living on a very strict budget that doesn't really allow me to spend a lot on food. I hope you understand."

"Oh, yes, I do," I reassured her. But I sure wished she didn't have to be so dominating and strict with a stern tone in her speech. I felt like I was in prison receiving the rundown of the inmate rules on do's and don'ts. What had happened to the Cynthia I *thought* I knew? This great loving fan of The Marvelettes who thought we could do wrong?

One thing I should have already known about fans was to never let them get to know what life is really like for you on the private side. If it is not up to their expectations, they only lose respect for you. I was a fool to think I had found a friend in an admiring so-called fan. She didn't seem to be so admiring and loving now. I just wondered if she had ever really been that kind of person from the get-go.

I had to stop and wonder about a lot of things now. Some things that were too late for me to change now. I had brought myself and my kids here to live with someone I had found I really didn't know at all. We were all at the mercy of the Hard Hannah commands and criticisms. How was I going to get myself out of *this* one?

The very next morning, I awoke to find her already gone to work, but there was a letter on the kitchen table waiting for me. It read:

> *Gladys,*
>
> *Please ask your friends to make sure they turn your faucets off completely after washing up. I don't need a bigger water bill than I already have.*
>
> *Signed,*
>
> *Cynthia*

I remembered what she said about the food, and I knew the kids were hungry. So, it was time for us to find the closest grocery store. Seeing the U-Haul truck sitting there in front of our house when we came outside made me realize that I also needed some neighborly help at once. The two elderly ladies who lived in the duplex right next to Aunt Cynthia's greeted us instantly. After I told them where we were coming from, they looked shocked.

"California!" They both repeated my words. "You mean you left California to move *here*?" They were serious with their desire to know why. Suddenly I noticed their smiles had disappeared. "Is she some relation to you?" they asked.

"No. Just friends," I answered.

"She ain't friends with nobody around here," they warned me. "I hope you know what you're doing, moving yourself and those fine-looking kids in there with her." The seriousness in their manner of talking to me made me want to hear more about the *real* Aunt Cynthia.

The kids were now playing with some of the other children who had welcomed them to the neighborhood. I knew it would be better for them not to hear what these ladies were about to tell me. I didn't want to alarm them. I was already a nervous wreck myself with worry now about what I had gotten us all into.

"She's mean and hateful to all of us neighbors," they told me. "She never even bothers to speak most of the time. I'm wondering why she let you come here and live with her with all of those kids. She hates kids."

While I was shopping for food, I couldn't shake the feeling that we were in real deep trouble coming here to live with the so-called Wicked Witch of Philly. Two guys who lived a couple of doors down offered to help me unload and move the furniture inside. They had seen me trying to tackle some items that were much too heavy for me alone. They also had similar stories of Aunt Cynthia's conduct around the neighborhood.

"She always looks like she's mad at the whole world," one guy mentioned.

I silently thought to myself, *I wish you both could have seen the big act she put on for us out in California. She's probably one the best actresses around.*

"Better hurry up and find you and those kids a place," they told me after we had taken all the furniture inside and turned in the truck at the nearest U-Haul.

"I can't tell you what to do," they told me. "If you know anybody else in this town, you'd better get in touch with them fast."

As if they were reading my mind, I had already thought about searching for the last address I had on Patti LaBelle. I knew she lived in Philadelphia, but I wasn't sure where or if she was anywhere in town.

There it was in one of my old address books: Patti Holt. There wasn't a telephone number listed, only an address. So, I began to write a letter hoping that it would get to her some way.

After a couple of days, I got a call from Jackie, one of Patti's sisters. I met her and Patti's mother back in the '60s when we frequently came to Philadelphia on show engagements at the Uptown Theater.

"Gladys, Patti's not in town, but when she called, I told her about your letter. She asked me to open it, and so it seems like you need help."

"I do, Jackie," I pleaded. "I'm scared and frightened, most of all for my kids."

"Kids?" Jackie seemed surprised. "How many kids do you have?"

"I have three boys," I told her. "Sammie, Vaughn, and Alphonso."

I quickly explained to her about the matter at hand and what a drastic mental effect I felt this had taken on the boys. They were so young. How do you explain to them that someone they felt had some loving feelings for them really had none?

"Oh, Gladys, I feel so sorry for you," Jackie said. "I'm sure the boys feel tricked and very confused by now."

"Yeah," I went on to tell Jackie. "You wouldn't *believe* the attention she gave to them before we came here to stay with her. She seemed so concerned about their feelings all the time." I told Jackie about all the times she sent them cards and money on their birthdays and holidays.

"I just wonder why she went through all of that to gain our confidence. Now she ignores them as though she never knew them. It's hard for the kids to cope with this type of situation. I think they resent the fact that she changed on them and now constantly argues about whatever they do. So they have become restless and stubborn on purpose. Every morning she leaves me a note full of complaints. She says she wished they wouldn't draw the neighborhood kids in front of her door to play. But whenever they play in the backyard, she complains about the dirt they bring back into the house. I am constantly mopping floors and cleaning up so she can't find anything to be upset about. Still, she always finds something else, something that I've overlooked."

Jackie laughed and said, "Gladys, it sounds to me like she enjoys the fact of having a well-known entertainer such as yourself, a Marvelette, doing her dirty chores like a slave in her home. These so-called fans are crazy. People, in general, are crazy, and they always have another side to them. That's why I have to protect Patti all the time from these fake fans who don't see you as real people with real problems. It distorts their daydreams of you to find out that you too have to breathe the same air as everyone else does. They imagine that life for you is full of star-studded lights, lots of money, big cars, parties, and streets paved with gold and silver. And when you show them you're a part of the *real* world, they hate you for waking them up to the truth."

Jackie went on to tell me that Patti would be home in

a couple of days because their mom was in the hospital.

"Oh, looks like I've come at a bad time," I told her. "I'm sorry I've added more problems to your already existing ones."

"Don't worry about that," Jackie said. "Patti will be glad to see you, and I'm sure we'll both try and give you all the help we can in finding you someplace else to stay. Please try and just hold on a bit longer."

Jackie's words spelled relief for me. For the first time since I had arrived there, I felt like I could relax. I didn't feel all alone anymore. Lucky for me, I had made some friends in Philadelphia a long time ago.

Aunt Cynthia didn't seem too pleased to hear the news that I had spoken to someone else I knew who lived there in Philly. The very next morning, we awoke to find out that she had turned off the water on us. How cruel could she be? Thankfully, the two ladies next door allowed me to wash the kids up over there and gave us some water for drinking later on.

"I told you that you were heading straight for trouble in dealing with her. Are you going back to California now?" they asked.

"No. I'm going to continue with my formal plans to move on to Detroit later on. But we will be leaving her house as soon as we can," I told them.

Patti called me as soon as she got into town.

"Miss Gemini!" she said. "What kind of mess have you gotten yourself into now?"

After explaining things over with Patti, she advised me to really be careful. "From what I hear, I get the feeling that she doesn't want the kids around you. She sounds like she may be after you as a lover and feels like she can't get to you mentally because of your devotion to your kids."

"So you mean," I said, "she may try to harm the kids?"

"Maybe," said Patti. "Let's not try to wait and find out. Jackie is asking a close friend of hers to rent you an apartment in her house. If she's ok with it, we're going to move you out of there tomorrow while that crazy lady's at work." Then Patti laughed out loud that laugh she's always been so famous for.

Thank God everything went along as planned. The next day, right after Aunt Cynthia went to work, some men drove up in a big truck and helped me to move my family and furnishings out of the dark, grim situation I had moved us all into.

I never looked back. I never even called Cynthia ever again to say anything else to her. A lesson I learned about almost getting burned. Some things are better unsaid and left alone, especially when you've got somewhere else that you can call home.

Patti LaBelle had helped me when she had problems facing her during those days that were even far worse than mine. Her mom had just undergone surgery and was in the hospital. A week later, when they called to tell me about her mother's death, I made sure I was there for her. I stuck by her day and night during that terrible period in her life. I think in many ways, it linked our friendship even closer and forever. Maybe I had found my real sister, my Gemini sister. Thank you, Patti. I'll always remember you and love you. Little did I know it then, the real soap opera days in Philadelphia had just started for us.

***

It took every penny I had saved to survive those first three months in Philly. We were living on the third floor of the house of a friend of Jackie's named Ronnie. Ronnie had just married an African fellow, and had a baby girl for him. She also had five other kids—three teenage daughters and two sons. The youngest was around the age of my boys.

At first, everything was super. I guess anywhere would have seemed like that to me after nearly escaping God knows what plans Aunt Cynthia had for us. My kids enjoyed daily recreation at the parks that the summer programs provided for the youth there in Philadelphia. Sammie couldn't hang out like the other two, but he and I would always find ourselves some entertainment. Many times, Ronnie's teenage daughters, Sam, and I would just sit around, chit-chat, and enjoy the latest music or TV shows. Sometimes they'd take us around on the trolleys and show us the shopping areas. Above all, there wasn't a dull moment to be experienced.

I think the first change came when the summer was over and school was about the start. Everybody was busy doing something. The girls were shopping for school, Ronnie's oldest son left for the military, and her African husband had made plans to move to Atlanta, Georgia, to further his education. I myself had the responsibility of getting my boys enrolled in school there in a new town.

We were from out of state, so sometimes this takes longer. But one great thing about the special schools for the handicapped is that all over the world, they make your job of finding the right program for your child as easy as possible. They offer any kind of information you may need and help keep you informed through hotlines and regional offices of all the opportunities and activities provided to each and every child or adult.

So finding a school for Sammie was the least of my troubles. Bus transportation to and from school was granted to him immediately. I was very proud of Sammie. He showed no fear of being in a strange city where we knew very few people. He acted just like an old pro and adjusted himself to his new school and transportation program like a champ!

Ronnie's youngest son, Shawn, who was around Vaughn's age, helped in getting us acquainted with the best and closest elementary school in our neighborhood of 51st Street and Chester Avenue. I enrolled Vaughn in classes there at Comegys Elementary School. Soon, he was on his way to attend one of the best educational systems in the country. That's what I later felt about the schools there in Philadelphia.

After seeing how Vaughn advanced so rapidly, I knew they were really on their job in this city. Because at first, he was termed as being below his grade level. "What?" I screamed when a counselor called me in to tell me that he was way behind the third graders there in Philadelphia. How does a parent deal with this type of academic pressure being placed on their child's learning ability? I knew that there was nothing wrong with Vaughn's learning capacity; it was just that he had not been pushed as hard during his years of school in California.

Education was something that teachers in Philadelphia made sure your child got. Dedication to the cause seemed to be uppermost in the people's minds running the schools there. I realized that there are good schools all over America. Still, if I had to do a commercial about the subject, I'd say that after that first year of going to school in Philadelphia, Vaughn gained strength and character in his learning capacity that kept him an honor student throughout high school. Alphonso never lost what he gained either. But that first year, he was only four years old, and that was not the school age for kindergarteners.

I needed a job fast because my rent had to be paid, and we were barely making it off the SSI check Sammie was still getting for his disability. That's when Ronnie offered me half off of my rent if I would babysit her daughter every day while I was watching Alphonso. Her husband was gone now, and he had been her help during the summer while she was working. So, of course, I agreed. That sure would help a lot until I could sort out my life and decide what would be next. A month went by smoothly with everybody and their daily schedules.

One evening, just before bedtime, Ronnie's little son Shawn and her baby daughter were both upstairs in my apartment on the third floor. My boys were getting undressed for bed when something new started. Vaughn was pulling up his pajama bottoms. Tanay, the little girl, ran up to him, trying to pull at his penis. Vaughn pushed her away, surprised like all of us that she would make such an attempt, being no more than two years old. Tanay persistently came at him as if she was well aware of what she was doing.

"Ooh! I'm going to tell Mama," said Shawn.

I stood shocked at the actions of such a small young child. I ordered Shawn to take her so that the kids could go to bed. I wondered if Shawn was going to report his sister's actions to his mother. I sure didn't want to be the one to present such a bad news story to any parent, especially a mother.

I do admit, though, that I was stunned. I had never seen the little girl act that way before, and I was with her most of the day. She seemed to know exactly what she was going for. She was so determined, so knowledgeable, so grown-up. I later just pushed it out of my mind as something that happened during her discovery that little boys were built differently than little girls. I also made sure that she was never around the boys again when they were preparing for bed.

It didn't occur to me at the time that Tanay would again soon repeat her actions. The knowledge came when Ronnie rudely called me to come to her room one evening. I knew by the tone of her voice something was definitely wrong, and she had never asked me to her room before. But I would have never guessed what she was about to say. The look on her face told me that all hell was about to break loose.

"Shawn tells me," she started out saying, "that Tanay tried to pull at his penis a few minutes ago." I then started to tell her about the same thing happening once up in my place when she interrupted me.

"I believe that you are letting your youngest son, Alphonso, teach Tanay bad habits while you are taking care of them every day."

I couldn't believe that I was being accused of such a thing. "No, Ronnie, no. Not Alphonso." I came to his defense because I knew that this was not happening.

She went on raving about how she saw him twirling her around by the waist one day. I still detested her convictions. I couldn't believe that she could even think I would allow such a thing to happen.

"Nothing's happening at all while I take care of your daughter. You're wrong now, real wrong. Whatever she's learning, it's not coming from any of my family."

It seemed to anger her to see that I was standing up for my son, who by all means was innocent. He had not even witnessed any similar sexual acts around me. I had been a single parent living alone for three years, without even an outside mate.

"I'm giving you three months to find someplace else to live," she said next, looking at me hard and fierce with anger in her eyes.

There was nothing I could say. She had reached her decision about how she thought Tanay learned about such a mature and grown-up sexual act. I knew that only time would tell her how and whom her daughter had gotten her training from. I knew that my boys were innocent, and *I* had not been rightly accused of such an act. It frightened me to feel like I was back out in the cold again, so to speak. Three months was a long time to look for a place. *I'd probably have a job by then,* I thought, *and we'll have met new friends and acquaintances who would surely show me around this big city of Philadelphia.*

This was one place where you really didn't need a car to get around fast. There were the trolley cars, subways, and buses about five minutes apart from one another. If you missed one type of transportation, you could surely catch another in just moments.

To my surprise, it didn't take long to realize I wasn't

going to have to worry about quickly learning the city in order to search for a new apartment. The very next day, someone was moving out of a flat two doors down from us. Alphonso was the one who first spotted the big moving van from our third-floor window!

"Mom, look, look! Somebody's got a big truck like the one we rode in," he called to me.

I immediately went over to find out who was moving out. It was the home of the girl who did everyone's hair on the block. Vi, they called her. We had seen one another many times in passing along the street, but now it was the first time we actually got acquainted. She was attending the Wilford Beauty Academy and doing hair in between school hours to help her studies.

She greeted me at the door with a big smile. "I've been wanting to meet you," she told me. "We heard that you were a recording star like Patti LaBelle, but I wasn't sure of what group you were with."

"The Marvelettes," I proudly answered, so happy that my music history sure came in handy whenever I usually got into a tight fix. I had to smile. She explained to me that she was not a landlord. Her cousin and his wife had been living with her but had now found a new place of their own. I quickly spoke up, saying I needed a place immediately.

"But listen," she said. "If you just need a place right away, I'd be honored to have you as my first tenant. One of The Marvelettes! I can't wait to tell all my friends at the beauty college. I'm going to have more customers here at home now than I can handle," she laughed.

She let me take a look at her third-floor flat. I had to marvel at how neat and clean her cousin had left it. "It's practically ready to be moved in today if you need it that soon," she said.

I couldn't believe my luck. A new place of my own already, in just a matter of hours since Ronnie's false accusations had rocked my world! Vi and I later discussed plans for me to pay rent which was also reasonable and quite affordable.

"I'll be looking for a job soon at one of these recording studios in the area," I promised. Vi smiled and wished me luck. She was so sweet and understanding. I couldn't have been a happier person that day.

I guess the news of my lucky streak of the day was too much for Ronnie's ears that evening. I would have thought that she would have wanted my boys away from her daughter as soon as possible. Instead, she was furious with me. The fact that I wouldn't be at her mercy for as long as she thought brought out a side of her that I never knew existed.

"You asked me to move. Now you're angry because I found a place already?" How jealous and evil human nature can be! I shook my head in pity. Why? Why do emotions like these have to exist in this world? I wish somehow they could altogether be eliminated. They made people act so ugly.

Ronnie made it clear to me that I couldn't just remove my washer and dryer from the basement during my move. For some reason, she remembered that she didn't have the key to open the door. Her husband had taken it to Atlanta with him, it seemed. Do you know that to this day, I have never seen my washer and dryer?

Well, I sure was learning *something* from our many moves, and that was that you have to just put the bad things behind you and keep on going. Vi had a happy home and happy family from what I could see from someone looking in from the outside. As radiant and as friendly as she was, I was a little afraid to really reach out to her and become very good friends. I had also learned from past mistakes that too much friendliness can sometimes cause a happy situation to end sooner than you expect. And so, I kept very friendly terms with her, but I refused to be downstairs in her apartment as much as she wanted me to be.

Plenty of female company was over all the time. Vi had a regular little intimate beauty salon going on right there in her house, and it was nice! I never lacked the need for conversation or recreation. I just didn't want to wear my welcome out. I'd just show my face every now and then and have a real good time laughing and gossiping with the different girls that were getting their hair done.

Vi's husband's name was Bill, and she had two boys and one little girl for him. It seemed like wherever we moved, my boys found new friends and things to keep them well entertained in between school hours. It wasn't very long before I got some help in finding myself a job. One day Bill's mother came over to the house, and Vi introduced us.

"So you're really an entertainer from the Motown family?" She seemed very delighted in meeting me, and for some reason, I felt very comfortable around her from our very first conversation. She wanted to know if I would listen to a song she had written a long time ago. It seemed that Mrs. Branch had once been a member of a girl group herself when she was a teenager. They had recorded a song called "Why Can't You Love Me."

"Of course, in those times, just like today, there was always a lot of talent," she explained. "But not always did every artist or group get the chance to experience having their very first recording be a big #1 like your song about the postman turned out to be. It's just a part of my life that I'll always remember. I enjoyed talking about the effect it made on me back in my early youth."

She was thrilled to hear me talk about my many travels and all the places where The Marvelettes had performed during my hot spell in the business. We also talked about the not-so-good year that followed for me.

"You can do it again, Gladys," she said. "I actually feel that it's not all over for you."

I told her about my future plans to go back to Michigan to regroup the girls.

"You've got a lot to do to get ready for that, young lady," she warned. "So many of the groups today are writing and producing their own material. Have you ever done any songwriting?"

"I sure have," I answered proudly. "I wrote our third release called 'Playboy,' and I also wrote the music to the B-side of our first recording called 'So Long Baby'."

"That's great!" she exclaimed. "Do you know what I've always wanted?"

"What's that?" I really wanted to know.

"To have that very first song I recorded and wrote for our group recorded over by one of the popular groups of today. Would you listen to it? If you like it, maybe when you get back with your girls, you can bring it back out on your new album. Or maybe even better, put it out as a single."

Her enthusiasm about the song really prompted me to want to try my hand at writing again. "All right," I quickly responded. "Bring it over. I really want to hear what a girl group of long ago sounded like."

"No sooner said than done."

The very next day, Mrs. Branch was over with the song on tape and a gift for me. "Open it!" she cheerfully smiled, looking at the dismayed look on my face.

"A gift for me?" I truly was surprised. As always, while opening a gift I hadn't expected, my mind was racing a hundred miles an hour, trying to guess what it might be. This time, she *really* caught me off-guard. I would have never expected such a wonderful but much-needed item if I was now going to start writing songs–a tape recorder! "Wow! What can I say or ever do to repay you for your kindness?" I asked her.

"Just work hard on using your gift of using your mind to write great songs. Maybe one day, you'll put my little old song on one of your albums," she smiled as she made her request.

"I sure will!" I promised her. "I'll work real hard on rewriting your song too. Just wait and see!" I vowed. "I won't stop until you're satisfied with what I've done."

That day started me on my real adventure into the world of writing songs. It was the very first tape recorder I had ever owned. Believe me, I guarded it with my very life. Somehow I knew my life's story depended on how much time and work I put into this little device that played back my every word. Every breath I took and every note and sound I made and sang made me closer to my goal. I began to hear music even in my sleep.

Sometimes, I'd wake up in the middle of the night with a song's melody in my head. I'd run to my tape recorder and put just enough of the melody on tape. After I got the kids off to school the next day, I could finish writing the song. I guess you would say I heard music coming from the depths of my soul. The miraculous thing about it all was that I began writing songs so fast, like a computer emptying out all of its data of melodies and lyrics. It was in my brain constantly.

The song Mrs. Branch gave me to listen to started it all. I was astonished at how fast I came up with a new concept and melody to go along with her song. I gained so much confidence in my ability to rhyme words and make lyrics into flowing patterns of short stories with catchy melodies. I realized that I should have been writing more songs during my career while on the road traveling between shows.

Mrs. Branch raved over how much she loved what I had done with her song until that even gave me more confidence in myself. "You seem to be very good with putting words together and making them tell a story," she complimented me. "I'd bet you'd be very good at writing poems. A lot of songs are derived from poems, you know."

I was all so new at this, but all I knew was that I felt like I couldn't stop now. Not a day went by when I didn't use my tape recorder to start or finish up some song I had created. I felt like I had found the part of me that had been missing for so long or just didn't exist because I failed to recognize and use it.

"Listen," Mrs. Branch told me, "I know a fellow who buys poems of all sorts for greeting cards and also song lyrics. I'm not sure if the pay is that great or even if you would be interested in such a thing, but it would be a way for you to make some extra cash if he accepts any of your work."

"Do you really think that I'm that good?" I asked. "I really need a job fast."

"Well, I could get you his number if you're interested. It sure won't hurt to give it a try."

I agreed, not really thinking that any good thing would come of it. But how wrong I was. I called to set up an interview with a Mr. Townsend.

"You need at least 10 different types of story-like poems with not more than 75 words on each," the girl over the phone told me. "They must be clearly written in print form on paper if you don't have them typewritten." That didn't seem to be such a tall order for me. By now, I thought I must be a word wizard with the mind of a genius. Songwriting does that to you. You feel as though you can tackle any situation on paper with a rhyme or a line.

Anyway, I had two weeks before I was to meet with Mr. Townsend, and believe me, I intended to work hard at getting my work approved. I had just about run out of funds from my latest royalty check. Although Sammie's SSI was enough to pay our monthly rent and buy some of our food, I always seemed to be needing more for unanticipated treats that teachers would ask the kids to bring for holiday parties, class picnics, or whatever the school's most recent projects would be. Too often, I found myself wondering where the money was coming from for that new pair of shoes or jeans for the kids. It's a good thing I didn't drink or smoke in those days while living in Philadelphia. Those vices alone would have taken a big bite out of my tight, tight financial budget. But after I met Mr. Townsend, that all changed. Besides him being a big fan of all my Motown memories, he seemed to love everything my pen put into writing form.

"Gladys, you were in the wrong profession," he cooed. "Don't you know the writers and the producers end up making the biggest portion of the money in the long run? Even with your own publishing, you would have received royalties year after year on those songs, even after you didn't hear them anymore on the radio. And my God, I'm sure you would have had two or three standards on file written by yourself by now. That brings in royalties for the rest of your life and even afterward!"

I explained to him that in those days, even if I wanted to, I would have been unable to apply myself wholeheartedly to writing and producing because of the energy it took to do all the shows. We were working the theater circuits most of the time, which meant at least three to four shows daily.

"They certainly kept you working hard," he said. "It seems as though the money would have been better than it was."

"Mr. Townsend," I said, "back in the '60s, $500 sounded like a lot of money to us. It was something new that we had never done before, so we didn't realize that our road expenses were going to eat up so much of our pay."

"I'm sure with you all being so young and all, there were a lot of things going on that you just weren't aware of. Now, on to what we want to call better days for you. I am what you call a middleman. I work for a big printing firm that sends out greeting cards of all sorts all over the world—get-well cards, thank you expressions, wedding notes, sympathy cards, holiday cards, and the whole works. What I do is employ writers or, to use another term, lyricists. I encourage my employees to write poems about everything they can possibly think of. The firm is always looking for fresh new bright ideas."

Then he explained, "First, I review your work, and only the best lines and ideas are passed on by me. Then the firm has the final words as to whether your material can be used or not. Because there are millions of rhymes and lyrics to be reviewed by them, I definitely recommend that you try your very best to be put on their list of top writers. This way, your material is put in a priority stack that almost always receives top billing from lots of other choices. There is an agreement you must sign that states that you agree to receive a flat price for any lyrics accepted. This, in turn, gives the firm the right to use your poems in any way they choose.

"For instance, a lot of times, some of your lyrics may be put with another writer's lyrics to make up a greeting note. So in that way, no one lyricist can claim complete rights to their material. So we pay you $500 a song for the complete rights to your rhymes. Maybe they'll even be using your words in as many as four or five different situations of greeting. That's why a flat price is paid to turn over the material to us to be used in any shape or form that we like, with all rights reserved by the printing company."

Then he reminded me again, "You'll want to be as creative as possible because there *are* other writers. Some are extremely good, especially if they've been doing this type of work for years. Now, my office works like this. We review your work at least once monthly, and we require that you have at least 15 poems ready to be interviewed every month. The first month is like a trial period where we want to help get you started and inspire your interest in the job. For as many poems we accept from your material, we will pay you upfront to show you that we have faith in your ability."

"Boy, that's really taking a chance," I said. "At $500.00 a poem, is it possible that you could pick all 15 poems?"

Mr. Townsend laughed. He was reading my mind. "Believe me, it hasn't happened yet. Come on now, I couldn't afford to give anybody $7,500.00 right from the beginning. But I've put $3,000 on the line before."

That was enough to boost my morale. "How many poems you get paid for is entirely up to how much thought and work you put into writing," he continued in a business tone. "If at any time all 15 poems are accepted by the firm, you will receive $7,500. But to my recollection, so far, I can't remember any employee of mine being *that* lucky. But thinking realistically, if only five poems are accepted, that's $2,500 a month. I'm sure you could use some extra cash. With your reputation and your class, this could be the perfect job for you."

"Mr. Townsend, I am so happy to have met you," I said. "And believe me, I am going to try my darndest to be the first employee with you whose complete list of poems are accepted sometime during my employment with you, ok?"

"That's the kind of spirit you'll need to make the job a success for you," he laughed. "And I never doubt any of my clients."

I walked out of his office that day in a daze. I just couldn't believe all the things that were happening for me since I had received that tape recorder as a gift. A very strong creative force had taken over my mind, and I began to write whatever it told me to. I forgot to mention it to you, but the day of my interview, Mr. Townsend chose three of my writings. The very next week, I received a check in the mail for $1,500.00! That was just the start. Every month thereafter, I got at least four or five of my poems accepted, and I felt like I was living on Easy Street again.

Mondays through Fridays during the school hours, I wrote and wrote. Then when the kids came home, I'd relax some, and cook their meals. Sometimes later on after they were all in bed, I'd do more writing. When the weekends came, the kids were ready to go to their recreation center right down the street. I'd pack up my pen and paper and take them there to participate in whatever activities were going on. While they were busy having fun, I'd sit at one of the picnic tables or park benches and write some more. That's how I met Darryl.

The moment our eyes met, I knew *instantly* there was something between us. He had been playing basketball with a crowd of other fellows when he caught my eye while watching them. At break time, he came over and introduced himself. As he got closer to me, I could see that my eyes had not fooled me. This was a real-life Adonis, right here reincarnated. Ladies, I called him Fine Mr. Brown from the get-go! He had all the outside qualities most ladies only dream about—tall, dark, handsome, and a nice tone of speech.

"Darryl is my name," he said to me in a deep baritone voice. "May I ask yours?"

"Gladys is mine," I smiled at the twinkle in his gorgeous brown eyes.

"I always heard that girls with dimples were kissed by an angel at birth." He had a big grin on his face now, as though he couldn't wait to hear my reply.

I thought to myself, *What a clever way to flirt, talking about my dimples.* I noticed that for some reason, he made me feel like I was extra cute. "That might be true, but that would mean that my mother was that angel, not me."

"Well, you've probably got a lot of those angel ways if she was your mother," he came right back at me.

Somehow, I knew that Darryl and I were going to spend time at this playground in the days and months to follow.

"You're new in the neighborhood, aren't you?" he asked.

"How can you tell?"

"Simply because I come here every day to play basketball or baseball or to swim, and this is the first summer I've seen you."

"Oh, then you've seen me before today?"

"Oh sure," he replied. "Almost every time you've come here. Aren't those your three boys over there playing with that group of kids?"

So he *had* been watching me, and I didn't know it. How romantically intensifying the whole idea seemed to be.

"What's wrong with one of your sons? I noticed that he walks as if he may have a bit of a handicap."

I explained to him about Sammie's condition since birth. "They call it cerebral palsy," I told him. I could see him waiting patiently and listening to every word I was saying. I was overwhelmed with feelings of compassionate thoughtfulness. I remembered how many guys never asked or ever even *tried* to talk to me when they see me with a kid that's different. "I appreciate the concern you have to want to know," I admitted.

He looked at me deeply. "How does that make you feel? You're so young and attractive, and to lose the attention of a lot of men because of this reason must really be hurting at times."

"No, it's not hurting to me at all." I suddenly felt a little angry. Not with Darryl, but with the ways of the world. People were so into being and looking so perfect all the time until they felt it would belittle them or take something away from their perfectionists' thoughts to be seen with someone with a handicap. "I really don't care because I haven't seen anyone I thought was worth spending any of my time with."

"Not anyone?" Darryl seemed to be asking me whether I felt he may be different from the rest or not.

"Well, almost not anyone." I managed to give him a big smile now.

"That's my girl," he said. "I don't like it when you get real serious. You look too mean."

We both laughed, and from that day, we did a lot of laughing together. We'd meet at the playground on the weekends and talk over the phone sometimes during the weekdays. What I like most about him was that he showed me right from the very beginning that he was more in love with my mind than he was with my behind. He never asked to follow me home after our visits at the playground or talk his way up to spending the night. Sometimes he spent time playing with the kids and just talking to me, mostly after the basketball or baseball games were over. He loved his sports, so I became one of the spectators who came to the playground to watch in between my writings.

Sometimes I'd think of songs to write about how Darryl made me feel. The first night after our first encounter of meeting, l went home and wrote a song called "Fine Mr. Brown," because that's *exactly* what he was, a fine brown-skinned, brown-eyed man. Then I wrote another one called "You Must Be Number One." Others that followed were entitled "I'm Hooked On You" and "You Give Me Happy Feelings."

When I'd sing some of the songs I had written about him, Darryl would just shyly blush and say, "Please, you're spoiling me, Gladys."

I fell head over heels, but I was afraid to tell him. I couldn't help it. He inspired me to some of my greatest thoughts in writing inspirational lines. He gave me so much feeling, and that's what every writer needs—to be able to feel many different emotions in order to write about them. Darryl was like fuel to my fire. He made every moment more intense and meaningful to me. I just didn't want to ruin it all and spoil our perfect relationship with sex.

In the past, it had never failed with my other male partners. After sex, they became that haunting lover who became jealous and physically overpowering. Darryl and I had never even quarreled since we had met, and it had already been six months or more into our friendship.

Sometimes I felt like he felt the same way I did about not wanting to lose what we had found through the interference of starting a sex life.

I invited him over one Sunday for dinner, and even then all we did was kiss and that was not until all the boys had gone to bed later on. I could see he really wanted to keep their love and respect of him. I never bothered to ask Darryl about his age, because there was a certain amount of privacy we still had between each other. I just figured him to be around 30 years of age because I was 34 at the time. I knew I was older than him, but I didn't know how much older until I had a conversation with his brother Ricky one day. I was devastated to find out that Darryl was even younger than his brother.

"I know Darryl has always looked older," explained Ricky. "Because of height and build, people always mistake him for the oldest."

I didn't discuss my age with Ricky because I'm sure he thought I was younger than Darryl. And Darryl, I found out, was only 24. I had never outright asked him his age, so I couldn't say he lied about anything. But sheer curiosity made me want to find out how old Darryl thought *I* was. So, when I got the chance, I asked him one day while we were talking on the telephone.

"Darryl, did you know that I am older than you?"

He was silent for a while and then said, "You could have fooled me."

"But Darryl, I'm serious."

"I know it. I know it," he replied. "I figured with three boys and the oldest one being 11, you must be between 26 and 28 years old."

"No Darryl," I said. "I'm 34 years old."

"Well, so what?" he said. "You look 24 or younger, and anyway, who's counting? You don't plan on not seeing me anymore just because of an age difference? Do you?"

My answer was no. There was no way I could stop myself now. Just seeing his face was like medicine to me. He was really too good to be true, treating me so nice without bugging me to do the "nasty." The only problem I was running into now was that I was beginning to want him in this way. Best believe I was not going to ever tell him, at least not yet. I wrote two or three songs about the feeling of wanting to have sex without telling your partner that you were feeling this way. One was called "My Hidden Desire." Another one was "I've Got A Secret", and the third one was "I Can't Tell Anyone About This Love."

In those early days of my writing career, I opened myself up to every emotion that the universe bestowed upon me. I wrote about every experience, every desire, every idea, every situation I was faced with. When I felt happy, I wrote happy songs. When I felt sad, I wrote sad songs. All of this helped me in my job of constructing lyrics for the greeting card firm. I was able to build up a bank account far beyond what I had ever imagined I would do.

I knew I really needed to be financially fit when the time came for me to move on to Michigan. Things were getting somewhat rough at Vi's house. Although she and I were still getting along like sisters, I could hear her and Bill at it early in the mornings and late at night. I really didn't understand what the problem was, but I knew problems were arising, especially when she told me one day that she was moving out.

Nothing had been a big problem to me. Still, now that Vi was threatening to leave, I knew I couldn't remain there in the house with him for more than one reason. When I first moved in, he had made sexual suggestions to me once or twice, and I politely put him in his place. I knew that with a beautiful and outgoing popular wife like Vi, he could only be trying to find out where my head was. So, I never mentioned to her or even gave it any real thought. Now, I was being faced with the problem of how could I stay on and not make myself seem susceptible to whatever may happen.

And really, there was no way. So, I decided that the boys and I would also be moving out. I sat down and explained things to Bill's mother, Mrs. Branch, whom I had grown to love and admire for her sweetness and kindness to me.

"Will you ever get your group back together?" she asked me.

"I'm sure going to try," I told her. "I've written so many songs now until we sure won't need to worry about that part of our comeback. It's just that I'm waiting on the proper time to make my move. Thanks to you, Mrs. Branch, I've got a job now where I'm able to save something every month in preparation for one day moving on to Michigan."

"You just keep the good work up," she said. "I'm sure the time will surely come for you to make your comeback."

"And one day," I reminded her, "you'll hear your song playing to a new beat and a new melody. But I'll make sure that your name is on the label for writer's credit."

She just laughed and gave me a big hug. We wished each other well, and I knew that some kind of way, someday I'd be able to thank her for befriending me through my days of moving on.

Yes, we seemed to be constantly moving from one place to another, each time for a different reason. This time, trying to relocate didn't bring on the fear. Nor did it seem to present as big of a problem as I had been faced with before, mainly because I had learned more about the city's layout.

Just getting around to different shopping areas, different school outings with the kids, out on the park, recreational programs, and picnics gave us the feeling of being at home in Philadelphia. The kids and I caught the trolley at the corner of our street every Sunday and went downtown to a movie.

In Philadelphia, on Sundays, all the means of public transportation were free. Sometimes to break the weekend monotony, we'd catch the El or one of the city's buses and just ride it to wherever it went. After looking around for a while and having a bite to eat, we'd catch the first transport we saw back to where we started from. I called it our "free sightseeing tour." Yes, we were meeting different people and making more friends all the while. I got to know the parents of the friends my kids were keeping. Just visiting their different homes and becoming acquainted with the different lifestyles helped to give us all more confidence in our surroundings, too.

But now that I was all ready to go out on my own and do some apartment hunting, something else miraculously happened. One morning after returning from grocery shopping, I noticed that there was a renovation construction crew working on the very last row of houses near the corner of 51st and Chester. Instead of turning up into my apartment house, I decided to walk down there and find out what was happening. I only had one light bag of groceries, so I wasn't in a hurry to put them down.

I approached one of the construction workers who was still out front and asked him. "Will this building be having apartments for rent soon?"

"I don't know, ma'am. I'm just employed to fix it up. But you can call this man. He owns the building, and he can tell you what's up with the place."

He gave me a card that read "Roberson & Sons, Inc."

I went home and called the number on the card immediately.

"Yes. I'll have three apartments ready to rent in about a month," the man on the other end of the phone spoke up. "Are you trying to move right away?"

"Well, a month from now would be soon enough for me. I'd like to have some reassurance as to whether I can actually depend on you for accepting me as one of your renters."

"Well, we can remedy all of that right now," he said. "Where do you live? I can get an application in the mail to you today."

"I live only a couple of doors down from your building being repaired."

"Well, how fortunate for you!" he replied. "Just meet me over there tomorrow afternoon, and I'll have some applications with me."

When I met Mr. Roberson, I found out that he had other property too. After finding out that I had a reasonably good job and would be able to pay the rent, he informed me that I had a choice of several other places in which I could move into even sooner. But the convenience of the property being renovated got to me. The kids wouldn't even have to change schools. I had gotten used to the neighborhood and all its surroundings, and I really liked my neighbors.

Another thing I must comment on is the good-hearted

people of Philadelphia, especially the older ones. These people were so full of love, especially when they saw you caring for small children. They offered their help so unselfishly at any instance where they saw you might need it. Many of these older couples had lived in the neighborhood for years, and they kept a lookout on *all* the neighbors—new and old. It wasn't like they were nosy or anything, but they were even better than a police patrol unit. They kept a neighborhood watch program in full effect.

One to mention was a couple on the block named Mr. & Mrs. Thurman. They were sweet and kind older adults. Along with many other mature neighbors, they seemed to admire my boys. They silently watched out for everything they knew was a daily happening on the street. One morning when Sammie's bus was late arriving, Mr. Thurman smiled and called to me from across the street after the bus had pulled off.

He said, "I was wondering what was taking the bus so long to arrive. I know your son loves leaving for school on time."

I looked and laughed along with him because he was so right. Sammie was having a fit because the bus was late. He hates to be ready and then have to wait. Then I recalled another time when the neighbors showed us their great hospitality. It was the first winter we were there. It had snowed overnight, and it was the first time the boys had ever seen any snow. Everyone knew that we had come from California and had guessed that the kids were still so young that they had probably never seen any snow before. So, a couple of them came over with shovels to show the boys what shoveling snow was all about. In a big city like Philadelphia, the snow never lasted too long with all the transportation options and people moving about. But one thing was obvious now: the boys and I were all going to have to start wearing some boots.

In a big, crowded city like Philadelphia, it's rare to find so many kind, caring feelings coming from strangers. Yes, I had grown to appreciate the love and concern coming from the people of the block of 5151 Street where we lived. I told Mr. Roberson that I wanted to wait for one of his places to be repaired because I wanted to stay around such nice people. He seemed to understand my sentiment, and I knew I had found another nice landlord.

It was the first time in my life that I had moved three times on the same block—first Ronnie's place, then Vi's house, and now this newly renovated apartment. It had only one bedroom, bath, living room, and kitchen, but it would surely work until I found my palace. I was daydreaming again because I knew that day was far off into the future.

***

Another summer had come and gone, and now it was time for school again. This was a very special year because Alphonso was entering kindergarten. Now, he and Vaughn would both be attending the same elementary school. Alphonso was so excited on the first day of school. He was also a happy-go-lucky type of child, always smiling and joking about something.

But this morning, for some reason, he had a grown-up attitude along with his usual personality. What a handsome face he displayed as he cheerfully greeted his kindergarten teacher! After filling out the enrollment paperwork, I walked back home feeling very proud at the thought of how all my boys were growing up to be real heroes in my eyes. As much as I moved them around from place to place, they could always quickly adjust to whatever circumstances they had to and keep on going.

When I returned at lunchtime to walk Alphonso home, the kids were lined up from the shortest to the tallest. And do you know where I found Alphonso? He was standing at the back of the line. The teacher had measured them all, and he was the tallest in the class. That was something for him to be proud of, even if it was just kindergarten.

Every day I walked Alphonso to and from school. This added something new to my daily schedule. I enjoyed seeing the joy it gave him to be making new friends of his own and learning new things about the world he lived in. I saw the new person he was becoming from the more grown-up feeling it gave him in attending school.

Sometimes he'd say, "Mom, I'm a big boy now! You

don't have to hold my hand all the time while we're walking." He'd see a couple of his friends running on ahead of their mothers, so he wanted to do the same.

I guess that's what it's all about—the children breaking away from the mother's apron and one day learning their self-independence, little by little. That school year was the greatest for me, too, because I had even more time now. Being alone at the apartment during the morning hours to write lyrics and record new songs I wrote was amazing. I even got a few bonuses from my boss. He said that since I had been employed by his firm, he had been given a bigger budget to work from, promoted to a top position, and awarded as one of their highest scoring departments.

"What are you going to do with all the money you're bound to make?" he asked me one day.

I told him about my plans to one day go back to Michigan. "I'm going to need a nice amount of cash to see me through until I can land a good record deal for my group," I explained.

"Well, I hope that won't be any time soon, because I'd like to keep you here with me forever."

It sure felt good to hear how much someone needed me.

***

Darryl and I were still seeing each other at the playground at least once a week. Whenever we could, we'd chat on the telephone. Then one night, it happened. Before now, he had always been reluctant whenever I mentioned him coming over to watch TV or just visit. I took his excuses as saying, "We'd better not." So, I never really pushed the issue. But because I liked him so much, I continued to ask just to let him know how I felt inside. Now, for some reason, he said, "I'll be right over."

It was so sudden and out of the norm from his usual behavior that it scared me. When he arrived, I took his coat and told him to have a seat. Feeling very nervous about what to do next or say, I somehow felt like a virgin again. It was a crisp and clear October evening, so the apartment was nice and warm from the heat. Darryl looked around the apartment and then said, "I liked your other place better."

Then I suddenly remembered the last time he had come over for dinner was when we were still living at Vi's house. He had never even seen my new place before now. "I did too," I agreed with him, mostly because it was larger.

We talked about my songs and poems and everything from the weather to how the kids were all doing in school. Then we tried to watch some movie on television. But for some reason, I knew neither one of our attentions was fully on it. So, when the kids were fast asleep, Darryl came over and laid on my bed. It was already in the living room because I had given the only bedroom to the boys.

First, he gave me a short, quick kiss on the lips. Then his eyes spoke to me, saying, "Oh, let's do that again!" This time, the kiss was longer and stronger. I could feel his grip tightening around my waist. Soon I found myself lying back on the bed, happily receiving all his kisses and hands, which were moving now in all the secret, private places of my body.

When it was over, Darryl said, "Wow! I never came that fast before with any girl. You're really something!"

It really felt good to know that he had enjoyed being with me. I kissed him again because I enjoyed being with him, even if that old familiar ending of mine was still the same old story. It took me too long to reach a climax, and I guess no man has been able to go that long yet. But just as before, it didn't matter to me. I loved Darryl for many other reasons that all made up for my unsatisfied climax.

***

I had been talking long-distance every now and then to a couple of my friends back in Michigan—Christine, Dolores, and mostly to Wanda of The Marvelettes. Today, I was telling her about my plans to record our group again.

"We can do it all over again, Wanda," I said. "I've got more hit songs than I can mention, and I'm still writing more songs every day. Here, let me sing this one to you over the phone."

> *We're gonna make it again, over again,*
>
> *Right to the top.*
>
> *We're bound to win,*
>
> *So keep trying,*
>
> *'Cause I ain't lying*
>
> *Yes, we're knowing just where we're going.*
>
> *We're gonna make it again, over again*
>
> *Again and again.*

"Don't you see Wanda?" I asked. "It will be our big comeback song. The fans will eat it up! It's so commercial and real for the public to relate to."

Wanda seemed to hold as much excitement and enthusiasm over the matter as I did at first. As usual, as our conversations would drag on and on, Wanda would start to air her depression to me about how bad the people in Inkster had been treating her since the group had broken up. It was hard to believe some of the things she told me were being done and said to her. I got the impression from the slur of her voice that she was drinking something right as she was talking to me.

"They keep asking me, 'Wanda, how come I don't hear no more hit songs from you?' Gladys," she almost cried out in tears, "they hurt my feelings so bad, I don't know what to do. They make me want to run away somewhere and hide. What am I going to do?"

"Just hold on for a little while longer, Wanda. I'll be there soon, and we'll get our thing back together again, ok? You'll see. They'll all be rooting for us again."

I think my pep talk at these times gave Wanda hope and something positive to look forward to. She and Bobby had finally divorced. Now that she was alone without a career, I think it made her realize that everything doesn't have to be over unless you want it that way.

"Take control of yourself, girl, and hold on!" I constantly told her. "Hold on tight to your dreams and ideals. They'll all come true."

She called me off and on to cheer her up and whenever she needed reassurance that I was still making plans to come there. Then one day she called, and I detected instantly another reason for her calling because of her quick, excited, and overpowering overtones to her voice.

"Gladys!" she called out my name in panic as I answered the phone. "You're not going to believe this, but Georgeanna died early this morning."

"No!" was my first word to the realization of what she was telling me. I didn't even know she had been ill until

Wanda explained everything to me now.

"She died in bed at her mother's house," Wanda said. Georgeanna had been in the hospital, and when she got out, she went to live with her mother to get the proper care. It was all still a shock to me as I explained to Wanda that I hated going to funerals. I just couldn't bring myself to go back there for such a sad occasion.

"Wanda, please understand," I said. "It means a lot to me to be able to remember Georgeanna alive."

I thought about the last conversation Georgeanna and I had when the boys and I were in Michigan vacationing in 1977. She had shown me that bad leg of hers. Now, here it was 1980, and she was gone. Only 36 years old.

***

It's hard to plan to make any moves during the cold season, especially to another city or state. But I think it was at this time that I decided that the boys and I would finally make our move on to Michigan when school was out in June.

Although my savings had grown, I still didn't have enough to buy any real property back there yet. And what I did have would soon run out if I didn't have any means of making more immediately. What I'm trying to say is that I'd need a job right away. I'd also need shelter from someone who could afford not to have to worry about the rent being paid on time. Maybe someone who owned their own home. The next time Wanda called me, I knew she was the someone who could help me in this way if only she would. So I asked her immediately.

"Wanda, can the boys and I stay with you for a while if we make plans to move there this coming July?"

"Yes, yes, yes!" she screamed. "You mean, Gladys, you're *finally* coming back here? Oh, I'm so happy! I'm so happy!" She was hysterical over the phone with joy. "I can't wait! I can't wait!" she screamed. "I'm going to tell my whole family as soon as I hang up from you. Gladys is coming home, and we're going to be The Marvelettes again! Oh, Gladys, please don't change your mind," she pleaded and begged. "Please don't change your mind. Don't worry about anything. You've got a place to stay right here with me. You and the boys!"

Well, that sure helped to make my plans final. Now all I had to do was find a way to tell Darryl I was leaving and then Mr. Townsend. *Maybe I could continue on with the printing firm through long-distance relations with Mr. Townsend,* I began to wonder. Then to my surprise, Mr. Townsend called and had some news for me that remedied the whole situation on my plans after moving away. He told me that he was no longer on the Advisory Board of the firm. Because of a big lawsuit, the firm was folding up. After April, it would all be over. The firm was filing for bankruptcy. He couldn't go into deeper details with me about the firm's legal matters. However, he told me that they still owed me around $3,000 and that he would make every effort possible to ensure that I got it before the April closing date.

Well, that was that. I didn't have a job anymore. But thank goodness it came only months before I was to move on to Michigan. I had enough saved to pay up my rent for months, pay my utility bills, and still be able to show the boys some fun on our weekend outings. I carefully checked and found out that after my moving costs and travel expenses, I'd be able to open up a bank account with something left over after I reached Detroit. With royalties twice a year and my son's monthly government check, I knew I'd be able to save at least $10,000 the first year while in Michigan after expenses.

So, I wasn't doing too bad. I decided to take it easy for a while and relax my mind. For two straight years, I had been a real live walking, talking, writing machine, always trying to make a song or a poem rhyme out of every incident I ran upon. I needed to let my mind be free. Plus, I wanted to see Darryl. I had already decided that I wasn't going to talk about me going back to Michigan until a week or so before we were scheduled to leave. That gave me at least four months to just really have a good time with him and enjoy life together.

Wouldn't you just know it? Darryl had decided to carry me through some changes I'll never forget. But now that I'm thinking about it, he really made the way for me to leave a lot easier than I had anticipated. It started the afternoon I went looking for him at the basketball court over at the recreational hall. For some reason, Darryl purposely ignored me throughout the whole basketball rehearsal. Usually, he'd glance over at me in the crowd of the onlookers and give me a smile. Today, our eyes barely met. Then, when I ran up to him after the game, he said he couldn't talk because he was in a hurry to go somewhere. I felt something was there that had not been there before, standing right between us.

I tried to clear my mind enough to figure out what I had done to instantly turn him off. I had myself in turmoil for the next two days trying to pinpoint the reasons. Suddenly, a very hurting thought crossed my mind: maybe he had met someone else closer to his age. It happens every time. No matter how you try to erase it from your mind, I know the thought does things to every female who has ever gotten involved with a younger guy. Even if no one else can tell your age difference, you have a deep-seated fear that maybe someone younger will grab his attention one day. So be it the case or not, you still never gain the confidence you need to chase that one fear away.

After three days had passed, I decided to call Darryl because he had not even once done that since our encounter that day. I heard him ask his brother, who had answered the telephone, who it was. When he said "Gladys," there was a long, quiet period where I think I heard some whispering in the background. Then his brother came on the receiver and said, "Darryl said he'll call you back. He's busy right now."

Now, all the hopes I had, had been erased from my mind and filled with nothing but doubt. It wasn't just that he had been feeling down that day at the recreational hall; he was having second thoughts about furthering our friendship. I say "friendship" because that's really all it had ever been. Our lovemaking that one time had never happened again. We both decided that we were in no condition to start another family when I already had one. So that recreation was ruled out. But I still enjoyed talking and meeting with him. Now he didn't even want to do that.

I knew that Darryl was a good person, and he must have some good reason to justify his actions. I just didn't know if I was strong enough to find out or to hear exactly what those motives were. The way he was treating me made me feel sad and lonely. I think for the first time in my life, I was really able to feel the emotion of real heartbreak and write about the pain—the pain that paralyzes you inside from head to toe, where you can't eat, sleep, or use your waking hours to find any happiness in anything you do because of the daze you find yourself walking around in.

Darryl made me realize that the sweeter the love, the worse the pain was. All I could do was count the days as they went by. I knew the only relief I would find would be by moving far, far away. As long as I was living there, I was going to ache to see his face and feel the touch of his hand—a face he no longer wanted to show to me, a smile I could never forget or erase from my mind.

One day, I decided not to torture myself any longer. I'd sit at the playground for hours after hours, hoping to get just one glance of Darryl, but he knew I would be there, and so he never showed up. Each time he never came, I left there feeling emptied of my heart and soul. I would soon just be a blank shell if I didn't get a grip on my life. I started planning other things for the boys and I to do so we wouldn't have to go there at all.

That Easter of 1980, I planned a trip to Atlantic City, New Jersey, during the holiday break. The boys and I really had fun. It helped to take my mind off the heartbreak hotel situation I had grown to know. The boys by now knew how much excitement came along with riding the bus to any destination. They reminded and encouraged me to do it more often. I could see that I was making adventuresome guys out of them. I knew later on in life, that they would never be afraid to venture out on their own and seek the far-away treasures of life.

It was now June, and school was finally out. We had about two weeks to go before July 1st, the famous date of our two biggest moves. First, from California to Philadelphia, and now, from Philadelphia to Michigan. I had already called the moving van and made the proper arrangements to have our furniture transported.

Since the trip was only 12 hours, the boys and I were going to make our journey by bus again. I had been talking with Wanda now almost every weekend. She knew what day we were scheduled to arrive there in Detroit. We were busy making future plans on how we were going to shock everyone with the news of our comeback.

I felt like I pretty much had everything taken care of business-wise and in packing up everything. For the time we had left to spend in Philadelphia, I wanted to use it to say our final goodbyes to some of the very nice people we befriended while residing there.

I didn't plan it this way, but the very last day before we were supposed to leave, I saw Darryl. The boys and I were walking past the playground. As if I heard someone call out my name, I looked over to the crowd watching a basketball match. My gaze seemed to go straight to his. Our eyes met and stayed locked for a short while. He wasn't playing in the match today. I wondered why. He was sitting at the top of the bleachers looking rather lonely. I hadn't seen him in almost 2½ months, but I knew instantly now that I still felt the same. Nothing had changed. And now, all our sweet memories started to crowd my mind again.

I knew I had to fight it and keep on walking. Although by now, the boys were asking "Can we go to the playground just one more time? Please, Mommy, please?"

I didn't know what to do. I had to stop for a while to think. I didn't want it to appear like I was on my way over to start up any kind of conversation with him. So, I said to the boys, "Only for a little while. We can't stay long."

They agreed. Vaughn and Alphonso ran on ahead of Sammie and me and quickly found some of their friends to play with. I looked up to see Darryl watching me very closely now. So purposely, I walked in the opposite direction to the other end of the playground. *That will give him the option to either come over to me to say hello or just leave things exactly as they have been for quite some time now,* I arrogantly thought to myself.

Even though we were a little distance from where he was sitting, I could still see his eyes clearly looking over to where Sammie and I were sitting. I wondered what thoughts were going through his head. Certainly, he knew that I had not been the one to call off our friendship from the start, so I had no reason to attempt a reconciliation now. We practically sat and stared at each other for a good hour. Stubborn, full of pride, and unwilling to break the ice, I guess that's what we both were feeling on the outside.

Truthfully speaking, I would have loved to run to him, wrap my arms around him, and say, "I hope you'll never forget me, sweetheart darling, because I'll always remember the guy I called Fine Mr. Brown."

Soon the kids and I were walking towards the way we came into the playground. I didn't turn around to see if Darryl was still watching until after we had crossed the street. I may be wrong, but it seemed like I saw him put his hand up as if to wave and say, "So long, my love, so long."

The very next day we were on a bus heading for Detroit, Michigan.

CHAPTER 7:

"INKSTER, MY HOME, SWEET HOME"

We pulled into the Continental bus station in downtown Detroit around 5:00 a.m. the following morning. After getting our luggage together, I went to the telephone to call Wanda. We had agreed that I would take a taxi to her house after letting her know we had arrived. The phone rang and rang. I knew it was very early, but she was expecting us, so she should have been awake by now.

I called back again. I let the phone ring and ring. *Maybe she was in the shower*, I thought, growing more impatient all the time. I hung up again and this time slowly, carefully dialed her number. Maybe in my haste, I'd been dialing the wrong number. This time I let the phone ring several more times. Just as I was about to hang up, I heard someone pick up the receiver.

"Wanda! Wanda!" l called. "Is that you?"

"Yeah, it's me, Wan-da" she slurred her words terribly as she spoke. How could she be drunk this early in the morning?

"Wanda, it's me, Gladys. The boys and I have just got into town."

"I know where you are," she came right back at me, angrily.

"Wanda, what's wrong?!" I screamed, becoming more terrified of what the situation was beginning to look like now that we had arrived. "What's wrong?"

"What's wrong?" she echoed my own words back to me. "What's wrong with *you*? Don't ask what's wrong with Wan-da. Ain't nothing wrong with this rich bitch."

Oh my goodness. She was really drunk. I knew for sure now. "Wanda, what about our plans? You promised me and the boys a place to stay when we got here."

Now she *really* performed. She screamed out loud, "Bitch, don't you dare bring your shit to my house! Do you hear me, Miss Gladys? I want you hear me good. Do you hear?"

She sounded so nasty and so mean-hearted that I just hung up the phone. The kids had been watching me all the while. They knew from my hurt facial expressions that something was dreadfully wrong.

"What's wrong, Momma? What's wrong?" They all seemed to be asking at the same time. "What's the matter? We can't stay with Wanda after all?"

I did the first thing that my mind told me to do. I flagged down a taxi and told the driver to take us out to Inkster, Michigan.

"I can give you a flat rate for that distance," the driver kindly notified me. "I'll take it, whatever it is," I quickly said. "Just get me there fast."

I thought about the mean nasty trick Wanda had played on me all during the drive out to Inkster. She had her nerve, playing games like this with me. I've got three kids to shelter. It's no fun thing to get me in the predicament of coming this far and then refusing to house my family. If I hadn't have grown up in this city and knew lots of people, right now my kids and I would be outside on the street. Wanda had gone too far now, for sure. This matter was far too serious for her to be treating it like she was, as though it didn't matter if we had a place to stay or not.

I had the taxi driver let us out over on Liberty Street at Christine's house. What was I going to tell her? She didn't even know that we had planned to come back here and live with Wanda. It was all supposed to be a grand surprise to everyone. Wanda and I had secretly planned over the phone a big welcome home party where we were going to invite everybody we knew. Now all those talks of good times and good cheer had been ruined by her old drunken spirit.

When Chris looked out of her window and saw us

all standing there, she screamed for joy. "Gladys! Gladys and the boys are here!" I could hear her coming down the stairs to let us in. "Isn't this a lovely surprise!" she sighed as she opened the door. "I just had you all on my mind the other day. Come on in and make yourselves at home. You did come to stay this time, didn't you?" She smiled at me as if to say, "Your last vacation just wasn't long enough."

"Chris...," I almost broke down in tears as I was about to tell what had happened. "We were supposed to live with Wanda, but she cursed me out this morning and told me not to bring my shit to her house."

"What?" Chris was appalled to hear how we had even made plans long distance to set up these living arrangements months ago. "Gladys, I wished you had called me from Philadelphia and told me about your plans first before you ever left there. I would have told you then everybody here knows that Wanda is a mental case and not to trust her word on anything. She's been in and out of the mental institutions since you left here way back in 1969. She drinks too heavily from what I hear, while she's supposed to be taking the medication that the doctors are prescribing for her, and it's driving her crazy."

Chris went on to tell me about the rumors going around in Inkster where people had seen Wanda in the daytime wearing make-up that was too heavy and some of our original stage gowns. "She's all dressed up, walking down the street this way. She's afraid that people are going to forget that she was once a singing sensation, it seems to me," Chris explained.

I couldn't believe the things I was hearing. I remember Wanda telling me over the phone that the townspeople were treating her unkindly. Now I knew why after hearing both sides of the story. I told Chris about my plans to reunite the group for another album.

"Well, I wish you lots of luck, because you're going to need it if you plan to do anything with Wanda. She needs a lot of help mentally, and you're not a doctor."

Chris didn't wait for me to ask. She knew we were hung up now for a place to stay, so she offered us refuge in her home for as long as we needed it.

"I don't know how I'm going to repay you for your kindness, Chris, but I'll think of something one day." We both laughed and a party soon began in Inkster.

"Gladys is back. Gladys is back to stay." The newstraveledd faster than tele-express. Everybody joined in for the big party. It was only a couple of days before the 4th of July holiday, and so Inkster was already in gear. Our being there just helped to escalate the excitement and fun already lingering in the air. In the courthouse-structured townhouse community where Christine lived were a group of just newly built places. All of them with almost the same three floorplan designs, which consisted of basements, main floors, and upstairs. Most of them were two and three bedrooms, with very modern kitchens and spacious living rooms. There were patios and green grass surrounding the whole area from front to back yards. This was a family development with lots and lots of children, children who went from one friend's house to another in just a matter of minutes. That's how close everyone was set up in the design of the houses.

The summer programs at the school yard playgrounds were in full effect here also. Every day they gave out free lunches to all the kids who played here. There were group activities of all kinds for the kids to get involved in. My boys were simply just having a continuous ball from one day to the next.

For the first two weeks from sunup to sundown, Christine had me visiting the many different townhouses of her new friends and some of our old friends. It was like having a party every day and every night. Music, food, and drinks, and I do mean *lots* of drinks. Beer, wine, vodka, rum, scotch—you name it and the people of Inkster claim it.

At first, I didn't realize it, but that one little can of beer for me was adding up to a daily drinking habit that I could have easily done without. Alcohol should have never been invented. It has a way of distorting your nice, clean, clear eyes and putting a foul taste and smell on your breath. But for the moment, I didn't care. I was having more fun than the law would allow—laughing, joking, and talking with everyone about my past Motown days, my biggest mistake of getting married, and my future dreams and desires to succeed again. That and whatever else was brought up to be the topic for the day.

"Hooray, hooray, the gang's all here," we sang.

Yes, we were all having the biggest party of the century when Mother Nature suddenly stepped in and put a stop to the whole charade. It was around 6:00 one morning when we were all awakened at Chris's house by something that sounded like a big explosion downstairs.

"What in the hell?" I heard Chris jumping to her feet and out of her bedroom. She flew down the stairs. I wasn't too far from behind her. I thought someone had broken in! The armored guard railing that she had put up on her front door had been blown right off the hinges and away from her house. It was now laying out on the front lawn. The wind was blowing hard, and the sky was a dark yellowish-green. Then it started to rain really hard. Electric power lines were blown down and trees were being uprooted and tossed everywhere. Then there was a large sharp crack of lightning, and all the electricity everywhere went off.

The Detroit area and all the surrounding communities were having the worst storm that Michigan had seen in 20 something odd years. No lights, no television, no music, no nothing—all the power was off everywhere.
No refrigeration for food and no cooking at Chris's house because she had an electric stove. But even for those who cooked with gas, the gas lines were down and needed repairing from all the flooding of the rain. Yes, everything had suddenly come to a standstill and the party was over.

Things were so bad in Inkster until meal lines were

set up at the community center for families to go and get something to eat. From breakfast to dinner, they gave out cooked meals. Community leaders also gave out free candles so people could see in their homes at night. Yes, it was a terrible time, but no one really knew how much damage had been done until after it was all over. Big trees had fallen on some houses and cars. There were cases reported where electric lines that were blown down had electrocuted some people who had walked on them, not knowing what they were or the danger. Someone had to bring up the fact that along with my coming back to town came this monstrous storm. I heard a few of the guys laughing and joking. "Out of nowhere, she came, and we didn't know what had hit us until we found out that she was Hurricane Gladys."

I laughed because it was all said in fun, but I knew now that it was time for us to get back down to serious business if I was going to stay in this town. I had to start paving the way for endurance. Somehow, I had gotten lost and caught in the spirit of the moment, but now I had to get back to basics and do my job as the family planner. Soon the boys and I were going to have to get out on our own and face the music back here in Michigan. I needed to start looking for somewhere to rent an apartment or a house.

Christine's family had been so nice to share one of their bedrooms with us, but the storm had put tension and stress in the air. I knew that things were becoming too crowded now, and we'd best be on our way. Chris's daughter Sherry and her son, Andrew, Jr., had both grown up so big I couldn't help reminding them of when they were only knee-high. Sherry had now already made Chris a grandmother with a baby daughter named Tasha. She was so cute and sweet that I knew I had overdone my share spoiling her during these few weeks of our stay.

Fortunately, finding a nice house for rent was easy there in Inkster. But what wasn't easy for me was finding out what our landlord had up his sleeve.

Here's what I mean.

I saw the ad in the paper: two-bedroom house for rent at $300 a month including all utilities. I arranged to meet Mr. Johnson at the house right away. I had no idea that the house was also totally furnished. I explained to him that I had furniture of my own in storage, just waiting to be moved as soon as I got settled somewhere.

He seemed reluctant about moving his furniture out, saying that there was nowhere else for him to store the furnishings. After agreeing to take the place as is, he promised me that he would make it possible for me to use my own furniture as soon as he could. So, as I said, it was a very easy move-in. All I had to do was get our clothes and move in.

I noticed that Mr. Johnson spent all that next first day changing the locks on the doors and checking for any plumbing repairs in the kitchen and bathroom. I saw that in one of the bedrooms, there was a pile a mile high of

Playboy and *Penthouse* magazines. That's what gave away the secret that some male had previously occupied the house. When I questioned him about it, he quickly acknowledged that he had been living there himself. Then he also provided me with the information that he would be occupying the basement.

"What?!" I almost screamed. "You mean you're going to be living here with us?" The surprise he had sprung on me seemed to give him delight in the total shock it had on me.

"Don't worry," he laughed out loud now. "I'm hardly ever even at home. I do construction work on vacant houses, and many of my jobs are too far to come back and forth every day. I usually camp out in the houses until my work is finished," he explained. "I've got a lot of tools, so I use the basement to keep all of my equipment. Whenever I *am* here, I'll be so quiet until you don't even know it."

So what? I thought to myself. *It's still like having an intruder and a stranger in my house.* It wasn't just because he was a young man who had already offered me something to drink earlier that I didn't trust him completely. It was because of an earlier conversation we had gotten into the same night we moved in. He hadn't connected the stove, so he offered to order pizza for us all that night. After we both had a few beers, we were really now off into some friendly conversation about each other's life's history. He happened to turn the conversation in a way that brought on the mention of people's sexual desires and behaviors.

He started by telling me that he didn't know what it was about himself, but that he had been often approached by just as many men as women. I wondered if he thought I was in any way attracted to him because I was now feeling enough effects from the beer to really be truthful about the matter. I didn't want to hurt his feelings on purpose, but I was getting a .0 on us ever being compatible. Something told me to make sure right away that I left no doubt on his mind what my preference was in the romance column. I explained to him that I was still very much in love with my boyfriend who I had left back in Philadelphia. And to add a definite final touch, I lied, but I summed it all up by announcing that we were getting married as soon as he finished getting his law degree.

"Well, congratulations," he said. "I hope you're making the right choice." His smile didn't seem to be so genuine now, and I could detect that maybe my words had somehow changed his plans or altered his direction in some way. But I just played it off. Soon afterward, he said goodnight and left. He had just come back this morning to finish up his work on the doors and the other repairs needed. So here it is. He just decides to tell me that he is going to be living with us. I wanted to ask him, "Where did you sleep last night?" but I was still speechless.

I suddenly noticed that there was no door that closed off the basement from the kitchen. He must have read my thoughts about not having enough privacy when he said, "There used to be a door there, but I took it down while I was here alone. I've been meaning to put it back long ago, but I haven't yet because I have to replace it with a brand-new door." Then to clear up all my doubts, he said, "I'll make sure all the needed work will be done around here this week before I leave to go up to Pontiac on a job." I could see him smiling underneath, all the while knowing what effect his talk about leaving soon was having on me.

When I told Christine about the living arrangements we had with our landlord, she told me to get a telephone turned on right away in case I had to call for help. We both tried not to jump to any hasty negative ideas too soon, but neither one of us could shake the feeling that something was not quite right about Mr. Johnson.

Just as he had promised, he left after a week of meddling and tinkering around. But I still felt uneasy about what the future would bring with him always in and out of my place. But fortunately, I didn't have to worry about that for long. About the third week we were there, a gas man came to our house and asked me if I was the owner of the property. I told him that I had just moved in as a renter.

"Well, ma'am, how did you get the gas turned on? Our meter reading shows that this property is not registered as far as having connections with the Gas Company."

"What are you talking about?" I asked, unclear as to what this was all supposed to be about.

"Ma'am," he went on to explain, "someone illegally turned your gas meter on. Now I have to turn it off because we are scheduled to start digging here with a land crew tomorrow. There is a big leak on this whole block."

"Oh no!" I screamed. I had been taken in by his ad that read all utilities included. "No wonder I didn't have to pay." The way he had it set up, nobody was paying, and now we had to move out. I thought about the $600.00 I had already given him for the first and last month's rent. He had probably lied about everything, and where he was now, nobody knew. I certainly didn't have time to try to track him down for my money. I had to look for another place to rent.

This time, I went straight to the rental office there in Inkster. I had to be moving somewhere else almost immediately. I got in touch with a Mrs. Harris, and I told her what had just happened to us. She was very sympathetic to my emergency needs. She had a bigger house for rent, with more room than the last house had, but there was no basement. There were two big rooms upstairs that could be used for anything (I thought of a playroom for the boys), plus two bedrooms downstairs, a large kitchen with enough space to put a table because there was no dining room, and a nice medium-sized living room.

I was really in no condition to be choosy, but I was thankful that her rental place was just what I needed. Her rent was also cheaper, but I had to pay my own utilities. But one nice thing about her was that she did not charge me first and last month's rent to get in, and I was glad that her place was unfurnished. Now I could get all of my furniture out of storage. It had been in there since we had arrived from Philly.

I had always opened up a bank account as soon as I could. Now after looking at my balance, I realized that I had been splurging much too much on all the partying and liquor. I had only been in Inkster for about two months now, and already I found out that I was buying at least a quart of beer and wine a day for just myself to drink. Even though it hadn't made me broke yet, I realized that I had to take the proper actions of getting off the booze and getting my career going or else we were going to be penniless.

I saw B.B. at the store one day, one of Wanda's sisters. I told her about the incident and what had happened the day we arrived, and she was really sad to learn about it.

"Wanda probably didn't even remember what happened the next day," B.B. said. "She gets that drunk. Have you talked to her since?"

I told her no, and she suggested that I call Wanda. "She's probably worrying about where you all are."

I wondered could that really be true, with Wanda not even realizing what she had done, so I called her up when I got back home.

The voice that answered the phone was certainly not the same drunken person whom I had spoken to at the bus station. "Wanda, this is Gladys. How are you?"

Wanda perked up right away. "Gladys? Gladys? Where are you? I've been going crazy with worry about you and the boys. Where are you? Where are you?" she repeatedly asked me.

"As if you even care, Wanda," I spoke up now. "Don't you remember what you said to me the morning I called to tell you we were here?"

"You mean you're here, here in Michigan?" she so innocently pretended not to know. "Oh, I thought you were calling long distance from Philadelphia."

"No, Wanda," I explained. "I'm staying out here in Inkster. I had nowhere else to come to after you turned us away, so Chris took us in for a while. Now I have a place of my own."

"Oh, Gladys!" she cried. "I'm so sorry. Really I am. I've been so sick and upset."

I couldn't help but to feel sorry for her and the condition she must be living with every day, and so I told her that she was forgiven. Right away, she started making plans to come out to Inkster to see me. "I'll call my friend Ricky," she said. "He'll bring me out there right away." I gave her my address and just waited for her to arrive.

It was a warm Sunday afternoon in late August, and so the feel of summer was still in the air. I hadn't seen Wanda since our vacation back in August of 1977, so it had been almost three years to date. I heard the car's motor as it pulled over to the curb and parked. I looked out to see Wanda and a very attractive guy with long hair walking towards the house. Naturally, I ran out to meet them.

Wanda had dolled herself all up for the occasion. She had on a long, white dress with a silver sequined hat and long silver lame gloves to match. I must admit that her outfit and make-up were much too extravagant for this typical Sunday daylight scene. But she did make me feel like she thought I was this important enough for her to go through such a glamorous treatment. I welcomed her graciousness and gratitude.

I was not paying any attention to what she was carrying as I gave her a big hug, and I almost knocked her drink on the ground. But this time, instead of her drink being any type of alcohol, it was a big mason jar of tomato juice. But now that I'm writing about it, and from knowing Wanda, it might have been spiked with something. I think they call it a Bloody Mary. Yes, Wanda has always been very clever when she wants to have her own way.

She certainly made a big impression on my boys. As soon as she walked in the house, they all sat down and gave her their undivided attention. Like I said, she was dazzling and sparkling quite a bit for the daylight hours.

Wanda introduced me to Ricky. "This is the guy I've been telling you so much about over the phone," she said. Ricky was very courteous and seemed quite pleased to be meeting me for the first time.

He said, "Gladys, I've been a fan of The Marvelettes since day one, and I've always bought all the Motown groups' records and albums. Plus, I saw you plenty of times on the famous Detroit's Christmas Motor Town Review. Oh, those shows were always a memorable event in everybody's mind. We lived the whole year long just waiting for the next review to come back." Like all the other dedicated fans of Motown and The Marvelettes, Ricky had brought along pictures, albums, and anything he could think of for me to autograph .

Then Wanda suggested, "Why don't we pay Katherine a surprise visit? It would do us all good to be together once more since it has been a long time."

Ricky nearly went out of his mind at the thought of getting all three of us together again. "Where's my camera?" he asked Wanda. "I did bring it, didn't I? In all my haste to get you out here, I never dreamed it would turn out to be such a fantastic day for me!"

With all the partying I had been doing with Christine and her family and friends, I had yet to find the time to get together with the group members until now. I knew I was going to cherish the moment too. Maybe now we could talk about that reunion album I had been working so hard on through my songwriting.

When we got to Katherine's house, at first we thought nobody was there. Although there were two cars in the driveway, no one came to answer the doorbell immediately.

"That's strange," Wanda commented. "Why would they be away without taking either one of the cars?"

Just as we were about to forget about our fun-filled day, Joe, Katherine's husband, opened the door, wiping his eyes as though he had just gotten out of bed. When he saw who it was, he was shocked.

"Both of you at the same time! I can't believe it," he laughed. "Katherine is going to be so mad when she gets back." Joe invited us in with the news that Katherine was to be gone all day. We sat down and talked for a while. I told Joe that I had moved my family back to stay for a while, hoping that maybe the group could get together and do something in the future.

"Well, you all are going to have to talk to Katherine about that. She's so headstrong, you know. But whatever she's always wanted to do, I've always supported her," he said.

Wanda stated that she was in no way in a hurry to get back to Detroit, and so we would probably stop back over later on that same evening. Joe agreed that he'd let Katherine know our plans as soon as she got in, and then we left only to come back later that evening around 9:00.

This time, Katherine was ready to meet and greet us with lots of laughs and hugs and a very cheery disposition. Ricky was constantly clicking away with his camera, making comments all the while to the effect that he alone was the honored fan to see this all happening again. "The Marvelettes, finally all together in one room after 12 years of separation." He looked adoringly at each one of us as he asked us to pose for some pictures.

She took us from room to room, describing what she called her and Joe's interior decorating plan for each room. They had surely done a marvelous job together.

Katherine and Juanita of The Marvelettes both had been lucky enough to still be married to the first man they had married. She and Joe now had four kids and so did Juanita and Larry. I had seen Juanita and her family during my run-around the first week we got here because she lived only a couple of streets over from Christine's house. But Katherine's visit had been delayed until now.

"I was wondering when you were going to get by here," Katherine brought up the subject now. "I heard it through the grapevine that you all were back in town." Then she said, "You know you can't keep nothing a secret here in Inkster."

"That sure is the truth," Wanda quickly agreed, and we all laughed, knowing that she was aware of the unwelcome rumors that had been going around about her.

"I'll tell you what..." I quickly wanted to change the subject now, hoping to start to try and regenerate some positive feelings going on about our future now. "Let's record a reunion album."

Wanda backed up my suggestion immediately, showing that she was all for it. But Katherine shrugged her shoulders as if to say, "I'm not so sure it's the right time for it." I could see that she needed some sales talk about the whole issue, and so I started.

"What have we got to lose but a million dollars if we don't jump for it? Our fans would welcome us back with open arms and open hearts."

"Yeah, but what company is going to get involved to promote such a deal on us?" Katherine asked. "Motown isn't here anymore. I don't know of any company here now that is doing as much or even anything in the way of producing wellknown artists."

I knew she was right, but I wasn't giving up the ship. "If we could just get ourselves together and start to rehearse, we could get enough on tape to even send off to another company, be it Motown or not. We'll need new pictures and new outfits. With a little routine practice, we should be able to stir up some action and start a few shows around the Detroit area, just to generate publicity on the fact that we are making a comeback. If we work hard on some of the new material I've written, I'm sure that there is a sure hit for us in the making."

Then Ricky, hearing and loving every word of our conversation, volunteered to get in touch personally with some club owners he knew that would be glad to get us some work in the different hot night spots happening in and around the city. Katherine still seemed reluctant to join in with our ideas and my great master plans. But thankfully, she was honest and did not lead us on to believe that she would participate in any way.

"You girls are going to have to count me out," she finally said. "It's been a long time since that last show. Joe and I have had to think about making plans that are a little bit more concrete than show business has proven itself to be for us. We want to open up a barbecue restaurant."

She explained to us that a lot of time and thought had already gone into their plans, and that she couldn't see herself giving up on their dreams now. "Besides," she added, "I can't even sing anymore no how. I've had a lot of trouble with my throat for these past years." That made the reason for her denial clearer to me now, for I was just about to suggest that the money made from our album would certainly help out a lot in securing that long dreamed about restaurant they wanted.

It now stood that Wanda and I would have to look for another girl if we wanted to get this thing of ours off the ground on the road and moving. When we later left Katherine's house, Ricky mentioned that he knew a girl who could sing and would fit in perfectly with us. Our talks had spurred Ricky on now, and he was willing to help us to get the ball rolling right away.

"I know the promoter who gives the record conventions in Taylor, Michigan, once or twice a month, and I'm going to try to get you on this very next convention date. But you all are going to have to start rehearsing right away," he warned.

Wanda and I were both all for that. The very next day, she came back out to my house. We started playing all our old records and singing them while trying to remember some of the old routines. It wasn't hard at all reminiscing through our old shows. Ricky made plans to bring Theresa Lockhart, the girl he spoke of replacing Katherine with, to our next get-together.

The convention date had been confirmed. Now Wanda, Theresa, and I were in full swing with rehearsals on the weekends and sometimes through the week. A day or so before the show, Wanda told me that she was going to buy a new wig. I waited on her to come over to the house afterward to show it to me. When she got there, she seemed to be so pleased with the fact that she had found exactly what she had been looking for. When she took the wig out of the bag, I watched as she slowly unrolled it. On and on she went until it looked like she had gone out and scalped Lady Godiva.

"Wanda!" I panicked. "You won't even need a dress on with that wig. It will surely cover your whole body."

Wanda laughed and put it on her head to let me see the new her. *A pint sized Cher,* I thought at first to myself. Nevertheless, it was still not the disaster I thought it would be. In fact, her make-up and costume on the day of the show turned out to be very becoming on her. It was a daytime event, and so we all wore pastel colors to give the effect of freshness and youth and of re-blossoming.

We all had to sign autographs during the first two hours. Later on, we lip synced four or five of our hit recordings, giving Wanda and me both enough songs to take equal leads on, with me ending the show with our first #1 recording of "Please Mr. Postman."

Theresa worked out fine that day. She was a great fill-in for Katherine. She had such a super smile and personality that no one even mentioned she was not an original girl, even though it was obvious to the fans who knew us. Katherine had been much taller and of a brighter skin tone.

Wanda's pleasing personality had not lost any of its magic and charisma. She was still able to stun her audience with her high falsetto lead on "Locking Up My Heart." Even though we were just pantomiming, you could still hear her singing out loud along with the record, gripping her fans with every step and note. It was such a fun day for me and all of us, I'm sure. I noticed that Wanda had not been drinking so much during the week before while we were busy getting ourselves ready, and I was so proud of her.

"You see, Gladys," she told me, "I wouldn't drink so much if I had something like this to do all the time. I'd be so busy until I wouldn't have the time to," she admitted. And so I knew this was the answer to helping her. We had to get more work.

The promoter paid Wanda and I both $500 a piece for our autograph party and show that day, and we then each gave Theresa $100 for her rehearsal time and appearance. Maybe I congratulated Wanda too soon, because the very next week, she called me drunk as a skunk. Her voice was the same as I had heard it that morning of our arrival in town. I now realized that something more had to be done.

This was another person I was talking to. It didn't even *sound* like Wanda at times. Whoever it was could curse like a sailor and use all types of nasty foul language. I hung up on her, and then she called me back and hung up on me. We did this on and off all evening until I couldn't take any more.

I called Ricky, trying to get some understanding of why Wanda went through drunken spells such as the one she was in now. Ricky told me of the many times she had also hurt his feelings and pride with her alcoholic harshness.

"When she gets this way, I just leave her alone. If I don't hear from her in two or three days, I just go over to make sure she's all right. She's gotten so drunk until she's passed out for almost a week."

"What?" I couldn't believe my ears. "A whole week?"

"Yes," Ricky said. Then he went on to explain how Wanda's paranoic behavior had ruined many plans he had made for her, long before I had even moved back here.

"Once or twice, I had set up radio interviews for her. When I went by to get her, Wanda either wouldn't let me in or refused even to go. She'd be drunk and talking about they were all out to get her. Sometimes she'd turn on me and say that I was nothing but the Devil trying to turn her out. Finally, I got tired and gave up trying to help her until you came back. Even now, you have to be careful. Sometimes she gets so bad and starts up so much trouble that she finds herself right back out at the mental hospital."

Ricky's description of all that had been going on previously to my coming back made me hesitant about really seeking the big, big shows for us immediately. I needed some time to see just how serious Wanda was about straightening up her own life. For the time being, I had three little lives of my own that I had to see about getting ready for school.

School was about to start there in Inkster, Michigan, where I had so many fun-filled memories. I was so excited that my own kids would be getting the chance to experience maybe even more joyous times than I had. Although I had attended Lincoln Elementary School, it was Douglas School where I had to enroll them because this was closest to our house.

Now it was the first grade for Alphonso and the fourth grade for Vaughn. Sammie, as usual, had to see a team of experts first to find out what special programs he was eligible for now that we were in another state. Each state, I might add, has done marvelous work in providing the proper care and supervision for these special kids in all of their classrooms. There has never been a lack of transportation or teachers with the skills for teaching these special kids and adults. Seeing this everywhere I go made me realize that there is a worldwide concern for the proper growth, physically and mentally, of these disabled individuals.

During that first school semester, I sort of went to school with my kids. I visited their school to see how many of the old teachers were still around. Inkster High School was the main course on my agenda. Gloria Nobles and Margaret Williams, two of my former classmates, were now teaching there. My oh my, how my old alma mater had grown! Inkster High School had expanded itself and now had a swimming pool and new auditorium, plus many more new built-on compartments. It really was a good feeling going there, the place that had started it all for my singing group.

I think that's when I first got the idea to relive the past steps I had gone through that March of 1961 when we first had the talent show. Speaking to the principal that day, I asked, "What would you say to me doing it all over again, and having a Marvelettes Revue Night, right here at Inkster High on that brand new Inkster High stage?"

"Would you be interested in doing it for us again?" he asked seriously.

"I sure would," I spoke right up. "It's a great opportunity to inspire the youth now who are musically inclined, plus it would put a lot of pride in my pocket just to be able to write about it one day."

"Well, it's all yours." The principal and I agreed on it that day. "I won't even charge you anything for the auditorium. Whatever you make, it's yours."

In no way was I doing it for the money, but I realized that I had to make something to pay whomever my hired help was. For instance, there would be the band, the MC, money on advertisement, the ticket money people, and whoever else helped on that big night. But I didn't rule out the possibility that maybe, just maybe, I'd be able to add something to my bank account if Lady Luck really decided to smile on me just a bit that night.

Plans had to be made, and I do mean *big* plans! I didn't want to pick a date for the affair right away. I needed time to put out flyers for a good audition on getting some of our own hometown talent for the show. And I had to make sure that my own group, The Marvelettes, was ready to make a repeat performance.

Yes, that night had to be no less than perfect. I knew a little about trying to get sponsors for donations for events like this. I knew I had to put on my businesslike voice and get on the telephone to interest the proper businesspeople around town who could back me with some funding or offer their support in any way they could. However, I knew I had a big job before me, but I also knew I could do it if I really tried.

The flyers read:

> *Come one, come all. It's your night to shine along with the stars. The Marvelettes are back for a repeat performance of that leg-*

endary talent show. Now is your chance to show off your stuff and let everyone see what you've got. For a special audition, call Parkway 1-2043 between the hours of 12 noon and 3 p.m., Monday through Friday.

The phone started ringing. Yes, it had all begun again. One of the reasons I think I had come back to Inkster was to give the people here their hope back, their dreams back, and their desires to stay up there at the top of the charts, like The Marvelettes had done so many times in the '60s.

From all the auditions I heard, I realized that if I had the money, I could have started another Motown in this talented city that once was called The Village of Inkster, when we first met Berry Gordy, Jr. Like Motown, it too had grown. It was now full of families who were all talented. One to speak of were The Lumpkins, who, from the father and mother to the youngest child, were all instrumental geniuses. They all played and sang, and gospel was their preference with jazz and modern overtones.

I met dancers, singers, musicians, comedians, and actors. Inkster was a real live show town, with more talent than you could shake a stick at. But there was no outlet for these artists to acknowledge themselves. After Motown Record Company left Detroit, this affected the young people who were waiting to get their chance to be heard. We were role models for them to watch and they had dreams of doing it the same way we had. But now there was nowhere to market all of this talent. And people were left with their God-given talents just sitting in their laps.

What a pity and a shame. It's just not fair. It's not fair at all to have so many dreams and ambitions crushed this way. Most of them, they never even got a chance. No wonder a lot of these people were absorbed in alcohol and nothingness. They felt scorned. So if it did nothing else, I knew a show like mine would raise everybody's spirits again.

I tried to get Wanda involved. Soon afterward, I heard that Wanda was back in the hospital from a nervous breakdown. So, I had to go on. I auditioned some more Inkster girls and called them "The New Marvelettes"—Judy Williams, Tanya Bullard, and Georgette Green. They all had very good voices that balanced out a very good blend, and they all had the good qualities for leading songs as well as backgrounding.

I also found a self-contained band with the name of Research. Together, we started practicing on my portion of the show. I decided that the talent show would be ready to be announced by early spring. That would give me at least seven months to prepare a real good show stopper. In the meantime, I would be polishing up my New Marvelettes act so that I could present a group as good as or maybe even better than I had in the past. The fellows in the band allowed us girls to come on in on their rehearsals every evening to practice hard until we got our show together. I had left a good note in the hearts of all the contestants who auditioned for our revue. I told them that I was not going to pick any acts for the show yet because there was plenty of time. I wanted to register the names and their numbers for the tryouts. Just before the talent show in April, we'd have the big, big, final audition to name the acts for the show.

"You must be good," I said, "if you want to be picked for the show. So please, everyone, go home and keep rehearsing. Only the very best will be chosen in the final test." They all left with stars in their eyes and the will to succeed in their hearts. I knew enough about the people of Inkster to know that when they really set their minds on accomplishing a goal, they worked hard towards it.

I also told them, "I know it's going to be hard to choose only nine or ten acts out of so much talent, but I can't say yes to all of you. It's up to each individual to stand out above the others."

Wow! I had surely gotten the competition going in this town. I even began to get calls from DJs and club owners for me to do some Marvelettes '60s shows at some of the surrounding areas that had Friday through Sunday entertainment. The news spread fast that one of the original Marvelettes had a group together again.

The girls and I had outfits made, and we took pictures with the band. We also did a couple of TV dance shows and videos, and I found myself on the radio again giving some of the DJs a personal interview.

"Well, Gladys," I was asked, "can we expect anything new from you in the days to come?"

"You sure can," I answered them quickly. "I've got a new revue together, and we're doing a lot of The Marvelettes recordings along with a bit of the new stuff."

"Any new record deals in the making?" they asked.

"Not yet." I was still very optimistic, though, announcing that I'm sure looking forward to that also happening.

"Well, Gladys," all the DJs would say, "we're all delighted to hear that you are on the comeback trail. And so, do come back and talk with us again."

I had to be careful now and plan my time very wisely. Even with all of my plans for success and talks about wanting a dynamic second chance to prove that I could do it all over again, my family's well-being and proper provision came first on my agenda. I deeply cared for my boys because they were all the only true and real substance in life I had. Nothing was going to take my eyes off of making sure that their needs were met constantly. In fact, my kids were definitely going to make sure that they got their portion of my attention.

So no matter what else was going on in my life, I had a permanent daily schedule, especially during the school months. From 6:00 a.m. to 8:00 a.m., it was getting the kids up in the morning with the proper dressing, a good breakfast, and then sending them out to school. From 8:00 a.m. to 10:00 a.m., I was making important business calls, setting up appointments for my music life, and sometimes for things that involved my kids' school and home life. These early hours might even find me writing a song or using my tape recorder for singing or adding new ideas in my head for shows or other musical endeavors.

Then mid-morning, somewhere between the hours of 10:00 a.m. and 12:00 noon, I got out of the house to do some outside chores, like grocery shopping, going to the malls, or just dropping in to say hello to a friend. Then it was back home to start preparing dinner for the kids. Usually by 2:00 p.m., that was all completed. From 2:00 p.m. through 4:00 p.m., the kids were arriving home from school. This time was spent listening to their many conversations about who did what at school, what the teacher had to say about that, and a question-and-answer period concerning their homework.

This time was very relaxing to me. I was always glad to see them safely back home and happy about whatever their school days had brought about in their busy lives. We talked to each other a lot during their elementary years, and I think I really learned to enjoy these years the most because I could hug and kiss the boys as much as I wanted to. Now on my schedule, somewhere between 4:30 and 5:00 p.m., the kids had dinner. After washing the dishes and cleaning up the kitchen, I got ready to go to rehearsals, which were only a couple of blocks away from our house. Most evenings, I was back home by 9:00 to get the kids off to bed for a good night's rest before an early rising again the next morning for school.

Although Sammie was the oldest, Vaughn was my big helper. He made sure that whenever I was away that all the doors were locked and that Alphonso and Sammie both behaved themselves. There never was any problem with my boys as far as them fighting one another as they were growing up. I used to call Vaughn my own private professor and detective. He always had a way of getting at the truth of the matter, with many remarks and questions he insisted on having answered. I remember once he came home from school all eager to talk to me about something he had heard.

"Mom!" he anxiously called out to me as soon as he reached the door. I could tell by the sound of his voice that it was something that he couldn't wait to get out in the open.

"What happened?" I asked right away.

"I heard some teachers at school talking in the lunchroom about the group you had while you were in school here in Inkster. They said they thought it was a shame that you girls never finished high school. Is that true Mom?" he questioned me good-heartedly. "Is it true that you never even finished school?"

The look on his face was saying in so many words that he didn't want a thing like that to be true about his Mommy. Believe me, for the first time in my life, I felt the terrible effect of what that really meant to a child that wants to think that their parents are nothing but perfect. I knew that no quick answer could be given about such a matter as this was, and so I had a lot of explaining to do today.

"Vaughn," I started out trying to find the right words to say, "sometimes people make decisions when they're very young that are foolish and wrong. In my case, I had a good reason for why I made a wrong decision. But later on, that wrong decision brought about certain circumstances that outweighed any good reason I might have had."

"What do you mean by that?" My little professor demanded an explanation.

"What I mean, Vaughn, is that I had a one-time chance for instant success, and I grabbed it when it came. I didn't think about all the years ahead of me, or even if I'd still have that same success forever. I just jumped into the skillet, not knowing the fire was so hot. And you'd better believe I ended up getting burned. But at the time, all I could see was being able to make a life for myself, and having money to spend that I made myself, in any way I wanted to. Only then, I didn't realize that I wouldn't be able to buy very much.

"Oh, I made enough to buy pretty clothes, shoes, perfume, wigs, and all the things I needed to do my job in show business. I was able to survive when I wasn't working, paying rent for a small apartment, but it's when you look to purchase the big stuff that your luck usually runs out. Listen, son, nowadays, without a college education, you certainly won't be able to buy the things that really matter in this world, like a house to live in and car to drive around to get you to and from your job. And many other things too, that you can only afford from a steady income. So please, Vaughn, don't do as I did. Stay in school and get your diploma. Quitting school is something that I'm not proud of. And bringing it to my attention today as you have done makes me wish even more that my good reason of being an orphan without a family had not gotten in the way of me making the right decision of staying in school. Now, do you understand?"

He seemed to be satisfied with the answers I had given him. But he said he still didn't understand why I couldn't have done both—stayed in school and sung on records too. I realized instantly what Vaughn was trying to say, and I knew that he was altogether right about his attitude to question another solution. Doing things that way would have benefitted me in a long run. The other way really seemed to only be a superficial solution that only helped the record company to reach its financial stature of greater assets. And me, just as an artist, I had everything to lose while our traveling and appearances gave the company even more recognition and establishment in society. Even now, they still had a big name in the business, while I was struggling, trying to feed and house my family off of what used to be.

"You're right, Vaughn." I agreed with him that he had

the right point of view about the whole situation. "I was really too young to make such a big decision like that all by myself," I told him. "And there was no one around to stop me from doing as I pleased." I sadly had to admit my foolish actions to my young child.

Even Mr. Gordy, Jr. and all the advisory committees he had set up in his organization did not warn us about what 20 years later could do to an uneducated teenager. He wanted us then because we were hot on the charts, making a lot of money. Again, I remembered his promise to us, that if we quit school to go out on the road, that we'd never have to worry about a job. The company would support us with jobs in the later years if we needed it. I saw it all now for what it was really all about from the beginning—Berry Gordy, Jr. was looking out for his own interests; what the later years would do for him financially, with all that money just building up with even more interest in time to come.

Yes, there comes a day when you have to take a look backward. I wondered how many of us were happy with what we saw. Or if that's what life was all about—constantly reviewing your actions and coming to grips and facing all of your mistakes. Was it always like this? With people usually being too far gone, all mentally choked up inside about the past, or too far away from your executioners to do anything about it when you finally realize how bad you've been had and used? I could feel the depression of everything driving itself back into my life again. *Oh, what I wouldn't do,* I cried inside, *just be able to do it all over again the right way.*

The yearning to have it all back again is what I think slowly drives you crazy. Then it's the mental abuse you have to endure with the whole world seemingly watching and waiting to hear about how you're able to cope with the fact that someone else has it all, while you're still trying to get back up on your feet after the rebound and the ones who keep knocking you down. I found myself weighing the pros and cons and do's and don'ts over and over and over and over in my mind. I had to snap out of it.

My remedy for feeling sorry for myself was always relieved by looking at the sweet faces of the children and holding them close to me. I thanked God that we had made it this far this safe, without any of them getting badly hurt or having to go into the hospital for any length of stay. Even Sammie, with his condition, was at least healthy and happy. Alphonso, Vaughn, and Sammie were enough reason to make me realize I had a lot to go on living for. Be it rich or poor, I had their love forevermore.

***

It was getting close to that time of year—the seasons of Thanksgiving and Christmas in Inkster. I remember while growing up here we looked forward to weekends of ice-skating up at the pond in Inkster Park. It had snowed overnight, and my boys were all excited about making a snowman in the field right next door to our house. I was busy putting on their mittens, caps, earmuffs, and boots. I certainly did not want the job of playing nurse this winter. Most people who lived here expected a few colds during the winter months, but the flu was nobody's favorite thing to catch.

I watched on and off that snowy Saturday from the kitchen window at what progress my kids were making with Mr. Snowman. In the final stages of his completeness, I had to marvel at how tall and big they had made him.

Alphonso knocked on the kitchen door, gleaming with joy all over his face as he said, "Now we need an old hat and some buttons for his eyes. I think we'll use a red and orange crayon for his mouth and nose."

After helping Alphonso to gather up all of these items, I watched as they brought to life a snowman that looked like he could have been on any Christmas card.

"That was a fantastic job," I told the boys as we now all watched Mr. Snowman together from inside. It had started to snow again, and it was getting dark outside. The streetlights had come on, throwing a stream of light right on the path of the snowman. It was a sight to behold. He was the biggest snowman I had ever seen any kids make. He was at least six feet tall. Vaughn said they had to stand up on the old picnic table in the yard to put him altogether. Mr. Snowman had on a knitted hat that sat off to the side of his big, round head. His eyes were black and for some reason, seemed to be twinkling from the light on the snow. He had a big orange crayon for his nose, and his mouth was filled in with a red crayon. The kids had even draped something around his shoulders that made out to be a coat. And by his left side, propped up against his arm, was an old broom.

Green buttons were coming down his front section made from some of their old Play-doh. And last but not least, they had placed two old shoes right down front at the bottom of the first big snowball that made Mr. Snowman look just like he had feet.

I wished I had a camera on hand to seal in that particular event and moment in our lives. It's like admiring a masterpiece of work after all the labor has been done and reaping the joyous feeling of its final perfection. I couldn't believe that the boys had done such an excellent job of building their first snowman, and might I add their last one, too. That winter, it didn't stop snowing until the snow was high enough to cover up Mr. Snowman. We're talking six feet or more of snow is what we got!

For the first time in my life, I knew what it felt like to be snowed in. We couldn't even go to the supermarket for a couple of days. Even after the salt trucks had plowed the streets open, there was still a maze to get through from the house to the curb. That was too much snow for me, especially after living in California for 10 years. During our stay in Philadelphia, it had snowed plenty of times, but the heat of the big, crowded city would melt the snow away sometimes overnight. But Michigan had fields and land between the houses in most areas, which gave the snow a resting place to harbor itself and linger on around. And that's *exactly* what it did here.

Sometimes it took months for just one day of snow to melt. If it snowed again before all the previous snow was gone, it just paved the way for the snow to last even longer. During most of the winter here in Inkster, you saw nothing but a picture of covered whiteness all over the land. Sometimes Mother Nature really got nasty, and it would decide to rain on top of the snow. It became cold, hard, slippery ice, with cars unwillingly sliding into each other. At these times, I was glad that I still didn't have a car or any other type of transportation while living in this winter madness.

But the good thing about all of this cold was that another season had to follow it. And the coming of spring is one of the sweetest delicacies of living in an area where the climate has four seasons. You learn to appreciate the warm, kind, gentle side of Mother Nature, right on into the hot spell of the summer and later the autumn leaves with the gold, yellow, red, and brown touch that they put all over the lawns.

Yes, the boys and I were enjoying it all together. These were memories that would last a lifetime with us, and there was nothing and still isn't anything I can compare with my kids' youth-filled days and the joy I felt just being with them.

The music for me never really stopped, not even during the dead cold of the winter months. It's just that business here in Michigan slows down a bit until the flowers start blooming again. Detroit has always been a party town, and so finding a party job to play here is easy. I found out you won't get rich quick from the pay. But it will keep some money in your pockets and keep you out of the unemployment line if you can maintain a good reputation of having a great show everywhere you go. That's why I continued to rehearse my girls as much as possible.

There was no way I was going to fall down on my job, even if they do say in show business "to break a leg." The time for the New Marvelettes Revue was getting closer. My band called Research and my girls were ready. We had worked together so much now until our show had been perfected and polished and was nothing less than what the pros would call a fantastic sensation. We got compliments everywhere we played, and I must admit that the whole organization, the boys and the girls, so richly deserved every comment of satisfaction they received.

I wanted to introduce my kids in our Revue in some unique way, and so I decided to start up a group of young kids including my boys and called them The Friend Kids. Getting the kids together was easy. They were relatives, sisters or brothers or cousins, and some of their own family members of my very own organization. It was 12 kids in all, seven boys and five girls. Now I had to come up with some great material to work with them on. I wrote a song especially for them called "Let's Be Friends." The second song came on a day when I heard Vaughn humming a certain melody.

"What's the name of that song?" I asked him.

"I don't know," he answered. "I just made it up."

I was so gratified to think that maybe my music traits were coming out in him now. So, I took the melody he was humming and put some words to it. We decided to call it "We Are Ready." The words went:

> *Ready, ready, we are ready.*
>
> *Ready, ready to dance to the music. Ready, ready, we are ready.*
>
> *Ready, ready to sing to the music. We are ready to go forward.*
>
> *Singing, dancing, playing to the music,*
>
> *Ready, ready, we are ready.*
>
> *Ready, ready to dance to the music. Ready, ready...*

The song I got from Vaughn's intuition turned out

even better than the previous one I had already written. It was a slower, universal type song whereas "We Are Ready" had a good beat for dancing, and as you all know, kids love to dance.

With my song, I wanted to get a message across with the words to "Let's Be Friends," so I wrote these lyrics:

Come on everybody! There's no time to waste.

We've got to make this world a better place.

So let's be friends right now. Let's be friends starting today.

Come on everybody. Let's not make the same mistake.

We're going to stand for love and never hate.

So let's be friends right now. Let's be friends starting today.

We're talking to the kids in China. We're talking to the kids in Africa.

We're talking to the kids in every place.

So hurry up, there's no time to waste.

Yes, let's be friends right now. Let's be friends starting today.

Let's be friends all of the way. Let's be friends, what do you say.

I took great pride in having my kids to participate in this event with me. I don't think anyone felt the depths of what I was trying to do at first, but maybe in later years, the meaning will be respected and understood clearly.
I wanted to prove that I could actually make time repeat itself in some manner as it had when I first stepped on stage for that historic talent show that later led to the beginning of my career, with the second time around, bringing with me three of my very own offspring.

The other kid's parents and I came up with the idea to buy the kids some silk jackets for the affair. The Friend Kids were going to look and sound great! I couldn't wait to give them their start in show business, even if it only turned out to be for just one night. It would be the night of all times for us all. I was making history.

First, I had a meeting with the school principal to confirm a date for our Revue. Later, I met with some of the students in the Art Department there who volunteered their help in making a big banner that went clean across the auditorium stage that read "Welcome Home Marvelettes Revue."

Now, the next thing I had to do was to arrange an individual private screening audition to pick the talent for the show. This way, nobody's feelings would be hurt for all to see or acknowledge if they weren't chosen. I made it clear to the ones that I didn't choose that every year a show like this would take place. If they missed out on this one, there was still another one to come next year. "So keep the faith everybody," I said. "Keep the faith, because you're all gonna make it one day."

I finally had all the flyers made up for the show. I decided to write the show invitation in the form of a letter. The New Marvelettes helped me to deliver flyers all around to the different schools there in Inkster and close-by residents of Taylor township, Romulus, Dearborn, and the Westland communities.

After talking to my hairdresser, the famous LaToya Pierson of Detroit about my Revue, I found out that she had an act using two big life-size puppets. She volunteered to go on-stage with The Friend Kids to spice up their portion of the show. I knew that having an adult on stage with the kids would give them the boost and confidence they all needed, this being their very first appearance on any stage. It worked out perfectly. I was already now give them all something to talk about for generations to come.

I had finally done it, placed my footprints in the Inkster sands of time, so to speak. No one could ever say I came back to Inkster and didn't try to bring out the best that I knew was still in them all.

There were more shows waiting for me to get involved in during my four-year stay in Inkster. The next big one came during the Christmas of 1981. This was the first big Motor Town Revue to hit Detroit again since Motown Records had moved to another state. It was being held at the Madison Theater. The headlining acts were The Marvelettes, Mary Wells, Martha Reeves & The Vandellas,

Marv Johnson, The Falcons, Sweet James & The Fantastic Four, The Valadiers, and The Contours! Wow! What a list of stars!

It was sure good to be together again after so many years had gone by. We still had it and knew it. The public would never forget our music of the '60s. Other changes had begun to happen now. Some for the best and some came just along with the rest. But I had begun to learn to accept the unexpected.

One of those unexpected changes was meeting Mr. Wright, and ladies, the spelling of that is not "R-I-G-H-T", like in being the right one, but "W-R-I-G-H-T", like the Wright Brothers. And believe it, he took me on a flying trip. For a while, I didn't know where I was going to land. But instead of using an airplane, he swept me off my feet into his Grand Prix Marquis.

At first, I saw him and his car as a means of getting me off of the street from walking everywhere I went. I was now being chauffeured, the way most people like to think that entertainers are supposed to be. It showed some prestige. Later, after experiencing the real nitty-gritty, I sat searching for the reason why I stayed with him for as long as I did, living under the pressures and changes I had to go through.

Because of the devastating nature of this time in my story, this portion of my book is dedicated to the millions of single female mothers who are constantly being told that your kids need the strength of a man in their lives to grow up with the right mental attitude in facing the barriers they may come upon their grown-up years. This may be true, but ladies, beware and be careful in who you are putting over them as a father figure. Any type of male image, be it an uncle, a cousin, an older brother, or someone else blood-related, makes a considerable amount of impact on your child's mind. Kids watch and remember adult actions.

For some strange reason, a male's action seems to have more impact on their minds than the females do. Maybe that's the reason they have always behaved faster for the father than the mother. Nevertheless, these actions are stored in their memory track, and actually become a part of their psychological make-up. It may take years, but one day you will see your children repeating some of the same things they saw their role models implicating to them as a child.

Whether the male was some kin of theirs or not, it doesn't matter. We are not talking about a "blood being thicker than water" situation here. We are talking about kids mimicking others and copying situations they have seen or experienced while growing up. And sometimes these things can be silently passed on to them without anyone saying or doing anything to the child. Remember, they are always watching.

For instance, say you have a boyfriend living with you that sleeps with you every night, gets up and eats the different meals you prepare for you and your family, and goes off to work every day. Although he is nice to the kids, he never likes to go anywhere with you and the kids together, like out on a family picnic or to the show or places where you all can enjoy and have fun. Say even though he does have a good job, he never helps out financially in the home, or never spends any money on the children. What mental message is he giving to your children without saying anything out loud?

These are the things that your children hear the loudest.

There are numerous situations that can send out negative vibes to children and do hurt their character in a long run. It doesn't always have to be a situation where the male is beating the mother up physically. He can be beating her even worse mentally. In most cases where the mother *does* remain with whoever it is, this gives out a worse message to kids. A lot of times there is nowhere to run to immediately, or fast enough for the results to not affect the child. You might as well say the damage is done as soon as they come into your kid's life.

So, I say from experience that most mothers would do less harm to their children growing up by remaining alone until they are able to see their own way because even getting the right man poses a bigger problem if he really is not the man you think he is. Maybe you see you don't allow any man to live with you, but you have a man you date occasionally. This sounds fine, but remember this action is also giving your small children a message. And more times than none, it is often a negative one. They worry while you're gone. They often imagine what may or may not be happening to you. They just may feel like being with you is not enough to keep you happy, and that's why you have to seek enjoyment out of the home. All of this only mentally sets up inadequacies of their own.

I realized that there have been rare cases where a single mother finds the proper and decent situation in which to raise her family. I respect, admire, and congratulate her. But all I'm saying is ladies, don't be in a hurry to surround yourself with another male, just because the father moved out, or because you need help with the bills, and your closest friends are telling you that you've been alone too long, or that you're going to end up all by yourself.

All I can say for myself is that I *knew* better. I had vowed, if you remember earlier in my story, that after Alphonso's daddy, I would never go through another common-law situation again. Even though this affair did not start off that way, I found myself starring in a brand-new episode with another younger guy driving a nice car with a lot of fast talk and charm for getting things his way, and a great thirst for that good old bottle of beer. Put all of those things together and it spells Keith, Keith Wright.

It all started from me needing a ride downtown to a special event. My designated driver had called me an hour before we were supposed to leave with the bad news that they couldn't get the car started. After calling around to a couple of other people who weren't able to help, I decided to look outside just to see if by fate someone was in the neighborhood who could help me. This was an event I simply just couldn't miss. I would have asked the milkman to take me if he had been passing by. I saw Kenny, a guy who often visited my next-door neighbor, standing outside. We had never been introduced properly, nor had I even found a reason to converse with him until this very day. I decided to go over and introduce myself so that I could pop the question after explaining to him what had happened.

"Hi. My name is Gladys," I said as I held my hand out in a friendly gesture. "And I already know your name is Kenny. I've heard your friends here calling you that." I could see that he was eyeing me with suspicion now and didn't trust my motives for suddenly introducing myself.

Suddenly, another car drove up, exactly the same make, model, and year as Kenny's maroon Marquis, only it was black with red trim. The guy driving got up and came right to us, smiling and laughing.

He said to Kenny, "Yo, bro! What's up?"

Kenny introduced me to him, "Gladys, this is my twin brother Keith."

I would have never guessed in a million years that they were twins. Kenny was short and Keith was tall. They were similar in facial features, but they did not look exactly alike. Keith was also a shade darker than Kenny.

"I'm so glad to meet you, Gladys." Keith was full of

mischief. I could tell by the twinkle in his eye that he was the livelier one of the two, the one who was shy in no way or meaning of the word. Keith had a way of stepping right and mastering the moment at hand, regardless of what was happening before he arrived.

"How about taking a spin with me?" he asked, smiling as if he knew I was ready to go somewhere, and how right he.

"That would be fine with me," I quickly agreed. "Only there's somewhere special I need to go." I started to explain to him how my ride was detained earlier, and how important my need was to attend this special event. In doing so, I had to tell him who I was.

"One of The Marvelettes?!" He was shocked to hear it. But he said, "I've been hearing about some of the things you've been doing around town. But because I work all the time, I haven't been able to attend any of your shows."

I continued on to tell him how Kim Weston, one of Motown's great female artists, had reached me through all the publicity from the appearances my band and new group of girls were getting, and asked me to be a judge at her yearly festival for the performing arts.

"A judge? Oh, you *do* have a special engagement, don't you?" he said.

"Yes, I do. And if you're going to drive me there, we need to be leaving right away. It's today."

"We?" He caught on right away that there was more

to me than what he could see.

"Yes. I've got three boys that are going along with me." I was hoping secretly that if he had any other ideas for later that the news of this would change his mind right away. But after meeting my boys, he seemed to really want their satisfaction of him. The boys were really impressed with Keith, his fun-loving attitude, and his black shiny looking car. It looked like he had been polishing it for days. There was not a handprint anywhere on it, and he enjoyed showing it off as his pride and joy.

I wasn't so much as impressed as I was happy that he had volunteered to get me to the event on time. That was the most important thing to me at the moment because I had never been asked to sit on a panel of judges for anything before, and I didn't want to miss this first and maybe last time opportunity. It made me feel important. I got the dress that I was going to wear and the kids and I got into the car and left.

All that Detroit talent was still around, and Kim Weston was doing a marvelous job in bringing it into focus and the public's awareness. It was all about the summer program she headed, dedicated to keeping the teens off the streets with something constructive to do. They had classes going on every day focusing on the arts of entertainment—singing, dancing, drama, modeling, and photography. It was an excellent program for everyone involved, with all the children actually learning to do the things they love to do best. And the great thing about it was that each student received a weekly salary like getting on a job. It was encouraging and inspiring to see what a big difference some of the government-funded programs made in the big cities.

After the Arts Festival was over, before Keith brought the boys and me back to Inkster, he drove us along the shores of the Detroit River, around through an ever-popular place, Bell Owl Park. He turned his music up loud and showed us a lovely moonlit night. He stopped and parked his car right there at the riverfront.

"Look!" the boys all shouted and pointed to a big, fun-filled passenger ferry boat making its way up the river. They were playing music aboard, and you could hear the cheerful laughter coming from the passengers.

"That's the Bobola Boat coming from Canada," I told the boys. "We used to take summer trip there all the time while I was going to school."

Keith saw that the idea of a boat ride was fascinating to the kids and promised them that one day, he'd get tickets and take us all. That right away made me realize that in no way did he expect this to be our last time together. The boys were now asking him about other places he knew of that they might want to visit. The zoo, the beach, and amusement parks were now all put on his agenda for the boys and me.

It all sounded so exciting, especially having someone with the means of transportation to carry us all to these different places. I must admit that until now, the boys and I just never thought of any recreational outings outside what the school or some of the churches offered families in the community. Something told me not to get my hopes up too high until I saw it all happening, but for now, I just laughed and coached the boys on. I didn't want to be a killjoy or put a disappointing sour note on their expectations.

Thus, the beginning of a new relationship had evolved. I wasn't in love, so I wouldn't be blinded by this affair. I didn't care how long it lasted, so it put me in the driver's seat right from the beginning. Keith was not what some females would call handsome, but he had charisma, charm, and a big, wide, powerful smile. He let me know right from the get-go that all of his earnings went into making his car his showcase. I didn't mind at first because I didn't need his money. I had my own, but I did expect to be taken wherever I needed to go if he was going to ask me for favors that involved sexual activity. What was I supposed to? Still be walking around town while he was gallantly riding by himself? I found out early in the relationship things that weren't exactly to my caliber of standards.

For instance, every two weeks, he got his paycheck, somewhere around the figure of $600-$700. After he had bought new things for the car or did what he called necessary repairs on it, he would either drink or eat the rest of it up. He would buy barbecue dinners, hot links, pork chops, chicken, beer, wine, vodka, or whatever else he could find to splurge his money on until every last penny was gone. Then he'd go broke until the next paycheck. I just couldn't understand a mentality such as this.

"Why don't you save some money?" I asked him.

"For what? I'm going to get another check on payday."

It was as though he thought there would never be a rainy day in his life. But there were plenty of those to come. First of all, I found out that his mother and sister lived right down the street from us. That's how I met him that day, right outside our house. I was becoming confused now as to where Keith really lived. He was only over to his mother's house on frequent visits and at mine whenever he wanted to get romantic. But where was he sleeping at night?

I noticed that during those first months of our relationship, he had to run off somewhere fast as soon as our nighttime fun was over. When I questioned him about it, he told me that he had an apartment in downtown Detroit. This is where I believed he was running off to until a female neighbor on the street approached me one day and spilled the beans.

"I see Keith is over to your house a lot lately," she laughed. "Are you two dating?

I really didn't know what to call it at the time. I knew I was not desperately in love with anyone, but I needed the convenience that Keith being around could give me with my active schedule and all. I started to explain that he was slowly growing on me when she advised me to beware of the fact that he was living common-law with another woman.

"What?!" I screamed. "You mean he is bed-slicking another woman and me at the same time?"

"Yeah, honey" she said. "He's out of your bed into hers and then out of hers and into yours." She went on with more information, telling me that she's been knowing Keith and his other lady friend for as long as she had been living on the street. "They've been going together for years," she informed me. "I'm surprised you haven't seen her over to Keith's mother's house before."

"Maybe I have," I told her, "but I didn't pay it attention, not knowing what to look for."

"She drives that brown Oldsmobile you see passing by here every so often, and her name is Glenda. They have a nice little home somewhere not too far from here across Michigan Avenue." She went on telling me the facts.

I can't say that I was deeply hurt inside or even in a jealous rage over the news. Up to now, Keith had given me no real reason to want to fall head over heels in love with someone of his nature. He had gotten me back to drinking more beer than I knew I should be. Plus, he was always asking me to support his habits in between his paychecks.

Truthfully speaking, I was tired of him by now. I rebelled against just lending him money, as he called it, because every cent I made was needed for taking care of my family. I loved them as much as he loved spending his money on his car. I was now even smoking cigarettes again, something I hadn't done since the last days of my travels with The Marvelettes. His bad habits were certainly rubbing off on me, a person known to have a strong will and constitution. I didn't know what had come over me, but it wasn't worth losing my pride and honorable lifestyle. I compromised myself, only trying to hold on to the convenience of a ride, especially after hearing what some people were saying about me around Inkster.

A good school friend of mine informed me that people were joking about how fast I could walk. They would see me walking at one end of town, and before they could drive to the other end, I was already there. The shame of it all was based on the fact that I had done something with my life and made a name for myself, traveling the world over. And most of my friends still living in Inkster were driving brand new cars, or at least had some kind of way to get around besides on foot. Now the spotlight was directly on me, and I had a reputation of a star, someone to be cherished and admired. And it broke people's hearts and tore down their dreams of me to see me trying to survive this way.

Keith, I think, was aware that I didn't want to go back to my days of a world without wheels. That's why he got away with most of his bad habits with me. His attitude now about me being a Marvelette was not encouraging either. Slowly but surely, I was beginning to learn more about the black man's ego than I wanted to. It's a pain for them to have a mate who is well-loved and popular, even if you don't have a dime. They'd rather for you to be rich than to be loved by anybody else. The power of a celebrity female is too much for them to bear, especially when they find that one monkey doesn't and can't stop your show.

I think what really got to him was that no matter how unimportant he tried to make me feel, I kept on stepping by booking engagements for our group all the time. He still refused to support my shows. He often made members of my group feel uncomfortable with his suspicious glances at them during our rehearsals or whenever he'd come back to pick me up after they were over.

One of my girls in the group mentioned to me on several occasions that he outrightly showed everyone that he was jealous of what we were trying to accomplish. At least once a week, I had to reassure him that none of the guys in the band were interested in me in that way. He appeared to be crazy about my boys, but we hadn't heard anything else about those trips he was supposed to take us all on. In fact, it was getting to the point where an argument arose every time I asked him to take me to do family chores, like to the laundromat or shopping for groceries. I should have been glad that now with this news, I had a good reason to shut my door in his face the next time he appeared. But it never happened that way.

I was confronting him with all the things I had found out about his private life. "You dirty sneak," I called him.

"How dare you two-time me?"

He just laughed and grabbed me and kissed me as though I hadn't said a word. "I love it when you get mad. Your eyes flash green."

"I'm not going to let you continue on with this nonsense," I warned him. "Glenda is going to find out, I promise you!"

He lied and said that he had already told her, but I knew it wasn't true. Why is it that men feel in control when they think that they have brought out the jealous streak in you? After he had gone, I decided to put a stop to his game. I only wished that I could get Glenda's telephone number when suddenly the answer came to me.

I ran and searched for an old telephone bill and looked for the number that was on the bill the most. I knew that would be the phone from where Keith had been calling me all the time. I dialed the number and a female voice answered.

"Glenda?" I asked. "Is your name Glenda?"

"Yes, it is," she said, "and who's calling?"

"This is Gladys Horton. You don't know me—"

"Excuse me, but I *do* know of you. And I have heard the gossip going on about you and Keith."

"Well, what have you heard?" I politely asked, trying to let her know that I did not want to challenge her or fight over Mr. Wright. I just wanted to clear up the fact that I never knew he was even attached to another woman, and that he intentionally never told me about her.

"Gladys," she said in a nice quiet firm voice, "it doesn't really matter what I heard. I am so sick of Keith and his foolishness until I'm glad he found somebody else, and I told him so."

"What did he say?"

"Then he told me that you and him were just friends and that he was not having sex with you. Because you don't have a car, he just comes over all the time to take you and the boys to different places so that you didn't have to walk around town, with you being a famous entertainer and all. Is that true?"

I could hear in her voice that she was hoping that he had not lied to her. Being a female myself, I understood how it can be with a man who's driving you up the wall constantly. You hate him for it, and you wish he would leave. That is until you find out that he is seeing somebody new. You know he's no good for you, and that you should just let him go. He's doing nothing but slowly killing all of your feelings about love and how it should be. *That's* what really hurts. The fact that he's now finding some kind of happiness and joy somewhere else confuses your true feelings, and makes you want to say, "Oh no, you're not going to be happy after you've ruined *my* life." So you keep holding on, secretly hoping that in doing so, he'll forget about what's giving him a new thrill in life, and stay on with you in your misery.

Sometimes situations like this even make the woman begin to fight for her no-good man. Not always fight physically, but mentally. She'll start wearing her hair differently, or shape up her figure now while paying more attention to her make-up and clothes. Sure, it happens. A little jealousy has sometimes made a new woman out of the wife. But I think in Keith's situation after knowing him, it would only anger him to see Glenda looking better. As I talked on with her, I began to realize that Keith knew he had her attention now, and he was going to keep it at any costs.

"Just tell me the whole truth," she asked again, taking my silence as an answer of "no."

"Glenda, Keith does nothing else but ask for sex," I informed her. "I can't understand why he would say we never have unless he really doesn't want to lose you."

I could hear a little tear in her throat as she responded by saying, "I actually believed him, because I figured a big star like you would only want him as a driver. He sure ain't no fancy face to look at and being a factory worker puts him in another class from you, so foolishly I believed him. I believed that big liar!" Then she started pouring the sorrowful times she had spent with him.

"Glenda, please," I said. "If you think he's treating me like a princess, forget it." I explained to her how he had helped me since I had met him, giving me rides to rehearsals, shopping, and other places I needed to go. But now even those rides weren't easy to get. I had to beg him and sometimes argue before I could go. By the end of our conversation, we had struck up a female understanding about the makings of Mr. Wright. Just from talking to Glenda, I knew she was a sweet person. Although she still cared for Keith, she gave me the impression that she didn't mind me continuing to see him if it meant having a way to get around on wheels to take care of my business.

We even made plans for her to come over and show me her Avon collection. "I sell Avon products," she told me, "and there's a sale going on now."

I met Glenda personally, and even though the mark of Keith kept us from feeling like bosom buddies, I knew that we didn't really dislike each other, deep down inside. Keith really got upset when he found out that Glenda and I had befriended one another. To hurt her, he moved out of their house and down the street from me into his mother's house. He knew that Glenda would realize that now he was even closer to me, and could see me more often. He was willing to do anything to keep her interested in him now.

I got the strange feeling that he was the one jealous now, jealous over the fact that Glenda was getting to me and conversing with a well-known entertainer like me. It was like two kids arguing, with him saying to her, "She's *my* friend. I saw her first, and you can't be friends with her."

Those indications alone made me know that they

were just like old married people who had gotten too used to one another. I even told Keith one day, "Keith, Glenda loves you, and you love her." He only denied that Glenda loved him. He never said that he didn't love her.

He only explained to me that, "Glenda acted like I wasn't even alive until she heard about you. And now that you woke her up to the fact that maybe somebody else does want me..."

Then I completed his story by saying, "You're afraid to show her your true feelings, thinking that she'll forget about you again."

"Gladys, don't you understand? She only wants me to leave you, so I won't have anybody. She still doesn't want me!"

"Well, have you tried to *make* her want you?" I asked. "It's hard to want someone who continues to act negatively on most matters."

He began to accuse me of trying push him aside, and now the bickering of who was using who had started up amongst us again. One thing was sure about being with Keith—you were going to argue every day about *something*. It was becoming tiresome to me.

"I've got to sing!" I screamed out at him. "How can I when you keep me hoarse from arguing all the time?" That kind of wear and tear on the throat was a threat to a singer. But now I couldn't get rid of him. He was around me most of the time that he wasn't working.

One night, around 1:00 a.m., early in the wee hours, we heard a loud hissing noise outside. Keith had not moved in with me, but he had fallen asleep while watching TV. He jumped up and ran for the door as if knew exactly what had happened.

"Glenda!" he screamed. "Glenda! The bitch done cut all of my tires."

I ran to the door to see Glenda in her car driving slowly down the street as if to say to Keith, "Catch me if you can." Keith was hysterical, and his eyes were like that of a wild madman. Sure enough, he started in pursuit of trying to run after her car.

It was a sight to see because she let him get as close to her car door as he could and then she'd drive off fast, only to come to another slow pace. He again started in pursuit of her. Each time he would get close enough to almost strike out at her vehicle, she'd take off again. Keith was so mad until I knew if she kept that game up, it could have given him a heart attack. But even I couldn't stop myself from laughing. She had really shown him what damage a woman's fury can do. No, Glenda was through playing. She left a note on his car that read:

This is for each time I catch your car in her driveway.

If you think Keith did not heed the warning, forget it! From then on, whenever he parked there, he was always by the window, sitting where he could watch his car. He never went to sleep with his car in my driveway again.

I called Glenda up a few days later, and we both had a big laugh about it. She told me that Keith had embarrassed her in front of another guy he had seen her out with recently.

"He's got his nerve not wanting me to have any fun. That's why I cut a little bit of his off." And she sure did. She hit him where it hurt the most, in the pocketbook. He had to buy four brand new tires.

***

One day after school, Alphonso walked home by himself. Usually, Vaughn and he came in together. As soon as he reached the door, he told me that Vaughn was coming; he just had to go by a friend's house first.

I couldn't imagine what could have made Vaughn alter his usual route home. I always told the boys to come straight home from school. Afterward, they could visit a friend or two if their homework was finished and I didn't have to go out. I wasn't a strict taskmaster of a mother, but my kids knew the rules and always obeyed my wishes. I was a little worried now until I heard Vaughn come in. I was in the kitchen, and he came straight to where I was. He was hiding something under his coat with a big, big smile on his face. Before I could ask what was going on, he slowly drew the item from beneath his coat and said, "Please, Mom, can we keep him? Please?"

He had brought home a baby puppy. He couldn't have been no older than a week or two. He was so cute and cuddly! I just couldn't resist saying "yes."

"Thank you, thank you," he said.

The kids all jumped up and down with joy. There was no way I was going to turn this little lonely looking character away. For some reason, I loved that puppy instantly. I wasn't too sure that I could even afford a pet now after meeting Keith. He had done more than just drain me of my energy to sing. He had put a big dent in my savings, and I was now back on a tight, tight budget. The kind where you knew where every penny had to go.

He had even begun to charge me for gas now because he had recently been laid off from the car factory. Remember I warned him about that rainy day? Keith's paycheck had been cut in half, and he was now only getting changed. In fact, they had only increased.

"I'll pay you back. I'll pay you back," he would beg and plead. Now that I was back under the influence of drinking and smoking again, he'd just come over all the time early, waiting for me to go and buy that first beer of the day. I had to start buying two at once now because he would casually help himself to most of the first one. And for some reason, we both smoked the same brand of cigarettes, so that was a solved problem for him also.

The lowdown dirty truth of the matter was that drinking and smoking can slowly rob you blind . If you spend only $10 a day on these vices, that's $300 a month, and sometimes more. And at an average of $3,600 a year, how does that sound for losers? Something I was fast becoming around Keith.

So now I had made up my mind to take on another mouth to feed, and I was too much in love to fight it, especially after looking into those "say you'll keep me" loving puppy eyes. Vaughn and Alphonso and Sammie were so happy and excited.

Vaughn said, "I thought you were going to say 'no.' All the way home with the puppy, I was wishing and hoping that you'd say 'yes.'"

I didn't know why myself, but I knew right away that I wanted to keep the puppy. The kids let me name him, so I called him "Sparky," because of his cute brown shiny eyes. He was black with a brown chest and brown paws. I wasn't sure of what breed he was at first, but we knew there was some German Shepherd somewhere in the mix. Later on, as he began to grow, we found out that he was a Doberman and Shepherd mix. He was a very beautiful and smart dog; one of the best guard dogs you can find.

Sparky changed all of our lives. I remember those first days we spent together after the kids had gone off to school. I felt like I had a brand-new baby in the home. He followed me everywhere. Sometimes he'd cry if he saw me leaving out to go to the store or the bank or wherever

I had to go, so I started taking him with me.

Once I was in the bank where everyone can read the big sign on the door that said "No Dogs Allowed," and guess what? Sparky was so small that he was sitting right down at the bottom of my big purse. I did that only once or twice, because he started growing so fast until soon, he was too big to fit anywhere but at home with us. I had special things for Sparky, and believe me, a dog knows when he is getting the royal treatment, and he adores it. I spoiled him rotten, just like you would do a little kid. I carried him around on a dark green velvet cushion while he was still small enough for me to hold in my arms.

The boys also did their share of raising Sparky and training him as best as they could. They played with him outdoors, teaching him to chase them until he caught them. Vaughn taught Sparky how to guard the house and my purse whenever he saw it, but I didn't have anything to worry about. I noticed that the larger Sparky got, the less company we had coming by. Like all puppies, his bark was bigger and louder than his bite. By the time Sparky was about nine months old, he looked like a sleek and slim black panther, because he moved so graciously and swift. I had treated his black coat with a small amount of oil daily, making him a beautiful sight to behold. Yes, we had added a new member to our family, and it was one that we were very proud of, and loved very much.

I had been looking for the mailman, so when the papers came in the mail, I wasn't a bit surprised. I just read them over carefully and put them away. They were from the courthouse. For the very first time in my lifetime, I was being evicted for non-payment of my rent. I was only one month behind, but the landlord wasn't hearing any excuses. Now that I had all of my rent saved up and was ready to pay it, I had decided to go ahead and move out with the money. We really needed a new place.

Sparky had taken his toll on almost every inch of the carpet. And although I had washed up spot after spot, the house had doggie odor. I bought carpet deodorizer and washed the corners down good with pure Pine-Sol, but Sparky's power was just a little bit stronger than any store-bought stuff. So, if we wanted to breathe fresh air inside our house again, we had to get into a new place.

My search had started again. Soon the boys, the dog, and I were on the move once more. This time we also had another follower: Keith himself.

"It would be just a like a brand-new start for us" he vowed. "I'll even help out with the rent as best as I can." He still had not returned to work. But even just with his unemployment benefits, he was collecting enough to do more than just keep up his showcase of a car.

Even if I had said no, he would have been over every day anyway. What was I going to do? I hated to admit it, but he was slowly growing on me. I found that I really need him around. I couldn't leave my ride behind, now, could I? Not only that, but I had also grown accustomed to his face, and like all silly females, we're always hoping for some big change of character in the guy that usually never happens.

Keith got along well with the boys and the dog. I never once saw him lift a hand to one of them or talk to them in any abrupt type of manner. I wasn't altogether against letting him in for that reason. It's just that for some weird reason, I felt obligated. Well, the real truth was about to unfold. I didn't know what it would be like shacking up with Keith. Before now, he had never moved in completely. And believe me, even if a man is at your doorstep 24 hours a day, and you think you know all of his little ways and attitudes, I got news for you! That guy you thought you knew is up and gone somewhere and a total stranger is the one who moves in with you.

Our new place was across Inkster Road, where the neighborhood used to be all white when I was a little girl growing up. Even now, we had white neighbors on one side of us. On the other side lived a girlfriend of Christine's named Lynnette. It was because of their friendship that I got to rent the house. She knew Mr. Ferguson. the landlord, very well and had talked him into renting me the place. Again, the fact that I was one of Inkster's Marvelettes played an important role in the deciding factor here. I just about had the place before I even met and talked with the owner because of my reputation and name here in town.

The house was nice and roomy, and like the other one, had a big room upstairs. It was even built somewhat on the same structure as the last house, only it was newer. Now, all we had to do was try harder in training Sparky.

We had to make him somehow realize that he was not a human being and not supposed to use the bathroom in the house. Sometimes the kids would walk him for nearly an hour and he would still wait until he got back into the house before he let my rug have it. I just couldn't beat him. I couldn't. He'd look so sad when I'd scold him until I'd soon apologize and take him back out in the backyard, trying to explain to him where he was supposed to potty. I knew that if I would just be patient a little while longer that my tolerance would pay off. But it was just taking so long for Sparky to get the message.

And so it was with Keith also. He just didn't understand that I was not used to staying in bed all day.

"Just because you don't have a job or anything else to do now doesn't mean that I have to lie around all day with you," I told him.

"I'm your man," he argued, "and all you do is think about your show, your fans, your outfits. Can't you give me some of your time?"

Then we'd start arguing about why we didn't make love last night. The truth being that drinking beer and wine mixed will definitely put anybody to sleep fast. To get back at me, sometimes he would wait until he knew I was ready to go somewhere important and he'd leave, saying that he would be right back. I'd end up having to walk or not go at all if it was too far away.

I tried hard not to argue in front of the kids, but he had a way of bringing the beast out of me, and I couldn't control my anger for long. I'd put him out and he'd come back late at night, calling my name out loud for all the neighbors to hear, saying, "Gladys, Gladys. Please let me in. Please. I'm sorry."

Just to shut him up and keep the neighbors from calling the police, I'd let him back in. Our living together was beginning to seem like a ridiculous setup for both of us. Something had to be done. I met a girl one day through an old musician friend of mine named Lance Finney. I told him that I had always wanted to find an all-girls band to work with. He gave me the telephone number of a girl he knew that played bass, and that's how I started working on a brand-new show.

I hadn't fired my other employees, so to speak, but we hadn't been getting along as well as we were when we had first started. And I knew that a change of characters would help boost my morale back up in the showplace. Tasha, the girl on bass, seemed to know some other girl musicians, so she took it upon herself to start a three-piece unit, consisting of bass, keyboards, and a guitarist. After they rehearsed some of The Marvelettes' material, we all got together so I could see what it sounded like. I was very impressed because these girls could really play. Girl musicians were really coming out of the closet now. They were forgetting their fears of being ridiculed by the guys who felt intimidated having to face a girl who really knew her stuff.

Tasha was a born leader. It was obvious by the confidence she executed on her bass. There was no half-stepping when she wanted to perfect a song. I also admired all the girls because they looked very feminine, even when playing their instruments. That was very important to me in the overall look of the group. I didn't want people coming to see me with a bunch of girls on stage that looked like men.

"Well, what do you think?" Tasha asked, knowing all the while that they had blown my mind that day at rehearsal.

"What do I think?" I said. "I think we should start looking for some shows to do right away."

To give the group some pumped-up inspiration, Tasha suggested that we all go over to a small club near southwest Detroit called Axle's, and catch Detroit's famous girl saxophone player, Billie Jean.

"She has other girls in her band that play also, and they have a dynamic show," Tasha informed us. I had never even heard about the chick before that night. After seeing Billie Jean's show, I realized why she had been packing the place seven nights a week for over a year already. She was super, she was great, and she was unforgettable. That was *exactly* what we needed to see.

Tasha had accomplished her mission of getting us ready. That night at Axle's, we met a show producer named Sears. Of course, he already knew Tasha. She invited him over to our table for a few drinks. After finding out who I was and our plans, he offered us a weekly rehearsal spot and promised us our first gig as soon as we were ready.

We decided to have a mixed group similar to Billie Jean's presentation, so we got two guys to join the group, one on drums and the other on lead guitar. So now, our unit consisted of five musicians and myself. Everybody was such a pro, and it wasn't long before Sears had announced that he wanted to start us off at a club called the Pyramid.

About a week before we were supposed to perform at the club, Keith and I had the biggest fight we had ever had. There had been other small rumbles every now and then, but this time he decided to mess my face up, knowing about my current show. Here it comes again, that favorite old landmark on my face: a big black eye.

Our show promoter was furious when I called him crying, telling him what had happened.

"I'll kill him! I'll kill him!" Sears screamed. "Where is he? I've spent big bucks renting the club and making the necessary arrangements and now this?"

"I can still do the show. But I'm going to probably have to use so much make-up to camouflage my eye until I am really going to look like an Egyptian mummy at this Pyramid."

It was nothing to laugh about, but Sears had to admit that I sure knew how to tell a good joke, regardless of how serious the matter was. The swelling had gone down some, but I'll never know how I got through that engagement. The whole side of my face was still sore. Every time I moved my mouth, I felt pain. Can you imagine how I felt trying to smile through every song?

I saw pity in the eyes of the girl musicians. "What kind of guy would do that to an important singer like you? He can't really have your best interest at heart. He must be a maniac." They all voiced their opinions.

I knew this was going to be the first and last gig for the girls and me and Sears. "I just can't take another chance," Sears sadly said to me as he was paying me for the show. "You sound great, but if you had been feeling better, you would have had a more professional-looking show. I think the band members feel the same way. When you get it together on the home front, maybe we can work something out."

But how long was *that* going to take? I certainly had no idea myself. I had hooked up with a madman who had begun to make threats of what he would do if I even said I didn't love him anymore. Of course, I knew clearly what had again taken place. My ghost lover was back. Now he had taken control of Keith's mind and body. He now possessed the same characteristics as all the kid's fathers had once had: extreme jealousy, beating me, and making terrifying threats.

How could I have been so stupid as to let this spirit get close enough to me again? For a while, I had forgotten how terrifying he could make my life. Now it was all coming back to me. Some kind of way this time, I had to outsmart him.

I began to look at Keith now as just a puppet. I realized that he and all the others were controlled by something or someone greater than themselves. Whoever this spirit was, it wanted me with him, and I was determined not to go. I knew if I angered him, he would cause whatever guy I was with to do me great bodily harm. So I played it cool while secretly planning another getaway for my children and me. I knew it wouldn't be easy, and I knew it would take some time. I needed God's strength to be strong and to keep holding on.

Keith was just like a giant ape. No matter what happened between us, he felt that we had been through enough for this long that we should always want to stay together. But I was so serious about my impending departure from him. I was anxious to be loosed from the hold he had on me. The first step toward my freedom was to cut out all the drinking and smoking. There would be absolutely no liquor, no cigarettes, and no marijuana! Without me buying, I wondered how long he would want to be around me?

I was determined to save every cent I could now. I'd have our transportation fare out of Inkster in a year's time or more. I couldn't breathe a word to anyone about my plans. No one could be privy to what I was up to.

"Come on, let's buy a beer," Keith said to me the next day.

"I don't drink no more," I told him.

"What? You can drink more than me."

"Not anymore," I swore.

"How come?"

"Because our drinking is ruining my life, my business, and I am losing my contacts. Nobody will want to hire me soon if the word gets around that you and I fight all the time. Remember how I looked because of our fighting on my last engagement?"

He just shrugged it off, thinking that I was just talking and still angry about that incident. But after a week or two went by with me sticking to my guns, he got worried. He had to try to find some kind of way to get me back where I was before.

He came in one night with the sad news that he had spent the rent. My blood pressure jumped sky-high.

"You what?!"

"Yeah, I was trying to double it at a gambling party and lost it all." I noticed that he had two 40 ounces of beer with him.

"I'm sorry, baby," he said. "Come on and have a beer."

I looked at him and realized now why he had done what he did.

"Not on your life, sucker!" I screamed. "You just want me to be an alcoholic forever. You're mad because I'm beginning to keep a clear mind all the time."

After I fussed for about an hour, he told me he was only kidding. "I just wanted to find out if you really had lost the urge to drink. Well, you've proved it to me. Now I believe you."

He slowly headed for the door and turned around and said, "Surely you don't expect for me to drink alone?" He was smiling now. "So now I have to hang out with guys to have a good time," he teased.

"Go ahead," I said. "I need my privacy anyway. I'm going to start writing songs again."

I got in touch with Sylvia Moy through Teddy Harris, a favorite musician friend from the old Motown days. He was raving about the beautiful studio Sylvia had there in Detroit. "You ought to give her a call," he said. "She could probably assist you in getting some of your songs on wax."

I didn't hesitate to call. I remembered Sylvia Moy and all the great songwriting she had done with and on Stevie Wonder's *My Cherie Amour*. It was one of her all-time greatest hits, and it had become what was expected from her. Sylvia had written many more songs, giving her the label of a genius female composer.

Masterpiece Studios, she told me, was the name of her business. And after hearing that, I was now trying my hand at songwriting. She was very interested in hearing some of them. So, we set up an appointment, and I was on my way.

Never will I forget the help Sylvia rendered to me right from the very beginning. Sylvia realized what had happened to many artists from Motown and tried to encourage me in any way she could. Most of my songs were not professionally recorded. It was only me singing accompanied by a guitar player from Inkster named Benny Lang strumming out the chords. Luckily, Sylvia had an ear for listening to the lyrics and the story of a song. She knew what could be done with maybe just a little bit of melody and a good punch line.

"Gladys, I think you've got something here," she smiled, "and I'm not afraid to take a chance with you."

Because she took this chance, I went on to become even a better songwriter, and she was the one who gave me my first try at producing. I worked with Sylvia as much as I could. The longer and more frequently I worked with her, the more confident I became in my songwriting ability.

As you may recall, I already had so much written material from way back in my earlier days of writing poems and lyrics in Philadelphia. But I didn't have the money it took to see some of these songs materialize in the form of recorded music. Believe me, there is no more incredible thrill for a novice songwriter than to hear that first song being done up with horns and strings and all the instrumentation that working with a professional producer can provide. I was lucky enough to have had Sylvia Moy do the production work on my first songs. I listened to her. I saw how she built the instrumentation around what I had already done. Then, I heard the final mix! It was a masterpiece of my own invention. A song that I couldn't believe I had written. She made me so proud of myself!

I had never been a big bragger before about anything until this very moment. I played my songs for all my close friends to hear—The New Marvelettes, my band Research, the girl musicians I'd met, my boys, and all of their friends and families. They all just flipped behind how great my work had turned out.

Sylvia reminded me that my excitement was a normal reaction for all first-time composers. As time went on and I wrote more songs, I felt some were better than those first ones. I began to relax. I remembered that every writer feels like every song they write will be loved or at least liked by others as much as you, the composer likes it. So I had to learn to be prepared for and accept criticism and continue with a strong positive attitude. I had to grow a thick skin and take it all in stride.

Sylvia was right. I still have so many songs now that I just knew would be #1 all across the nation, and they're still sitting in my tape file. Every year, I try to update some of them, giving them new modern beats or changing a few lyrics here or there to keep up with the times. My sincere desire is to have some of the contemporary artists of the '90s record some of those tunes Sylvia helped me with: "There's A Brand New Station Coming On The Air" and "Come Fly With Me." It wouldn't be fair to not share such genius work with the world.

Speaking about moving on, in June of 1984, the boys and I finally left Inkster. Since we first arrived in 1980, can you believe we moved around and lived in six different houses? Some of my closest girlfriends from my school days were beginning to tease me about acting just like a gypsy. I had become infamous for not staying in one place too long. My close friends, whom I confided in a lot, would always come to my rescue whenever I needed a favor. My foster cousin, Christine, who was closer to me than even a sister could be, was always there to help in any way she could.

I had a host of friends who made coming home a pleasure for my boys and me. But just like in any other soap opera or, for that matter, life, there are some moments that you wish you could erase. One such memory that comes to mind is our class reunion of 20 years. Unfortunately, someone on the planning committee got jealous and turned down the offer to have my group and me perform at the reunion's dance. So what could have been more proper and fitting than for me to be able to sing for my classmates? I hadn't even planned it that way to be there right at that time; however, fate saw it fitting for me to be right there. I'll never stop feeling like that cancerous emotion called jealousy cheated my friends out of their proper due. But even with the regrettable times, life goes on.

Sparky had just gotten all of his necessary shots to fly with us on the airplane. That's right! I wasn't leaving our dog behind to grieve our absence. He was coming to California with us. I felt proud of my progress in the last couple of years. I had fought the alcohol and cigarettes and built my savings back up. As soon as I had saved the money for the airline tickets, I bought them immediately and made reservations as early as way back in April. I wanted to ensure that nothing got in the way of my departure.

Sometimes I had to hide money from Keith. That's how bad things had gotten between us before we left. Once or twice I even feared for my life. I did not know what to expect from him once he realized I wasn't playing his game anymore. That last month in Inkster was like waiting for a time bomb to explode. I even had to have police security around my house to make sure he didn't break in and try to attack me. I saw Glenda before we left, and she wished me the best. I'm hoping that maybe today, she has gotten Keith back to being the man she wanted him to be.

As to what my kids had to say about it all, that day we were about to board the plane, Vaughn said, "Mommy, promise us one thing."

"What's that?" I asked.

"That when we get to California, you won't try to find a "That when we get to California, you won't try to find another boyfriend." I knew they had seen and been through enough. The date was June 30, 1984, and I've been celibate ever since, by my own choice. nother boyfriend." I knew they had seen and been through enough. The date was June 30, 1984, and I've been celibate ever since, by my own choice.

CHAPTER 8:

"MOVING ON—CALIFORNIA, HERE WE COME"

Several months before we were scheduled to leave Inkster, I got in touch with Alphonso's grandparents. Mrs. Morris answered the phone when I called. The whole family had not heard from us since 1975 when Alvin and I separated. She couldn't believe her ears when she heard my voice on the other end of the telephone.

"Thank God you've finally called us," she said. "I have spent many a day worrying about how my grandson was coming along. How old is he now?"

"He's the perfect age of 10," I answered. "He's right here. You can talk to him."

Alphonso was a big boy now but was still quite shy as he spoke to his grandmother. Mrs. Morris was even happier to hear the news that I would be returning with the kids to California very soon. I was sorry to hear that Al was back in jail. He had been doing just fine working as a youth counselor for the city, dressing conservatively and carrying a briefcase to work every day. I was so proud of his accomplishment. The sad part was he violated his parole by forgetting to report in one time, and they wrote him up and sent him back in to do some more time. It was heartbreaking to hear about how strict our justice system can be on some, especially those that need a chance to make their lives worth living again. "Oh, but he'll be so glad to hear that I've talked to you and his son now. I'm sure he'll want to write to you himself."

It wasn't long afterward that I received a letter in the mail. It was from Al asking me to forgive him and to marry him. Oh, how sweet his letters sounded to me during this period of my life. A period when there was no sexual intimacy and none in the foreseeable future. I didn't believe he was the same Al I knew 11 years ago.

I even wrote back and said that I would marry him, especially after reading some heartwarming scriptures he quoted me out of the Bible. I felt like he must have been a brand new person inside spiritually.

For some ungodly reason, I had forgotten all about those dark, terrible days of me wanting to commit suicide if that was what it took to free me from our life together back then. Now here I was, ready to run to his arms again, even if it meant marrying him in jail. Was I this hungry for love, or had these days in Inkster taken its toll on my mind, causing me to take leave of all of my common sense? Whatever it was kept me under its spell long enough to see us all safely out of the snake pit I had fallen into.

We were about an hour away from landing at LAX. Mrs. Morris and her youngest son and daughter, Steve and Penny, Alphonso's aunt and uncle, were all waiting there at the airport for our arrival. Alphonso was meeting his relatives for the first time since he was very young. We made plans to stay with the Morrises until I could find us a place of our own.

Boy, it sure felt good to be back on California soil. The 1984 Olympics were being held in Los Angeles, and the whole city was getting ready for all the participants and tourists that would surely be here soon. The 4th of July was right around the corner; we were just in time for a month or more of The Olympic games to be celebrated in the city.

Until I visited Al, I hadn't realized how all the beer-drinking back in Inkster helped me pack on unwanted pounds. He noticed it right away but refused to comment on it until we had a conversation on the phone the following week. Then he hit me with the truth.

"Girl, you sure were showing that big behind of yours in that summery outfit you had on the day you came up here to see me." His words made me feel like a big fat cow. I tried to defend myself by denying that I hadn't even noticed any change in my shape, but I had. I was now carrying 10 extra pounds or more around with me. I tried camouflaging it all by buying clothes that were a size and a half too big, but I couldn't fool Al when it came to hiding the meat. I knew him well enough to know that Al didn't like any fat on his girls anywhere.

Just to feed my curiosity, I asked Mrs. Morris, "Do you think that I've gotten fat?" I knew she would tell me the truth.

"No, Gladys," she answered. "You're not what some people would call fat, but you were a little more petite in size the way I remember you being the last time I saw you."

I told her that I thought maybe Al was having second thoughts now about marrying me after seeing that I had gained some weight. She just laughed, saying that it sure wouldn't be a big enough reason for him to feel that way. Still, I knew better. I'd better get in shape and get my weight back down for more than just one reason. These California girls certainly believed in staying fit and trim, and nothing was wrong with that. It's good for your overall appearance, attitude, and most of all, it's good for you mentally to feel good about yourself.

Well, California, here we are, back to where we started. I had to reestablish myself and pick up where I left off. Getting Sammie signed up for whatever government benefits and programs in whatever area we lived was the first assignment I completed whenever we moved. This time the regional centers were recommended to me. Like always, before I could even feel comfortable working on any projects, I had to ensure Sammie's educational and physical needs were provided for. Then, in the fall semester, when school started, he'd be ready to be placed in any district's schools without delays. I had become an old pro at the business of caring for a child with a disability. I knew how to avoid the many pitfalls that could arise. Having a disabled child does not have to be the burden everyone imagines. As the parent, you have to provide stability and be consistent. Always put the little things they cherish the most at the top of your list. Attending school daily or workshops was the most significant part of Sammie's life, just as it was for millions of others with disabilities.

It was mid-July, and I felt really good about the appointment I had made to see someone in the publisher's and writer's department at Motown Records. I had given it some long thought-out attention and had decided that songwriting would be a new avenue to venture down in the music business for me. It would be a career where I could still sing to keep my vocal cords in shape and demonstrate my ability to deliver a message musically. But most of all, it would be one where I would start earning a living of which I could be proud and make a name for myself in this field.

I packed up the two songs I had done in the studio professionally with Sylvia Moy and a few others that I had only on a rehearsal tape. I also took along a book full of newly written material that had yet to be recorded but had strong lyrics and good punch lines. I thought I was ready to make a presentation to become one of the company's future songwriters.

Everything started fine. I caught the bus to Hollywood and got off at Hollywood and Vine. I was about an hour and a half early, so I wanted to visit the Motown business offices at this corner first. My meeting was scheduled to take place at the company's recording studios located on Romaine near Santa Monica Boulevard. However, I wasn't sure of my way there, so I intended to find out from somebody here.

I was standing at the light waiting to cross the street when I heard my name being called. I looked around to see her smiling face right in front of me, standing at the corner where I was about to cross over. Of all people, it had to be Cindy Birdsong. Cindy Birdsong had once been a member of Patti LaBelle's Bluebelles and later took Florence Ballard's place with The Supremes.

"How long has it been?" We both acknowledged our years of not seeing one another. "Do you know," I told her, "that you are the first person in show business that I've met since I've returned here to California?"

"Well, you're in luck," she informed me, "because Betty Kelly of Martha Reeves and The Vandellas works right in that bank in front of us, so she'll be number 2."

"What?" I was shocked. Two entertainers in one day!

"Come on, let's visit her."

I asked Cindy to accompany me, but she informed me that she was on her lunch break and had to take full advantage. "I'm working as a secretary at the Motown office building. So come up and visit me soon. That job helps to keep me up with the better times in this town." I didn't know what she meant then, but I would soon find out.

Meeting Betty in the bank that day was a big shock for both of us. She was not just a mere bank teller; she was now a bank assistant who had her own desk. In addition to satisfying the needs of long-time customers who were seeking new ways of making their money grow, Betty took care of the more challenging aspects of banking.

We talked and talked about old times and good times. She caught me up on all the happenings in Hollywood and the Los Angeles area and even talked me into opening up a bank account. Then, before I had to rush out for my interview, she invited me to come along to the Legendary Ladies show being held that same weekend at the airport Sheraton. On the bill were Mary Wells, Martha Reeves, Shirley Alston of The Shirelles, and Arlene Smith of The Chantels. What a host of legendary ladies it was going to be!

"I'll call you later on for more information about the show," I promised Betty. But now, I was off to my own engagement of seeking a job for myself.

Raynoma Gordy Singleton and Don Johnson were the next two familiar Motown faces I saw. "Ray," I said, "look at you! You haven't changed a bit. How on earth have you been able to keep that same size 5 figure?"

"It's all in the mind, my dear girl!" Ray laughed; she

was the same sweet, humble, intelligent person I had known her to be from the '60s.

Don wished me luck with my songs. He told me the most essential trait needed in this business would be perseverance and confidence to survive and have longevity.

I took his advice in stride, but I can't say that I received much inspiration from that interview that first day. "There's a million hit songs being recorded every day all over the country. So what makes you feel like yours will be the ones from the chosen few to be listened to?"

Now *there* was a question I couldn't answer. Then I heard, "Do you know how many tapes we listen to in one day around here?" I was told, "If I had a dime for every songwriter that knocked on my door, I'd be rich."

The number of people seeking to do the same kind of work I wanted was overwhelming. The thought of it alone began to overpower my thoughts and depress me. My will to succeed began to diminish. After leaving that interview, I felt like the whole world had suddenly fallen on me. It would be so hard and so long before I could get up again. I wanted overnight success just like I had in the '60s, but it wasn't coming that easy for me this time. This whole city had so many people standing in line waiting to be in the business; I felt like a tiny dot in the crowd. Being recognized instantly was becoming a dream. To be brought out in front of a big crowd was something that you just had to wait for, and maybe that took forever.

I knew worrying about how I would make it here now would only cause me to have the biggest headache of my life. I decided to give my brain a rest and concentrate on meeting some more of my favorite friends at the Legendary Ladies show. Maybe I'd meet someone to help me there. It was too late to change my mind or my plans. I had to jump in there and ride the bumps and bruises that were trying to thrive in this city and business.

The next day, Betty Kelly advised me to call Mary Wells. "Maybe she can get you on that same show. You certainly are a legendary lady yourself." Mary Wells did her best to get me my first job almost immediately after arriving in town, but it failed. The show's producer was thrilled to hear about my presence here, but the contracts were already signed. Too many important details had already been finalized. There was just no way of adding another person to the bill.

"But Mary," he said, "please ask Gladys if she will make a guest appearance on stage during those nights because there will be many important people there. It will be a great opportunity for her to announce that she's back in town."

Yes, I was back, and I definitely needed a way to shout it out loud to the mountaintops if I wanted a job here doing anything. It was no big thing to anyone here just how much you had contributed to the world of music or in the field of entertainment. Unfortunately, people here seemed to forget too quickly or just refuse to remember anything or anyone for too long unless they were deceased. Californians were hot on whatever was going on at the moment. Everyone was looking for the next big thing in California, the next crowd pleaser!

"Of course, I'll make a public appearance on the Legendary Ladies Show," I assured Mary and thanked her for her efforts. I already knew the road here in California would not be easy to navigate. The one feeling I think I was looking for now is the feeling of security: knowing where you're going to be living, how you're going to be eating, and where you're going to be working. It is so gratifying for the soul's peace. These things in life ensure one of at least a good night's sleep.

The night of the show came, and I wanted to look my very best, so I adorned myself in copper lame from head to toe. There was no way I wasn't going to be extra-appealing in my hopes to catch the eye of the onlookers. I had worked with Martha Reeves and Mary Wells while I was doing shows back in Michigan, but it had been nearly 17 years since I had seen or heard from Shirley Alston of The Shirelles. So now, I had my first opportunity ever to meet any of The Chantels. The introduction of Arlene Smith was a welcomed one that night. The Chantels had been one of the earliest cherished sounds around in my teen years. Yes, a real inspiration to all girls trying to sing during that time.

I sat in amazement as I listened to her sing their big record, "He's Gone." She sounded just like she did on record. She was fantastic on and off stage.

Shirley Alston had not lost a thing either. She was still sparkling onstage with the sound that sold millions of The Shirelles's records. After not seeing one another for many years, our meeting again was so gratifying and fulfilling. It did wonders for my somewhat low self-esteem as I was unsure of where my place was and if I belonged.

"It's been different for all of us," said Shirley. She sadly told me about the three groups of The Shirelles of which she, Beverly, and Doris were all now leaders. "The business is just not as dedicated to the cause of why we are still doing it," Shirley explained. "Instead of all of the entertainers sticking together more now, everyone is looking out for #1: themselves. You can't blame them, though," she went on to say. "It's a big struggle now to survive in this field with the cost of living rising as fast as it is."

Shirley and I caught up on what had been happening on the home front and what we both were looking for in the future. Seeing her again was an absolute delight. One thing was for sure. We were still sisters from the '60s.

When Mary Wells announced that she had a surprise for the audience and invited me to join her on stage, I was stunned by the welcoming applause I received. People actually stood and cheered my appearance! She then asked me to accompany her in an ad-lib on the song "Shout." We had never even rehearsed or talked about doing anything more than just taking a bow. Still, I was flattered at the opportunity now to show off my vocal cords.

"You know you make me wanna shout! Shout! Shout! Shout"

Back and forth she led me in a duo chant of the ever-popular Isley Brothers recording. Mary Wells was such a pro you couldn't help but feel any other way while being on the same stage with her.

Martha Reeves starred that night and woke everybody up to the fact that there is only one Martha! The electricity went off on the bass amplifier without warning, and she had to improvise for about 30 minutes on stage. But, wouldn't you just know it—Martha came through with flying colors! She started telling jokes and talking about secret matters that brought the house down in laughter. It's at times like this when a true entertainer has to prove to the audience that it's not just the singing that makes them a star. They can reach out and touch people's hearts and minds even with their words. Then, of course, when the trouble was all cleared up, Martha gave an excellent performance, just like she always does. But Martha Reeves has the magic and natural charisma like no one I've ever known at Motown, and I've always enjoyed just being in her company.

That opening night also put me in touch with others I hadn't seen for so long. There were Motown faces like Harvey Fuqua of The Moonglows; Hal Davis, who first came to Motown with Brenda Holloway as her producer; Mary Wilson of The Supremes; Bobby Sanders of Greater Entertainment Enterprises; several disc jockeys from KRLA who were big sponsors of the show; and a host of other Legendary Ladies' fan club members and its president Manuel Esparza.

"Just call me 'Spooky,'" he announced while introducing us. That is how all the fan club members know him. It was definitely spooky because of the impact he had when first meeting. Spooky immediately offered me the chance to be on the cover of the next edition of his newsletter. His newsletter reached fans all other the world. "The fans have been writing me for years now, Gladys, asking if I had heard anything about the whereabouts or what The Marvelettes are doing these days. So, I've just got to interview with you as soon as possible." I agreed, and for the rest of the evening, I took loads and loads of pictures for his newsletter.

Another terrific fan I met was David Haury. David later supplied me with all the missing Marvelette tapes and pictures I had lost through my many moves around the country. "Gladys," he said, "I'm sure you're going to need a lot of that old material pretty soon if you're going to re-establish yourself and your place in music history as one of the all-time greats. People like to know that you've still got plenty of the original stuff around, still sitting in your cabinets and files and up on your walls."

Just from hearing him talk, I knew that his place looked like a museum. David was a well-known journalist and photographer for a West Hollywood magazine publication, but he offered to play chauffeur for me as much as possible when he had some free time.

Yes, the night was full of meeting and greeting new friends, faces, and fans.

Lee Griffith, Martha Reeves's bodyguard during the show, offered to assist my group and me in any way necessary during future appearances. Later on, when I got my show together, I used him as the postman during our comedy acts and nearby tours. Lee loved to dance onstage, and he was so fat and jolly until I recognized him right away as the twisting postman.

My coming to and being seen at the Legendary Ladies showcase really proved beneficial to my career. I heard that several of the DJs in the audience mentioned the next day on their shows that I was back in California looking good and could still stir the crowd up with my voice. "She hasn't changed a bit," one of the announcers at KRLA raved over the airwaves.

Spooky, the fan club president, called me early the very next day. I wasn't even surprised when he informed me that he had not even been home or been to bed yet. "Gladys, I just had to find out a couple of things from you immediately on who's behind this phony business of all of these fake Marvelettes working all over the place."

How the news had escaped me until now, I'll never know. "What fake Marvelettes?" I asked.

"You mean you don't know about all the girl impostors that are doing shows and calling themselves The Marvelettes?" he asked.

"No, I don't," I answered, "and I'm afraid I'm going to have to find out more about the situation before I can give you a statement on the matter."

Spooky went on, prying for more juicy gossip. "Gladys, do you know a lot of the fans were upset with the fact that The Marvelettes didn't make an appearance on the 25th Anniversary show of Motown. Can you tell me something about that and why?"

"Well, the truth is I was also baffled that I didn't even get an invitation to just sit in the audience. I've always felt that Motown had no reason not to respect the fact that it was our group that gave them their first certified #1. So it was disrespectful for them to not even offer us a chance to make a guest appearance, even if they didn't want us on the show to perform."

"Well, why not?" Spooky continued with his questions. "Weren't you doing shows at the time in Detroit?"

"I sure was, and I'm sure they could have gotten in touch with me, even just to find out if I would be available. But I heard nothing from anyone responsible for getting the acts together for that televised event."

"Were you hurt behind this action?" Spooky was asking very serious questions now.

I had to laugh. Thinking back to when it was all happening, I remembered that I didn't even know anything about it until after it was all over. I couldn't feel hurt. I think neglected was a better word for it. I explained to

Spooky that after the anniversary show was televised, I received some very negative critiques. But the fact that Wanda was not well may be one of the reasons that Motown felt as though the group was not prepared to make a contribution to the program.

"So you don't think that Motown's actions were deliberately motivated against you?" Spooky was now trying to arouse my anger about something I hadn't even given much thought to until now.

"You know Spooky," I answered, "I've thought about things in a different light now, and I agree with you. I've sat back and just taken this mental abuse without putting up a real fight. It's time now for me to take a stand and show them all what I'm made of. So be sure to put this in your news report."

I *really* wanted to throw some dirt now. "Motown, with all its high quality and standards, never even gave the group who gave them their first #1, a gold record. How's that for a company held in such high esteem?"

Spooky choked. "Gladys, it's unbelievable! Didn't they even show their respect and appreciation to you girls in this most accustomed manner?"

"No!" I screamed, "and believe me, they haven't heard the last from me yet!"

Spooky then informed me that if I wanted more information on the girls who are going around working as Marvelettes, Bobby Sanders might be able to enlighten me. I had met Bobby the night before and had his telephone number, so I called him. He was glad to fill me in on what he had heard.

"Mr. Larry Marshak is the name of the guy who claims that Berry Gordy, Jr. sold him The Marvelettes name. That's why he uses it whenever he likes to advertise phony girl groups."

"How long has this been going on?"

Mr. Sanders informed me that ever since the late '70s, he had gotten responses from someone having the proper license to use the name. "A trademark is what it's called," he told me.

"But why would Mr. Gordy take the liberty of just giving someone else the privilege to use our name and take away our livelihood without even informing any of the original members of our group that this was happening? It's got to be against the law."

Then Bobby Sanders asked me the big question. "Is it true that Mr. Gordy named your group?" Without even answering, the truth was revealed in front of me to see in a flash

"So that's why he insisted that we change our group name from the very beginning, giving him a chance to rename us and put his legal claim on our name forever." It must have been a long, thought-out plan by a group of higher-ups in the company so that we would not have the rights to it if we ever decided to leave the company and try to continue our recording elsewhere. It was like Mr. Gordy was putting a lock on our future and lives from then on. How heartless and cruel are their motives to determine our futures by devising traps for us to fall into farther on down the road? We were oblivious to their evil motives.

Bobby Sanders could hear over the phone how frustrating this entire matter was becoming to me. "You're going to need a damn good lawyer. But, needless to say, with no job, no money, and no earnings in the foreseeable future, how on earth was I going to be able to afford one.

This was just the beginning of some of the hidden facts that I was also about to find out. Somehow, the conversation got pivoted, and we began discussing my wanting to embark upon the field of songwriting. "Didn't you write "Playboy" for The Marvelettes?" Bobby asked.

"I did," I told him, "and I was still receiving writer's royalties for the song since its release back in the '60s."

"That certainly must have helped you out a lot," he remarked, "receiving your performance and writer's royalties all those years."

"What performance royalties?" I questioned him seriously now. "I've only been receiving one writer's royalty check from Jobete, Motown's publishing, as a writer on the song."

Now we were getting into the deep stuff. Bobby realized I was telling him that I had not received any performance royalties from the song I wrote. "Gladys, can you meet me at the BMI office in about two hours? I've bet you've got royalty checks due you from way back. If they haven't been sending them to you, they still have the money on file waiting for you to claim it."

I couldn't believe it. Back payment from 1962; it was 1984!

"I'm going to be rich! I'm going to be rich!" I kept telling myself while quickly getting ready to go to BMI. I had finally struck it rich, and all my problems would soon be over. I was too excited even to breathe a word of what was happening to the boys. I had a time just keeping my own lid on.

Control yourself. Control yourself, Gladys, I kept thinking. It was bound to happen sooner or later—that glorious moment of truth. I would finally get my proper dues out of all of this.

Bobby was as excited as I was riding that elevator up to the 21st floor. "Girl, this is the money you need to get back on your feet," he said. "I'm so happy I helped you to realize that you had something coming after so long of being in the dark about it."

We talked to a consultant about what had been happening to me now for over 20 years.

"You mean you wrote "Playboy" and never received a check other than your writer's allowance since 1962?"

"That's right. I never even knew that I was entitled to a performance royalty check until Mr. Sanders here informed me about it today."

"I have to check the computers on this matter. I'll be back with an answer soon."

His answer quickly eradicated my dreams of becoming a millionairess overnight.

"I don't even see your name on the computer as a writer on that song. I have a Robert Bateman, a Brian Holland, and a Mickey Stevenson—the only three names registered."

"What! How could that be? They only produced and arranged the song. I was tricked into putting their names on the record with mine because they said they had helped with it, so they were entitled to the writer's share. So now you tell me that they were receiving something from BMI all of these years off of my song, and I wasn't?"

"I think what happened in your case is that you were too young to sign yourself up for BMI or ASCAP performance royalties. None of these other parties named informed you of your right to have one of them sign you up? They could have done that for you, you know," he informed me. "It's hard to believe that they never set you down and explained to you all of your rights as a songwriter. I'm sure you were too young to really know all that you should have known at the time. I'm sorry that you had to find out like this. Do you have a lawyer or an attorney who could recoup some of your monies due you from these three guys?"

I told the consultant that I didn't even have a job yet to pay my rent, so an attorney and attorney fees were out of the realm of possibility. Getting those three guys all together now would be a job within itself. It would probably take more time than I had to waste right now. But one day, I'll catch them all. I just don't know if it'll do any good or if they'll even be willing to pay me back any of the money I never got.

Honestly speaking, if I didn't have any children to leave behind, I think I would have jumped right off the top of that building that day. *That's* how used and betrayed I felt at that moment, especially since I was unable to do anything about it because the statute of limitations had run out. I remembered how hopeful I had been on my way there. And I now felt like I had been smacked in the face by an iron fist. It hurt so bad…so bad to really need your money and can't get it, knowing someone else has had the joy of spending it.

A couple of days later, I went to see a copyright lawyer who explained to me some of the important do's and don'ts for writing a song. "There are things you should know if you expect to become a professional writer who gets their proper payments for their songs. Listen to me. The first mistake that so many writers make is that they put a bunch of names on the writer's agreement that don't belong there. If you wrote a song one night, and the next day you ask a guitarist to add something to your song, you offer him a percentage of a songwriter's income from the song. You never put anyone else's name down as a writer unless you two were together when you started writing the song. That alone entitles you both as being the writers of the composition. Otherwise, anything added afterward deserves only a percentage credit, not a name credit."

He explained that millions of writers unknowingly make this mistake every day. The rules to songwriting should be known by all who hope to be successful composers. If you do it wrong, you're going to get messed around each time. We also talked about the proper ways to protect your songs and receive all the benefits that are due to a writer.

This is something I should have educated myself on long ago, back in the '60s before I ever sat down and decided to write a song. We were ignorant about the music business and blindly trusted everyone back then. We did everything to have fun and for the love of music. Many of us can never be repaid appropriately, even if it came back to us double in due time. It's what we've lost emotionally that can never be replaced, something that money cannot buy.

Yes, coming back to California this time had opened my eyes to many hidden truths. Of course, I had no way of knowing it at the time, but I was in store for even more news and finding out who did this and who did that. Somebody was really trying to get a message to me. Yes, God was trying to tell me something.

I had no idea that there was so much thieving and lying going on for years behind the scenes of big record businesses. Also, while I had all this newfound information, my savings was bound to be gone if I didn't find a job fast. But where and with whom?

In this town, you needed an agent to work unless you had been here long enough that the club owners knew it was ok to take a chance on you because you could bring in the crowd. And even bringing the crowd never lasts for long. The following week someone else is the star of the show, and the only bill you see your name on is the unpaid utility bills they continue to pile up.

Yes, it was time for me to either give up show business and get a 9-5 job or sign up for public social services—the Welfare department—to keep some funds flowing while I got my act together.

"If you're going to wait to book shows, you're going to find yourself standing in the soup line, lady," one employer told me. "You'd be surprised to find out how many entertainers are receiving some type of aid, even with the shows they do. Even the hottest acts don't work every day of the year."

I had to do something fast because Mrs. Morris had given me until April 1st to find a place of our own, and that date was only a week away. Mary Wells laid out the welcome mat days after I had first talked to her. "Gladys," she said, "if you ever need shelter, you can come and stay at my place until you find your way."

I appreciated her thoughtfulness, but I wanted to see what I could do on my own. I remembered getting a friend's telephone number from some of her relatives before I left Inkster. They told me then, "if you get a chance, go by and see Ann Montgomery while you're there. She's the choir director of a big church now and has married the preacher's brother."

I planned on calling Ann sooner, but so many other things seemed to be more important. I knew it would surprise her to see me again after all these years. She had been my choir director back in Inkster when I was only 12 years old. Her voice had inspired me to want to learn to lead gospel songs in the church. I learned the technique and gained the confidence that goes along with it.

Soon after my success with Motown began, I moved off to Detroit to sing and record rock & roll music, or maybe I should call it the dance music of those days. Now, here I was calling her up. I knew after telling her who I was, that it was going to knock her off her feet.

"Gladys!" she screamed. "Where are you, and how did you get my number?"

I explained everything to her, quickly telling her how I went back to Inkster to live and had talked to her cousin Ruth. It didn't seem the most appropriate time to do it, but I had to let her know right away that I hadn't settled into a place of my own yet. She immediately knew what I was asking of her, and questioned how many were with me.

"I have three boys and a dog," I told her.

She laughed, saying that she couldn't wait to come and get us.

Before we moved out, Mrs. Morris reminded me that only reason she had opened up her home to me was that she was under the impression that I had to come to California to marry her son Al. Since I had shown no signs of even trying to get in touch with a minister to perform the ceremony, she took it as it meaning that I had changed my mind. And so, the right thing to do would be for me to move on.

She was right. I knew that marriage now would be like romance without finance—there was no way it was going to work out.

Ann had a lovely home on the west side of Los Angeles. She recently remarried, and they were now Mr. & Mrs. Taylor. Although she was the choir director of a much bigger church now, she claimed that her voice was not as good as it had been years ago. She was also involved with a school program that served the handicapped. She was very helpful in giving me some advice on what schools were best for Sammie.

Every day now she was leaving work early to drive me around to look at different rental properties. "Our church always has a couple of rentals," Ann informed me. "If they would ok it, you probably wouldn't have to pay as much as an average apartment holder would. We try to offer refuge to the ones really needing it. And with a handicapped child, you definitely would qualify first on the list."

We took a look at them. The good news was that they were clean and the rent was reasonable, but the sad news was that they didn't allow dogs on the church property.

"Why?" I begged, hoping to somehow change their minds.

Ann said that the preacher had mentioned to her that the dog's barking might interfere with their Sunday services, since the apartments were right next door to the church.

"It's up to you," Ann stated. "You can get the apartment, they said, but the dog has to go."

"No way. I don't want it if Sparky can't come with us."

"Really, Gladys," Ann sarcastically remarked. "You are not in a situation where you can afford to be choosy. I don't know how much longer I am going to be able to house you. Two weeks have gone by already, and we've had no luck anywhere else."

"Well, I'll just sleep out on the streets before I give up our dog."

Ann just ignored my suggestion and said we'd look around some more.

Another week went by without us having any luck when Ann's husband started drilling her about just how long we were going to be there. He had gotten tired of houseguests already. Ann started to complain to me about some of the things he was riding her back over.

"Gladys," she began telling me one day, "Ira says he can't even eat seeing you walking around with those halter tops on. So can you cover yourself up more?"

One complaint led to another. I knew it was time to go, especially after Ann voiced her open opinion one day after hearing me talk about all the fans we had as a group. "The Marvelettes!" she snorted. "What have you got left from that group? If you've got so many fans, why won't some of them give you a place to stay?"

It wasn't just what she said that shook me, it was the overpowering truthful manner in which she was now expressing herself. I never knew that she resented my past success until now. I really do believe that all the while, even long ago, she felt that it should have been her that became the superstar from Inkster. She really did have the greater sound and the better voice. Now I felt like she secretly thought I had in some way robbed her of what should have always been her chance at becoming a famous singer.

It was startling to me to hear any type of jealousy coming from her. I always thought that she was 100% behind my success and really felt good that I had made it. Now I was awakened to the realization that there had always secretly been some animosity growing within her. Boy, oh boy. Time has a way of revealing people's true underlying feelings. I took it all in stride, feeling like it was something that I needed to know to keep on going and become an even stronger person in life. So, in our parting, I had no regrets.

Our next move was to Mary Wells's house. I had only been in California for one month and three weeks, and already we were on our third move. I'm kind of wondering now if moving around is a pre-destined thing over which I have no control. I certainly had been moving from day one through all the stages of my life and now as a young adult struggling to raise three kids. If we could stay in one place long enough, maybe I could make some progress.

Things started out great at Mary's house. Mary and I reminisced over those early years with Motown when everything she released was a hit: "Bye Baby", " Two Lovers, "You Beat Me To The Punch", "The One Who Really Loves You", "Old Love", and "Laughing Boy." I could go on naming lots more of her chartbusters. I couldn't help but look at her as an angel because Mary really rescued my family and me from the sharks that were beginning to bite.

She told me right from the beginning that we all had the rest of the year to get ourselves situated. "That's all the time I have left to remain here in this house," she explained. "We've had numerous problems with our landlord and the neighbors, and Curtis and I are really ready to get a move-on ourselves and find someplace else to live."

Mary was now living in West Hollywood, close to all the fabulous Melrose shops and restaurants specializing in French cuisines. There were plenty of other stylish and fancy restaurants and places of business in West Hollywood. The Pacific Design Center, the Beverly Center, the banks, the post offices, parks, and recreational centers made this one of the more exquisite, classier neighborhoods in the City of Los Angeles. There was nothing about Mary's house that we didn't enjoy.

Sparky, our dog, seemed to really be enjoying his time at Mary's as well. Unlike the other places we stayed, Mary allowed Sparky to stay indoors with us. Now, *this* was Sparky's way of living! You should have seen him grinning! He had always been allowed to stay indoors with us from the time we took him in as a baby.

"I love his big bark," Mary commented on how she wouldn't have to worry about any intruders from now on. "Even the landlord will leave me alone now," she laughed.

Mary and Curtis took to Sparky so much until she asked me if she could take him on some of her travels. Of course, you know the answer I gave her—the boys and I would miss him too much.

Everything seemed so perfect here for a while; it was almost too good to be true. Mary's kids and mine got along fine, and I took advantage of her patio with the barbecue pit; I played chef as much as I could.

Mary and Curtis were like two peas in a pod. Many

evenings, they would sit around with me and we'd joke about almost everything: music, shows, and entertainers we both knew. Sometimes we'd get into deep conversations, like how we got to where we were now. Mary talked about her mistakes in the business, and I talked about mine. Curtis always joined in, adding his opinions and giving us advice. Mary and I had always had a deep respect for one another, so we knew how to give each other the privacy we both deserved.

We sat down and devised a living arrangement that would be suitable for both of us. "Listen Gladys," Mary said, "I need someone to watch the place while Curtis and I are gone, like answering the phone, writing down important messages, and just keeping things in order around here. In return, you can stay here and save up your money for wherever or whenever you move into a place of your own. From now until January 1985 should give you plenty of time to look around. We can help each other in this way. Ok?"

That was a good enough deal for me, and exactly what I needed. So, I agreed. "Do you have any type of income now?" Mary asked.

I told her about Sammie's monthly SSI check and my artist royalties checks that came twice a year. "That's all I'm receiving right now, which adds up roughly to around $10,000.00 a year, and that's not very much. Without me booking any shows, I'm not going to be able to afford the high cost of living in this state of sunny California." I even confided in Mary about my plans to file for money on welfare.

"Do whatever you have to do until you get your name out there in the public again. You've got to continue to pay your bills, so don't be ashamed. I'll try to help you as much as I can. I'll let some of the club owners and show promoters I work for know that you're getting your act together and that you need work right away."

Things were still running smoothly. Mary and Curtis spent most of their weekends out on engagements and I played house secretary; making sure everyone had a good home-cooked meal. Then suddenly, our seemingly perfect living arrangement was brought to an abrupt halt. It happened one evening while the kids, the dogs, and a couple of kids were visiting. I was barbecuing some hamburgers and hot dogs over the open pit fire on the patio. Mary and Curtis had just returned home earlier that day and were asleep in their bedroom. I can't say why or how it all began because my back was turned when the chaos began.

All the kids were laughing and teasing and drawing pictures at the patio table. All of sudden, we heard a loud growl from Sparky. I turned to find him chasing Shorty, Mary's youngest son. Sparky chased him so vigorously that in order to try and get away from him, Shorty had to jump over the studio sofa. Alas, it was too late. Sparky had already lodged his teeth in one of Shorty's legs, and now he was bleeding all over the place. We were all screaming loudly now from the shock of what had just occurred. Mary and Curtis came running out to find out what had happened.

Seeing her son lying there holding his leg in tears and in pain drove Mary back into the house in pursuit of her shotgun. "I'm gonna kill him. I'm gonna kill that dog!" she screamed repeatedly.

I found myself by her side pleading and begging her not to. "Shorty must have done something," I told her. "Shorty had to do something to Sparky!" I screamed. "He's never bit anyone before. I'm sure Shorty did something, maybe unintentionally."

Mary raced to the back door leading to the patio with Curtis and myself right behind her. Thankfully, when we got there, Sparky was nowhere in sight because it gave Mary some time to calm down and think. She helped Shorty up and Curtis drove them to the nearest hospital.

Alphonso had saved Sparky's life by taking him for a walk, but we could never erase that night's memory from our minds. All the joyous feelings and sounds of happiness coming from the house were silenced. The party was over again for us. Words could not express the sadness that prevailed over all now. We all waited up patiently for Mary and Curtis to bring Shorty home, hoping and praying that the doctor said that he was going to be all right.

Shorty came in with his leg all bandaged up. He had required ten or more stitches. Mary knew in her heart that there was no way that we wanted such a thing to happen. She was more sympathetic than I ever imagined that she would have been at a time like this. I was a mother myself; I knew the consequences of messing with a mother's child. The signs always read danger.

I had no clue what Mary was going to say, but I knew she would be against letting Sparky remain indoors from now on. "Gladys," she spoke sincerely now, "believe me, if that had not have been your dog, he would be dead by now. I'm only grateful that Shorty is not hurt any worse than he is, but due to the circumstances, Sparky is going to have to stay outdoors. I know you understand why."

We chained Sparky outside that night, but something happened only hours later that caused another change in our housing situation immediately. While we were all asleep inside, Mary's older sons attacked Sparky with bottles, cans, barbed wire, and anything they could find to throw at him from the roof of their garage. Sparky found shelter somewhere behind the guest house and shielded himself from all the broken glass and wire.

When I went out to him the next morning, he was quivering and shaking from fear and loneliness. I looked everywhere on him for bruises and cuts, but there were none. Later, during a big, big argument, I cried and plead that Sparky was innocent. I asked Mary if I could clean out the one-room guest home she had in the back. That way, the boys and I could sleep outside near Sparky for the rest of our time there. It was a win-win situation for everyone.

I wasn't taking any more chances with our dog's life,

even if we all had to live in one room. Why should he die because of someone's else carelessness? I had to take Sparky to the vet to get tested for rabies. Thankfully, he received a clean bill of health.

Things slowly got back to normal around there, but there was still an aloofness and coolness in the air. The boys and I were in the back most of the time, with me honoring our original agreement. I only came inside while Mary had to be away for an engagement.

When September came, it meant school time again for my guys and some free time for me. I spent the early morning hours searching the papers and walking around the area looking for rent signs.

As I looked through application after application, I realized that on the lines that read "occupation" and "name of employer" I wasn't going to get very far telling the truth. I was only going around in circles, ending right back up where I started from, and that was nowhere. Several applications distinctly read NO PETS ALLOWED. I tore those up and threw them away immediately. People who don't like animals don't have a heart, and I could care less about their rules.

On one occasion, I lied and told an apartment manager that I was on low income already. It was the only thing I could think of to say when she asked why I had not filled in the information about my years of employment.

"Really lady," she told me, "there are places where you can easily afford the monthly rent payments. But I'm afraid our $1,500 a month for your size family is a bit too much for you." I asked her where some of these places were, and she told me to look closer to the Compton area. I guess in many ways she was trying to tell me that I was on the wrong side of town if I was receiving welfare.

Wanda of The Marvelettes must have picked up on my negative vibes and sensed that I was not having much luck in this city of bright light. She called Mary Wells's house one day, all boozed up and ready to talk that talk of hers.

When I answered the phone, Mary picked up at the same time in her room. All three of us were on the phone at the same time.

"Gladys," Wanda called my name, low down and gritty, as if she was laughing at the same time. "What in the hell are you doing at Mary Wells's house?" she drunkenly flopped the question at me.

I tried to answer, but before I could complete any statement, she sneered. "I bet you miss this sweet old country town of Inkster now. Don't you, bitch?" Now she really laughed out loud, as if she knew I wasn't having the same luck in finding shows to do out in California as I did in Michigan.

I came back on the defense by claiming that I couldn't and would never miss a place that didn't know how to treat me or respect who I was or what I had done to better thousands of lives.

"They ran you crazy Wanda," I told her, "always reminding you that the good times for The Marvelettes were over. But when they started in on me, I think I showed them who was boss. I left. I just refused to stay in a place where many were satisfied with nothing, and others hated you if you got something. I want to advance, and I've got no time for drinking alcohol all day long. And that's exactly what you've been doing, haven't you?"

Mary stepped in now and said, "Hi Wanda. It's Mary. You don't sound so good, girl."

Wanda right away seemed to get really wired up at the sound of Mary's voice. "Mary Wells, now you want to be a Marvelette, you bitch you!" she yelled out over the phone.

Mary was shocked at the welcome Wanda was giving her. I could hear Mary trying to talk some sense into Wanda during the course of the conversation despite Wanda's incessant babbling about how Mary was nothing and would never be a Marvelette.

"To hell with you! Go jump in a lake, you bitch," Wanda cursed on.

We sounded like a bunch of cackling hens talking over one another over the telephone. Nobody's message was getting across. We wanted to be heard but did not want to understand. Finally, Wanda hung up, slamming the telephone, leaving Mary in almost tears.

"I could help her, Gladys," Mary repeatedly said afterward. "I know I could help bring Wanda out of this terrible dilemma she's in. She's fighting inside for the life she used to have."

"I think we all are," I told Mary, "in some way or another, we all are."

That evening, Mary suggested that we both sit down and write Berry Gordy a letter asking him to help us get our careers at Motown Records back. *It certainly wouldn't hurt*, I thought. Letters have been known to cure many a situation. Like it has been said, the pen sometimes is mightier than the sword.

I don't know what Mary said in her letter, but I simply told the truth. I told Berry that I had come as far as I could, and now I was here in California without a job and no permanent place to live.

> *I have three sons now, one handicapped with cerebral palsy. If you could just help me out by getting me in touch with someone in the real estate business who can help me to put at least a roof over our head I think I can do the rest on my own.*

Never did I ask him for any set amount of money. Really, I didn't know what it would cost, but I did know I didn't have nearly that amount in the bank. I went on writing.

> *Mary Wells has been so kind as to open her doors to me, but even this time is limited. That job you offered me years ago that would never run out at the company would surely be appreciated now. I am still singing along with now writing my own material.*
>
> *Please don't turn away now. I need your help, Berry.*

I then enclosed a tape of a few songs I had recorded. I closed the letter with my name, address, and telephone number where I could be reached. Mary and I both mailed our letters at the same time. That was around October of 1984. As of 1991, I had yet to receive a reply.

Oh, yes, after a month or so had gone by, I received my tape and letter back in the mail. On the front were the words in big bold letters: UNSOLICITED MAIL. It looked as though it had not even been opened. How's *that* for gratitude? It was as though Berry Gordy, Jr. had no time to listen to our tales of woe. If we lived or died apparently meant nothing to him. He had what he wanted and in the process had managed to diminish both our pride and honor.

I had begun to drink again. I could see how the beer was putting those extra pounds back on me, but I didn't care. I was caught up again and in a very depressed state of mind. I was hoping that alcohol would make me forget what had to be done: get on welfare or leave California.

One fact was for sure now. I could not work a 9-5 job even if I found one. Caring constantly for a handicapped child didn't leave much time to do anything else during the day. I had to put Sammie on the bus every morning and be there in the afternoon when the bus brought him home. Sometimes the hours varied. There was just no way of getting around it. I needed a job with flexible hours, so a 9-5 job was out.

The kids were growing like weeds. Being in California made them suddenly fashion-conscious, and so they complained. "The kids here don't wear that, and the kids don't like this. And I need a new this and a new that, and another way to express myself."

They constantly demanded a change. Yes, they were in those in-between years and everything was a battle. Naturally, they didn't mind expressing themselves verbally to demand what they wanted. I felt like a total loser at times. It used to be that a good meal would satisfy them all and keep a smile on their faces. Unfortunately, cook didn't rate so high anymore.

The holidays came—Thanksgiving and then Christmas—and I still had not applied for public assistance yet. Despite my vices, I managed to still have some sort of savings. It wasn't much, but it was enough to enable me to get a room at the Tropicana Hotel for the boys, me, and luckily the dog, when we finally had to move out of Mary Wells's house.

As a matter of fact, we all moved up to the Tropicana on Santa Monica near La Cienega Blvd. in West Hollywood. It was Mary and her crew and me with my crew. I was so afraid that they weren't going to let Sparky in, but it was just my luck that the manager at the hotel loved dogs just like I did.

"Of course, you can bring your dog in with you," he smiled the day I went in to book us a couple of rooms in advance.

He didn't know that Sparky was as big as he was, though, until one day he saw the maid running from our suite in pursuit of the nearest exit. "I don't mind you having such a big dog," he called up to my room and said, "but please make allowance for the maid to get in and clean your room every day."

The Tropicana was slowly but surely putting the biggest dent in my pocketbook. Our weekly rent was $350. I could only handle those prices for about a month, and I knew it. I prayed for a miracle, and I got one.

One day while I was out still searching for a cheaper place for us to exist, I saw Cornelius Grant, another familiar friend and face from my Motown years. Cornelius had once been The Marvelettes's guitar player, but was taken away from us by The Temptations; they made him a better offer. We sure hated to lose him, but we had remained friends throughout the Motown era. In fact, he was one of the musicians there that I had a long time crush on. He was now happily married to a beautiful girl from India and lived right around the corner from us.

I told him my money problems and how I needed to reach someone from Motown who could help me financially so that I could get settled in this town. I quickly explained to him about monies I hadn't received from "Playboy," which really could help me out now if I only knew where to find the Holland team.

"That's easy," Cornelius told me. "They've got offices in Hollywood on Highland Avenue. Call information for their number."

Before we parted, Cornelius invited me over to meet his wife one day after I myself together. "And I wish you all the luck," he added.

It sure seemed strange to see Cornelius all settled down now and raving over one woman. He had once been what any girl would have called the playboy of the '60s. All The Temptations, even the musicians, had left a string of broken hearts wherever they played.

Brian Holland was still the same old sweet fellow he had always been. He still had a calm, reserved way about him as he took in whatever was said. Brian was always relaxed and maintained the utmost control. He gave you the feeling like he was saying, "It's no problem. Let's just work it out."

After hearing my story, Brian said, "Gladys, things were happening so fast in those days that I could only remember what was brought to my attention from time to time. I'm sure we didn't purposely leave you out of the performance royalties from the song."

He offered to help me in any way he could now, which made me realize he was genuinely innocent in this matter. "How much do you need? I'll help you," he said. It was as easy as that.

"Brian, you sweetheart! I could kiss you!" I said. "Thank you, thank you so much."

All the guys with the Holland group joined in and gave me a check, enough to get me into my first apartment there in West Hollywood. I had to pay first, last, and security. Believe me; they had been quite generous with their help.

"How can I repay you guys for being so kind?" I asked. Brian, Eddie, Chris, and the rest of the team told me to bring some of my songs in for them to listen to. "Maybe we can help to get you back into the stream of things."

We were now moving out of the Tropicana Hotel into a one-bedroom apartment only moments away. I had really pulled it off, and I was proud of myself! Finally, I had found a place still located in this swanky, high society area of West Hollywood, close enough to all the luxurious stores and restaurants.

My kids and I were still living on Easy Street, only now I knew I'd better make sure that we had a way to remain here. So, I finally made that call and got an appointment to come and apply for you know what. Why or how I still had any pride left I don't know. The wear and tear of the whole ordeal really rocked me. I lied about almost everything I knew would bring me and who I was to shame. I never mentioned my past as an entertainer. I claimed that my husband had disappeared and left us with nothing. Hearing about the three kids, one having cerebral palsy, made them realize that this was my only solution.

Getting on welfare did not give me a welfare mind, though. I didn't just sit around and collect my payments every month. It just gave me self-respect because I no longer had to kiss ass to pay my bills. I knew where the rent was coming from, we would have food to eat, and my utilities would not be turned off. It was only enough money to supply our basic needs.

Soon after settling in the apartment, I met some people who helped me start a small songwriting business. I was going to slowly but surely work my way up the ladder of success. I called my songwriting business Songs For Success. It was geared toward writing songs for success-oriented artists. I wanted artists who were recording and had songs on the charts constantly. Patti LaBelle, The Pointer Sisters, Stevie Wonder, and Gladys Knight & The Pips were a few of the first artists I looked towards pleasing. I thought having a relationship with a few of the artists may increase my chances of working with them. Unfortunately, it didn't work that fast.

My landlord had gotten upset when she found out we

had a dog, but she continued to let me stay and raised my rent by $50.00. Now, because she heard music constantly coming from my place, she knocked on my door to voice her displeasure. I met a couple of musicians who had just gotten into town and had a studio full of equipment and no place to put it. So naturally, my front room looked like a recording studio.

"Are you actually recording in here?" she asked as she looked around the room.

I knew what was coming next and assured her there would be no more playing after 9:00 in the evenings and none before 10:00 in the morning.

Once we cleared that up, she then informed me that my neighbors living above me were complaining about the dog barking each time they passed by. "Can you try to keep him calm? They've threatened me about moving out, and I wouldn't want to lose them. They've been here for a long time."

Sparky had a way now of scaring everybody who he thought showed any fear of him. But what could I do? A dog was going to be a dog. And no matter where I moved, people were going to hear from Sparky. Besides, Sparky was the best guard dog any family would want. I felt extremely secure knowing that I didn't have to worry about my place getting robbed. I had musical equipment here valued at over $150,000—synthesizers, drum machines, microphones, guitars, speakers, and loads of tapes and recording supplies. I don't even know how my two work colleagues got all of this stuff into town.

I met Chafielle first up on Hollywood Boulevard one weekend when taking the boys in to get a haircut at one of the barber colleges. He and I happened to get into a conversation about show business. I told him about my success as the lead singer of The Marvelettes. Come to find out, he was right out of Gary, Indiana; the same hometown as the Jackson 5.

"I wish you could see the house where they all grew up." He was speaking of the home site of the Jacksons before they experienced the fame and fortune that they had now come into.

After finding out that he and another partner of his from New York were sleeping on top of the Palladium roof there in Hollywood, I offered to give them a place to store their musical instruments, which was now in a friend's garage.

After seeing the recording studio they made out of my living room, I decided to form a songwriting and recording team with them. They had everything I needed to make a professional recording without ever leaving my apartment. I took full advantage of such a rare opportunity for a struggling artist like myself. Never before would I have been able to create musically. Not only was I able to complete music from the past, but I could also begin working on future songs too. Ebony was the musician of the two. Chafielle was the singer, but he was good at computerizing the drum machines for different hi-tech elaborate sounds and rhythms. They were both back and forth at my place, carrying all their hopes and desires of making Songs For Success live up to its name.

One night it was raining so hard that I couldn't send them back up on that roof to sleep. So, from then on, they found a permanent space in our recording studio to sleep. It seemed like the right thing to do at the time, offering them some warmth from the cold. Before I moved out of that apartment, we had almost 10 homeless friends of theirs shacking up with us from time to time. First, their two girlfriends stayed with them for one night, which eventually led to them staying over every night. Then, for many reasons, all different from the last, there were a host of other relatives and friends of friends that needed a day, a week, or more for someplace to hold up.

It was getting so crowded that the only privacy I had was in the kid's bedroom. I told Ebony and Chafielle that they could pack 'em up to the ceiling if they wanted to, but our one bedroom was off-limits for anyone else but the boys and me. It was the only space we ended up having to call our own for a while.

"It won't be forever," I told my kids, "It's just that people have helped us so many times before when we've been in desperate need. In a way, I'm only giving back and paying it forward to someone else who's now in need."

The kids said they didn't care because they loved hearing the music and songs we were working on. It was exciting to always have people around who wanted to become big stars.

For a while, I had things working like an actual professional studio. I even had a secretary answering the telephone. It was Ebony's girlfriend Candy from New York City. And if you've ever heard the real New Yorker's dialect, you can just imagine her voice time as the calls came in.

Yes, you would have thought you had reached a business located on the highest floor in some skyscraper with a high-end clientele. I mean, I really had it going on. You should have seen me carrying my new briefcase. Every day I was getting more people interested and involved in my project. I had business stationery, cards, envelopes, and this was all done for me free of cost by two of my teammates.

They were a husband and wife team who flipped over my singing and writing ability. They had faith in our success after seeing our setup and hearing some of the material we were creating. They knew my being a Marvelette meant something, so they offered to put some big bucks behind my project and helped promote my new establishment in any way they could.

I felt so confident when I went to see Patti LaBelle later that year. She already had a hit single called "A New Attitude." However, I knew she needed to keep the fire burning. I offered her a tape filled with a couple of real foot-stomping, hand clapping numbers.

"Aren't you going to continue your singing career?" she wanted to know.

I explained to Patti that my need for a comeback was not as critical now as finding a way to see my family through this economic crisis.

"Patti," I begged, "you're still going strong, and you could take a song I've written and make it a super hit. You can sing anything and make it sound good. Please sing one for me, and I promise you that I'll be back out there going strong when the time allows me."

Patti offered to help me, but it was not by recording one of my songs like I wanted. Instead, she sent me four beautiful gowns that she had worn with the group La-Belle. "Gladys," she said, "you're going to need these dresses one day soon, I know. There is no way the fans will let you become just a songwriter. They want to see you again up there on stage. So go on, girl, and do it!"

We were in Patti's dressing room at the Paramount sound stage studios, where she was filming a segment for *Solid Gold*. I had the privilege that day of meeting Whoopi Goldberg. She had not yet filmed the movie *The Color Purple*. In·fact, it was that day that she told Patti and me something about the script that she was studying. "I'm going in for an interview for the part today, and I'm hoping that this will do it for me. I really need it."

She had been such a down-to-earth, warm, funny person that I found myself in her corner, rooting for her without knowing her and her abilities. So when I later heard from Rudy Calvo, Patti's make-up artist, that Whoopi had landed the part in the movie, I told myself right then that I wanted to see what that movie was all about. Rudy Calvo was another crazed ladies of Motown fan. I met him from visiting Patti off and on that year.

"I've just imagined to myself," he said to me one day, "how thrilling it would be to do all the ladies' make-up one day. And Gladys, you are one of the ones that I've just dreamed about making up."

"Maybe one day," I agreed, not knowing just how long it would be before I got to show off my make-up or face to any audience. I was obsessed with writing songs and getting some prominent name artists to record them. It was too late in the game to start off with unknowns, although I would eventually seek to write material for as many as possible. But first, I had to make some money in this new career.

Another artist I tried to get to sing one of my songs was Gladys Knight. Back in the '60s, when our song "Please Mr. Postman" was riding high on the charts, her group was also singing about the postman with a song called "A Letter Full Of Tears." When we first played in Atlanta, Georgia, her whole group came down to the club to meet us. After that, I felt like we would be friends forever. The Marvelettes constantly met up with Gladys & The Pips on one-nighters and shows at the Apollo Theater in

Harlem, New York. We saw Gladys through both of her pregnancies during the '60s and even visited her home while she still lived in Atlanta. Those days were the early days before her success; she still lived in the projects.

Sometimes, we would get together and see her performances even if we weren't performing. Yes, The Marvelettes admired and felt a real kinship with Gladys Knight & The Pips. I can remember how I longed to see them get their propers one day in the business. But, even though they were dynamic on stage, they just couldn't seem to get the big break they needed.

We, as a group, begged and begged them to come to Motown. Unfortunately, it took a while because, like most of the groups during that time, they were afraid of the power Motown executives had over their artists. Eventually, it did all happen for them. Consequently, almost simultaneously, I decided to leave Motown to become a full-time mother to my first-born, and Gladys Knight got her first real big break. I can remember how happy all of us girls were that Gladys & The Pips were now riding in style and living on Easy Street.

Now, I was asking Gladys, just as I had Patti LaBelle, to help me out by putting one of my songs on their future albums. "I'm trying out my hand at this end of the business because I can't travel right now. I told Gladys how I needed to care for Sammie and my two other sons. I explained how it would help me financially to receive a writer's royalty check in the mail. I really needed my old friends' help now.

"If you would consider recording this song, I know you could make it a hit." The name of the song was "A Special Feeling." And like many of the songs I had written with particular artists in mind, I had written this one especially for Gladys, using her same style. *This made the song unique to the person,* I thought.

But for some reason, I was deceived into thinking that Gladys still remembered those early years and how close our groups were. She promised to do everything she could to help me with the song, but I never heard from her. Even as I sit writing now, I wonder what made her so uncaring about my desperate situation. I understood that she didn't owe me a thing, but I felt like this was one situation where it was a sister begging another to help her regain her life back.

I wasn't asking to join her onstage. I was only asking a favor of her. I would have never turned her away or let her down the way she did me.

Another well-known artist I accidentally ran into and later sent her some of my songs was Miss Diana Ross. Our meeting took place at the Bohdi Tree Bookshop on Melrose Avenue, right down the street from my apartment. I saw someone with her distinctive features entering the bookshop as I was crossing the street. I was tempted to go inside. *I'll just look around, hoping to get a closer glance at whoever it was,* I thought.

At first, I couldn't believe that it was really her. Now I've never been one to put anyone so high up on a pedestal that I felt like seeing them walking around on Earth was impossible. But here she was, mid-afternoon in broad daylight for all to see, Diana, unless it was one of West Hollywood's drag queens. I think Diana spotted me before I could spot her because I heard her yell in surprise; she was only a few feet away from me. Before me stood a soft, sweet girl I knew from a long time ago. Looking at her now reminded me of how she would look after a performance while basking in the approval of fans. There was no trace of the personality many had labeled her with over the years. To me, that was all hearsay and gossip. Her behavior now was only proving them all to be big liars. She was nothing but gracious toward me now.

"Gladys," she called out my name with outstretched arms to embrace me. We hugged each other and then stood back to take another look as if we both just couldn't believe we were face to face.

"Girl, you never change!" Diana said as she complimented me on my girlish face. "You look the same as you did years ago. So what's your big secret?" she laughed now openly.

By now, we had caught the attention of almost everyone in the shop. I could hear their whispers. "That's Diana Ross of The Supremes and Gladys Horton of The Marvelettes."

I looked at Diana. She had on a cute matching white blouse and skirt. She wore her hair long, her usual style. On her face, there was not a stitch of make-up. And talk about looking young, she very well did! "Your skin looks good too!" I threw back the same compliment to her.

She grabbed me by the arm and proceeded to walk around the bookstore. "Tell me, Gladys," she said, "tell me about everything that you've been doing. It's been so long. I've often wondered where and what your group was up to now."

I felt like I had only minutes to fill her in on my life. I didn't know how long she would be there, so I talked fast. I told her about the kids and Sammie, about going back to Michigan and trying to help Wanda, and now about my adventure into wanting to become an established songwriter.

Standing there with her made me recall a dream I had about her once. I had not given much thought about it until this very moment. Even if Diana didn't have much time, she didn't show it. She dropped everything and begged, "Gladys, please, you've got to tell me all about the dream. I want to know what you dreamt about me?"

Dreams are one subject where almost anyone will listen intently to what you have to say. The suspense of it all is always too great for them to pass up. And so, I told Diana about the dream.

"I saw you riding in this car, made of see-through material, like hard plastic. It looked like it could have been a car from the future. It was circular and looked like a mini-spaceship riding on the street. The sight of it drew everyone's attention. And when I looked, I saw you. Unfortunately, the car had other people in it, too, so it was hard for me to catch your eye. You all had stopped at a red light, and when you finally looked my way, it was about time for the car to drive off. 'Give me your telephone number,' I yelled out to you. You called out some numbers to me. Somehow, even in the dream, I felt relief after seeing you. I felt that if I could only get in touch with you, maybe you could help me get away from the place I seem to be unable to leave in my dreams. I called and called the number, desperately hoping for you to answer. Each time, it just rang and rang and rang."

As I regaled Diana with the retelling of my dream, she seemed amused. She smiled that wide grin of hers that she never revealed to the cameraman or when the TV lights were on. It was the Diana *I* knew, though. She wasn't playing a role or putting on heirs to further her public persona. Instead, she was totally enjoying herself that day, and so was I.

Before we went our separate ways, Diana invited me to see her next performance at Caesar's Palace in Las Vegas. "Come on up," she said. "Just tell them who you are, and I'll make sure you get accommodated."

She promised to listen to any tape of songs I sent her and begged me to write her a letter, even if I couldn't make the show. I never heard any reply from her or anything about the songs I sent to her. Finally, I was beginning to realize that everyone was so busy in their greatness that they just didn't have time to think about doing anything to help me. Still, I didn't give up. I sent songs to The Pointer Sisters, Stevie Wonder, Smokey Robinson, Eddie & Brian Holland, Cornelius Grant, and other well-known producers, writers, and recording artists. But Mr. Postman was just not delivering any mail from the important ones nowadays.

I can't say the postman hadn't begun to play a significant role in my life now because he had. There was one thing that soothed the people's minds in a hurry, and that was the 1st and the 15th of every month. They were all waiting for the postman to deliver those welfare checks.

It seems like my song, regardless of everything else, was very popular on those days. And if your check or food stamps were late or didn't come, I could hear a lot of people singing, *"Wait a minute, Mr. Postman. Wait a minute. Please check just one more time for me."*

In the meantime, Bobby Sanders had offered to do a benefit show for me to help raise some money. My landlord was done with all the traffic and the noise coming from my apartment, and she had asked me to move. "It's not the music," she said, "it's because of the dog; he's scaring my tenants."

The benefit show was supposed to help me raise money to move into a bigger house. The flyers we had made for the benefit read:

```
         GREATER     ENTERTAINMENT
         PRODUCTIONS  PRESENTS   A
```

```
BENEFIT FOR GLADYS HOR-
TON, ORIGINAL LEAD SING-
ER OF THE MOTOR CITY'S
LEGENDARY   MARVELETTES,
SATURDAY,   OCTOBER   26,
1985. 8:00 P.M.
```

Bobby and I worked for about a month on this event. He even got the press to come out and advertise for the show. We met with Mr. Dennis Hunt of *The Los Angeles Times* and one of their photographers, Brian Gadburry. They gave us a big layout story in *The Los Angeles Times's* calendar section two weeks prior to the engagement.

I had rehearsed with two female background singers recommended by Bobby Sanders himself. We even did a commercial for a cable TV show advertising the benefit. Everything spelled "go," and I was ready to at least let the fans know that I was still willing, able, and qualified to sing those old familiar Marvelettes tunes. Then out of the blue, the show was canceled. Without warning, Bobby Sanders had canceled the show on me. Now, what was I going to do?

After going to court and winning the case against my landlord, the judge ruled that the dog's barking wasn't justification for eviction. However, after considering how crowded our living conditions had become, I had decided that I wanted more room for my kids. I, therefore, decided to move out. But even after the court hearing, the judge gave me until the middle of November to stay there until I had saved up enough money to cover the costs of my moving expenses somewhere else.

Now here I was. I was depending on this event to be a success and provide for me financially. I was hoping to move to a bigger place and have a better living style. And now that there wasn't going to be any show, there wasn't going to be any money.

Thankfully, I had been saving my rent payments along with the royalty checks as I was planning to purchase transportation. It was supposed to be a Christmas surprise for the boys after moving into our new home. But now, it looked as though I would have to make some significant changes to my plans. It was no use in trying to rent another small apartment. My family was growing rapidly, and moving into another small house would only frustrate everyone. I needed space and lots of it.

I looked for an apartment diligently with no luck. Finally, one apartment manager approached me one day and told me why I wasn't having much luck finding a place to rent anything. "Miss Horton," he said to me as I was returning an application, "may I make a suggestion, if you don't mind?"

Of course, I was ready for whatever help anyone could give me. I was exhausted mentally from apartment hunting. I was all ears.

"You're a well-known entertainer. With a growing family of your size, you should now try buying a house by getting on a rent option plan. For the first several years, your payments will be put towards your down payment in purchasing the property. Here, let me show you. I have a partner who sells houses this way all the time. If you can come up with about $25,000 down, you will easily qualify. Otherwise, you'll just be going around in circles looking for an apartment now because your name is on a "hot list" from going to court recently."

"How did you know that?" I blurted out.

"Gladys," he smiled and patted me on the shoulder as he revealed how he knew what he knew, "I'm a landlord. Whenever I get an applicant's name, I call a reference number available to all landlords. Landlords are informed on your rental history: have you ever been evicted, how many times you've been to court on non-payment of rent, and all of that good stuff."

"What?!" I screamed. I couldn't do anything but feel defeated. "This system of tenants and landlords is nothing but a big trap!" I shouted.

"No, no," he protested, saying that I shouldn't feel angry about it. "I'm just telling you as a friend. I know you'll need a place soon, and you won't find one at this rate. We, as landlords, take a considerable risk every time we rent out a home. So we have to have something that protects us too. So don't look at it as us being the bad guys.Here, I'm going to call my partner up and set up an appointment for you two to meet. He's all off into that '60s music, and when I tell him who you are, I know he'll go out of his way to make sure your needs are met."

The desire to have my own home a stable place for my kids and me sparked the idea of having Bobby Sanders sponsor a benefit on my behalf. I was a struggling artist with a disabled son. Everything was already worked out with an agent for the house I wanted. Now, all I needed was the money to back my plans. Now, everything was ruined, including my reputation. My name was now synonymous with a canceled show. I had to make an open apology of some kind to the public. "No, that won't be possible," Mr. Hunt told me over the phone. "Just make sure next time that you're dealing with more professional people who have integrity. Ensure you're working with someone that will care a little bit more about false advertising and contributions made by the public.

Then, he brought up the most important fact. "Not only does it put a bad light on you, but I get a lot of feedback coming from me being the news reporter."

I felt awful. My big comeback show ended before it even had a chance to start. There was nothing left for me to do now but buy a car so I could leave California.

"Do you know that taking me to court has ruined my chances of ever finding another decent apartment here in California?" I argued the point with my landlord. "I should take you back to court and sue you!" I threatened her. But I knew the damage had already been done, and it would take years for me even to collect off such a suit.

Time was of the essence, so I decided to go and look

for a used van. I needed to buy something big enough for Sparky to ride comfortably in if we were moving out of town. I *definitely* was not going back to Michigan, though. Someone had told me that Northern California was beautiful, and the cost of living was much cheaper than it was down here in Los Angeles.

I had passed the driving test and was now waiting on my picture ID in the mail. I hadn't had much practice driving since my early Motown days when I drove a friend's car whenever he was out of town. I knew how to drive; it's just that it had been over 20 years since I had gotten behind the wheel. Now, I was going to have to refresh my memory really fast.

I met the man who was about to change my life on the used car lot.

"That's a good one right there." He pointed to the bronze-colored van sitting across the lot. "If I weren't going to buy this truck, I'd buy that one myself."

"Is it really in good working condition?" I asked.

"I don't know all details about the automobile, but you sure can't beat the price. He's selling it for $1,500 as is."

I looked up to see another man coming towards me.

"Do you think that van over there is in good enough condition to take me out of here and on the road?" I asked the salesman after he had come up and volunteered to show me the interior.

That's when the first guy I had met asked me where I was headed. "I don't exactly know yet," I answered him, "but my family and I are unable to find a place to stay now after going to court, and I've got to move to another town."

"Hold on a minute before you make that move." He took out his wallet. "My name is Mr. Charles Banks, and I own a realty company."

He passed me one of his cards.

"But I thought you worked here as a salesman," I said.

"You *thought*. I never said that. I'm just here on business myself. Jim, the owner, and I've been good friends for years, and I send him many of his customers. Now back to your situation. You say you need a place to stay. Well, I'm the man to see," he smiled.

"The place where my wife and I stayed is going to be up for rent in about two weeks or less."

"Are you sure?" I asked, not knowing whether to believe this fast talker or not.

"Am I sure?" he laughed. "Of course, I'm sure. We are moving into a new home I just purchased. My wife just had a baby. We already have a son and need a bigger place. Listen, after you've finished here, I can show you the place today if you've got some free time."

"Right now! I'll come back and get the van later," I told the salesman. "I need to take a look at Mr. Banks's place right away. It could mean me being able to stay in Los Angeles after all." Mr. Banks's place was a large duplex sitting in a tranquil, well-kept neighborhood between San Vicente and Pico Boulevard. I was shocked to see how big it was inside. Downstairs, there was a living room, dining room, half bath, and a gigantic kitchen and family room combined. Upstairs, there were two bedrooms with a full bath, a backyard that would have made any teenage boy proud to call it their home, and a basketball net and hookups.

The house was too good to be true. The place was super big and clean, with beautiful, thick moss green carpet throughout the house. The kitchen cabinets and low dropped ceilings had all been remodeled and done by Mr. Banks himself; he bragged about it with pride. The entire house was a showcase. I knew that I would certainly have a heart attack after seeing this dream place and finding out that I couldn't afford it. It was time to talk about money.

"How much?" I asked him without batting an eye.

"$2,000 to move in and $700 a month," he answered. "Your move-in fee covers first and last month's rent along with a security deposit of $600. If you've got that, the place is yours in two weeks."

I should have known something was funny about the deal when he didn't even require a credit check. "But what about an application?" I asked. "Don't you want me to fill out an application?"

Mr. Banks seemed to know the ropes in the real estate business and had decided that credit checks and applications didn't mean anything. "Your money is what speaks to me," he answered. "I've been all through the long, drawn-out ordeal of running credit checks and checking applications. None of it matters but receiving your rent when it's due. Can you afford $700 a month?" he asked me.

"I've only been paying $550 a month up until now. However, if I could put my boys in a lovely home like this, I'd gladly make the sacrifice and find some way to come up with another $150 toward the rent. It would certainly be worth it."

"Well, how soon can you get me the cash? The sooner the better. I have other clients who have seen the place and want it too. You wouldn't want me to accept anyone else's money before yours?"

I sure didn't, so I had Mr. Banks take me directly to my bank.

"I'll need a witness for this transaction," I told him, "because lawfully, I should receive a key from you upon your receiving my money."

"You'll have a key a day or two before you move in, and I'll put that in writing on your receipt," he promised and did so.

Betty Kelly handled the transaction for me, so I introduced her to Mr. Banks. She was so happy to hear that things were finally working out in my favor. I also kept Betty posted on the latest happenings. She knew the battle I had been fighting and what I was up against so far.

After paying Mr. Banks, I realized that I could still get the van without going totally broke. I needed some transportation anyway. It was time for me to stop begging for a ride to get here and there. I figured I'd better jump at this low price for such a good used van.

I had Mr. Banks drop me off at the used car lot. I was about to purchase my first set of wheels.

CHAPTER 9:

"THE STREETS OF L.A.—SOCIAL SERVICES OR STARVE"

The boys couldn't believe that I had finally done it. "Now we can go to Disneyland and Knott's Berry Farm and Magic Mountain!" Oh, they were making big plans to have fun already.

"And guess what?" I told them. "I've got an even bigger surprise for you that's gonna make you really happy," I told them about the duplex and then drove them around the neighborhood so that they could check it out for themselves.

"Wow!" Their eyes were wide with excitement."We're going to be living in that big house?"

"Yes, we are," I happily and excitedly smiled at them all. For once, I felt like I was giving them a chance at a real life, the kind of life boys should know before becoming men and have to face stronger obstacles. The kind of life I always dreamed of giving them.

Then one of my boys asked, "Who's going to be living next door?"

Until now, I hadn't given the duplex next door much thought. Now I was looking it over closely.

"It doesn't look like anyone is living there," I said after noticing that there was paper up on the windows. Anyway, that was not my concern now. What I wanted to do was start packing up at the apartment.

Ebony and Chafielle had already moved their equipment out a week ago. They were in the process of making arrangements to go to New York City to find a backer for a live album they wanted to record. Even though my dreams of becoming a great songwriter had not died, we all decided that now was not the best time. Maybe further down the road, we might be able to hook up again and complete our project.

About three nights before we were scheduled to move into our new place, the kids and I decided to make another unannounced trip to the duplex to see how far Mr. Banks was coming with his moving out. Boy, were we in for a big surprise. It was nighttime, but even the kids noticed that the curtains were still neatly hung and that there still seemed to be people living in the house.

"Mom," Vaughn started right in with his observations, "It doesn't look like they are moving to me."

It didn't look that way to me either. So I went up to the door and rang the bell. Mr. Banks answered. As soon as he saw it was me, he stepped out on the porch and closed the door as if he didn't want his wife to hear our conversation.

"Mr. Banks," I said, "it doesn't look like you're moving, and we are supposed to be settled in here in three days."

"Listen, honey," he said, "my business also moves houses in a matter of hours. So moving furniture is no big thing to me. I'll have everything out of here in no time. So you don't have to be alarmed by what it looks like. You just let me handle everything, and don't worry," he insisted. "I'll call you and give you the key in a couple of days. All right?"

The only thing I could say was, "All right." But still, there was an uneasy feeling beginning to grow inside me. Something wasn't right about this man. Why didn't he want his wife to hear the conversation, and why hadn't he offered to introduce us? It would have been the perfect time. I would soon find out that my soap opera days in California were just beginning.

When I got the call from Mr. Banks, I wasn't surprised to hear about the delay in moving plans. "Darn those big corporate realtors," he cursed. "They've messed me all up now. The paperwork on my place is still not complete, and they say it's going to be another two weeks."

"Two weeks!" I screamed. "The court papers say I have to be out of here by tomorrow. You've got my money, and now you're telling me..."

"Hold on, hold on," he said. "If you'll give me a chance, I was just about to tell you that you can move into the duplex next door to me until then. I own that side of the house too, and it's no problem. I won't charge you anything else. You won't begin paying rent until you move in here."

There was no way that I could even argue the point. I had to move into something, and he knew it. He had me just where he wanted me.

The duplex was just as big as his place was downstairs, but it didn't have an upper floor. Instead, there was a large living room with a fireplace, dining room, smaller but newly remodeled kitchen, and one bathroom at the end of a long hallway with two big bedrooms. It didn't look bad, but it in no way compared to his more modernly decorated home we were supposed to move into.

Our duplex did not even have any carpet on the floors. They were all hardwood, except for the kitchen, where he had freshly laid some new brown brick linoleum. We had a washroom where I could put a washer and dryer hookup. Instead of the revolving glass doors like his place had, we had to reach the backyard from a long, narrow sidewalk. There was no doubt about it. This side was not as modern, cozy, or as comfortable as the side I had paid for my family to live in. But it would do for now. It *had* to.

I also had to deal with some serious setbacks right

from the beginning. The first real problem I had was that there wasn't a refrigerator available for about a week. Mr. Banks and I had an understanding that the stove and refrigerator came along with my apartment. However, Mr. Banks said that because he didn't realize until the very last moment that he would have to put us up in the duplex next to his, he had not arranged to have a refrigerator delivered. In return, he mentioned that the house was freshly painted and the kitchen had a new floor.

"Do you see all of this work? A few partners and I did all of this just yesterday. We all worked overnight in a hurry to have the place ready, and I just didn't have time to think about anything else. I'm sorry," he said," but I'll have a refrigerator delivered by tomorrow."

Well, that tomorrow turned into about a week. There was one excuse after the other. First, the appliance store he went to didn't have the correct size refrigerator in the store. Then the guys on the delivery truck were all tied up with other deliveries and so on. So in the meantime, I had to go back and forth over to Mr. Banks to get this or that. We had to share his refrigerator until mine came.

The next big problem was I didn't have a telephone for almost three weeks. Thinking that his place would be mine, I had the phone company turn the phone on there on my expected move-in date. Even though he knew he would not be moving out, he didn't disconnect his phone service. Eventually, the telephone company disconnected his line and put my number at Mr. Banks' place.

I was so taken aback after discovering that things were not starting off as I had anticipated that I forgot to call the phone company and have the services transferred to the correct address. And when I did finally think about it, I figured that it would only be two weeks. Why transfer the service over to my side and then have to switch lines back to the other side? After two weeks and he still hadn't moved out of the duplex I was supposed to rent, I called and had the services switched over.

"I'm sorry, ma'am, your service has been on now at that address since November 18th." I realized my negligence. After clearing up the matter with the operator, she arranged for my service to be connected. This is when I found out that there was another problem with the connections on my side of the duplex. "The lines are down," they told me, and a special crew would have to come out to hook up my service. That took another week. Finally, my phone was on, but yet another problem surfaced.

The kids and I had been smelling something off and on since we moved in, but now the smell had gotten stronger. I called it to Mr. Bank's attention. He looked under the house, which only had an opening on my side. That's why he was unable to smell the sewage.

"There's so much water under there you can swim in it," he complained after he came from under the house. "A water pipe must have broken," he said. "I'll have some plumbers come out now and go under there and fix it."

Sure enough, in a couple of days, a crew of men came

out to fix the problem. Before they left, one guy knocked on my door to inform me of the potential health hazards.

"Ma'am," he said, "that water is coming from your toilet, and it's been broken like that for some time. Now that someone is living here, the toilet is constantly being flushed. Water will remain under the house until the pipe is fixed.

"Well, what's the problem?" I asked. "Isn't he going to have you guys repair it?"

"To be truthful with you, lady, I think he got upset when we told him how much it was going to cost. And believe me, we gave him a big discount on the price. There's just no way that he can get by with paying just a couple of hundreds of dollars on a job like this. He's let the condition get too far out of hand, and it needs immediate attention if he is going to have tenants living here."

I thought about the matter. Mr. Banks knew about this problem even before we moved in here. *That's* why the place was vacant. Before the plumber left, he told me that I had the right as a renter to report him if he didn't have the work done right away.

"The smell is going to get worse, believe me," he said, "creating a public health hazard."

I confronted Mr. Banks about what the plumber told me, and he assured me that the problem would be fixed.

"Mr. Banks, please hurry," I added. "You can't smell the foulness on your side like we can, and I'd hate to find lizards coming up into our house."

I must have really put something on his mind, or maybe he was terribly afraid of lizards. Within a few days, two or three of his beer drinking buddies were roaming around the property and examining the conditions under the house. You know the kind of men, naturally handy with tools and have an innate ability to fix anything, but also have to stop every two or three hours to have a beer and fool around. They came back two or three days in a row, but finally, the problem was cleared up. The smell was gone, and the pipes were fixed.

Each day that the mailman stopped by our house, I noticed that he left tons of mail. We had a slot that let the mail directly into the house, and I could hear it as it slid onto the floor. At first, I paid no attention and politely picked out my mail and threw the rest away. Then one day, I stopped and started reading some of the names addressed to this duplex: Harris, Franklin, Jones, Williams, Smith, Toliver. *My goodness*, I thought, *a million people must have at one time rented this duplex from Mr. Banks.* I didn't find out what this was all about until one evening when a couple came to the door and rang the bell.

"May I help you?" I asked, looking through the peephole on the door.

"How long have you been living here, may I ask?" the lady spoke to me.

"For about a month and a half," I answered.

"Well, ma'am, we know it's none of your business, but we gave the owner of this place a deposit several months ago, and we never heard from him again."

"Well, why didn't you get your money back?" I asked.

Then the man spoke up. "We came by on several occasions, but there was never anyone home over there, and this place was still vacant. But now we've noticed that someone is living here and realized that he must have finally rented it out."

"Well, surely now he should be willing to give you a refund."

"That's just it. We've written Mr. Banks letters and called him, but he hasn't responded to us. Can you give him this card when you see him? Tell him that our attorney will get in touch with him if he doesn't get in touch with us and refund our deposit."

I agreed to relay their message. My eyes were open, and I could see the whole picture now. That's why there was mail with so many different names being delivered here. Mr. Banks had been getting away with highway robbery for a mighty long time, it seemed. I knew for a fact that lots of people leave deposits on places and never get them back. Reasons for this vary. Whatever it may have been just helped increase the con artist's confidence to prey on these victims.

I gave Mr. Banks the message glaring at him suspiciously. He knew I was suddenly onto his game. To change the subject, he said, "It won't be long now. The wife and I will be moving out the first of the year."

Yes, the kids and I had gone through the holidays under the pressure of living with a swindler. Would we ever get to move into the side of the duplex that we paid $2,000 for?

I didn't have much of the holiday spirit that year. I was just thankful that my kids were all healthy and we had a roof over our heads. Sparky was still doing his job too. Besides being the best companion in the world, he always hugged us whenever we felt lonely and discarded.

That's what I love about dogs and cats. They have a way of constantly filling up those empty spaces in our lives. It almost scared me when the day came that it finally happened. Mr. Banks knocked on my door early, asking if he could plug in an electric cord.

"My electricity is already turned off," he said. "We're moving everything out today."

I gladly opened my door and let him use one of our plugs, never even asking him why he needed electricity. Then, I saw the big truck and the two men helping him move pull up.

I briefly met his wife earlier, but I never saw too much of her because of her job. She was gone early every morning. I never knew what time she arrived in the evening. So, we had not done much getting to know one another.

But, now, seeing her standing outside as they were loading up the truck made me want to extend my hand in friendship to her, even if we were just saying goodbye. I just felt friendly anyway. I was so thrilled about us finally moving into that beautiful duplex next door.

In a way, I wished I had just stayed inside; she seemed to be upset with her husband about something. She held the baby while their little boy was playing on the lawn. I was glad that my kids were in school, so they weren't in the way of the movers.

I commented how fast the baby was growing and how cute both kids were. But I could see her mind was on something else far more important, so I quietly slipped back indoors.

I watched the truck leave and return a couple of times, and then I saw Mrs. Banks gather the two children up and drive off in her car. Mr. Banks's truck was still in the driveway, so I knew he was still finishing up with something inside. Then he came over to unplug his cord and said his last goodbyes. That's when he informed me that I would have a new landlord.

"Yes, I had to sell the place," he told me. "But don't you worry. We've got rent control in this area, and the new owners cannot go up on your rent for at least a year. If they even decide to, you've still got your receipt, don't you?" he asked me.

I told him I did.

"Well, whenever the new owners do get by here, that's your proof that you have already paid your move-in fees to live here. Now, have a good time and good luck."

He bid me farewell and left the key. I couldn't wait for him to pull out the driveway. I was going to run over there and kiss the ground! I was so glad that they were gone. As I saw his truck slowly turn the corner, I slowly turned the key and walked inside.

At first, I didn't see what devastation lay ahead of me because the living and dining rooms were untouched. But then I saw it as I entered the kitchen and the huge family room. Mr. Banks had destroyed all the beautiful work he had done to that part of the house. He took an electric saw, cut up the kitchen and wall cabinets, and tore down all the material used to build the electric lighted drop ceiling. Tiles on the sink were torn, and the floor was full of glass.

He had ruined the place. He had even torn up the electric wall sockets so that no electricity could flow in there until it had all been remodeled and rebuilt. The place was in shambles. It was a total disaster. I couldn't believe my eyes. He made sure that there was no way I could have moved in there after him.

"Don't feel bad, and don't worry Mom," the kids told me after they took a look at what this man had done after they had returned home from school. "We like the other side next door. Really we do," they said, trying to look convincing.

"At least it's a whole lot bigger than that one-bedroom apartment," Alphonso said. He was always so optimistic.

"In fact, it's the biggest place we've had in a long, long time," Vaughn reminded me.

I just loved my kids for always trying to make the best out of a bad situation. But deep down inside, I knew it wasn't fair for them to have to see how cruel grown-ups could be. They were still young, and these shouldn't have been the lessons they were being taught from the outside world. Kids don't forget. It's hard for them to do. But they easily forgive. Being a mother all these years taught me two important lessons: give your time and show your children your love. They needed to have and know that you got them regardless of whatever else happened.

At this moment, I realized the bond my boys and I developed. Sticking together was our specialty. We knew how to do that. All the moving around, meeting that big, bad wolf from time to time, and having to escape the grip of disappointment made us all strong. Surviving and doing so the hard way has taught us many lessons. Each lesson was a little harder than the last. But here we were, still fighting the battles and winning.

For the next two weeks, I was out of sorts. My world had been turned upside down by Mr. Banks's duplicity. Right away, I had real estate company representatives knocking at my door, asking what seemed like a million questions. The number one question, "What was I doing there?"

One lady who showed her card from Century 21 said they were taking over the property. Another gentleman from Fred Sands Realty stated that the property had been offered to them and was up for bid. In all, at least five or six different real estate brokers were baffled by how they all were under the impression that this piece of property was soon to be in their possession.

I was standing my ground. Whenever any of these representatives found the need to explain why I had to move out, I quickly reminded them that I had also been a victim of this con artist and had my rights violated.

"That's easier said than done with my means of support," I told them all when they seemed to feel like I could just find someplace else to live. I went on arguing my point. "I'm a struggling mother on welfare with three kids to feed and support and keep a roof over their heads."

Hearing my plea, along with the fact that one of my kids was disabled, further proved that it wouldn't be easy for any of them to get a sheriff's order to lock me out. Showing them all my receipts where I paid $2,000 to move into the dilapidated duplex surely buried any complaints they felt they could bring up in any courtroom against me. They were caught off-guard by my determination to reside in the duplex for which I was currently paying to occupy.

"But you can't do that!" one realtor shouted. "It's going to be harder for us to sell this property as long as there are tenants on the premises."

Another realtor agreed with my decision to fight the wrong committed by Mr. Banks. "You've definitely got a court case," he told me.

Now, for many reasons, it seemed as though everybody's hands were tied at the moment. How many companies had been conned out of their money, I didn't know. Nobody told anyone what or how much they had lost.

About a month after the realtors stopped bothering and questioning me about my right to remain on the premises, I received a telephone call from a bank in Northern California. Unfortunately, it seems like the real owners of the property were an elderly couple who had lost the property to one of Mr. Banks's scams.

"He never owned the property where you are staying," they told me, "and he had no rights to be living there himself or to rent that side out. It's all been illegal, and no court would justify any of his actions. Can you tell us anything about where he might have moved?"

"No," I said. I truthfully had no knowledge of his whereabouts. I learned that day that these old people were forced out by him five years ago, and it had taken them this long to regain the title on their property.

"If and when you do find him, he's got a lot of legal complaints and suits to answer to."

No wonder Mr. Banks had left me no forwarding address.

My final conversation that day was with the Savings & Loan Division. I planned on informing them of my plans.

"I certainly can't move out now," I told them after hearing that the actual owners might be thinking about renting the property and remaining up north where they had been forced to move. "I'd like to see the place where I originally paid to move properly repaired so that we can move over there," I told them.

They then informed me that they would confer with the owners and get back to me as soon as possible. I didn't hear anything from them for about three weeks. When they finally called, they had an entirely different outlook on the matter and my involvement. Mr. Matthews was introduced to me as the representative working toward settling my housing situation. I was offered the opportunity to remain where I was, but I had to start making rent payments of $650 a month immediately.

I could immediately tell that there was no plan to renovate the mess next door and give me what I initially paid for. Instead, they probably were going to try to sell the property with me still living there and get as much rent from me until the dispute over the property was settled.

I sensed that something was missing in their proposal. I had no guarantee of what came afterward for my family and me. I knew somebody was stalling for time, and it should have been me.

"Mr. Matthews, if your bank expects me to pay rent for something I didn't want, I'm going to need something from you. I want this side of the duplex remodeled inside and out: a new paint job, drapes, and new carpet throughout the house because I don't have any at present. Also, I'd like repairs on... "

"Wait a minute. Just hold it a second." Mr. Matthews had heard enough. "Are you telling me that your side of the house was unfinished when you were forced to move in there?"

"I certainly am," I said.

"Well, I'm sorry," he apologized quickly. "I was under the impression that everything was in tip-top shape and completely remodeled, with carpet and drapes and all the standard amenities at the time of your move. I'll have to get with the owners and the committee to discuss what you have told me and then let you know our decision. Until then, I suggest putting your rent payments in escrow or a personal savings account. You will be required to make all back payments on the rent after our decision is made."

"Absolutely," I agreed. "But Mr. Matthews, if I'm going to have to pay for second best, it's going to have to look like first class."

They all knew that they had a pro on their hands now, someone who had been financially screwed but still had all of her marbles upstairs. It was going to be more than just a mental trip. I quickly became one hell of a determined choicy bitch who made them feel the effects of me saying "no." And until I said "yes," there was nothing they could do.

I expected to see a cleaning and remodeling crew out in a couple of days. But to my surprise, the whole summer went by that year without a single peep out of them. What I figured happened was they didn't want to spend any money, but they wanted me to do so. Their lawyers probably advised them that after a specific amount of time had gone by without collecting any rent from me, it would increase their chances of having the court remove me from the premises.

I knew they were just waiting, and so was I. I even consulted a legal aid lawyer to determine what I should do. I was told to write the Savings & Loan company a letter stating that I am willing and able to pay rent at the address as soon as the property is updated to rentable condition.

"Send them a copy and keep a copy yourself' I was also advised. "If a court does decide in their favor, you can appeal, and you'll have proof that rental payments were agreed on by you and that you were amenable to the payments, but they were the reason why the payments could not be sent."

I sent the letter registered mail and received the card showing that someone had signed for it. Still, no word from the bank. I wasn't going to allow their silence to depress me or stress me. I knew that legally, I had time on my side. No one could just *make* me move out. There would have to be a court date set for a hearing. And because their offices were located in Northern California and not in Los Angeles, that gave me more time.

That summer, the kids and I had a ball. Having transportation opened up Los Angeles to us. We visited many of the beaches and a lot of amusement parks. The boys joined a swim team, and that took us to many fun-filled tournaments, with my boys bringing in a handful of first, second, and third place ribbons and trophies. We barbecued in the backyard almost every weekend and took trips to Disneyland, Knott's Berry Farm, and Sea World. Yes, we were living it up.

I wasn't just splurging and squandering money. I saved some when I could, but I had to keep the van in working condition with our busy schedule now. Quite a few times, I found myself having to replace a cylinder here and there or buy a rebuilt carburetor, not to mention new shocks and tires.

Once, we were miles away from home when I had a busted water hose. I can remember having to pay a tow truck to bring us all the way back to Los Angeles and then pay a pretty penny to a mechanic the next day for not only new hoses but a new radiator also.

It seemed like I had to spend some of my savings on car repairs every month. Once, my battery was stolen while in Compton. It was midnight, and we were trying to replace it. Lucky for me, gasoline was no more than 79 or 89 cents a gallon for regular then. That's all I used on my 1971 van; it worked perfectly fine. A steering gearbox, a rebuilt engine, new brakes, fuel injector, points and fuses, a new body paint job, and lots of other parts; you name it, and I had to replace it. In less than a year's time of owning the van, I think I had bought almost all new parts. Now it still had an old body, but with brand new parts. But what could I do? We had to keep it moving.

There was no stopping us now.

The calls from the Savings & Loan in Eureka, California, began coming in around the last week in September of that same year. They had someone new handling the case this time, a lady named Mrs. Shelby.

It's funny how men love to dominate the workplace, but when dealing with really tough customers, they always turn that job over to women. Well, this time, it was lady versus a lady, and she had her work cut out for her if she thought she could out-talk *this* lady. I was ready to hear the plan.

Mrs. Shelby had one of those soft, timid voices. This time, they had plans to smother the cat with kindness.

"Ms. Horton," she whined, "it's been nearly a year since you've moved in there, and you've been living rent-free all this time."

"Yes, I know that. But it doesn't mean a thing."

After listening to my argument and questions about why the owners had not made any efforts to respond to my demands yet, Mrs. Shelby said she couldn't understand why I hadn't spent any money fixing up the place myself by now. I had an answer for anything she threw at me.

"Ms. Shelby," I said, "I've been sitting on my hands without knowing what to do. The first gentleman that called me advised me to save up my rent because I would have made back payment whenever an agreement had been reached. Now I couldn't very well spend that money on remodeling and have my back rent payments too!"

Then Ms. Shelby went on to ask, "Well, now that you have all that money saved up, won't that be enough to help you to relocate someplace else?"

"No," I sharply insisted. "I want the place I paid to rent. Why should I go through the torment of finding someplace else? I'm perfectly satisfied with this location now."

"Ms. Horton," she called out my name as her voice got sweeter than before. But I *knew* what was in her heart. "Let me be truthful with you now," she continued. "The owners are too old to have the task of being landlords. They really can't afford what it would cost them to have our bank collect all the monthly payments and do the taxes and paperwork. So they've decided to sell the property. They don't want the problem of remodeling or doing whatever it takes to make your place livable.

"So we're taking it off their hands and selling it for them. And the buyer that we've found wants to use the property to start a preschool. They do not intend it for rental purposes at all. They are willing to settle with you out of court by giving you, on top of all the free rent you've had, $2,000 to relocate. We thought that might solve the problem fair and square. What do you say to that? They're even willing to give you ample time to look around for some other property. Now you can't beat a deal like that!"

Oh, she was *so* sweet and convincing. It was hard for me to engage in a verbal fight with her as I had planned. I knew even a legal aid lawyer would have advised me to move under those circumstances, especially without the hassle of going to court. But, yes, Mrs. Shelby had me thinking real hard, and she knew it. And I could feel her confidence rising as she awaited my ok in agreement.

I didn't want to tell her the truth; that $2,000 was just about all I would have to move with. So if it never happened again, I made sure my boys had fun that summer, lots of expensive fun. And now I didn't have the year's money in back rent, so what the heck was I to do?

Now I had to get back down to business and face paying my dues again. I should have been prepared for it. Nothing that good was going to last forever. It was a pre-paid vacation. Now it was over and back to work and back to moving. This time, our move took us deep into the really tough streets of L.A. We now lived on 17th Street, between Venice and Washington Boulevards.

It wasn't that easy even getting here. I had forgotten about my name being on the hot sheet for landlords' inquiries, so it took about a month of filling out applications before I was able to find a place. Then one day, I even scared myself with the luck I had. I was just about ready to give up the ship again when I happened to call a number listed for a rental and reached a lady that was working in the Motown offices in Hollywood.

She was shocked when she heard that I was Gladys Horton, the original lead singer of Motown's Marvelettes. And I, in turn, was shocked to find out that she worked for Motown's Hollywood offices out here in California. She just about told me over the telephone that I could get the place if I wanted to. So my search was finally over. And believe me, I was so worn out and tired now that whatever the place looked like, I was going to take it. Being on that hot list, my name wasn't exactly helping me anyway. I wasn't about to be choosy. It was now or never for me.

When I got to the place, I was surprised to find out that it was a big house on a lot all by itself. It was designed and built like those houses back east—a basement, main floor, upstairs had two bedrooms and a full bath, a large formal living and dining room, and a dressing room with another full bath and bedroom downstairs.

The kitchen was the highlight of the entire house. It

was full of windows that gave terrific views of the city and the surrounding neighborhood. The house sat atop a hill, and I could see that familiar Hollywood sign painted on that mountain behind Sunset and Hollywood Boulevard. It was pretty visible, even that far away. I could see it from our kitchen area, exceptionally well on a clear day.

Connected to the kitchen was an outdoor patio which also made a perfect view of the scenery. Even in the Hollywood Hills, the house had more room than most California houses. So when she quoted me the rental price of $1,000 a month, I accepted it. I knew my best bet would be to get me some renters for the upstairs area. The kids and I had more than enough space and room on the main floor. Renting out the two bedrooms upstairs would help me keep my rent manageable.

It certainly wasn't hard for me to find my first renters, either. I knew some relatives of Bobby Womack's who had been looking for an apartment. They had a good manager who had assured me that he would be taking care of their rent. Right away, that problem had been solved for me.

Now that I had squared away all the tasks I had to complete after moving into someplace, I was free to think about my career again. I couldn't keep this moving from place to place all my life. I needed to search for some solid ground and stay there.

The songwriting business had not provided me with

the big break that I thought it would. And my first comeback show had left me without an audience and still broke. It was then that I decided to join the fray and begin writing my first book.

I wanted to tell my story differently and make it commercial and more marketable than some other Motown artists had done. So I thought of a way to do a record album storybook. I'd tell my story on tape with words and songs between chapters and include both new and old songs.

It was also going to be a way to introduce the public to my songwriting ability. *Oh my,* I thought as I started on the project, *it's going to be different, and it's going to be original.* No other artist has told their story on tape before. I seem to be able to come up with new brilliant ideas all the time. I just never got around to seeing them through to completion. I vowed that this time would be different. I'll make them all sit up and take notice of my story. Just you all wait and see.

I needed a great title, a title that would speak for itself. So I thought about a lot of things. Then something said to me: name it what you need most right now. The words help came to my mind.

"That's it!" I shouted out loud. A title short but straight to the point: *Help.* I need help. Help me, somebody. I wanted to mention to the listeners from the beginning of my story how people always seem to stop whatever they're doing at the call of someone screaming for help.

It was the one word to which everyone seemed to yield.

Once more, I knew I had hit the jackpot and had come up with a million-dollar idea. I would find out later that it would take more than 15 different tapes to record my whole life's history. Even with the songs and poems, I'd still only be skimming the surface of my story. I wanted to dig deep, go back into my past, and tie it into my future.

I worked on this project for about nine months or more. I let a couple of people who I knew would give me their honest opinion on how they felt it would go over with the public. They all agreed that it was a unique and different style of telling my life's story, but it really didn't come off as being a serious, sincere story like I wanted to present.

One friend told me that it would be a terrific idea to present it in this way for people who have reading disabilities or other handicaps, enabling them to not read for themselves. God knows I had met many of these kids and adults in different group homes and schools everywhere we had traveled. These people, including Sammie, my son, would never pick up a book and read it themselves.

So, no, I wasn't throwing away this tape idea at all. I could surely use it to follow up on my first book, dedicating it to those disabled citizens who wanted to read but couldn't. But for now, I decided to keep all of my recordings on tape until I could find the time to sit down and just tell it all like it was in the book version.

***

It was 1987 in LA, and now more than ever, I just wanted to let all of my ambitions go and get out into these streets and find out what my boys were learning.

After hearing rounds of nightly gunshots more often than I had been accustomed to, I was awakened to the fact that we were living in a part of town where the people talked less and showed more action.

I didn't have to worry so much about Sammie; his main concern was only getting on that bus daily in the mornings and going to school. When he returned home in the evenings, I had no problems trying to keep him off the streets. He was ready to watch television, have dinner, and enjoy his home life until school began the next day.

Vaughn had not yet posed any real problems for me, but it was now 1987, and he was 17 years old. His likes and dislikes had changed drastically. He was going to high school, and I knew for sure that girls were becoming a favorite with him. This was never a problem for me. I wanted girls to be interested in my son, and I wanted him to let me know that he had similar feelings for them. Any real mother looks forward to seeing her children have children.

The kissing game and lover's lane opened Vaughn's eyes to what the birds and bees mean. Of course, he was shy and didn't want to bring his female acquaintances to the house, so hanging out at other houses was the cool thing. But even now, Vaughn showed himself to be very conscious that he would have to make a salary one day on his own. It was this year that he started work on several jobs.

Being a member of his school's Cadet Corps instilled him with pride. He kept his uniform clean 100% of the time. Neatness and cleanliness were significant for him as he began his junior year of high school. He was an honor student and was placed in a class of A students. In addition, Cadet Vaughn won first place for California at the drill team workouts. So, this and other positive attention gave Vaughn the motivation to keep his head in the right direction, no matter what was happening around him.

It seemed as though finding work was never a problem for him. His first job was an office job filing and bookkeeping at an Army Recruiting Station close by. The musical entitled *The Gospel Truth* was one of his first jobs as a theater usher. Later, he worked at several other theaters on Hollywood Boulevard after moving there.

Once, he even tried working at a popular fast food chain, but he couldn't hack it. Vaughn came home with his hand blistered from hot grease. From then on, he stated that cooking was not his deal. Vaughn landed his highest paying job yet as a security guard just before he graduated. I couldn't be more proud.

Wearing a uniform was something he seemed to be destined to do. Soon after graduation, he signed up and enlisted to go into the United States Army. I recalled one night while we lived on 17th Street, I had to get into the van and get Vaughn from the basketball court. I had told him many times not to worry me by staying out after dark. I'd heard stories from the kids about how some of the older men in the neighborhood had been bullying the younger teens—showing them guns and making threats of what they had coming if they ever came down wrong with them. I didn't mean to embarrass Vaughn by showing up in front of his friends in a rage, but I just couldn't understand why these boys would knowingly lay themselves out as targets for these neighborhood thugs.

"Why do you guys keep playing after it has gotten dark, knowing what danger is out there?" I screamed at him as he got into the van.

"Mom," he cried, "all the guys are laughing at me! I'm tired of you treating me like I'm still a baby. Why don't you just leave me alone? If I get hurt, I just get hurt!" he screamed back.

Deep inside, his words tore me up. Had I spent all of these years with my kids only to lose them to these streets? I was wise enough to know that it was all due to the environment. Along with all of Vaughn's excellent qualities, he had to survive with this type of attitude because of where I had us living.

There was no doubt about it—we were right smack in the middle of the streets of L.A., the hood. So, I had to realize something. When you're in Rome, you must do as the Romans do. And when you're in the ghetto, you must live as the people in the ghetto do.

I can't tell you how many times throughout my life traveling around with my boys that I had to think back to the root of the *real* problem. I wouldn't have constantly suffered these setbacks or had to beg for a place to live and worry about food to eat if I had been given my proper due from the very beginning.

If I would have received my rightful piece of the pie off "Please Mr. Postman" alone, I could have bought my castle a long time ago. My boys could have been raised like the royal princes they were. I won't even mention all I could have given them and myself if only Motown would have paid me for all the other successful hits the Marvelettes made.

These kids of mine are a blessing. With all I had accomplished in my life, I should have been able to do so much more for them. I think in many ways they were special and deserved to live their lives in their own special haven that I should have been able to provide for them. Now, I can't help but be furious at the people who in many ways were responsible for them being tricked into coming into nothing but hell because that's all I could provide since my rightful share of monies had not been given to me. How could I give them what they should rightfully have when all rightfully owed to me had not been given? All I had was experience. Experience with no money!

There was no doubt about it. The innocent years of my kids' youth during which they expected and loved my protectiveness were becoming a distant memory. Instead, they were growing up and fighting to find their strengths and develop their character. My fears grew more intense as they got older. I sure didn't want them to discover who they were in those L.A. streets. No sir, not at all.

Alphonso, now 13 years old, was still pretty naïve and innocent. While he was getting older, he still enjoyed playing with younger children. There was something unique about Alphonso's personality. He enjoyed leading the younger kids. Alphonso reveled in teaching them to play games and taking them out for different adventures. I marveled at how the children hung on his every word. It didn't matter where we lived; something about his personality made children flock to him. The neighborhood kids would be at my door, knocking and wanting to play with Alphonso. His friendship after meeting the kids seemed invaluable to them.

While in the midst of growing up, you don't think about it, but if you reflect back, you'll recall an older kid that took the time to make you feel accepted. That's how you learn. That was Alphonso's role in our family. His attitude was that life would be nothing if you couldn't laugh, have fun, and enjoy being alive. Alphonso carried this attitude into the classroom. He enjoyed being the class clown so much that he spent a lot of time in the counselor's offices in whichever school he attended.

It wasn't that Alphonso wasn't smart; he was. He had *lots* of smarts. In many ways, I believe he was a genius. He didn't have to study to remember what he had read. He could definitely carry on an intelligent conversation with anyone. All of his teachers knew this about him too. Often during parent-teacher conferences, they would convey to me that if Alphonso only took his studies seriously and applied himself, his potential was limitless. His teachers believed he could be the class valedictorian and attend any university he chose. "But he seems to get bored easily with the class work," one teacher stated as the reason for his behavioral problems in the classroom.

But one thing was clear: all Alphonso's teachers loved him. He was charming and charismatic; he melted everybody's heart. He touched everybody's life that he met with his kindness and genuine ability to understand people's differences. Sometimes he'd see me just sitting around moping and drowning in my sorrows, and he'd start doing things to garner my attention and change my gloomy disposition. At first, I was grouchy and said things like, "Alphonso, stop playing so much and go clean up your room." But, then, I'd see his light. He was only trying to make me laugh—trying to show me that I didn't have to take it all so seriously.

"Let's have some fun and forget about the bomb that was about to drop," was Alphonso's philosophy on dealing with the worst situations. He was always the life of the party, making and keeping friends forever every place we lived.

Alphonso had an energy that exuded all around him. That's why there was always company over to our house to see and be with Alphonso. He had a way of making you feel alive.

***

Our dog Sparky had been gaining so much weight he began to look like he was pregnant. I knew something was wrong because he could hardly walk. We had to take him to the vet.

"It's heartworms," the veterinarian told me. I had never even heard of it before. But the fear of losing Sparky quickly made me educate myself on the disease.

"Oh no, not my dog," I cried. "We love him so much. Can't you do something?" I begged.

The vet told me about the treatment options for heartworms, and it was shocking. First, the dog had to be injected with a poison called arsenic. By doing this, the arsenic kills the worm, causing it to release its grip from around the dog's heart.

"You're taking a mighty big chance," the vet warned me. "Some dogs make it, and others don't." The vet explained that this is because the worm may have already done too much damage to the heart.

With eyes full of tears, I looked at Sparky. I already felt the pain of what it would be like losing my dog. I didn't want to think about it. Not *my* dog. He just had to live. With all the love we all had for Sparky, I knew that it would surely be enough to pull him through.

Yes, Sparky was a big strong dog. There was no reason for us to doubt that Sparky would be okay. So, I asked the vet to give Sparky the treatment he needed.

The next three days were filled with tension while Sparky was in the hospital. I think I called the veterinarian every hour on the hour to get a progress report on Sparky.

"He is doing fine. He's just great." Then we were told, "He'll be ready to go home tomorrow."

Thank God! My dog had made it. He had been cured of heartworms, and I would bring him home the next morning. What a relief! We had all been sick with worry over Sparky's outcome. Now we could relax.

Sparky was so glad to see me; it was as though sparks filled the air that day. I hugged and kissed him, and I knew happiness had put a glow all over our faces. I never knew how much love could exist between humans and animals until now. Undoubtedly, an unbreakable bond is created by the closeness and loyalty between a pet and its owner.

I have a habit of thinking deeply about that which interests me. For example, Sparky was my first dog, and as I observed him, I wondered how dogs learned to charm humans. I think it's because there is no speech, just body language, and energy. The way humans and animals interact demonstrates that silence truly is golden and true feelings and emotions are easily communicated. The silent message creates an impact on your nervous system.

Love seems to have more meaning when you can just look across the room into someone's eyes and *feel* that they love you. It's a spiritual connection and requires no explanation. I can remember how good it made me feel just to have Sparky come across the room and sit down beside me and rest his head by my foot. Nothing was said because dogs can't talk, but ooh, they know how to make you feel loved!

So, I paid the bill and brought Sparky home that day. But, boy, oh, boy, did he have a lot of medicine to take. I felt like a nurse on duty, keeping up with the correct time and dosages to give him.

That first day, everything seemed fine. But I noticed that Sparky had lost weight. I never mentioned in all my talks about Sparky, but he did not eat dog food. I knew my meals would have him back up to his normal size in no time. He ate whatever we ate. In fact, he refused to eat dog food.

After tasting my pot roast with gravy and potatoes, he would rather go hungry than eat dog food. I had hooked him on hungry man meals, and from then on, so to speak, I had a man living in my dog's body—an all meat and potatoes man at that. Even in the mornings, it had to be Rice Krispies, Corn Chex, or flakes. He was definitely spoiled, but I loved him just the same. Now, I noticed that he didn't want to eat much of anything. I was able to give him his medicine, so I didn't worry. I figured that the treatment had diminished his appetite some. Still, as long as he took his medication, it would be enough to keep him healthy.

After a week had passed, I was due to take Sparky back to the vet for a final checkup. I'll never forget how Sparky looked at me that day and ran under the table, not wanting to get this one shot. I questioned the doctor what the shot was for, and he said it was only vitamins.

That same evening after I brought Sparky back home, he began vomiting blood. I called the vet, but they had already closed. There was an emergency number to a facility that Sparky could be taken immediately if I needed help right away, so I called the number. It was a 24-hour emergency room in Culver City.

"Please, lady. Calm down and explain the dog's symptoms," the person on duty asked of me over the phone.

I told him all about Sparky's heartworm treatments and how he had come home and was doing fine until the doctor gave him that shot.

"What could have been in that shot?" I screamed, wishing that I could have been at least 10 feet in front of that vet right now. "He was just jealous!" I got louder over the phone with whoever was on the other end. "He was jealous because my dog had lived," I accused the vet openly.

"Now, ma'am," the voice said to me over the phone, "I understand that you're quite upset. But believe me, we vets love animals. That's why we're in this business. So I doubt seriously that your dog's doctor would have *intentionally* killed him."

"But why? Why now? Sparky was doing just fine," I cried as I was trying to tell him that Sparky didn't want that shot. "I could feel him begging me not to let that doctor give him that shot."

The attendant at the emergency facility said, "That was probably due to Sparky's fear of needles after his three-day stay in the hospital. They had to administer him at least three doses, and he probably didn't take too well to getting those many shots. Watch him carefully tonight, and then either bring him here or back to see your own vet in the morning."

Sparky seemed to stop spitting and was resting peacefully, so I laid down beside him and went to sleep. When I woke up, Sparky had moved under Alphonso's bed and now gagging, and then he vomited something up. I looked and saw a big blob of blood. When he came from under the bed, he could hardly stand up. I knew it was that time. While he was still alive, I wrapped him in a sheet and gently rubbed his head as I repeatedly said, "I love you Sparky. I love you. I love you so much. I love you."

We all knew what was happening. That morning, we said very little to one another, but the pain was written on all of our faces. We were losing our very best friend and guard. Vaughn usually walked to school, so he got ready and left. I put Sammie on his bus. Every day, I drove Alphonso to school because he was still attending Bancroft Jr. High, and it was farther away.

"Let's take Sparky to the vet first," Alphonso told me, "before you drive me to school. You can write me a note for being late. The counselor will understand."

I could hardly stand to see the sadness in his eyes too. It was a wet, dark morning. It was definitely was going to rain. We all knew that. All that day it rained, and when it stopped, I knew Sparky had died. Later on, the sun came out, and there was a rainbow in the sky. Wouldn't you just know it? For some reason, Vaughn had bought a new camera. He ran outside and took a picture of that rainbow, and I put it in his book. I knew my dog had gone to Heaven, but it still didn't stop the terrible pain I carried around in my heart for months afterward. You just don't lose that much love without it hurting really bad.

I still carry Sparky everywhere with me today, in my heart and in the jar where I have his ashes stored. Sometimes, I even dream about him. He comes and lets me pet him awhile, and then he walks away. I know his spirit will never die, just like true love never does.

***

Before moving off 17th Street, I think I made a name for myself outside of the entertainment industry. I had made a name for myself amongst landlords anyway. I had become infamous for allowing roomers and boarders to stay with the kids and me. As quick as one set of roomers moved out, another set moved in just as fast. If they didn't pay the rent, they were gone just as quickly as they had come. Some lasted a week or two, and some hung on a month or more. To my recollection, I think I rented those two bedrooms out to over 12 different people during my stay there.

I learned a big lesson the hard way about collecting the rent on time. The thing I didn't want ever to be known as is "that crazy old landlord." Thank goodness I still had friends who wanted to ensure my singing career got back on track.

"You're an entertainer, Gladys; you can't afford the rumors associated with that lifestyle." Rudy Calvo heard rumors and complaints about who I put out the house every other week. He offered to help me have some professional pictures taken. "You need to start preparing a dynamic promo pack and sending it out to all of the agents."

Spooky had also offered his help by advertising in the *Legendary Ladies* magazine that I would be making a big comeback soon.

"Gladys," he said, "even if you don't have any confirmed dates yet, you have to advertise that you do. You have to get it on the fans' minds that you're on your way back to stardom. If they see it, then they will believe it." He also took some personal photos for his newsletter to help promote my comeback.

In so many words, my caring friends were trying to tell me, "Hollywood is where you need to be." Okay, I could take a hint. And so, we packed up the van and moved.

Yes, we were moving again, but this time, right in the middle of Hollywood. To be exact, Hollywood Boulevard and the Wax Museum. I could see the sign from the front of my apartment building. Movie stars and tourists— it was like a never ending party from noon until 2:00 a.m. daily. On weekends, the party lasted even longer. I saw so many people; New York Times Square didn't have anything on the streets of Hollywood.

The tourists came and trampled all year long on the star-studded boulevards of Hollywood and Sunset. I felt like the cameras were everywhere, watching and filming all the action taking place. We were surrounded by theaters, restaurants, and shops. There was never a dull moment.

Oh, don't get me wrong. I knew I wasn't a star on top yet. I was just glad to be able to live so close to all the happenings. But, with all the glamor around me, I was still keenly aware that Hollywood Boulevard was not immune to homelessness. So in that way, it was similar to the rest of Los Angeles. The homeless were here too, just like I had seen them everywhere else in L.A.

I still had a long way to go. I was, however, finally getting to know the right people. In Hollywood, sometimes knowing the right people means more than having that extra buck all the time. These people were going to stick with me and bring me back. That first year in Hollywood opened up many avenues of opportunities for me. I was able to see the light at the end of the tunnel in more ways than just one.

The awful truth of how Mr. Larry Marshak had robbed the Marvelettes of their livelihood was finally revealed. I heard various rumors about how Mr.Marshak trademarked the group's name. I was now getting first-hand accounts from Katherine Schaffner, an original group member. Katherine had just gone to court in an attempt to settle some problems she was having with receiving her record royalties. She called long distance one day, eager to tell me what information had been revealed to her during her court proceedings.

"Gladys, if you're standing," she said, "please sit down because what I'm about to tell you is going to knock you off your feet."

At this time, it was finally revealed to me who was the real evil, sinister person behind all the bogus Marvelette groups. It seems an investment deal had gone sour between Marshak and Smokey Robinson of The Miracles.

The deal was supposedly settled for Motown by giving Mr. Marshak the authority to use The Marvelettes name to make up for the financial difficulties he was facing.

Whether it was supposed to be only a temporary agreement or not, I'm not sure. But I am sure no original group member was informed about this course of action or was even offered the opportunity to at least make a percentage of the money to be made off the name that we had popularized. It was dirty and underhanded, and absolutely nothing could be done about it at this time. It demonstrated a total lack of respect for what we had done as a catalyst for Motown's ascension in the world of music.

Several reporters told me that it had taken years to get Smokey Robinson to even admit that "Please Mr. Postman" was Motown's first certified #1 song. He argued on many occasions that he deserved credit for giving Motown its first #1 hit, "Shop Around." Unfortunately, it was not considered Motown's first certified #1 because the song had been released and was doing fine on the charts until it suddenly began to fall down. They released another song because The Miracles felt it was slipping on the charts and losing its popularity. In the course of the two songs now being on the charts, "Shop Around" slowly moved back up the charts and later went on to reach the #1 spot.

I had no problem accepting that Smokey made this contribution to Motown. However, the people who decided who received credit for having #1 hits took issue with Smokey's claim. This must have hurt his ego immensely. Smokey had been with Berry from the start. He had all the knowledge and experience in recording, producing, and songwriting. So for a bunch of country girls with no previous experience to come in and go straight to the top without any struggle while he worked so hard had to hurt him.

Deep inside, he must have hated us all along. Discovering The Marvelettes had a little misfortune, he took this opportunity with Mr. Marshak to thwart whatever chances we as a group might have had to make a comeback. He knew about my disabled child and even more about Wanda's drug problem than I'm sure he would be willing to talk about. I could see the light very clearly now. If there had been any genuine concern about how we were going to live in the future, we would have been handled differently. We would have had the opportunity to decide with the assistance of a lawyer before any actions could have been taken to trademark our name. But, no, someone didn't care if we lived or died, and the proof is in the pudding.

When something like this is done, you know that greed, not love, is the real motive. No person with a conscience could do this to five females starting their own families. We were all having children whom his decisions would affect.

These revelations didn't drastically change my opinion of Smokey Robinson. I knew the truth about how sneaky and underhanded he was. I saw how he was unfaithful to be lovely wide Claudette.

When I first saw them together, I idolized them both. What a handsome and gorgeous couple they made, on and off stage. Claudette added so much shine to the act and the look of The Miracles. But even with all their success then, she was willing to be a wife only to him if he demanded it. And, of course, he did. Unfortunately, from what I saw, the reasons were not what Claudette was led to believe.

Smokey Robinson seemed to be intent on letting The Marvelettes know right from the beginning that he was not the loyal, devoted husband Claudette bragged to us about all the time.

I was really impressed with what I thought I saw in them at first. When you are an orphan, you often imagine the characteristics you would want your parents to have: loving, caring, and faithful to one another. I think every female fantasizes about a love affair where the man wants no other woman but her.

Well, I just knew I had lucked up and found a couple like that in the Robinsons. Reality set in when Smokey brought a beautiful girl named Lorraine into our dressing room. He asked if she could stay in the room with us because they had no privacy with Claudette being on the road too. I couldn't believe my eyes. As perfect and beautiful as Smokey's wife Claudette was, he still needed to be unfaithful. He had ruined my idealistic teenage dreams about marriage by showing me his. I resented him for destroying my faith in whether true love existed.

Smokey Robinson was really a dog. He even got Lorraine a room at the same hotel where we were all staying. Yes, with Claudette, the other guys in the group, and all the other Motown acts on the tour were lodging. I felt so sorry for Claudette; everyone knew what was going on behind her back. She was oblivious and continued telling everyone what a good guy Smokey was.

I despised him in those days, so it didn't take much to awaken those same feelings again after learning the part he had played in minimizing my ability to earn a living to support my family and me. As the old adage goes, "What you don't know won't hurt you." But it's what happens *after* you find out that you have to learn to deal with the dirty truth.

As I watched Smokey Robinson put on airs for television and claim to be the focal point of Motown's operation during the '60s, I just shake my head at that snake. While he may never be given credit for providing Motown with its first #1 hit, he was Motown's #1 drug warlord.

I'm speaking to all you delusional Smokey Robinson fans It's only living proof how much deception television provides the viewers with. The medium loves showing the public the real snakes in the grass and glorifying their names out front, leading the poor people to believe in nothing but trash and total lies. Then you ask why? Why is the world becoming such a rotten place in which to live?

Well, you can give some of the thanks to Smokey Robinson, who will never be #1 on the record survey charts for giving Motown its first certified #1, but he was the #1 drug warlord of Motown in the early '60's. The way I feel right now. If you don't like what I've said, you can go to Hell with Smokey because he'll never see the likes of any place else!

***

Many good things were happening at school for my boys. Sammie had graduated and was now in a workshop program for adults with disabilities. Vaughn graduated next. His graduation exercises were held at the famous Greek Theater in Griffith Park. The setting was beautiful, and we had a great time. He later signed up for the Army and went away for basic training. Alphonso was the big man around the house now. He proved his ability to help me keep things organized and constantly cared for his brother Sammie. Alphonso got a job working as a locker room attendant at a well-known Los Angeles indoor pool.

Things in the streets of L.A. were getting dangerous. More drive-by shootings were being reported on the news daily. Then, one night, Alphonso was held up at gunpoint, and it scared me so bad that I decided to get him that car he had been begging me for. He was taking driver's education at school and would soon take the DMV test.

"If you study and get your license, I'll get you transportation!" I promised him. He needed something so he wouldn't have to walk the streets.

On several other occasions, Alphonso's handsome good looks had gotten him a few unwanted whistles not just from older females but some of the men whose preferences weren't women. Yes, times had really changed a lot. Not only on the streets of L.A. but all over the world. Being a parent has never been an easy job, but now, for sure, you needed a master plan.

I finally found my way out of the beautiful but dangerous bright lights of Hollywood Boulevard. In November of 1990, I moved to the Valley Village area of North Hollywood. It was more suitable for families with children. Aside from another move, nothing had changed with me except my show business career was on the rise again, and I was no longer on welfare.

I felt so much more in control now. Not only was I no longer drinking alcohol, I'd also stopped smoking marijuana. I'm elated to say that I was clean and sober for two years at this point in my life. I even lost the beer belly weight, and I'm back to my slim self again. I'll never go back, and I wish I could bottle the determination to others who find it difficult to leave their vices alone.

I still have one flaw that I just couldn't seem to shake. Believe it or not, as I write, I'm still a nomad. I can't seem to stay in one place. I think my best bet will be to just buy a motor home and move around for the rest of my life in my very own wheels!

PART 3:

"THE BEST TIME AROUND"

CHAPTER 10:

"SPOTLIGHT DATE: 1988"

April 17, 1988. It was my time to shine again. It had taken me 20 years to get it all back together, but here I was, once again about to take center stage. I felt like the whole world would be watching, and they wanted to see me do it alone.

So for my comeback debut, there were no background singers, no musicians, no opening act, no one to add to or take away from what I still had to offer. It was just me. It was called the Gladys Horton Expo, held at the hottest nightspot on Sunset Boulevard. Back then, the place's name was Carlos & Charlie's. All the big-timers in the business hung out here on the Strip.

I did a little bit of it all—dancing, acting, and singing live to a music track. Then, I took the audience back to the past and sang all of The Marvelettes hits. The place was packed with promoters and record personalities who wanted to hear what I sounded like after all these years.

Everywhere I turned after that, I met and heard from people who wanted me to perform. My next date was also a solo event. Mr. Rich McCain, author of the book *Let's Get Rich*, asked me to appear at The Palladium to do a show for the Black Businessman's Convention. This convention was held in honor of the new black businesses coming up around the Los Angeles area. So, whether you were opening a new restaurant or selling a newly written novel, here was the ideal place to showcase your product and put your goods on display.

The convention started in the morning and lasted well into the evening hours, with our show being the last event of the day. There was a marvelous fashion show to top it all off, and I got my message across to all the businessmen with our "Too Many Fish In The Sea." When one customer says no, another one will.

Next on my calendar of events was an establishment I never thought I would be playing. The songs I made famous back in the '60s weren't exactly the type of music a high-end supper club like this was noted for. But here I was, on the bill at the Vine Street Bar & Grill, a popular legendary jazz spot in Hollywood. So, what did they want with me? Word was spreading like wildfire that I could surely handle it all. No song or style was too difficult for me! I had matured enough and knew how to adjust my voice to whatever style the songs called for. I could still sing my very own songs in that teenage voice and then jump right on to a contemporary jazz sound and other genres. I even wrote an original jazz tune for that specific engagement called "I'm A Lady, And A Lady Don't Stand For That." Yes, Vine Street was the spot where all the heavyweights had played. It was like I was finally able to reach out and touch the sky, and even that was not the limit. Eartha Kitt, Duke Ellington, Carmen McRae—they all had been standing right where I was now. Now, I *really* had something to brag about.

Rich McCain was working as my publicist now, and was able to generate attention nationwide that I was on my way back. There was a write-up in Cashbox and Billboard announcing my comeback. Rich immediately set up radio interviews for me with Tony Hart of KGFJ and Spider Harris of BRE Exclusive Radio. Rich knew a lot about the business and how to get that little extra push we all need to get the motor started and running.

The first two female background singers I was introduced to were recommended by Rich McCain. My phone had started to ring, and it was people in high places calling.

My first national televised TV show came soon after the publicity had started. I flew out to New York City to tape the *West 57th* saga. The topic of discussion was very important to me; bogus groups touring using group names that weren't their own. Doris Jackson and Shirley Alston of The Shirelles were going to be on the show as well. Yes, I was right on time to not only discuss my personal experience but what should be done about it.

1988: My California Comeback

Program from the Vine Street Show.

Doris, Shirley, and I were on live. Because this problem wasn't unique just to us, on the same show were clippings from a taped conversation with Charlie of The Drifters. He was also finding this impostor group business a problem.

Beverly Johnson, another original Shirelle, had been interviewed earlier. She was shown on a taped conversation discussing how we were robbed of our ability to earn a living.

I was so happy to find out that many people were willing to do all they could do to stop this nonsense. The first thing was to alert the public to what was happening. Unfortunately, it seemed as though many people involved in paying to see these phony groups were not aware that they were being tricked, and the promoters who booked these acts were getting away with it. Illegal name fraud is what it is called when someone claims to be someone that they are not. The sad thing about all this duplicity of some in the music industry is that it has given the industry a dirty reputation and damaged the very people that have done the most for music—the artists. Executives getting away with theft makes you wonder for whom are the laws written for. It was just another type of corruption that plagued the entertainment business. In the 60s, it was payola. Who knows what it will be in the 90s and so on?

Los Angeles is one city that blasts their "Oldie's But Goodies" stations year-round. I interviewed with several radio stations in L.A.; KRLA, KRTH, and KODJ. I also sat for an interview with the extremely one and only, handsome Rick Fields. I even had the opportunity to go on a cable TV show called *The Rock & Roll Record* featuring DJ Steve Probe.

KGFJ, another radio station in the area, had really done a lot of broadcasting that I was back in the limelight again. So, November of 1988 found me appearing in one of their biggest events of the year at The Speakeasy Lounge in West Hollywood. They went all out and gave me a grand introduction. Then, on the night of their event, a limo was sent to pick me up. When the car arrived, I stepped outside to find a cream colored Rolls Royce limousine waiting for me at the curb. Talk about classy! I felt like I should have been on my way to attend a ball!

Later that year, I was privileged to perform at the very famous Rock Around The Clock nightclub in Montebello, California. That New Year's Eve found me in the luxurious resort town of Palms Springs, California. It was then that I had the honor of performing with Mr. Great Balls of Fire himself—Jerry Lee Lewis. Yes, I was on my way back to the big time, and this time was going to be the best time around.

1989 kicked off in an even bigger way. For the first time in 20 years, there would be a Motown artists' reunion. For about two or three years now, prior to the reunion, Ian Levine, a European producer, had revived and dug up the whereabouts of almost every group or artist that had recorded with Motown Records. In addition,

Ian had backed the remakes of a lot of the old recordings. He worked with some of Motown's original hitmakers: Sylvia Moy, the Hollan brothers, and Mickey Stevenson. They had come up with fantastic new material.

When I first heard about this guy trying to round us all up again, I rebelled. It all sounded too good to be true. I, for one, did *not* want to be used again. What if we all get burned twice and have nothing to show for it? Other artists were suspicious at first, too. Still, Ian slowly but surely gained enough of our confidence to get us back into the studios, recording, and singing together again.

Our ability to re-track and do a repeat performance was evident. Our voice structure and tones had developed to even greater consistency over the years. When I heard Brenda Holloway's remake of "Every Little Bit Hurts," I knew that she had not gotten her rightful due in her heyday. Brenda's voice was a wonder; there had never been a voice like hers! I had been looking forward to this reunion for some time now and had even often dreamt that we'd all get back together to do something one day. And now my dream had come true.

For the first time since 1968, I saw Claudette Robinson. In addition to Claudette being there, many former Motown artists were there: Pete of The Miracles, The Originals with Freddie Gorman, Mary Wells, and a host of other artists. Raynoma Singleton Gordy, who was the real force behind Mr. Gordy's success, was also there. Ian Levine managed to reunite many artists that were integral to the success of Motown.

1989 Back on the road again

Many of these people I hadn't seen for quite some time. I busied myself collecting new addresses and telephone numbers. We all felt what coming together could do for us all at this stage in the game. And so, we didn't want this to be the last time. Let's keep in touch and help each other out whenever we can.

We all gathered around the piano, joining in on the different songs from various Motown artists. We listened to some of the new songs Ian Levine had already recorded with several artists currently involved in the project.

I listened to a tune that Wanda had recorded for Mr. Levine while conducting the same reunion in Detroit for the artists who were still residing there. The song was called "Holding On With Both Hands," and Wanda sounded great.

This boosted my morale. I later recorded some of the songs we had released back in the 60s, like "Too Many Fish In The Sea" and "Beechwood 4-5789" for Ian and the Motor City Record label. Many of the artists involved in the project had perfected their craft and become better musicians. Several of us had become good songwriters. I also got a chance to record some of my own original writings: "He Used To Be A Playboy," "Hey What's Your Name" (a contemporary song), and "You Bring The Love Into My Life."

Yes, the opportunity to do it all over again was unfolding in front of my very eyes. But this was a new day and age in the life of an artist, and the fears, the jealousies, and the people now running the business at the top weren't ready. No, they weren't prepared for Motown to dominate the scene again like we had done back in the '60s. Ian had produced a trillion-dollar package with all of us legends. The deal was too much for one company to take on. It proved we still possessed the power to invade the world with our sound that still lived on. No, it had not died at all. The sound of Motown was very much alive. I'd like to thank Ian for making it all happen. After meeting up with Raynoma Gordy that day at the reunion, she offered me my very first engagement out of L.A. I would fly out of town and work on a fabulous show. It was first-class for me all the way.

June 1988, there was a worldwide convention book fair in Washington, D.C. Raynoma Singleton Gordy was working on an upcoming novel about her roots at Motown. While the book wasn't done, she had a preview on display at the convention. Raynoma's publishers had backed her in providing the conference conventioneers with a premiere show allowing Raynoma to host the grand affair herself. Raynoma came up with the idea to have the first three artists that gave Motown its first three #1 hits to perform on the show: Marv Johnson, Mary Wells, and The Marvelettes. My first comeback show so far out of town could not have been more delightful or memorable.

Washington D.C.'s newest Sheraton Hilton laid out the welcome mat for us this weekend. All transportation, meals, and rooms were paid for by Raynoma's book publishers. After singing to a crowd of 5,000 people or more, I was ready to get back to catching planes, living in hotels, and tipping bell captains. I couldn't wait to sign thousands of autographs everywhere we went. This trip certainly reminded me of the good old days. I could never thank Raynoma enough for giving me such a big send off. Plus, the pay enabled me to take a break before doing it again.

Brian Beirne, disc jockey for KRTH radio station, had my group of Marvelettes on that year's 1989 Home & Garden show held at Dodger Stadium. Chubby Checker headlined with me that year.

By now, I had already begun to see problems surrounding the use of different background singers. I never realized what a beautiful understanding we Marvelettes of the 60s had until now. I was in for quite a surprise, thinking that all females got along that smoothly when they just don't.

Because times had changed, the humble nature of people just didn't exist anymore. Everyone wanted to be a superstar, and they wanted it overnight. So a lot of these girls audition wanting to be in the background, but before the show is over, the roar of the applause changes their minds. All the applause, excitement, and extra attention has introduced them to the spotlight.

After that, taking a back seat is out of the question for them. So if you ask to use them a second time, they have this "you must need me" attitude, changing the mood of your whole show. In their minds, *you* should be trading places with *them*.

I was thought it fair for me to be dressed in sparkles and glitter while the girls in the background stood there in what appeared to be a housedress. They were only heard but rarely seen. I wanted to also give my singers a chance to excel. I'd let them take different leads to show off their voices and always made it clear to them that if an opportunity came along for them to be on stage with me, to take it. I also wanted to give each of them the chance that someone gave me. I wasn't at all about standing in their way or possibly holding anyone back. I thought this would foster a serene work environment, and loyalty would avail. I hoped they would be dedicated and help make each show be the best show ever. But, unfortunately, oversized egos abounded.

So, background singers came and went with Gladys Horton's Marvelettes group. I was the boss, and I didn't want any employees that behaved like children and would throw tantrums when they couldn't get their way. So, if I couldn't be nice to you without you feeling like I didn't know how to run the show, I let you go. I didn't need background singers with whom I had to argue and put in their place before and after each performance.

I got wise to the game of Hard-Handed Hannah being played on me by some of these girls. I was supposed to become hard, rude, and old from the incessant bickering, complaints, and obstacles they were purposely causing me to face.

They played the soft, sweet roles of gentle, feminine ladies onstage. They knew it was hard to smile and be your charming self for the public if there was fighting going on behind the scenes. Oh, no! That wasn't going to work on me. No, they had to bring their jealousy, lies, and evil intentions into my business life. That didn't work either. I think that's what most of them hated the most about me. Becoming a diva with me never worked, no matter how hard they tried.

During my career, I have hired various types of female background singers: tall, short, fat, slim, cute, ugly, dark, light. I even found myself with two fairies once. Oh, I'm telling you the truth! I thought their real names were Donna and Sue, and it turned out to be more like Bobby and Lou. Yes, finding people to replicate the original Marvelettes, people with our charm and class, seemed an impossible task. While mounting my comeback, I was continually on the hunt. In doing so and going through background singers, I earned a reputation I didn't deserve.

I'm not hard to get along with, but it is hard to fool me. The humbleness that was prevalent amongst entertainers when I started out was gone. It had been replaced with everyone wanting money and fame instantaneously. They were spoiled and rotten.

***

July of 1989 found me flying back home to where it all had started, Detroit, Michigan. I was scheduled to appear live on the Kelly & Company morning talk show. However, this morning, their program would be very different from most of their morning shows. Instead, they were presenting an hour-long live Motor Town Revue that included The Marvelettes, Martha Reeves & The Vandellas, Mary Wells, The Contours, The Elgins, and G. C. Cameron.

I was glad to be back in Detroit again, especially since it was still summer. I had no desire to stay there anymore as the warm climate of Califonia had spoiled me. I was also scheduled to do some recording with Wanda while in town. I was hoping to get the chance to visit the Motown Museum. I had heard how Mrs. Edwards had remade the old building, Hitsville, USA. People came through daily for tours of the legendary place.

I arrived in Detroit on the eve of July 20th, but I couldn't do much sightseeing because of the time of day. From my hotel window, I could see that new high-rise buildings were being built all over the city. I hadn't forgotten my old telephone book, so I got on the phone and made calls to my school friends who were still living in Inkster and some now residing in the city.

It felt good to hear all the well wishes from familiar voices. Almost everyone had seen the advertisement on television about the big Motown day Kelly and his wife were hosting. They assured me that virtually every family member's face would be glued to the set that following day. I was so excited I could hardly contain myself.

As always, Mary, Martha, and I found ourselves humbled and feeling grateful to be doing something together again. We had proved ourselves as three of the strongest females ever to set foot in Motown's offices. We had all survived under the pressures of this industry who failed to give any female artists—with the exception of Diana Ross—their flowers or accolades. Yet, so many more of us gave it everything we had in those days.

I had gone unrecognized for so long that I had become immune to it. I refused to allow it to make me grow old and bitter. Instead, I basked in the fact that I was still alive, feeling and looking good, and could do it better than I had before. No. Along with countless other artists that had been unappreciated and stepped on, Motown was never able to bury my spirit. That day, the show brought back some of that life and inspiration that had left Detroit when Motown moved their main office to California.

The telephone lines were jammed with calls from viewers from all over Michigan. Each group performed a song and interviewed the show's hosts, mainly talking about that group's future plans for recordings and travels. Finally, we closed the show by everyone joining in on "Someday, We'll Be Together," an old Supremes song. It was definitely an early morning treat to Michiganders.

I hadn't planned it, but on our way back to the St. Regis, I asked the driver whether we could surprise the old Motown Museum with a visit from me and my girls. I hadn't called or seen Mrs. Edwards since I had been in town, and I knew she would be delighted to see me again. She had been a mother figure for me and my legal guardian's wife while I was with Motown. I felt this visit was meant to be more than just a tour of the building again.

When we first arrived, Mrs. Edwards hadn't gotten there just yet. However, John, the tour guide, offered to give the ladies and me a look around about the old familiar landmark. The background girls with me weren't expecting such a treat.

I can't say that I was too impressed with anything I saw initially. The place was dark due to bad lighting, and the atmosphere wasn't as happy as it once was. Walking through these doors, we could feel the hope and joy in the air. Knowing Mrs. Edwards like I did, I realized that she wanted to keep the original décor. The same old steps, floors, and ceilings were on display for the tourists to see, feel, and get a tiny glimpse of what Motown was like in its heyday. She wanted the public to see the actual walls behind all that timeless music. That was understandable to me.

What wasn't understandable to me was walking into the legendary doors of Motown, a place that made so many artists from the 60s dreams come true, and see a life size portrait of El DeBarge. That was extremely odd to me. This was very surprising, especially considering Mrs. Edwards was the museum's curator. Her goal was to keep Motown's legacy alive. I would have expected to see Jackie Wilson's face, Marv Johnson, Mary Wells, or even Mr. Berry Gordy, Jr. himself standing there representing this iconic institution. There was so much great history made here; DeBarge shouldn't have been the first person you see when walking through the doors of Motown.

Even though I love the group and their sound and realize they made a significant contribution to the world of music, it was all *after* we put Motown on the map. If I had the honors of decorating that main lobby, I would choose 8 x 10 framed glossy black and white portraits of Motown's early pioneers. On the walls, I would have included producers, writers, and outstanding employees who treated the job like it was more than just a paycheck. I would have had all of these pictures beautifully framed in the lobby greeting the tourists to show respect for their contributions.

I could see right away that someone's head was not on straight based on the setup of the displays. Before the tour was over, I really had to shout, "Wait a minute! Where are The Marvelettes?"

There were small portraits of different artists surrounded by the Gordy family on picnics, Christmas parties, and social gatherings. I could see that Mrs. Edwards wanted to display that everything was centered around family. Yes, we all were a great big happy family. And until that day, I really had felt like Mrs. Edwards really liked me a lot. Now, I knew that I was just another foolish artist she had to deal with and keep in order. It's not that I expected to see my face all over the place, but come on. The only trace of The Marvelettes was a 45 record jacket and tiny pictures. You had to squint to tell that it was us.

The two female background singers with me saw how embarrassed I was. They took the opportunity to inform me that unless someone had told them that The Marvelettes were a Motown act, they would have never known by looking at the museum display. Their smiles were like a knife in my back. One girl asked, "Where are the big portraits of The Marvelettes?" after seeing a gigantic photo of The Velvelettes up on one of the display walls.

Here is where Motown should have put the gold record we never received as a group for our greatest achievement. Even if they would've ordered one and kept it for themselves, it would have been better than nobody having one. They could have hung the album on the wall with a plaque, "Here is the gold record commemorating Motown's first certified #1 song, "Please Mr. Postman." I wouldn't have minded at all. At least it would have shown me that they respected us in some small way. But no, they were intent on never giving The Marvelettes credit for anything. No wonder the place felt haunted and cold. There wasn't a feeling of life anywhere here in this place.

Well, Mrs. Edwards finally arrived, and she wasn't in a good mood, and neither was I. She was upset about some remarks made on Kelly & Company that morning about why some of the artists had left the company so early. When I questioned her about why The Marvelettes were not on display in a manner that acknowledged our legacy, Mrs. Edwards gave me a quick answer. She said she didn't have any pictures of us in her possession. Excuses, excuses.

Then boldly, I said, "Why don't you take that big picture of Smokey Robinson down and put our picture up? You have more than enough of his face around here."

She could sense my animosity towards Smokey, so I told her. She, of course, took up for Smokey, telling me not to believe everything I heard. I had a few more things to say to her before I left. I let her know that I no longer worshipped some of those men who had led me to believe that they deserved my respect.

We didn't part with me feeling good that day. I had been misinformed and disillusioned for a long time. Now I had seen the truth. Mrs. Edwards had not loved me the way I thought she had. Her job was to be my guardian, and seemingly that is all it was to her. When I left the museum that day, I vowed to myself to never again grace that building with my presence. I had been shown the truth, and the truth had set me free.

All was not lost in my visit, though. The next day found Wanda and me recording again. It had been years since we had both been in a studio singing together. Wow! It was good to see her again. Our group was releasing a new record with Motor City Records. We spent the next two days recording songs and taking pictures for our album cover.

I came back to Los Angeles only to leave right away again. This time, it was on to Canada. It was late August of 1988, and I was about to star in my very first professional motion picture. Mr. Ron Mann, the film's producer and director, had reached me several months before the actual filming. We had discussed the film's purpose. It was to be a film documentary on the life and times of the era of the Twist. It seemed as though Ron had done some research into the period when the Twist craze was sweeping the country. Songs were being released by certain artists in those days to go along with the dance the Twist. It was such a happy era. Through much research surveys, Mr. Mann discovered that people said they were seldom depressed during this period, although there was a war going on.

Mr. Mann wanted to recreate the mood of that time with his documentary. His documentary would include interviews with artists that recorded a song with twist in the title. If you remember, The Marvelettes had a release out about that time called "Twisting Postman."

Now, here I was 27 years later, dancing and singing about the Twist with the cameras moving. It was a royal treat to me, just to be there again in the country of my mother's birth—sweet, calm, peaceful Canada. And now, to be here retelling history once made by us all!

Yes, every available artist was on hand that summer to play their part in this documentary about the Twist.

Along with The Marvelettes, Chubby Checker, who made a remake of the original *Let's Do The Twist* was on hand for the documentary. Hank Ballard made the original *Let's Do The Twist* was also there. I had the honor of meeting and working with him for the first time in my career.

Dee Dee Sharp was there, singing the duet she and Chubby Checker had recorded called "Slow Twisting." Joey Dee of The Starlighters, whose Peppermint Twist had opened the doors to New York City's famous Peppermint Lounge during that magical time was there. I saw Gary U.S. Bonds, the handsome teenage idol. All the girls fawned over him. Gary performed his recording "Dear Lady Twist" and "Twist, Twisting Nora." Some go-go dancers valiantly gave the Twist all they had to songs like "Twisting The Night Away" by the late Sam Cooke and "Twist & Shout" by The Isley Brothers, who were not available for the actual filming.

I made an important discovery that may have been obvious to others. I was truly blessed to have been a part of history; it was without question a fantastic era. Our music not only made people happy, but it gave them life and a reason to live!

Lulu's, one of Canada's largest nightspots, is where the documentary was filmed. I looked up and was happy to discover that my career had taken a big twist, and I loved dancing my time away.

September of the same year found me around the

Bay Area of San Francisco. It was Santa Cruz, California, on the boardwalk when Pepsi Cola sponsored a series of one-nighters during the entire summer. Their theme that year was "A Blast From The Past." That summer, the shows on the boardwalk included a host of groups and artists from the '60s, including The Marvelettes.

I had begun constantly traveling again. The timing was perfect; my kids were all big enough to look after themselves. While Sammie had come a long way with his cerebral palsy, he still couldn't be left alone entirely. He spent many hours well supervised in the care of the staff at Respite Group Homes. The homes had living quarters for clients to be cared for while their guardians or parents were away.

The rest of this year, 1989, included fun dates like KGFJ's Breakfast Party, a Sunday afternoon benefit show after the famous Rock Around The Clock in Montebello, and a pre-holiday house party sponsored by the Colonel up in Benedict Canyon for the kids of the victims of the San Francisco earthquake.

I played the Las Vegas strip for the first time to top off this monumental year. And guess what? It was the high rollers' private New Year's Eve party at Caesar's Palace. Wow! I had *never* seen Las Vegas the way I saw it now. The bright lights of the strip outshone any and all the places I had ever been.

The Temptations and Paul Robey's Platters were headlining that night along with The Marvelettes. Yes,

Caesar's Palace was the place to be for me. I saw it all.

In 1989, I picked up my pen and began writing the long awaited book you are currently reading. My many shows and frequent touring made it possible to end my story happily and something good to look back and remember.

1990 was the second year of my comeback. And the good news that an original member of The real Marvelettes was out there on the circuit and putting on a good show had begun to spread. Despite many promoters that refused to work with artists from the 50s and 60s, I was beginning to thrive. Booking agents like Mark Young and Dennis Condon from Dick Clark Productions, Barry Kass from B & K Productions, and Bill Trout of Monarch Productions helped me maintain my livelihood. Thank you!

Several bogus groups of Marvelettes worked everywhere around the country for cheap. So, while I hadn't gotten rich yet, I was able to pay my bills, keep a roof over my family's heads, and food on the table.

What was happening to me because of these imposters was criminal. Finding a good lawyer was also easier said than done. I'm sure if I could have put up a $10,000 retainer, some lawyer would have quickly taken a chance. Under the present circumstances, there was much speculation that someone in authority from Motown Records had advised my present persecutors to do what they had done.

One of my background singers, Melinda Chapman, had worked with Doris Jackson's Shirelles and appeared with some of these phony groups. She suggested that she might be able to get in touch with Mr. Marshak. She hoped to propose a deal where he and I could assume some type of business relationship. Instead of booking the bogus groups, he could invest his time and money in the real deal: me. But there was no way I would accept the small salary he was paying his girls. Just like a greedy investor, there was no way he wasn't going to make the biggest piece of the pie or split the biggest portion of the money with me. The attempt to correct a wrong was incomprehensible to him.

Mr. Marshak, like many people, couldn't imagine seizing an opportunity to right a wrong. His love for money and propensity for greed came easy to him. It feels good to them. So I just continued performing and working on my book. I knew in time, the book would reveal many truths.

My 1990 calendar for working show engagements went somewhat like this:

January: Ventura Beach Fair Grounds. I started the year off on a Just Say No To Drugs for the We-Tip sponsors. I was so happy that while performing in front of this crowd for two shows, I could genuinely say I was a role model clean from all alcohol and drugs. I did not just appear for the money. I was actually out front for the sponsor's cause. No drugs or alcohol had been in my system now since July of '89. While this was not long, I resolved not to consume either again. I had all the proof I needed that life can be more incredible when you are entirely in control of your actions. If you're not sick, you don't need drugs. And you will be if you indulge yourself in alcohol. It's as simple as that

March: Gladys Horton's Marvelettes performed at the annual Graffiti Fest in Modesto, California.

April: We performed at San Bernardino's Orange Show.

July: We did a private beach party at the end of July for all the year-round beach goers.

September: The Taste of L.A. is an annual event in Los Angeles. The Marvelettes were honored to appear. The Taste of L.A. is a food festival held over the course of 2-3 days featuring various restaurants from the area.

Show engagements were spaced out during the first half of this year, but I was still working hard on my book and trying to make ends meet. I knew that a great deal of my financial success depended on the sales from my book. I spent countless hours piecing together chapters and monologues. I knew I had a different but exciting story to tell. I wanted to break it down and make it as simplistic as possible. I wanted even the youngest readers to read and understand all that I was trying to convey in my story. It was taking more time than I expected, but I definitely did not want my book to be picked up and read at bedtime only or used to escape real life.

One day, I got a call from Raynoma Singleton Gordy, whose book had finally been released. It was on bookshelves everywhere. She wanted to let me know that she had recommended me for a spot on Geraldo's popular daytime talk show. Raynoma told me that she knew it would also be an excellent opportunity to announce the release of my book. I didn't know quite how to thank her for being so helpful to me as I mounted my comeback. I knew the time would surely come when I could show her my gratitude. I was already planning a book tour for whenever I found a publisher. I told Raynoma that I definitely wanted her to host my show, similar to how she had conducted the preview of her book during that big book fair weekend in Washington, D.C.

"It would be great," I suggested, "if by that time we could have all the present and former novels on exhibit that have been written by Motown artists."

Raynoma agreed and accepted my invitation. "Just let me know when, my dear, and I'd be glad to be a part of your project."

Just her approval of my plans was enough to make me work that much harder at achieving my goals. Raynoma Gordy had been such a strong person from the earliest days of Motown that I knew that with her on anybody's side, success was bound to happen.

It was "The Ladies of Motown" hour on Geraldo! And what a show it was, with Raynoma Singleton Gordy, Martha Reeves, Sylvia Moy, Syreeta Wright, Kim

Weston, Janie Bradford, Mabel John, and myself.

Two great ladies from Motown were missing. One was Claudette Robinson. She definitely had been another one of the role models that had made me, even as a teenager, sit up and take notice of myself. Mary Wells was also scheduled to be on the telecast, but sickness had taken its toll on her voice, and she could not attend. But she was in no way forgotten. Personally speaking, I felt good being included with this group of gifted and talented ladies. The world was finally waking up to the fact that Motown had a large group of female powerhouses that could sing.

After returning to Los Angeles, I gave a farewell show at Carlos & Charlie's. I was departing for London soon for a month long tour. I had not been to Europe since the original Marvelettes had performed there way back in 1964. So, I had plenty of fans awaiting my arrival there.

On October 10, 1990, I finally set foot again on European soil. I was in for a terrific time. Europeans still had that flair for hospitality that was hard to beat. I was glad to be here. It was to be an all-girl group revue featuring The Marvelettes, The Crystals, and The Shangri-Las.

It was my first time working with The Shangri-Las, but Dee Dee Kennibrew, the original lead of The Crystals, and I had met on several occasions back in the '60s. We started the tour right out the gate, spreading the joy we felt touring again. Both of these girl groups had been New York based, and I've always found their personalities so pleasant. It was a wonderful experience.

Henry Sellers presents
ALL AMERICAN LEGENDARY LADIES

THE **CRYSTALS**
DA-DOO RON RON. THEN HE KISSED ME.

THE **SHANGRI-LAS**
REMEMBER, WALKING IN THE SAND. LEADER OF THE PACK.

THE MARVELETTES
PLEASE MR POSTMAN. WHEN YOU'RE YOUNG AND IN LOVE.

UK 1990

After 26 years, I returned to England to perform on a tour

The Shangri-Las—Marylou, Betty, and Bo, and The Crystals—Dee Dee, Darlene, and Marilyn—made that month-long engagement a memorable time in my life. I felt like I had found my long-lost sisters. I enjoyed every show, every song, every laugh, and every moment on that tour. I'm sure that they'll never forget our newfound friendships made there in Europe.

By the first of November, I was back in the United States. But two weeks before I had left for Europe, I had booked an engagement with Mary Seymour, once an agent with the Banner Booking Agency out of New York City. It was for a big yearly event with the Rochester branch of the Urban League. So, after two days of being at home, I was on a plane again on my way to upstate New York.

It was November, and the weather was cooling off some now, so holiday feelings were beginning to set in. The Urban League dinner was honoring Motown this year. The theme was Motown Memories. The original Marvelettes were their special guests for that night.

I felt proud, especially after seeing the effort spent on the decorations for the evening. A 45 record sat in the middle of each table; they served as the centerpiece. Of course, on each 45, there was a title of a song recorded by The Marvelettes. There were also programs with our pictures and a biography of the group's leader and only original working member, me!

The year wasn't over yet. To my surprise, I was called

by BET programmers to be a guest on Tanya Hart's Live In LA. Of course, Raynoma Gordy had again given me a chance to talk about my upcoming book.

We both had been slighted after giving so much of ourselves to Motown. We had gotten nothing in return. The more I thought about it, the angrier I got. I wasn't going to be Mrs. Good Girl anymore. I wasn't going to spare the feelings of others anymore either. So I called out a few lousy names right on the show. What did I have to lose? Nothing! Nothing at all!

No amount of money could pay back the losses I had suffered at the hands of dishonest people. My pride and honors I earned throughout my life had been bought and sold.

1991 marked The Marvelette's 30th anniversary. 30 years in the making for that big, big hit that put Motown and its sound on the map and on everybody's mind.

Strange but true, this momentous occasion went without notice from Motown. There was no press release, TV special, or anything. What successful business allows history and significant milestones to happen without any kind of acknowledgment? Maybe now you readers can sympathize and understand why Motown is a broken establishment today. I bet even Ford Motors still has the first car on exhibit. The car that launched their success. The big question on the minds of many was why did Motown purposely not acknowledge The Marvelettes?

Not only had we been denied an appearance on the

TV specials, but we were rarely mentioned in newspaper articles by Motown writers. The disrespect was so blatant that even fans observed how Motown had isolated us.

For many reasons, writing letters and looking for mail from loved ones and people just waiting on the postman, in general, was prevalent during this time. So I decided that a thank you letter to the postal carriers all over California would be an excellent way to say "Happy 30th Anniversary" from us all.

I spent most of this year writing and working on my book. But when I was called on to do *The Joan Rivers Show*, I made sure I announced to all the viewers that day that it was also the big 3-0 for The Marvelettes. Joan Rivers's topic for our taping was "Motown Artists From the '60s Who Had Ended Up With Nothing." While this topic was very personal for me, I still felt a need to turn a bad situation into a moment of gratitude. So, I announced to the audience that we were in the middle of The Marvelettes 30th anniversary, a fact of which I was incredibly proud.

Mary Wilson talked about her setbacks on the show. Raynoma Gordy, Mary Johnson, Bobby Taylor, Frances Nero, and I spoke about the triumphs and tragedies we confronted during the Motown era as well. Mary Wells's interview with Joan Rivers was taped earlier. While she was barely audible, she made it clear to viewers how rotten the record company treated us and left us strapped for cash while they prospered.

This year, I taped a few more TV shows—two for a cable dance show called *Dancing To The Oldies* and another TV talk segment with *The Roy Firestone Show*. Raynoma Gordy, Freda Payne, and I were celebrated as women of the '60s and subsequently interviewed by Roy himself. So, again, I was able to talk about our group's 30th anniversary and about the many imposters pretending to be Marvelettes.

Late August of '91 found me up in Solvang, California, performing at a benefit for the Humane Society. The organizers somehow discovered my deep love for all animals. I still think about Sparky all the time. His death had only made me an avid dog lover. It's as if we speak a unique language. I look at them, and they look at me, and we're suddenly pals forever.

October of '91, I met Donnie Brooks and Don Kurtz, founders of the 30th Anniversary Rock & Roll Shows. Our timing could not have been better. We made plans to do some professional shows, and on December 28th, I appeared on their preChristmas private show in Ventura, California. They loved my performance and offered me a spot in their '92 Summer Tour. I'm certainly looking forward to it, if it's going to be as rewarding as it was working with some of the regular acts had been that night.

Al Wilson, Jewel Akins, Pat Upton, Jerry Corbetta, Otis Day & Amelia Jessie, Eddie Serrano, Phil Miles, Tiny Tim, Donnie Brooks, and a host of others all performed. The show was great and brought back memories of how professional Dick Clark's tours were. Donnie Brooks and

Don Kurtz offered me the opportunity to be part of this type of professionalism and togetherness again.

Soon New Year's Eve was going to usher us into 1992. And where was I going to spend those last hours commemorating The Marvelettes' 30th anniversary? Yes, you guessed correctly—Caesar's Palace in Las Vegas. My group was on the bill again. It just goes to prove that I hadn't been half-stepping at all! I'm still in demand and loved by the fans!

Oh, guess what? They want me back in Europe again too! This time, for three months, starting March of 1992. So you know what I'm going to do? I'm going to keep in touch with you.

Forever,

Gladys Horton

BACK ON TOP!

An Afterword by Vaughn Thornton

Guess what? Gladys headed to Europe in March 1992, and it was a complete success! This was definitely the best year she had since leaving Motown, and it was well deserved.

Despite all the setbacks with the Marvelettes' trademark and the passing of her younger son, Alphonso in 1991 who was only 17 at the time, Gladys managed to get through all the stress and depression she was in. After years, she had finally made it back on top.

Also, in 1992, Vaughn, Gladys's second son, and his wife Mickey had their first child, a baby girl, they named Miracle. Miracle was truly a miracle for Gladys because she brought her so much joy and happiness. A joy and happiness that had not been seen in her since Alphonso passed away. Soon after came her second grandchild, a boy they named DeVaughn. Being a grandmother for Gladys definitely eased the pain of losing a son at such a young age. It gave her a different outlook on life, and that was a miracle in itself.

Being a proud grandmother, she appeared on the daytime talk show, *George and Alana* in 1995 to perform. It had to be sometime in November because she gave a special birthdate wish to her granddaughter, Miracle, who was turning three at the time. It was happening again. Gladys's voice was being heard all around the world, but this time, in a different aspect. She had become a true spokeswoman on the "dos and don'ts" in show business. As successful as she was, she still was very passionate in helping others achieve their goals. That is what motivated her to write her life story.

Sometime during 2006, my mom, Gladys, woke up one morning and noticed that her face on one side was drooping. She did not tell me right away because she knew I would worry. She finally called and told me, and I went to visit her immediately. The first thing I thought upon seeing her was I thought she had a stroke. She quickly informed me by saying, "Vaughn, I already went to the doctor and they diagnosed the condition as Bell's Palsy." I knew my mom despised going to see the doctor about anything, but I wish we had at least gotten a second opinion. One thing about Bell's Palsy, it can happen to anyone; age is not a factor. However, the face usually restores back to normal. In my mom's case, her face was never restored completely. Appearance-wise, it got better, but never the same. She was very conscious about her smile. Nevertheless, my mom got herself well enough to continue performing for approximately four more years. Unfortunately, as her condition continued to worsen, she had to stop performing.

It was at this time that I contacted Marvelette member, Katherine Schaffner, and I regret that decision greatly to this day! Many fans wonder, "Why does Vaughn have such a problem with Katherine?" Well let me explain. Let's start from the beginning. As I mentioned, my mom's condition was getting worse, and I really needed some support from someone that could also offer some advice on how to handle my mom's situation. Someone from her past that she knew and personally trusted.

The first person that came to my mind was Marvelette member, Juanita Cowart. Unfortunately, I could not find

Juanita's contact info at the time, but I found Katherine's info instead. I must admit, I did not feel totally comfortable calling Katherine about this matter because I knew my mom and her had challenges with their relationship in the past. So, I called Katherine and spoke to her about my mom's condition, and she was on the next flight out here to California. Initially, I thought she was just being supportive, but I quickly figured out she was here on business.

Once Katherine saw with her eyes how really sick and vulnerable my mom really was, she had the nerve to present to me a Power of Attorney form for me to sign my mom's rights over to her for some projects she was working on. She was not clear about whatever projects she was mentioning but warned me that it would be in my best interest to sign the form. The reason is Katherine told me she really did not have to share anything with me pertaining to The Marvelettes. Why would she bring a matter like this up now? My wife and I were offended, so of course, I did not sign her fraudulent paperwork. I am pretty sure that Katherine traveled home unhappy and angry on that day.

Shortly after our encounter, on January 26, 2011, my mom, Gladys Catherine Horton passed away peacefully in Sherman Oaks, California. She was 66 years old. I was emotionally destroyed but relieved at the same time because she was no longer suffering. Thank you to all of the fans that sent condolence cards during that time, although we did not receive many of those cards thanks to Katherine.

Without my knowledge, Katherine set up a Marvelette fan page and directed all of the fans to send their condolence cards there. Well, at my mom's service, Katherine approached me and gave me a few condolence cards which all had been opened. She immediately walked away. I was confused why the letters were already opened? I will not mention any names, but a very credible person that I consider a Motown alumni, who was standing there with me at the time said Katherine was most likely looking for money. I felt extremely disrespected and hurt at the same time. I could no longer trust her after this. I hope she found what she was looking for.

Some months had passed when Katherine approached me again. This time it is was regarding The Marvelettes' trademark. I am the executor of my mom's estate, so Katherine needed my help in getting petitioned on The Marvelettes' trademark. Another mistake I made. We had made a verbal agreement to split all profits made from The Marvelettes' trademark between the two of us.

Now, why did I believe she would keep her word when I just mentioned, "I could no longer trust her?" Well, in the beginning, we split three payments. After that, she just stopped. Katherine had once again taken advantage of my kindness and vulnerability at the time. She was now performing at cheap venues and had even formed her, "New, (phony) Marvelettes". I realize Katherine is an original member, even though it has been alleged that she did not sing background on 90% of The Marvelettes' songs. Wow!

My mom had to battle with phony Marvelettes groups like Katherine's when she was building her career back up. If Katherine wants respect, she has to pay up! But for now, they look like phony Marvelettes, and sing like phony Marvelettes. They are phony Marvelettes. Case closed! Katherine is no different than all the other fraudulent promoters my mom had to deal with in the past. I am happy to announce that I have legally secured myself on The Marvelettes' trademark.

It has now been 11 years since my mom passed away. I want everyone to know that my older brother, Sammy, and the rest of the family are doing well. Many of you all know of Sammy because my mom left the group to become a full-time mother for him. She was still performing during the months she was pregnant until her departure from the group in 1968 at the New Year's Eve show.

Her husband at the time, who is also my father, told me my mom had been wearing a girdle to hide her pregnancy. Katherine and Wanda would argue with my mom to cover her stomach up while on stage. Berry allegedly had a big problem with my mom's pregnancy showing when they were performing. Remember, Berry and my mom had a big argument about this when she departed from the group that New Year's Eve night in 1968.

A few months later, Sammy was born with cerebral palsy. It is a shame that my mom felt she had to wear a girdle to please Berry at the time. This is no different than the body shaming that goes on in today's time with female artists. I wonder if Berry feels guilty about Sammy being born handicapped. He was definitely invited to my mom's service in 2011, but he responded back, saying he could not attend because he was in New York working on his Motown play. How could a group like "The Marvelettes," who were such a vital part of Motown's success, just be forgotten about by the CEO himself? The Marvelettes are seldomly mentioned or seen on any Motown anniversary shows.

Berry forgot The Marvelettes had a smash #1 hit before the "no-hit Supremes." I have not seen Berry's Motown play, but I heard he did not give The Marvelettes their proper dues as usual. Berry should be ashamed of how he continues to neglect and ignore the history of this marvelous group. He once called it, "The group that put Motown on the map." Hopefully one day, he will give these girls the respect and recognition they so greatly deserve! I will continue to support (promote) The Marvelettes' legacy in any way possible, and I encourage (urge) everyone to do the same but please, no "Phony Marvelettes."

Thank all of you who read and supported my mom's book. Now, spread the word.

R.I.P. Gladys Catherine Horton
May 30, 1945 - January 26, 2011

You were loved by many, and you taught us to never be afraid to live our lives to the fullest. The seeds that you planted while you were here will continue to blossom and grow in your memory.

R.I.P Wanda Young Rogers
August 9, 1943 - December 15, 2021

We send our sincerest condolences to her loved ones. Wanda was very special to our family, and we know she is in a better place singing with Mom.

Many Blessings,

Vaughn Thornton

A Tribute to Al
By Gladys Horton

Alphonso, my third son's friends all called him Al. However, I never called him anything but Alphonso from the day he was born. And believe me, out of all of my boys, he's the one that made me scream the loudest. Because of it, my lungs were even stronger when I returned to the stage.

Yes, my singing career was great and exciting, but the best chapter of my life began with my three boys. My first son Sammie taught me that there were other ways to give of myself. He woke me up to the world of the disabled. It gave me more compassion and a more profound concern for the lives of others.

Vaughn came next, and with his arrival, my constitution was strengthened, and my will to succeed fortified. Even from an early age, he would not allow me to wallow in my weakness or complain about what we didn't have. Instead, he would say angrily, "Mom, stop saying that we're poor. Don't you know we're not poor?" He strengthened my character and made me feel rich even when I didn't have a penny. With him, I *knew* we could win the fight.

Alphonso, my third son, taught me just what true love is all about. Yet, even now, after almost three years have passed, I still find it terribly difficult to write about it. Where do you begin? How do you start? What do you say to describe the emptiness, the loneliness, and especially the pain you're forced to live with each and every day after a tragedy?

I think so much of me left with him that day until now, I'm just somebody wandering around in search of what lies ahead. But, remember, there was a time when I wanted to live forever. I was full of joy and happiness and lived solely for my three boys. Them laughing and joking with one another and always filling every moment they could find with lots of fun was all I needed. So many good, good memories. Thank goodness there were so many good ones; as you think about those happy times, it helps heal the pain a little.

I can remember when breathing meant something to me. But that was when I felt alive. That was before the evening of September the 12th, 1991, the last day I saw my youngest son Alphonso, who was fatally wounded in a drive-by shooting that evening. Now it's June of 1994, and this is the first time I've picked up a pen to write about it. Death had never been a part of my story because its reality had never hit so close to home. Because I was an orphan, never knowing my kinfolk, I was a novice and had no idea how to contend with what I was about to contend.

I don't like using certain words, so that's why I don't talk about it to anybody but his older brother. Alphonso's leaving changed the meaning of life for me. I woke up to the reality that we all are taught to believe as we are told. But no, I say no, there should not even be a word called DEAD. Every time we describe our loved ones with this word, we brand them. I prefer to use the word INVISIBLE, mostly because I know that just because we don't have the power to see them, it doesn't mean that they're not around us. They can come and go as they please.

Many times I've known and felt Alphonso's presence still around me. My heart and soul could hear him saying to me, "Mom, don't be sad. I'm having fun in my new existence. It's not like everybody thinks it is. I'm free, happy, and I still love you, Vaughn, and Sammie very much. I'm glad I'm done with all the pain of life on earth." Yes, body aches, headaches, colds, hunger for material things, trying to do the right thing when the world's full of wrong things.

Every mother knows when their child is changing. Alphonso was 17 years old, his fifth year of being a teenager, and he was still a sweetheart, but I knew the streets were getting too rough. He had to survive. Alphonso had to learn who his friends were and who was not. I think this was his hardest lesson for him because of his happy-go-lucky nature. He thought everybody was his friend and most everybody was, or soon discovered they wanted to be. Something about him would turn even an enemy into a companion. But Alphonso's handsome features made some of his friends leery of what girls they brought around him.

I witnessed a scene that depressed me deeply. I realized how vital having true friends was to Alphonso. He and one of his buddies had met a girl while out one evening and had given her our telephone number. His buddy had been staying over the weekend, and I guess that was why she was given our telephone number. When Alphonso and his friend got in that evening, he asked me as always, "Who called?"

I said, "Some girl named Keesha; she asked for you."

Right away, I felt the tension mounting between Alphonso and his friend. His friend looked down as if his whole world had fallen apart. Alphonso, whose skin color was the lightest of us all, quickly flushed a red tone, indicating that the entire situation was quite embarrassing. He was lost for words as he tried quickly to turn a bad situation around. Finally, he said, trying to cheer up his buddy whose feelings were obviously quite hurt, "Man, she's got her nerve, trying to play slick. I'm not even going to call her back." I was convinced now of what I previously suspected. They both were led to believe that the girl was interested in his friend, but all the while had chosen Alphonso.

***

Alphonso was the kind of person who was determined to have fun no matter how down or depressed the world around him seemed. He was going to have a good time. He even brought me out of my weariness at times with his constant joking and playing around. Sometimes I didn't want to be bothered. I was worrying and wondering if we were going to have all the rent on time or if the food I purchased would last until I got my food stamps again. Alphonso was determined to play hide-and-go-seek or ask me silly little questions about things that were supposed to make me joke back and forth with him. I'd say, "Not now, Alphonso, I'm busy." Still, he'd continue with his clowning, playful nature until I'd stop and look at him. I had to smile back.

He was always a great-looking kid with a great smile that made me admire his humor. Something in my heart would say, "Why don't you relax and don't be so serious all the time? He's only trying to make you smile to brighten your mood. So you can enjoy life more. *Things can't be that bad,* I'd finally tell myself. So I'd end up playing Alphonso's game with him, and I'd begin to feel good about myself.

This is what kids do for us naturally, you know. That school play you attended or that swimming team tournament that they got you to come out and see was all God's plan to make you feel good about the lives you have brought into the world. So as a parent, all parents, future parents too, please make sure that your children have lots of fun while growing up because that's the times when they are truly yours.

When they become full-fledged teenagers, they tend to want to become someone else at times. Someone unrecognizable to you. They still love and cherish you, and thank you for all the help you gave to them to get this far. However, this is when they begin to explore freedom and are deciding who they want to be.

With all they are exposed to, it doesn't take long for our children to feel like they are grown. Can you understand that? The older they get, the more they need our protection, even when they refuse to let you provide it to them. So what can you do? Your hands are tied in a sense.

***

May 30th, 1989, my birth date. Still, like always, I never made a big fuss about it to anyone. No cake, no ice cream, and no party. I realized a long time ago that this was just another day and had stopped celebrating. If it were your birthday like everybody has been programmed to call it, you would be a brand new baby, and I knew I was *nobody's* baby.

Vaughn, who was still away, never forgot special

dates. I had already received a call from him earlier, but I was shocked right out of my seat when I found out Alphonso also remembered. It was late in the evening, around 10 p.m. Sam and I had already gone to bed. As usual, as soon as Alphonso came home from work and would stick his key in the door, I would wake up. A lot of times, I didn't say anything to him; I'd just sigh with relief that he was home safe. But that night was different. Instead of going to his bedroom, I noticed that he walked over to where I was quietly playing sleep. I slept on a cot in the corner of our living room, right by the big picture window, so that I could feel the cool California night breeze on my face as I slept.

At first, he didn't say anything. He just stared quietly out of the window as if something was deeply on his mind. This lasted for about three minutes, and then I made it apparent that I had been watching by sitting up. He didn't seem surprised or anything. He just took a gold box out of his pocket and handed it to me, saying, "Happy birthdate," showing me he remembered me telling them all that it's only a birth date that's being celebrated. "Ooo, Alphonso," I called out his name, acknowledging his grandest surprise. I was totally blown away. It's not like he had never given me anything because he always gave me cards on special days. I was happy with whatever he gave because I knew it came directly from his heart, and he didn't have much money to spend.

I'd always tell them when I gave them money at Christmastime for gifts to not waste it on me. I was just fine with what I already had, and that was them. But this was the first gift he has given to me where he had worked hard for it himself. I knew he wanted me to be proud. And I was proud! Happy, surprised, grateful, and shocked all at the same time.

I went out of my mind at the beautiful gift. I jumped up and down, ran, and turned on the light as I opened the gold box. I saw the inscription. It said, "And may you have many, many more." When I saw the delicate gold chain bracelet, I knew he had spent about $50 or more on it. "Alphonso, I love it. I love it," I kept saying as I gave him a big hug.

I think I scared him, showing so much emotion that night. He smiled; I could read his eyes as he thought, "Wow, I didn't know she was gonna like it this much." My kids never see me release emotions this way. Not even on the days that I received my royalty checks, and those were the times that they *knew* I was extremely happy. I never fell apart over anything. Just as they hardly ever saw me cry, they never saw me jump up and down and scream for joy.

I wasn't a hard-hearted mother. I used to kiss and hug them a lot when they were younger, but not as much that they were mansized. I understood that too much outward expressions make boys maturing into adulthood feel like you still think they're momma's little boys. But tonight, Alphonso had changed all of that. My quiet, reserved nature was now that of a wildcat. I think I thanked him every day for a week.

***

I have watched a lot of things corrode since we can no longer feel that energy. September 12th, 1991, was the beginning of the end. At first, I thought it was just for our family, but as I watched the news and read about tragedies, I knew that I should not have had to join the broken hearts club.

Alphonso was only 17. 17 seemed to be the age when the teenage tragedies occurred. Why are so many youth today leaving this world at that same age? Something strange is happening. This just can't be a coincidence. I think now more than I talk. I think about how thankful I was that he was not in an automobile accident. I could have never forgiven myself for buying him that car if he had been.

I'm grateful to have made a man out of him. He was a strong, determined, and sometimes stubborn man, but nevertheless, he was a man now—a man with a mind and a will of his own. I know now that it's very important to have that. It makes your spirit strong, and a strong spirit never dies. Our love for him will let him live on forever and ever.

I think about other things too. Like the two years, 1961 and 1991. 30 years exactly. 1961 was the year of my triumph, the beginning of a successful career, and the year I recorded a #1 song. Then, 1991, the year I experienced the worst tragedy of my life. One of my sons was INVISIBLE.

That year I can remember how hurt I was that Motown did nothing to celebrate the 30th anniversary of their first #1 recording. I asked myself, "Do successful companies do things like this?" I would be lying to you if I said that we were not angry because now we were, my three boys and myself. They were older now and knew about all the credit their mother hadn't received.

One day Alphonso said, "Mom, they dogged you for years. I wish I could get my hands on them." It was embarrassing now for them also, seeing their friends' faces go sour after learning how much I had contributed to the music world and was still living in an apartment.

Today, I thought of a way to make the tragedy of 1991 a triumph on behalf of Alphonso. Because he cared so much about me never getting appropriate credit from Motown, not even a thank you after 30 years, I decided to write a letter to him since my career began on a song about a letter.

A letter for Alphonso:

Dear Alphonso:

You've become somewhat like a religion to the boys and me because we worship our thoughts of you. Not just on Sunday but every day. To say we miss you is just not enough because we've all experi-

enced the magic of you still being everywhere we go.

We wish we could see you and touch you as we did before. With you always being the life of the party when you left, you sort of took the party with you, it seems. But you brighten up the hours that we spend talking all about you and your habits. It's the only way that we have now to keep a party going on here.

This world's become a sad, sad place without you, your smile, and your laughter. A lot of your close friends are lost, and a lot of them have died. Sometimes I wonder if you all are together, still enjoying life as it is on another planet.

I admire you for the way you refused to let this old world get you down and depressed. You brought fun and enjoyment to all who were fortunate enough to meet you.

I'm sure you're pushing all the right buttons now. I'm glad nobody is ever going to be able to boss you around. I'm looking for-

ward to seeing and being with you again, but I can't say when or how. But I can say, "I love you now, and I'll love you even more then."

Your Mother,

Gladys Horton.

***

It took nearly two years before Alphonso's case finally came up in court. Our small family now had grown a bit larger in numbers. Vaughn was now married to Michetta, and they had a daughter named Miracle, my first grandchild. We were still a united family but still mourning our loss. I think every family's wish is to see the person face-to-face who turned your dreams upside down and who also took away part of your life. So many strong feelings and emotions are all stirred up again with court proceedings commencing. Still, we stuck it out and saw it through to the end.

We heard testimonies from all the guys in the car that night of the driveby. We heard arguments from both lawyers, saw pictures and exhibits, and listened to every bit of circumstantial evidence presented. Nobody denied the fact that a big mistake had been made. The judge was a lady, and every now and then, our eyes would meet. I tried to read them. All I could see or hear from them was a lot of pity accompanied by streaks of anger. The attorney handling our case was also a lady and together gave the defense attorney a difficult time. A wrong decision can never make a right reaction. Truly, I was hurt and angry, but I couldn't quite harden my heart the way maybe many people do in cases like this. I kept trying to understand how I would feel if the shoes were on the other foot. I'd stick in my son's corner till the bitter end, just as this boy's parents were doing for him.

I sat in the courtroom shivering. There always seemed to be a damp coldness in there, as though you're at the bottom of a dry well. So much went through my mind. Seeing Alphonso's body just before his autopsy made me cry out loud. He was still so beautiful, even in this lifeless state. I knew he was somebody special. When he walked into a room, you felt like a million people were suddenly there and when he left, so did the crowd. You knew for sure you were alone again.

As I listened to the boy's parents testify, I could see how hurt they were by all of this as they sat with slumped shoulders. Their eyes were apologetic; they doubted it would ever be accepted. My son's assailant had recently become a father himself. I saw the boy, and I wondered, *What was all this going to do to his life?* As parents, we never think about what our babies will grow up to do to shame us later.

Why I felt so much forgiveness is beyond me. Maybe

it was because I realized I needed some forgiveness myself—forgiveness for not being a stricter parent.

My mind harkened back to the warning shot, the first time he got in serious trouble. Alphonso was put on probation due to an incident at one of the shopping malls involving a fight between his friend and a girl. From the very first visit we made to the probation officer, I realized that instead of him wanting to do better, he began not to care at all. Before this, he would at least *attend* school. Alphonso's only problem was that he liked to be the class clown. He enjoyed making his friends laugh and wanted everybody to have a good time. Fun, fun, fun, all the time! If learning wasn't fun, he didn't want any part of it.

I used to tell him, "Alphonso, you're going to have to get serious and choose an occupation one day." I knew it was all going in one ear and out the other. Being on probation had indeed put a bad mark on him. The mental strain from being told you can't do something makes them want to do it more. I tried not to worry about his laissez-faire attitude about the future. I just told myself that I wouldn't give up on him; I'd help him out by giving him a job helping me.

"Alphonso, you'll be the one to help me with Sammie when I go out of town. I'll create a job out of it for you and pay you well." He agreed that would be fine but never stayed home long enough to show me that this was even something he would consider doing as a future job. He had lots of buddies over all the time. He made sure that his friends had lots of fun with him. He took them along with him on all of his fun-filled activities. I guess they all knew they would never have a dull moment with Alphonso around. I was beginning to get another message from the whole rush.

All the while, he seemed to be telling me something. He seemed to be saying to me, "I've got to hurry up, mom, and do all the things I want here on earth because I won't be here long." It may sound unbelievable, but sometimes, there was a sadness in his eyes as he looked at me. I could hear him talking to my soul, and he was saying, "Just let me go, I'll be back." And so, I let him party as much as he liked. I still argued about school whenever I got a call informing me that Alphonso was truant. Something deep inside me would not let me fight with him long over these calls. I knew I was wasting all my energy trying. The stress and the strain were getting to me. Only when Alphonso was home for the night could I relax my mind and body.

Being in a courtroom can make you weigh the pros and cons, the dos and don'ts, the rights and the wrongs. I had to fight with the question, "Who gives us the right to be born?" Is life the blessing it's made out to be? I listened in court as the defense and the prosecuting attorneys were now delivering closing arguments. I felt a sense of relief after reliving my son's last hours with testimonies from people who were there. One point that was clear and set the record straight was that Alphonso was an innocent bystander. He was not the intended target. He just happened to be in the wrong place at the wrong time.

Silently in my mind, I went back to the last couple of weeks that led to that awful night. They stand out in my memory like a sore thumb. It was the last days of August, and we as a family were celebrating the thrill and joy we felt of having Vaughn back home from the Army now, for good. The war in Saudi Arabia was over. Because it had been so costly to the American government, the Army cut spending by sending some soldiers home immediately.

It had taken me writing many letters, but they seemed to have worked. As a single parent alone, trying to cope with the pressures of raising two sons with different visible behavior problems was my rationale for asking for Vaughn's release. Now that Vaughn was home, I was getting more respect from Alphonso, and even Sammie was more mild-mannered. When school started that September, Alphonso even agreed to and enrolled in continuation classes at our neighborhood high school. His attitude about doing homework even improved. I felt it, and I knew we all felt it in our hearts. We were a happy family, together again.

I even got a chance to see the brothers together enjoying one another, like they had before Vaughn enlisted in the armed forces. It was just like their high school days all over again, where they used to hang out together and party on the weekends. I was always proud that my boys really loved one another. It's very rare in cases when siblings have different fathers.

Vaughn and I pled with Alphonso to leave the old

neighborhood alone, where he still found time to go. But he just wouldn't listen. "All of my friends live over there," I remembered him saying so many times. I had a dream that I warned him about, never knowing it would come true.

The truth about what really happened on September the 12th, 1991, before Alphonso was in the neighborhood, was revealed in court. A couple of Alphonso's buddies got into a confrontation with another guy who didn't live in that section of town. They had embarrassed him in front of some girls he knew and then ran him out of the area.

Later that evening, after Alphonso had arrived on the scene, the guy came back with some more guys in a car with a gun. I still say Alphonso did not have to be there. He *chose* to be there. Alphonso was the only one hit of all those kids there who were all in harm's way. After hearing that the bullet was a silver-tipped hollow point, the intent to kill was obvious.

Well, all his worldly pain is all over now. It kind of makes me wonder just who are the lucky ones because *we're* the ones left to suffer. And whoever said the pain lessens as time goes on, they lied. Grieving becomes life's task; you just learn to do it graciously. There's always something there to remind you every day of the emptiness.

The trial lasted about a week, and then we took a short break. Before the end of that next following week, the verdict was read. "Guilty on the count of second-degree murder," which automatically constitutes a sentence of 20 years to life without parole. Justice had been served even though nothing could console us or compare to having Alphonso with us. I was truly grateful that many others were concerned about ensuring that this crime did not go unpunished.

I had not touched the gold urn holding my son's ashes now for weeks. That day when I returned home, I lifted it down from the top of the bookcase in the living room and looked at all the pictures of him I had carefully glued all around it. I was so happy that I had never buried his body. Here it was, with me, every day, to hold whenever I wanted. I spoke to him softly and said, "Today, justice has been served on your behalf, my son. May you continue to live on peacefully with all of our thoughts and love keeping your spirit alive forever." I believe that anyone who has ever walked this earth and given so much light to life should never be buried under the ground.

To say that it's all over now is a fallacy. The statement is simply not true. I can't stop here. I have to attack this problem and many others from the seed before it is ever planted. It's not enough to just teach your child right from wrong. Those rules may apply to running your household, but what about the world outside that doesn't live by those rules? Someone said, "What the world needs now is more love." I say we first, we have to heal minds.

Right now, today, we've got to wake up and realize that it's up to us to stop this foolishness. Our minds have been corrupted for so long. Yes, we've created lots of beautiful material things. But what can we say about the body? The mind? The soul and the spirit? The things that really matter?

For instance, Santa Claus, from birth, we've ruined and planted a seed of deception in every generation's mind right from the beginning. Believe me, it has grown. It's a very ignorant race of people who cannot think of any other way to have their children experience the joy of surprises and giving and getting gifts without having to make up a big lie to go along with this.

When one individual stands up and says, "Let's stop lying to our babies because afterward, it's hard to get them to believe anything we say," we get a group of fixed minds tearing them down, blaming them for taking away the fun of being a child when there is no fun in being tricked or lied to. Especially before you've learned the truth about many other things around you. I never told my boys that big lie, and when they came home from school and asked me if a big, fat man wearing a red suit comes down the chimney bringing lots of toys, I told them, "Hell, no. That was just an old fable. Christmas is a holiday set aside to show your love and gratitude for people who have been nice to you all year long. You buy gifts, and you receive gifts to make others happy." Thanks to me, none of my boys were ever held prisoner to that lie or any other lie.

Yes, I've always seen the light, but now I see it from another perspective. We should all be tired of making the same mistakes repeatedly. Yes, now that I see the light in a new way. I've come to realize that some of the behaviors you're taught are continually passed down from generation to generation. And so, some people should not have children, no matter how much you love them. You know, I think I'll change that statement to, many people should *think* about having a child before they have one.

I still dream about Alphonso from time to time. Strangely enough, he's always around the age of 8 or 10. A few times, he was in his teens. For some reason, I can't remember all of those dreams. Alphonso is a young spirit and was never meant to experience the life of an elderly person. That's why I dream of him in his youth when he was so pure and untouched by the world's sins.

It took me almost a year and a half to let the tears flow. I kept denying the fact that half of me was gone. I kept finding reasons in my heart why I wanted to believe that Alphonso was lucky to be out of this rat race. I refuse to break down. I refuse to let a society that had fast become back-stabbing, ill wishers and blood-hungry animals gaze upon my son's remains. That's why there was no funeral. I simply told his friends, "I'm sure Alphonso would love for you to remember him as he was, alive and vibrant."

Alphonso, Alphonso, I knew
this hero. So strong, so brave, and
not afraid to face a destiny already

made.

Alphonso, Alphonso, you are always that young man, with pride, with a purpose, with whom we understand.

Alphonso, Alphonso, this name rings a bell of victory and honor. Right on, right on, Al.

It wasn't the time or how long you were here. It was all the good cheer whenever you were near.

It wasn't the way or what you'd say. It was just having you with us each and every day.

Alphonso, Alphonso, what a friend indeed. You made us remember the forgotten seed.

Alphonso, it's known, you were the prince, and there hasn't been one to come like you since.

Alphonso, Alphonso, I know there's no end to angels who come here and then descend.

To angels who know which way to go, Alphonso, Alphonso, we all love you so.

Alphonso, Alphonso, are you watching me now? Well, I wonder if you could tell me how to mend this broken heart, somehow.

Alphonso Bruce Morris.

May 19, 1974-September 12, 1991.

LETTERS FROM

GLADYS

Dear Mom and Dad,

Thank you for giving me all the chances I probably would never have had if you had have done things any differently. But you both have so much faith in me right from the very first breath I took. You knew I didn't need anything else but life and you had already gave that to me. What else could I or anybody else ask for in this world?

But I still want you to know that I saw you many times in those complete strangers who came up to me and helped me over some of those stumbling blocks that got in my way from time to time. And I heard your voices many times when I was about to go in the wrong direction and couldn't figure out just why the way was blocked. Somehow, I knew you were there, even in the darkest hours when I couldn't see the forest for the trees.

You never said no. You never said yes. You left those decisions up to me. Now I hope I have made you proud of me, and I hope I am half of what you thought I would be. And here's one thing I've always wanted you to hear. I love you mom and dad, and thank you. Thank you for letting me be me.

Your daughter,

Gladys

To Mrs. Sharpley,

Not a year goes by where I'm not asked the question, "How did your group get started?" The public sure has a way of not letting you forget your homework :-)

I bet you millions of people you never thought of have read books and newspaper articles and reviews which included your name because I never forget to tell them all about the teacher who felt like my group had done such a wonderful job on the school's talent show but hadn't won. And so, she asked the principal to break the rules and let one of the losers attend the audition that day at Motown Records. Because of you, those losers turned out to be mighty big winners before it was all over with.

Words that say "thank you" sometimes just don't seem to be enough. I hope that in many ways your concern and consideration that day for me has rewarded you with blessings over and over time and again. Some people like you are just unforgettable.

Always,

Gladys

Dear Mr. Gordy,

After all has been said and done, I only have one question for you: why did you say that we were all like a big family and that you wanted us to feel like this? Whether you knew it or not, the word family was like the magic password for me, because I was an orphan, and I had never known one. So you really hit the jackpot and got my attention when you use the word family.

But tell me if I'm right or wrong. When family members go away or make a big mistake, when they do finally see the light and come back home, doesn't a true loving father welcome them back in with open arms?

I noticed that when some of your sons like The Temptations and The Four Tops left you and went to another company and didn't do so well, they came back to you and you let them right back in the door. But no female artist has ever got this type of return welcome from Daddy, the father of the family. Why? Is this the way you soften them to treat your daughters, the female artists?

Just wondering why,

Gladys Horton of the Marvelettes

To the Marvelettes fans all around the world:

Thank you for still loving us, even the many years that went by when you had at one time lost complete sight of our whereabouts. A lot of you wrote letters that went unanswered, made calls that never got through, and simply were unable to gather up any information on whether the return of The Marvelettes would ever be a visual event or not. But you still continue to buy our albums and you still requested our songs to be played in our towns or whatever old but goody stations there were.

Thank you for remembering all the fun we try to give you and for keeping our image alive in your minds and in your hearts. Because of your prayers, I'm back. And since my come back debut in 1988, you all have shown me everywhere I've played and performed that you still got the power to keep the love of it all going on strong. I'm talking about all the excitement, all the joys of remembering every word to every song of that era, all the happiness we felt in that time, all the kindness and consideration, and the real brotherly and sisterly feelings we all had in common each and every day. It must be something more to it all than I can explain because the influence of our musical generation has also keep kept us all young and love.

Now and forever, Gladys Horton

P.S. I hope you enjoyed my story now let me say thank you for buying my book.

To Wanda Young Rogers, an original member and a lead singer for the original group of The Marvelettes.

Dear Wanda,

I still love your voice and all the effort you put forth in making all the songs you and I had the pleasure of updating back in 1989 from Motor City Records a big success. I haven't given up hope that you maybe will make a complete recovery and join me on stage one day for a reunion tour. Gee whiz, how I wish things would have turned out differently for our group. But I have reached the discovery that instead of trying to find the old pieces of a puzzle to rematch them, that we should take on the challenge of solving the mystery of a new chapter in life and work on putting that new puzzle together. I'm going forward, keeping the progress in motion. When you are ready, don't hesitate. I would always welcome you back.

Wishing you the very best from now on,

Gladys Horton

Dear Katherine,

Finally, after all of these years, you've shown your real colors, and your green stands for envy, not money. There aren't too many situations that I've come upon that left me in the dark for long, and so it is to with your recent actions.

Even though you refused to sign the letter giving the lawyer, Mr. Stephen Brown, the rights to act in our favor in bringing justice from our imposters on behalf of our legal rights for being original Marvelettes, you could have at least wrote some type of comment to me as to why your denial was so inevitable.

I've known from the very beginning that you were totally against me ever trying to continue on with the show without you being a part of the group. I would like at fault and sorry for you if I had not have come over to your house and asked you personally to join up and do something with us again. But I did, and you refused. So why all the jealousy now? Did you actually think that I needed you to go on? Did you actually think that you had the power to stop me? Must I bring it to your attention that I started the Marvelettes, not you?

Going back to that day in school I even recall now that I asked Georgeanna to bring some girls over to my house to try out for the talent show. I never even talked to you from the beginning. The thought of you never even entered my mind, and you never would have traveled all over the world with the Marvelettes and made a name for yourself if it hadn't have been for me choosing you that day. Look how one person can make a change for the betterment in our lives. And although I never have even asked you for it you certainly have shown me your gratitude.

Now for what I really want to say in this letter. I started the Marvelettes, and only I will be one to give the go-ahead to sue anybody on our behalf. I have informed the proper legal people at Motown Records that no money will be collected off of my group whatsoever unless I say so, unless I also receive a share of whatever monies that are requested. So you can throw your lawsuit out the window along with Chuck Rubins, who I'll get to next.

Yes, this is in retaliation for you refusing to sign my letter, thinking that it was going me some percentage of monies being made by whatever bogus Marvelettes groups were performing. No, you were dead wrong. We all as living Marvelettes could have demanded a rightful percentage of whatever work was being generated in our name. So now you see sometimes in life, you must learn that we have to help each other out if we want to achieve our utmost goals. So don't even try it. Just forget about it.

"G"ladys speaks out.

Lastly, to my three sons — Sammy, Vaughn, and Alphonso

My dear boys,

Nothing can ever come between the love I have for you all. Not life, not even death. No man or woman. It is hard holding on to anything in this world, but I vow that we'll always be together even through eternity.

Your only mother,

Gladys

VAUGHN

ACKNOWLEDGMENTS

Well, we finally did it! Gladys Horton's story is finally here after a long journey! I want to thank all of the Marvelette fans around the world for your patience and support. This book is a "MARVELOUS " read.

Please allow me to give a special thanks to:

First of all, my wife, Michetta Thornton, but let's call her "Mickey." Our journey together began over 30 years ago and still counting. My mother loved you dearly. She groomed me from a young age on how to treat a good woman and she must have done a phenomenal job because you're still here. Thanks for your patience and persistence throughout this journey because without you, we would not have found Bianca Scott, our editor.

Because of you Mickey, my Mother had the pleasure of being a Grandmother to our two children, Miracle and De'Vaughn. She loved them dearly. She may not have had a chance to meet her Great Grandchildren, Jaylen and Zara, but she is smiling down upon them with much love. Thanks for being my "ride or die wifey," I love you so much. You have been such a blessing in my life.

To my children: Miracle and De'Vaughn, when my brother Alphonso, your Uncle, passed away, my Mother was heartbroken in the true sense. You all gave her a second life. As you know, she loved you all with all of her heart and more. And now that love extends to her Great Grandchildren, Jaylen and Zara. Miracle, you are the splitting image of your Grandmother. De'Vaughn, you remind me so much of your Uncle. Thank you for being my journey and motivation in life to succeed. I am Blessed to have children like you all in my life. I am proud of you all and love you both.

To my Brothers Alphonso and Sammie: Alphonso, I hope Mom and yourself are at peace there in Heaven. And Sammie, I am so happy after all these years to find out that your Father is also mines. Even though our Father is not a nice guy, I was more excited to find out that we're full siblings. I'll never forget the fun times we had as a family growing up. I love you all forever.

To Mark Rowland at TVONE and everyone that participated on that "MIND BLOWING" episode about the Marvelettes on "UNSUNG," GREAT JOB!

To The official fan club of the classic Marvelettes: Thanks to all of the administrators for keeping the Marvelette's legacy alive!

Patricia "Sweet Pea" Washington, Marlo E. Waters, Barbara Croskey, Jeff Brody, Mary M. Anderson, Michael Miller, Shannon Gordy.

To: Deanne Fabro, Marcus Eley, Raina Shaw, Ron Brewington, Stephen Wood, THANKS for your special contributions and dedication to this project.

To the original Marvelettes: Gladys Horton, Wanda Young, Juanita Cowart Motley, Georgeanna Tillman, Georgia Dobbins, and Katherine Anderson, Thanks for being a vital part of Motown's history and success! And for putting Inkster, Michigan on the map.

And last, but definitely not least, to our editor Bianca Scott: You went above and beyond on this project and my wife and I thank you sincerely. Your professionalism and attentiveness in bringing this book to reality was and is superb! I would recommend anyone needing a book self-published? Look up Bianca Scott at BusyB Writing! Definitely the way to go!

Printed in Great Britain
by Amazon